Stimmt! 1

Übungsheft B

Malcolm Pacey

ALWAYS LEARNING

PEARSON

1 Hallo! (Seiten 8–9)

1 **Two of the words in each set have a sound that is the same. Circle the word with a different sound from the other two.**

1	*Schlange*	*Porsche*	*Buch*
2	*Bär*	*Löwe*	*Röntgenbild*
3	*Wildwassersport*	*Auf Wiedersehen*	*Tür*
4	*Biene*	*heiße*	*Eis*

2 **Join up the sentence halves.**

1 Gut, danke. Und
2 Auf
3 Ich heiße
4 Hallo! Wie heißt
5 Ich heiße Nadia. Wie
6 Nicht

a Wiedersehen.
b Ben. Wie heißt du?
c geht's, Ben?
d du?
e schlecht.
f dir?

3 **Write the sentences from exercise 2 in the correct order for the conversation. Then translate them into English.**

1 ______________________ ______________________
2 ______________________ ______________________
3 ______________________ ______________________
4 ______________________ ______________________
5 Nicht schlecht. ______________________ Not bad. ______________________
6 ______________________ ______________________

4 **Unscramble the inventions. Look at the definite article (word for 'the') for each word. Then write each invention with the indefinite article (word for 'a').**

1 sad ngbönReltid das … ______________________ ein … ______________________
2 erd reelmiDtoos ______________________ ______________________
3 sda toF3rMmPa- ______________________ ______________________
4 sad PeuAsotrcoh ______________________ ______________________
5 ied sAMrkdadiae ______________________ ______________________

2 Eins, zwei, drei … (Seiten 10–11)

1 The bank has sent texts to customers with their coded PIN numbers. Solve the maths problems in German to work out the PINs. Then write each customer's new PIN below the phone.

1

2 7 _ _

2

_ _ _ _

3

_ _ _ _

2 Write the winning lottery numbers in words.

1 

______

2 

______

3 

______

4 

______

5 

______

6 

______

3 Write two sentences for each speaker. Give the speaker's age and the age of his/her friend.

er ist = he is
sie ist = she is

1

Ich bin dreizehn Jahre alt.
Sie ist zwölf Jahre alt.

2

______
______

3

______
______

3 Ich wohne in Deutschland (Seiten 12–13)

1 **Read the dialogue and complete the table with the correct forms of each verb.**

Melanie: Hallo! Ich heiße Melanie. Wie heißt du?
Marco: Ich heiße Marco. Ich wohne in Straubing. Wo wohnst du?
Melanie: Ich wohne in Braunschweig. Wie alt bist du?
Marco: Ich bin zwölf Jahre alt. Wer ist das?
Melanie: Sie heißt Jessie. Sie wohnt in Leipzig und ist dreizehn Jahre alt.

wer = who

	heißen (to be called)	**wohnen** (to live)	**sein** (to be)
ich (I)		*wohne*	
du (you)			*bist*
er/sie/es (he/she/it)	*heißt*		

2 **Write the missing word in each sentence and complete the crossword.**

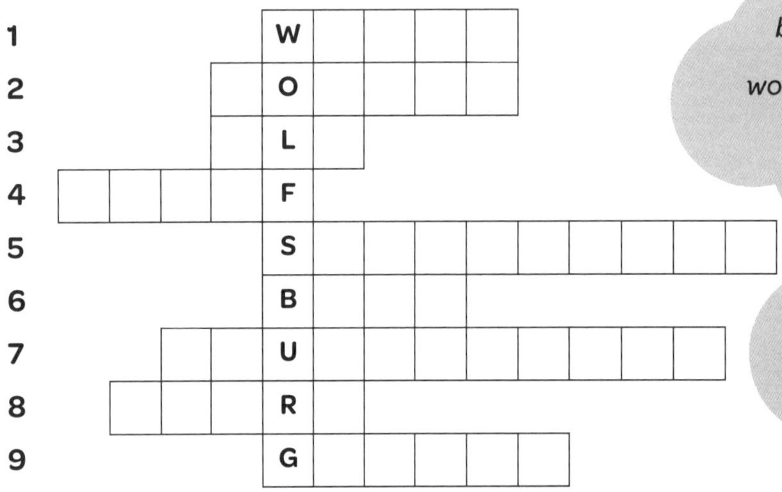

bist *zwölf* *wohne* *wohnst* *Jahre* *Schottland* *Deutschland* *geht's* *alt*

1 Ich ____________ in Manchester.

2 Wo ____________ du, Nick?

3 Wie ____________ ist er?

4 Er ist ____________ Jahre alt.

5 Glasgow ist in ____________ .

6 Wie alt ____________ du?

7 Ich wohne in Berlin. Das ist in ____________ .

8 Ich bin elf ____________ alt.

9 Wie ____________ ?

3 **Research why the city of Wolfsburg is important to Germany.**

1 **The printer has made four mistakes labelling the illustrations. Write *richtig* or *falsch* under each caption.**

1  Ich bin musikalisch. ____________

2  Ich bin sehr launisch. ____________

3  Ich bin ziemlich freundlich. ____________

4  Ich bin kreativ. ____________

5  Ich bin laut. ____________

6  Ich bin lustig. ____________

2 **Rewrite the false captions from exercise 1, correcting them so that they are true.**

____

____

____

____

faul
lustig
musikalisch
sportlich

3 **Separate out the words to form three sentences.**

meinelieblingsfußballmannschaftistbayernmünchen

meinlieblingssportisttennis

meinelieblingszahlistsieben

Remember that each sentence must start with a capital letter. Also, remember that nouns start with a capital letter.

1 ______________________________

2 ______________________________

3 ______________________________

4 **Write a sentence about your favourite ...**

1 football team: ______________________________

2 sport: ______________________________

3 number: ______________________________

5 Meine Sachen (Seiten 16–17)

1 Write the German question word under its English translation.

Who?	What?	How?	Where?	Where from?

Wie? Was? Wo? Woher? Wer?

2 Write the correct question word in each question. You may use each word more than once.

1 ________________ bist du? Sportlich?

2 ________________ wohnt Shiva?

3 ________________ heißt du?

4 ________________ kommst du?

5 ________________ ist das? Ist das Max?

6 ________________ alt ist Michael?

7 ________________ ist Hannover? *Hannover ist in Deutschland!*

8 ________________ ist deine Lieblingsmusik?

3 Read the paragraph below. Pretend that you're Gabi, and answer each question in a complete German sentence.

Hallo! Ich heiße Gabi und ich bin vierzehn Jahre alt. Ich wohne in Kiel, in Deutschland, aber ich komme aus Swansea. Das ist in Wales. Wie bin ich? Ich bin sportlich, lustig und auch sehr laut! Mein Lieblingsmonat ist Dezember und meine Lieblingssendung ist ‚Die Simpsons'. Ich habe ein iPad und auch einen Computer. Tschüs!

1 Wie heißt du? ________________________________

2 Wo wohnst du? ________________________________

3 Woher kommst du? ________________________________

4 Wie bist du? ________________________________

5 Wie heißt deine Lieblingssendung? ________________________________

6 Was hast du? ________________________________

Ich über mich (Seiten 18–19)

1 Complete the table with the correct words.

	the	a	my	your
masculine: Sport				
feminine: Musik				
neuter: Auto				

2 Write each sentence or question in German. Tick the boxes when you've checked each part of your work.

Part of writing accurately in any language is going back over your work to check that there aren't any mistakes. Get into the habit now and watch both your English and German improve!

1 I'm called Osman.

____

2 I live in Germany.

____

3 I'm quite friendly and also creative.

____

____

4 I have a mobile phone.

____

5 Where do you live?

____

- ☐ Spelling of key phonics sound 'ei'
- ☐ Name has a capital
- ☐ Spelling of key phonics sound 'eu'
- ☐ Full stop at the end
- ☐ Check the qualifier
- ☐ Check the connective
- ☐ Capital on the noun
- ☐ Right word for 'a'
- ☐ Correct question word
- ☐ Verb in second position

3 Write a short paragraph about yourself. Use the sentences in exercise 2 as prompts. Check your work against the checklist below.

- ☐ genders
- ☐ qualifiers
- ☐ connectives
- ☐ verbs
- ☐ capital letters
- ☐ spelling
- ☐ question words

____

____

Wiederholung 1

1 Fill in the gaps by writing the German for the words in brackets.

Hallo! Ich __________ (am called) Marie und ich __________ (live) in Walsrode. Das ist in __________ (Germany). Ich bin fünfzehn __________ (years) alt. Ich bin __________ (very) sportlich und __________ (quite) intelligent, __________ (but) ich bin __________ (also) faul. Mein __________ (favourite sport) ist Hockey und __________ (my) Lieblingsmusik ist Pop. Ich __________ (have) einen Vogel aus Amerika. Er ist __________ (very) freundlich, aber __________ (not) laut!

2 Crack the code and write the sentences correctly.

a 18/24/19 4/12/19/13/22 18/13 20/28/7/7/18/13/20/22/13

Ich wohne in Göttingen.

ä = 27	ü = 29
ö = 28	ß = 30

b 22/9 18/8/7 20/26/13/1 21/9/22/6/13/23/15/18/24/19

____

c 14/22/18/13/22 15/18/22/25/15/18/13/20/8/14/6/8/18/16 18/8/7 14/12/1/26/9/7

____

____

3 Make up a coded sentence in German for a classmate to solve. Don't forget to provide a key.

4 Write the questions you would ask to get these answers.

1 *Wie heißt du?*

Ich heiße Elaine.

2 __________

Mein Lieblingssport ist Tennis.

3 __________

Sami ist musikalisch und intelligent, aber sehr launisch.

4 __________

Alwin ist vierzehn Jahre alt.

Wiederholung 2

1 Read the website entries.

Ich heiße **Franzi** und suche Freunde aus England, Irland oder Nordirland. Ich habe eine Schlange zu Hause! Sie ist sechs Jahre alt. Ich wohne in Wien. Das ist in Österreich. Ich bin sehr kreativ und intelligent! Schreib mir bitte!

Hallo! Ich heiße **Hannah** und ich wohne in London, in England. Ich lerne Deutsch. Ich suche Freunde aus Deutschland, Österreich und auch aus der Schweiz. Ich bin sportlich und spiele Fußball und auch Tennis, aber ich bin sehr faul! Meine Lieblingsmusik ist Rock. Schreib mir!

Mein Name ist **Felix** und ich wohne in der Schweiz, aber ich komme aus Dortmund in Deutschland. Zu Hause habe ich eine Wii und mein Lieblingsspiel ist FIFA. Meine Lieblingsfußballmannschaft ist Bayern-München. Ich suche Freunde aus Schottland und Wales.

Hi! Ich bin **Muhammad** und ich wohne in Cardiff. Das ist in Wales. Ich bin sechzehn Jahre alt. Meine Lieblingssache ist Technologie. Ich habe zu Hause einen Computer, ein Handy und auch ein iPad. Ich bin nicht sehr sportlich, aber sehr freundlich. Mein Lieblingsland ist Deutschland und ich suche dort Freunde.

Write the name of the person who …

1. is looking for friends from Switzerland. Hannah
2. supports a football team. ______
3. has a pet. ______
4. is just looking for friends from Germany. ______
5. lives in a different place from where they were born. ______
6. does not particularly like sport. ______
7. lives in Switzerland. ______

suche = seek
Schreib mir (bitte)! = Write to me (please)!
dort = there

2 Write your own profile for the website. Use as much German as you can from *Kapitel 1* to describe yourself.

____

____

____

____

Grammatik (Seiten 22–23)

1 **Write a sentence using the correct German word for 'a' for each item.**

1 
2 
3 
4 
5 
6 
7 
8 

1 *Das ist ein Computer.*
2 ______________________
3 ______________________
4 ______________________
5 ______________________
6 ______________________
7 ______________________
8 ______________________

die Gitarre
der iPod
das Skateboard
der Fußball
das Handy
der Computer
das Keyboard
die Wii

Grammatik
masculine – *ein*
feminine – *eine*
neuter – *ein*

2 **Circle the correct verb form to complete each sentence.**

1 Lukas **habe / hat / hast** einen Computer.
2 Ich **heiße / habe / hat** einen Vogel zu Hause.
3 Wo **bist / ist / wohnst** er?
4 Er **ist / komme / bin** musikalisch und sportlich.
5 Julia **bin / ist / wohnt** fünfzehn Jahre alt.
6 Wie alt **wohnst / bist / bin** du?
7 Wo **hast / bist / bin** ich?

Grammatik
You can use the pronouns *er* ('he') or *sie* ('she') instead of writing someone's name. Both need the *er*/*sie*/*es* form of the verb.

3 **Complete the table with the correct forms of each regular verb.**

wohnen (to live)	**kommen** (to come)	**heißen** (to be called)
ich *wohne*	ich	ich
du	du *kommst*	du
er/sie/es	er/sie/es	er/sie/es *heißt*

Now use the table to write the correct verb in each gap.

1 Mein Handy ____________ aus China.
2 Meine Schlange ____________ Sissel.
3 Du ____________ Gabi.
4 ____________ du aus Berlin?
5 ____________ Monika in Hamburg?
6 Deine Lieblingssendung ____________ ‚EastEnders'.
7 Ich ____________ Wolfgang.
8 Wo ____________ du?

Mein Fortschritt

1 **Record your levels for *Kapitel* 1.**

2 **Look at the level descriptors on pages 59–60 and set your targets for *Kapitel* 2.**

3 **Fill in what you need to do to achieve these targets.**

Listening 	I have reached Level ______ in **Listening**. In *Kapitel* 2, I want to reach Level ______ I need to ____________________
Speaking  	I have reached Level ______ in **Speaking**. In *Kapitel* 2, I want to reach Level ______ I need to ____________________
Reading 	I have reached Level ______ in **Reading**. In *Kapitel* 2, I want to reach Level ______ I need to ____________________
Writing 	I have reached Level ______ in **Writing**. In *Kapitel* 2, I want to reach Level ______ I need to ____________________

Wörter

Hallo! • Meeting and greeting

Wie heißt du?	*What's your name?*
Ich heiße ...	*My name is ...*
Hallo!	*Hello! / Hi!*
Guten Tag!	*Hello!*
Wie geht's?	*How are you?*
Gut, danke. Und dir?	*Fine, thanks. And you?*
Nicht schlecht.	*Not bad.*
Tschüs!	*Bye!*
Auf Wiedersehen!	*Goodbye!*

Die Zahlen 1–19 • Numbers 1–19

eins	*1*
zwei	*2*
drei	*3*
vier	*4*
fünf	*5*
sechs	*6*
sieben	*7*
acht	*8*
neun	*9*
zehn	*10*
elf	*11*
zwölf	*12*
dreizehn	*13*
vierzehn	*14*
fünfzehn	*15*
sechzehn	*16*
siebzehn	*17*
achtzehn	*18*
neunzehn	*19*
Wie alt bist du?	*How old are you?*
Ich bin ... Jahre alt.	*I am ... years old.*
Wie alt ist (Julia)?	*How old is (Julia)?*
(Julia) ist ... Jahre alt.	*(Julia) is ... years old.*

Wo wohnst du? • Where do you live?

Ich wohne in ...	*I live in ...*
Er/Sie/Es wohnt in ...	*He/She/It lives in ...*
... England	*England*
... Irland	*Ireland*
... Nordirland	*Northern Ireland*
... Schottland	*Scotland*
... Wales	*Wales*
... Deutschland	*Germany*
... Österreich	*Austria*
... der Schweiz	*Switzerland*

Wie bist du? • What are you like?

Ich bin ...	*I am ...*
Er/Sie ist ...	*He/She is ...*
faul	*lazy*
freundlich	*friendly*
intelligent	*intelligent*
kreativ	*creative*
launisch	*moody*
laut	*loud*
lustig	*funny*
musikalisch	*musical*
sportlich	*sporty*

Lieblingssachen • Favourite things

Mein Lieblingssport ist ...
My favourite sport is ...

Mein Lieblingsmonat ist ...
My favourite month is ...

Meine Lieblingsmusik ist ...
My favourite music is ...

Meine Lieblingszahl ist ...
My favourite number is ...

Meine Lieblingssendung ist ...
My favourite programme is ...

Meine Lieblingsfußballmannschaft ist ...
My favourite football team is ...

Mein Lieblingsspiel ist ...
My favourite game is ...

Mein Lieblingsland ist ...
My favourite country is ...

Mein Lieblingsauto ist ...
My favourite car is ...

Was ist dein Lieblingssport?
What's your favourite sport?

Was ist deine Lieblingszahl?
What's your favourite number?

Was ist dein Lieblingsland?
What's your favourite country?

Hast du einen Computer? • Have you got a computer?

Ich habe ...	*I have ...*
einen Computer	*a computer*
einen iPod	*an iPod*
einen Fußball	*a football*
eine Gitarre	*a guitar*
eine Wii	*a Wii*
eine Schlange	*a snake*
ein Handy	*a mobile phone*
ein Keyboard	*a keyboard*
ein Skateboard	*a skateboard*

Fragewörter • Question words

Wie?	*How?*
Was?	*What?*
Wo?	*Where?*
Woher?	*Where ... from?*
Wer?	*Who?*

Oft benutzte Wörter • High-frequency words

und	*and*
(und) auch	*(and) also*
aber	*but*
sehr	*very*
ziemlich	*quite*
nicht	*not*
Was denkst du?	*What do you think?*
Ich denke, ...	*I think ...*
Ich auch!	*Me too!*
Ich nicht!	*Not me!/That's not what I think!*
Was? Du spinnst!	*What? You're joking!*

1 Extreme Haustiere (Seiten 30–31)

1 Complete the sentences about the pets. Write the correct words in the gaps. Remember to think about the gender of each animal.

1. Ich habe _ein_ ______ Pferd. _Es_ ___ ist groß und heißt Romeo.
2. Ich habe __________ Kaninchen. ______ ist niedlich und heißt Timmo.
3. Ich habe __________ Katze. ______ ist intelligent und heißt Mieze.
4. Max hat __________ Schlange. ______ ist zwei Jahre alt.
5. Gabi hat __________ Pferd. ______ ist launish.
6. Ich habe __________ Hund. ______ ist freundlich und heißt Prinz.
7. Susi hat __________ Goldfisch. ______ heißt Nemo.

Grammatik
Remember: after *haben* the masculine word for 'a' changes from *ein* to *einen*.

Grammatik
m. der / ein → **er**
f. die / eine → **sie**
n. das / ein → **es**

2 Tina Tierfan has lots of pets! Write Tina's answers to the interviewer's questions about how many of each animal she has.

Grammatik

Hund (-e)	Pferd (-e)
Katze (-n)	Goldfisch (-e)
Schlange (-n)	Maus (Mäuse)

1. Hast du einen Hund? _Nein! Ich habe drei Hunde._
2. Hast du ein Pferd? ______________________
3. Hast du eine Katze? ______________________
4. Hast du einen Goldfisch? ______________________
5. Hast du eine Schlange? ______________________
6. Hast du eine Maus? ______________________

2 Supertiere (Seiten 32–33)

1 **Complete the sentences about the animals. Write the correct name in each gap.**

Hermann 
Minnie 
Sisi 
Kizzi 
Moto 
Millie 

1 __________ ist schnell.
2 __________ ist süß.
3 __________ ist gemein.
4 __________ ist superintelligent.
5 __________ ist cool.
6 __________ ist kräftig.

2 **Write a sentence to say what each of the *Supertiere* can do.**

1 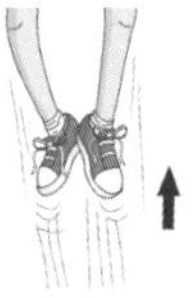
Hermann

2 
Sisi

3 
Minnie

4 

Kizzi

5 
Millie

6 
Moto

1 Hermann kann springen.
2 ______________________________
3 ______________________________
4 ______________________________
5 ______________________________
6 ______________________________

Grammatik
The verb *kann* is always followed by an infinitive verb.

3 **Read the text below, then translate it into English.**

Günther Goldfisch ist mein Lieblingstier. Er ist ein Jahr alt. Er ist sehr lustig und kräftig, aber auch ziemlich süß. Er kann schwimmen, springen und auch im Aquarium tanzen! Günther hat einen Freund: er ist sehr cool und schlau.

3 Meine Familie (Seiten 34–35)

1 **Find the numbers in the puzzle, and write them next to the correct numeral.**

v	i	e	r	u	n	d	s	e	c	h	z	i	g	m	e
b	a	l	c	o	e	z	n	f	w	i	r	d	s	k	s
s	e	c	h	s	u	n	d	d	r	e	i	ß	i	g	a
q	g	n	a	j	n	x	i	n	d	m	h	t	g	ü	o
h	a	c	h	t	u	n	d	f	ü	n	f	z	i	g	i
u	e	i	n	u	n	d	a	c	h	t	z	i	g	p	b
n	t	e	r	i	d	f	b	n	ß	e	d	z	g	d	s
d	r	e	i	u	n	d	v	i	e	r	z	i	g	w	e
e	v	h	f	r	e	a	m	ß	p	l	s	j	a	q	c
r	d	r	e	i	u	n	d	z	w	a	n	z	i	g	h
t	z	a	n	j	n	x	o	u	e	y	g	r	e	v	z
k	c	p	f	s	z	d	l	b	n	l	a	i	h	m	i
i	b	z	w	e	i	u	n	d	s	i	e	b	z	i	g
a	g	b	n	ü	g	y	i	a	z	o	m	e	d	h	e

100 ______________

64 ______________

99 ______________

43 ______________

72 ______________

36 ______________

58 ______________

81 ______________

60 ______________

23 ______________

2 **Describe each of the families. Fill in the gaps for the first family. Write the whole description for the second family.**

Tom

42 7 14 5

Oban

Ich heiße Tom. Ich bin vierzehn Jahre alt. Es gibt vier Personen in meiner Familie. Meine Mutter ist ______________ Jahre alt. Ich habe einen Bruder. ____ ist ________ Jahre alt. Ich habe eine Schwester. ______ ist ____________ Jahre alt. Wir wohnen in ________.

47 51 Katja 12 10 19

Köln

____

____

____

____

____

____

3 **Write about your family (real or imaginary). Use the descriptions in exercise 2 to help you.**

der Stiefbruder = stepbrother
die Halbschwester = half-sister
Ich bin Einzelkind. = I am an only child.

4 Die Farben der Welt (Seiten 36–37)

1 Describe each person's hair and eyes.

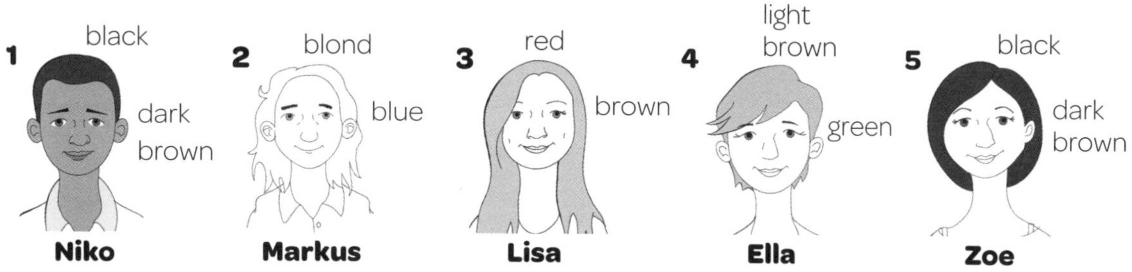

Grammatik
When you describe hair and eyes, the adjectives (colour, length) need an ***e*** on the end.

hell = light — **hellbraun** = light brown
dunkel = dark — **dunkelblau** = dark blue

1 *Er heißt Niko. Er hat kurze, schwarze Haare und dunkelbraune Augen.*
2 ______________________________
3 ______________________________
4 ______________________________
5 ______________________________

2 Complete the text by choosing the correct words from the cloud to fill the gaps. There are more words than you need.

Es gibt fünf __________ in meiner Familie. Wir __________ in Braunschweig. Das ist in __________. Meine __________ heißt Emma und sie ist neunundvierzig __________ alt. Sie ist sehr freundlich und hat __________, schwarze Haare. Mein Vater __________ auch neunundvierzig und er hat kurze, dunkelbraune Haare und braune __________.

Ich habe zwei __________: einen Bruder und eine Schwester. __________ Bruder heißt Mehmet und er ist __________ Jahre alt. Er ist launisch aber __________ lustig. __________ Schwester, Isla, hat grüne Augen und __________ Haare. Sie ist sechzehn Jahre alt, sehr klein und __________.

Deutschland alt Augen Personen braune wohnen sportlich Meine Mutter Jahre lange Geschwister zwölf auch Mein blau ist

Read the text for gist first. For each sentence, think about whether you need a noun, a verb, a connective or an adjective.

5 Alles Gute! (Seiten 38–39)

1 Reorder the words to make correct sentences. Don't forget the full stop!

1 am Mai Ich Geburtstag habe neunzehnten

___

2 hat Oktober am Oma Geburtstag elften Meine

___

3 Geburtstag Stiefbruder Dezember am Dein dritten hat

___

4 hast Geburtstag einunddreißigsten Juli Du am

___

5 und Geburtstag haben achten am Michael Juni Monika

___

2 Complete each sentence by writing the date. Write each holiday in English.

Neujahr ist am *ersten Januar*. *New Year*

Der Maifeiertag ist am ___. ___

Der Tag der Deutschen Einheit ist am ___. *German Unity Day*

Weihnachten ist am ___. ___

Silvester ist am ___. ___

3 Read the short profile about Yannic and write a summary in the table.

Er heißt Yannic Spiller. Er ist dreizehn Jahre alt und kommt aus Trier. Trier ist in Deutschland. Yannic hat am siebten Januar Geburtstag. Er hat einen Bruder, Tim. Tim ist achtzehn Jahre alt. Yannic hat auch eine Schwester. Sie heißt Steffi und ist sechzehn Jahre alt. Die Familie Spiller hat zwei Haustiere: einen Hund und eine Katze.

Name:		Geschwister:	
Alter:			
Wohnt in:		Haustiere:	
Geburtstag:			

4 Now write a short profile about yourself.

6 Eine Superfamilie (Seiten 40–41)

1 Rescue the question words from the alphabet soup. Write each one on a line and use it to write a question.

Wie viele Brüder hast du?

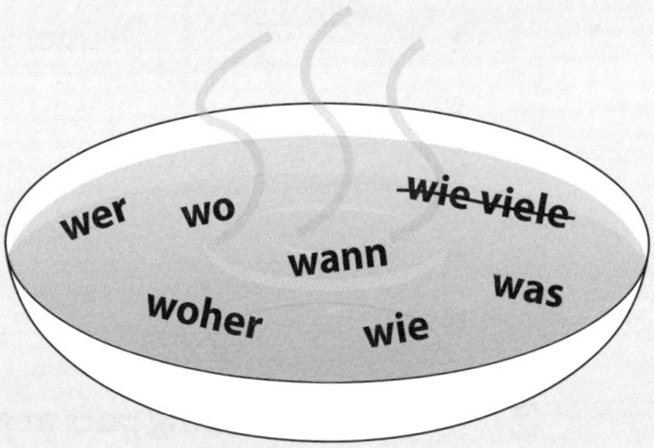

2 The police have written a summary about a crime suspect. Write six questions for a journalist to ask the suspect. The questions should cover all the information in the summary.

1. Wie heißt du?
2.
3.
4.
5.
6.

Martin Kolwitz ist 24 Jahre alt. Er hat am achten November Geburtstag. Er wohnt in Hamburg, in Deutschland. Er hat einen Bruder. Er hat auch Haustiere: zwei Hunde.

Remember: the verb usually goes straight after the question word.

3 Use these notes to write questions to Martin about his accomplice, Sophie.

1. Wie heißt sie?
2.
3.
4.
5.

Sophie Meyer
19
Ebbingen, Deutschland
Haare – kurz, Augen – blau
Geb. 21.10.

Remember to use the correct part of the verb with the pronoun *sie*.

4 Write a summary about Sophie, like the one the police wrote about Martin in exercise 2.

Wiederholung 1

1 Complete the sentences. Choose the correct word from the cloud to fill in each gap.

1 ________________ Mutter ist sehr freundlich und intelligent.

2 Hast du ________________ Meerschweinchen?

3 Wir haben ________________ Haustier.

4 Wo ist ________________ Vogel?

5 Ich habe ________________ Bruder.

dein *kein*
ein *meine*
einen

2 You are describing pets at a pet show. Use the owners' notes to write what sort of pet they have, what the pet is like and what it can do.

Mareike

mouse
Pippa
cute, fast
fly, swim

Mareike hat ________________.

Sie heißt ________________.

Sie ist ________________.

Sie kann ________________.

Aaron

cat
Mieze
intelligent, cool, mean
jump, play football

________________.

________________.

________________.

________________.

________________.

3 Decscribe the animal you'll be entering in the pet show by writing a similar description.

Example: Ich habe ...

Wiederholung 2

1 Read the texts below.

Hallo! Ich heiße **Anna** und ich bin fünfzehn Jahre alt. Ich habe am elften Februar Geburtstag. Ich wohne in Klagenfurt, in Österreich. Ich bin ziemlich groß und schlank und habe kurze, schwarze Haare und blaue Augen. Ich habe keine Geschwister – ich bin Einzelkind. Ich habe einen Goldfisch und einen Wellensittich. Ich kann Flöte spielen und Italienisch sprechen.

Hi! Ich bin **Noah** und ich komme aus Aachen. Das ist in Deutschland. Ich habe am zweiten November Geburtstag und bin vierzehn Jahre alt. Ich liebe Haustiere! Ich habe zwei Hunde, drei Katzen und eine Maus. Ich habe eine große Familie. Ich habe einen Halbbruder (er ist ein Baby) und zwei Schwestern. Mein Halbbruder ist sehr süß und klein. Er hat schwarze Haare und blaue Augen.

a Complete the sentences by writing *Anna* or *Noah*.

1 __________ lives in Austria.
2 __________ can play the flute.
3 __________ 's birthday is on the 02.11.
4 __________ has a half-brother.
5 __________ is 15 years old.
6 __________ has cats.

b Write *richtig* or *falsch* next to each statement.

1 Anna hat einen Halbbruder. __________
2 Anna kann auch Englisch sprechen. __________
3 Noahs Halbbruder hat blaue Augen. __________
4 Klagenfurt ist nicht in Deutschland. __________
5 Anna hat am fünfzehnten Februar Geburtstag. __________
6 Anna hat keine Geschwister. __________

2 Translate these sentences into German.

1 My birthday is on the first of May. __________
2 She can speak German. __________
3 My guinea pig is very cute. __________
4 Your sister has light blue eyes. __________
5 My grandparents live in Southampton.
____
6 My brother can fly.
____

Grammatik (Seiten 44–45)

1 Complete the table by writing the correct form of *haben* for each pronoun.

haben *hast* *habt* *hat* *habe* *haben*

Words for 'you':
du (speaking to one family member or friend)
ihr (speaking to two or more family members or friends)
Sie (speaking to people you don't know or adults)

ich	du	er/sie/es	wir	ihr	Sie/sie

Now complete the sentences with the correct form of *haben*.

1 Katja, hast ______ du eine Katze?

2 Tom und Niko, ______ ihr einen Hund?

3 ______ Sie eine Schlange, Herr Brand?

4 Ich ______ ein Pferd.

5 Frau Gerber, ______ Sie eine Maus?

6 Herr Alexander ______ ein Pferd.

2 Join each pronoun to a verb. There is more than one possible verb for some of the pronouns. Then write a question or a sentence with each pair.

1 ich	a macht	1 ______
2 du	b heißen	2 ______
3 er	c wohnst	3 ______
4 wir	d heiße	4 ______
5 ihr	e spielt	5 ______
6 Sie	f spielen	6 ______

3 Rewrite the sentences so they include the verb *kann*.

1 Mein Bruder fliegt. Mein Bruder kann fliegen.

2 Ich spiele Flöte. ______

3 Meine Mutter schwimmt. ______

4 Mein Vater springt. ______

5 Ich tanze. ______

6 Er singt gut. ______

Mein Fortschritt

1 Record your levels for *Kapitel* 2.

2 Look at the level descriptors on pages 59–60 and set your targets for *Kapitel* 3.

3 Fill in what you need to do to achieve these targets.

Listening 	I have reached Level ____ in **Listening**. In *Kapitel* 3, I want to reach Level ____ I need to ________________ ________________ ________________ ________________
Speaking 	I have reached Level ____ in **Speaking**. In *Kapitel* 3, I want to reach Level ____ I need to ________________ ________________ ________________ ________________
Reading 	I have reached Level ____ in **Reading**. In *Kapitel* 3, I want to reach Level ____ I need to ________________ ________________ ________________ ________________
Writing 	I have reached Level ____ in **Writing**. In *Kapitel* 3, I want to reach Level ____ I need to ________________ ________________ ________________ ________________

Haustiere • Pets

Hast du ein Haustier?	*Have you got a pet?*
Ich habe ...	*I have ...*
einen Goldfisch	*a goldfish*
einen Hamster	*a hamster*
einen Hund	*a dog*
ein Kaninchen	*a rabbit*
eine Katze	*a cat*
eine Maus	*a mouse*
ein Meerschweinchen	*a guinea pig*
ein Pferd	*a horse*
eine Schlange	*a snake*
einen Wellensittich	*a budgie*
kein Haustier	*no pet*

Eigenschaften • Qualities

Wie ist er/sie/es?	*What is he/she/ it like?*
Er/Sie/Es ist ...	*He/She/It is ...*
dick/schlank	*fat/thin*
frech/niedlich	*cheeky/cute*
gemein/süß	*mean/sweet*
groß/klein	*big/small*
kräftig	*strong*
schlau	*cunning*
(super)lustig	*(really) funny*
Er/Sie/Es kann ...	*He/She/It can ...*
Italienisch sprechen	*speak Italian*
fliegen	*fly*
Flöte/Fußball/Wii spielen	*play the flute/ football/on the Wii*
(schnell) laufen	*run (fast)*
lesen	*read*
Rad fahren	*ride a bike*
schwimmen	*swim*
singen	*sing*
springen	*jump*
tanzen	*dance*

Die Zahlen 20–100 • Numbers 20–100

zwanzig	*twenty*
dreißig	*thirty*
vierzig	*forty*
fünfzig	*fifty*
sechzig	*sixty*
siebzig	*seventy*
achtzig	*eighty*
neunzig	*ninety*
hundert	*hundred*
einundzwanzig	*twenty-one*
zweiundzwanzig	*twenty-two*

Meine Familie • My family

Es gibt ... Personen in meiner Familie.	*There are ... people in my family.*
meine Mutter	*my mother*
mein Vater	*my father*
mein Bruder	*my brother*
mein Stiefbruder/ Halbbruder	*my stepbrother/ half-brother*
meine Schwester	*my sister*
meine Stiefschwester/ Halbschwester	*my stepsister/ half-sister*
meine Eltern	*my parents*
meine Großeltern	*my grandparents*
Hast du Geschwister?	*Have you any brothers and sisters?*
Ich habe zwei Brüder.	*I have two brothers.*
Ich habe drei Schwestern.	*I have three sisters.*
Ich bin Einzelkind.	*I'm an only child.*
Ich habe keine Geschwister.	*I have no brothers and sisters.*

Die Farben • Colours

schwarz	*black*
weiß	*white*
grau	*grey*
braun	*brown*
rot	*red*
orange	*orange*
gelb	*yellow*
grün	*green*
blau	*blue*
indigoblau	*indigo*
violett	*violet*
lila	*purple*
rosa	*pink*
bunt	*brightly coloured*
hellblau/dunkelblau	*light blue/dark blue*

Haare und Augen • Hair and eyes

Er/Sie hat ...	*He/She has ...*
schwarze/braune/ blonde/rote Haare	*black/brown/ blond/red hair*
kurze/lange/ mittellange Haare	*short/long/ mid length hair*
blaue/braune/grüne/ graue Augen	*blue/brown/green/ grey eyes*

Die Monate • The months

Januar	*January*
Februar	*February*
März	*March*
April	*April*
Mai	*May*
Juni	*June*
Juli	*July*
August	*August*
September	*September*
Oktober	*October*
November	*November*
Dezember	*December*

Das Datum • The date

Wann hast du Geburtstag?	*When is your birthday?*
am 1. (ersten) Januar	*on 1 January*
am 3. (dritten) Februar	*on 3 February*
am 7. (siebten) März	*on 7 March*
am 8. (achten) April	*on 8 April*
am 15. (fünfzehnten) Mai	*on 15 May*
am 29. (neunund-zwanzigsten) Juni	*on 29 June*
Ich habe (heute) Geburtstag.	*It's my birthday (today).*

Oft benutzte Wörter • High-frequency words

und	*and*
aber	*but*
oder	*or*
ziemlich	*fairly, quite*
sehr	*very*

1 Bist du sportlich? (Seiten 54–55)

1 **Look at the survey results in the table. Then answer the questions using full German sentences.**

Ahmed	😊😊			☹			😐
Nicole		😊😊			☹		
Christa	😊		😊😊				😐
Torsten		☹		😊😊		😊	
Herr und Frau Meyer	😊😊			😊	☹	😐	

😊😊 = sehr gern 😊 = gern 😐 = ziemlich gern ☹ = nicht gern

1 Wer spielt sehr gern Fußball? Nicole spielt sehr gern Fußball.

2 Wer spielt gern Tischtennis? ______

3 Was spielt Christa sehr gern? ______

4 Was spielen Herr und Frau Meyer gern? ______

5 Wer spielt Basketball nicht gern? ______

6 Wer spielt ziemlich gern Handball? (2) ______

7 Und du? Was spielst du gern? ______

2 **Write three questions and three answers about the other people and sports in the table in exercise 1. Use the questions above as a model.**

______

______

______

______

______

______

2 Freizeit ist toll! (Seiten 56–57)

1 Write the words from the cloud in the grid. Translate the code word into English.

furchtbar
Eishockey
schlecht
spielst
irre
stinklangweilig
langweilig
Tischtennis
toll

2 Read about all the activities Hannes and Lola are involved in. Then write *richtig* or *falsch* next to each statement.

Hallo! Ich heiße **Hannes**. Ich finde Sport fantastisch. Ich spiele Tennis und schwimme. Schwimmen finde ich total super. Ich reite mit meiner Freundin, aber das finde ich langweilig. Fußball finde ich cool. Ich fahre auch gern Skateboard und lese sehr gern Sport- und Fitnessmagazine.

Meine Freundin heißt **Lola.** Sie findet Tischtennis toll. Lola fährt auch gern Rad – das ist sehr gesund! Sie findet schwimmen auch gut, aber Fußball findet sie nervig. Sie kann nicht Ski fahren. Im Winter spielt sie Eishockey und sie sieht sehr gern Eishockey im Fernsehen.

meine Freundin = my girlfriend
gesund = healthy
Fernsehen = television

1 Both Hannes and Lola participate in winter sports. ____________
2 Lola watches ice hockey on television. ____________
3 Hannes really likes swimming. ____________
4 Lola thinks skiing is fantastic. ____________
5 Lola plays ice hockey in winter. ____________
6 Hannes doesn't enjoying horse riding. ____________
7 Lola thinks football is exciting. ____________
8 Hannes watches sports programmes on television. ____________

3 In meiner Freizeit (Seiten 58–59)

1 **Separate the words to form five time phrases and write them below. Number the phrases in order of frequency, starting with 1 for the most frequent. Translate the phrases into English.**

jedenTagdreimalproWocheeinmalproMonatamWochenendesechsmalproMonat

☐ ______________________ ______________________
☐ ______________________ ______________________
☐ ______________________ ______________________
☐ ______________________ ______________________
☐ ______________________ ______________________

2 **Use the time phrases from exercise 1 to answer the questions about yourself. Write your answers in full sentences.**

1 Gehst du ins Kino? ______________________

2 Machst du Sport? ______________________

3 Gehst du einkaufen? ______________________

4 Hörst du Musik? ______________________

5 Spielst du Wii? ______________________

6 Chillst du mit deinen Freunden? ______________________

nie = never

3 **Join up the sentence halves. Rewrite each sentence so that it starts with the time phrase.**

1	Ich höre am	**a**	Tag Sport.
2	Ich chille am	**b**	Abend Musik.
3	Ich spiele sehr	**c**	pro Woche Pizza.
4	Ich mache jeden	**d**	Monat ins Kino.
5	Ich esse einmal	**e**	oft Xbox.
6	Ich gehe einmal pro	**f**	Wochenende.

Remember the 'verb in second place' rule.

4 Ich bin online (Seiten 60–61)

1 Unscramble and write down the time phrase in each sentence. Then translate the sentences into English.

Grammatik
You can use the present tense with a future time phrase to say what you are going to do – just as in English.

1 Wir machen ähncset eoWhc Filme. *nächste Woche*

We are going to make …

2 Ich suche ma Mtanog Infos im Internet. ______

3 Wir sehen ma eneneoWhcd Katzenvideos auf YouTube. ______

4 Ich chatte nejde denbA auf Facebook. ______

5 Stefan spielt ni iezw cnoWhe Wii Sport. ______

6 Ich lade gomrne Musik herunter. ______

2 Underline all the verbs in the text. Circle the words that are in first position in the sentences. Write a sentence about what you notice.

Hey du!
Franzi hier! Jetzt sind wir Freunde auf Facebook! Jeden Tag spiele ich Wii. Jede Woche schreibt mein Vater ein Blog, aber das finde ich langweilig. Am Abend lese ich gern E-Books. Morgen telefoniere ich mit Freunden in Kanada über Skype. Das finde ich cool! Im Sommer fahren wir nach Vancouver. Fantastisch! Was machst du am Computer und wie oft?

______

3 Reply to the question Franzi has asked you in his chat.

Use as many time phrases as you can in your reply.

Brieffreunde (Seiten 64–65)

1 What type of word is needed to fill the gap in each sentence? Complete each sentence by writing an appropriate German word or words in the gap.

verb *noun* *time/frequency phrase* *connective* *adjective*

		Type of word
1	Ich finde ______ Tennis toll.	verb
2	Meine Schwester findet Tischtennis ______ .	______
3	Wir sehen ______ fern.	______
4	Herr Peters spielt nächste Woche Tennis ______ Fußball.	______
5	Mein Bruder schreibt ein ______ .	______

2 Answer the questions about German grammar.

Use the sentences in exercise 1 to help you answer these questions.

1 Where in a sentence do verbs usually go?

______

2 What often goes after a verb? ______

3 What can you expect to go after *ein/eine*? ______

4 Which German verb suggests you're giving an opinion? ______

3 Replace the underlined word(s) with something else: a different noun, adjective or time phrase.

1 Ich finde Tischtennis furchtbar. Ich finde Tischtennis langweilig.

2 Ich spiele nicht gern Fußball. ______

3 Micha spielt gern Wii. ______

4 Er macht einmal pro Monat Judo. ______

5 Olli findet E-Books fantastisch. ______

6 Ich sehe jede Woche fern. Meine Schwester sieht jeden Tag Videos auf YouTube.

______

Remember that you'll keep the reader's interest if you use a variety of different words and phrases.

4 Write about your friends' hobbies.

Remember to include:
- opinions
- connectives
- time/frequency phrases
- 'verb in second place' rule

Wiederholung 1

1 Put the words in the correct order to make sentences or questions. Don't forget to insert a full stop or question mark.

1 fern | gern | sehr | Ich | sehe ____________________
2 einkaufen | er | Wochenende | geht | Am ____________________
3 Hausaufgaben | Ich | Infos | lese | die | für ____________________
4 in | Wie | Stadt | oft | du | fährst | die ____________________
5 Woche | Kai | Wasserball | Nächste | spielt ____________________
6 herunter | Videos | Ich | lade | Musik | und ____________________

2 Rewrite each sentence, beginning with a time phrase. Then translate the sentences into English.

1 Ich spiele Volleyball. (at the weekend) *Am Wochenende spiele ich Volleyball.*
At the weekend I am going to play volleyball.

2 Er spielt Basketball. (on Monday) ____________________

3 Du spielst Tischtennis. (every week) ____________________

4 Rosa spielt Fußball. (today) ____________________

5 Ich telefoniere mit Sam. (next week) ____________________

6 Sophie liest das Buch. (tomorrow) ____________________

3 Underline the regular verbs and circle the irregular verbs.

Ich spiele nicht gern Tennis. Ich finde Tennis langweilig. Fußball spiele ich dreimal pro Woche. Mein Bruder spielt sehr gern Tennis. Er fährt auch gern Rad. Radfahren findet er toll. Meine Schwester sieht ziemlich gern fern. Meine Mutter liest ziemlich gern. Oft liest sie Blogs im Internet. Ich lese auch oft. Mein Vater fährt gern Ski und spielt Gitarre.

Wiederholung 2

1 Read the email. Find the German for the following words and phrases in the text.

1 I think ______
2 about ______
3 but ______
4 New Zealand ______
5 comedies ______
6 Best wishes ______

Lieber Anish,

wie geht's? Danke für deine E-Mail.

Ich denke, Technologie ist toll. Ich bin sehr oft online. Ich chatte sehr gern mit Freunden auf Facebook. Facebook finde ich super und ich sehe oft Videos über Fußball auf YouTube.

Ich spiele Computerspiele nicht gern, aber ich suche ziemlich oft Infos für die Hausaufgaben. Meine Cousine, Connie, wohnt in Neuseeland und wir telefonieren ziemlich oft über Skype. Kannst du auch über Skype telefonieren?

Ich mache viel Sport mit meinen Freunden: Wir schwimmen zweimal pro Woche und wir spielen am Abend Basketball. Im Winter fahre ich auch Ski.

Ich esse manchmal am Wochenende mit meinen Freunden Pizza, und dann gehen wir ins Kino. Ich sehe gern Komödien. Nächste Woche sehen wir *Skyfall*.

Liebe Grüße,

Tibor

2 Answer the questions in complete German sentences.

1 Spielt Tibor gern Computerspiele? ______
2 Was macht Tibor auf Facebook? ______
3 Wer wohnt in Neuseeland? ______
4 Wie telefoniert Tibor mit seiner Cousine? ______
5 Wie oft schwimmt Tibor? ______
6 Was machen Tibor und seine Freunde am Wochenende?
______

3 Write a reply to Tibor's email about your hobbies and activities.

Grammatik (Seiten 68–69)

1 **Complete the verb table.**

	fahren (to go/travel)	**sehen** (to see)	**lesen** (to read)
ich			
du	fährst		liest
er/sie/es		sieht	
wir			
ihr			
Sie			
sie			

2 **Complete the sentences by writing the correct form of the verb in brackets.**

1 Ich ______ das Auto. (waschen)
2 ______ du gern Mangabücher? (lesen)
3 Er ______ im Schlafzimmer. (schlafen)
4 Thomas ______ nach Stockholm in Schweden. (fahren)
5 ______ du morgen Torsten? (sehen)
6 ______ du eine Schuluniform? (tragen)

Verbs like fahren:
tragen = to wear
schlafen = to sleep
waschen = to wash

die Schuluniform = school uniform

3 **Write the question for each reply.**

1 ______ Ja, ich spiele Gitarre.
2 ______ Nein, ich spiele nicht gern Wasserball.
3 ______ Ja, Michael schläft im Bett.
4 ______ Ja, ich fahre nach Bremen.
5 ______ Ja, ich lese gern E-Books.
6 ______ Nein, ich sehe nicht gern fern.
7 ______ Ja, ich bin sportlich!
8 Was ______ Ich trage morgen Jeans und ein T-Shirt.
9 ______ Michael trägt eine Schuluniform.

Remember, to form a question you put the verb before the subject:
Du spielst gern Tennis. → Spielst du gern Tennis?

Mein Fortschritt

1 Record your levels for *Kapitel* 3.

2 Look at the level descriptors on pages 59–60 and set your targets for *Kapitel* 4.

3 Fill in what you need to do to achieve these targets.

Listening 	I have reached Level _____ in **Listening**. In *Kapitel* 4, I want to reach Level _____ I need to ______________________________ ______________________________ ______________________________ ______________________________
Speaking 	I have reached Level _____ in **Speaking**. In *Kapitel* 4, I want to reach Level _____ I need to ______________________________ ______________________________ ______________________________ ______________________________
Reading 	I have reached Level _____ in **Reading**. In *Kapitel* 4, I want to reach Level _____ I need to ______________________________ ______________________________ ______________________________ ______________________________
Writing 	I have reached Level _____ in **Writing**. In *Kapitel* 4, I want to reach Level _____ I need to ______________________________ ______________________________ ______________________________ ______________________________

Bist du sportlich? • Are you sporty?

Ich bin (sehr/ziemlich/ nicht sehr) sportlich.	*I am (very/quite/ not very) sporty.*
Was spielst du?	*What do you play?*
Ich spiele ...	*I play ...*
Ich spiele gern ...	*I like playing ...*
Ich spiele ziemlich gern ...	*I quite like playing ...*
Ich spiele nicht gern ...	*I don't like playing ... playing ...*
Badminton	*badminton*
Basketball	*basketball*
Eishockey	*ice hockey*
Fußball	*football*
Handball	*handball*
Tennis	*tennis*
Tischtennis	*table tennis*
Volleyball	*volleyball*
Wasserball	*water polo*

Was machst du gern? • What do you like doing?

Was machst du gern?	*What do you like doing?*
Ich fahre Rad.	*I ride my bike.*
Ich fahre Skateboard.	*I go skateboarding.*
Ich fahre Ski.	*I ski.*
Ich fahre Snowboard.	*I snowboard.*
Ich lese.	*I read.*
Ich mache Judo.	*I do judo.*
Ich mache Karate.	*I do karate.*
Ich reite.	*I go horse riding.*
Ich schwimme.	*I swim.*
Ich sehe fern.	*I watch TV.*
Ich spiele Gitarre.	*I play the guitar.*
Ich tanze.	*I dance.*

Wie findest du das? • What do you think of it?

Ich finde es ...	*I think it's ...*
Es ist ...	*It's ...*
irre	*amazing*
super	*super*
toll	*great*
cool	*cool*
gut	*good*
nicht schlecht	*not bad*
okay	*okay*
langweilig	*boring*
nervig	*annoying*
stinklangweilig	*deadly boring*
furchtbar	*awful*

Was machst du in deiner Freizeit? • What do you do in your free time?

Ich chille.	*I chill out.*
Ich esse Pizza oder Hamburger.	*I eat pizza or hamburgers.*
Ich gehe einkaufen.	*I go shopping.*
Ich gehe ins Kino.	*I go to the cinema.*
Ich gehe in den Park.	*I go to the park.*
Ich gehe in die Stadt.	*I go into town.*
Ich höre Musik.	*I listen to music.*
Ich mache Sport.	*I do sport.*
Ich spiele Xbox oder Wii.	*I play Xbox or on the Wii.*

Wörter

Ich bin online • I'm online

Was machst du am Computer?	*What do you do on the computer?*
Was machst du auf deinem Handy?	*What do you do on your mobile?*
Ich chatte mit Freunden auf Facebook.	*I chat with friends on Facebook.*
Ich lade Musik herunter.	*I download music.*
Ich mache Fotos oder Filme.	*I take photos or make films.*
Ich sehe Videos.	*I watch videos.*
Ich simse.	*I text.*
Ich spiele Computerspiele.	*I play computer games.*
Ich suche und lese Infos für die Hausaufgaben.	*I look for and read information for my homework.*
Ich surfe im Internet.	*I surf the internet.*
Ich telefoniere mit Freunden.	*I call my friends.*
Ich mache ziemlich viel auf meinem Handy.	*I do quite a lot of things on my mobile.*

Oft benutzte Wörter • High-frequency words

Wie oft?	*How often?*
(sehr/ziemlich/nicht so) oft	*(very/quite/not so) often*
einmal/zweimal/dreimal pro Woche/pro Monat	*once/twice/three times a week/a month*
jeden Tag	*every day*
jeden Morgen	*every morning*
manchmal	*sometimes*
immer	*always*
nie	*never*
Wann?	*When?*
am Wochenende	*at the weekend*
am Abend	*in the evening*
heute	*today*
morgen	*tomorrow*
am Montag	*on Monday*
nächste Woche	*next week*
in zwei Wochen	*in two weeks*

1 Ich mag Deutsch! (Seiten 76–77)

1 Write a sentence for each illustration.

1

2

3

4

5

6

1 Ich mag ______________________

2 ______________________

3 ______________________

4 ______________________

5 ______________________

6 ______________________

ich liebe
ich mag
ich mag ... nicht
ich hasse

2 Read the forum entries giving people's opinions about school subjects. Then answer the questions below.

Hallo Leute! Mein Lieblingsfach ist Englisch! Ich liebe Englisch, weil es total interessant ist. Ich lese sehr gern Bücher auf Spanisch und auf Deutsch. Mathe finde ich langweilig. **Pedro**

Hi Pedro! Ich mag Englisch nicht. Es ist sehr schwierig, aber ich mag Mathe und Naturwissenschaften. Ich finde Mathe supercool. **Nadine**

Grüezi aus der Schweiz! Ich liebe Theater und Kunst. Ich mag Kunst sehr gern, weil ich total kreativ bin. Informatik finde ich sehr langweilig, und Geschichte und Erdkunde sind nutzlos. **Marta**

Who ...

1 is very creative? ______________

2 enjoys reading? ______________

3 doesn't like English? ______________

4 thinks ICT is boring? ______________

5 likes maths? ______________

6 can read Spanish? ______________

7 loves art? ______________

8 doesn't like geography? ______________

3 Rewrite each sentence in exercise 1, adding *weil* and an opinion. Use the examples in exercise 2 to help you with word order.

2 Was und wann? (Seiten 78–79)

1 **Look at the timetable. Write *richtig* or *falsch* next to each statement.**

	Montag	**Dienstag**	**Mittwoch**	**Donnerstag**	**Freitag**
8.15	Mathe	Erdkunde	Englisch	Deutsch	Technik
9.15	Englisch	Informatik	Theater	Mathe	Deutsch
10.45	Kunst	Mathe	Deutsch	Kunst	Naturwissenschaften
11.45	Naturwissenschaften	Mathe	Naturwissenschaften	Geschichte	Theater
13.30	Deutsch	Sport	Technik	Musik	Englisch

vor = before **nach** = after **die Doppelstunde** = double period

1 Am Mittwoch habe ich Deutsch. ____________

2 Wir haben am Freitag nach der Pause Technik. ____________

3 Am Montag vor der Pause haben wir Englisch. ____________

4 Theater ist am Mittwoch und am Donnerstag. ____________

5 Ich habe am Donnerstag nach der Mittagspause Musik. ____________

6 Am Dienstag habe ich eine Doppelstunde Mathe. ____________

2 **At what time do you have the following subjects? Write a sentence for each.**

1 *Ich habe Englisch um neun Uhr zehn.*

2 ____________________

3 ____________________

4 ____________________

5 ____________________

6 ____________________

um acht Uhr = at 8 o'clock

3 **Look at the timetable in exercise 1 and describe one school day. Try to add interest to your sentences by giving opinions about some subjects.**

Example: Am Montag um acht Uhr fünfzehn habe ich Mathe. Ich mag Mathe, weil es interessant ist.

Ich finde Mathe ... = I find maths ...

3 Lehrer und Lehrerinnen (Seiten 80–81)

1 Write a description for each of the teachers.

1 Mein Sportlehrer heißt Herr Huber.
Er ist cool, aber sehr unpünktlich.

2 ____________________
____

3 ____________________
____

4 ____________________
____

Use some qualifiers in your descriptions: *sehr, zu, ziemlich, ein bisschen, nicht*

2 Complete the text by writing the correct word from the cloud in each gap.

Mein ____________ an der Schule ist Geschichte, ____________ meine Geschichtelehrerin sehr lustig ist! Sie ____________ nur ein Haustier, aber ihr Haustier ist eine Schlange!

Am ____________ und am Freitag haben wir Kunst. Ich finde Kunst ziemlich langweilg, weil es schwierig ____________. Mein Kunstlehrer ____________ Herr Ackermann. ____________ Schwester ist auch Kunstlehrerin an meiner ____________! Sie heißt Frau Ackermann! Meine Sportlehrerin ist ____________ freundlich. Sie heißt Frau Krause und ____________ Lieblingssport ist Volleyball. Ich mag Sport, weil ich sehr ____________ bin.

heißt hat Mittwoch Lieblingsfach ist
sehr Schule Seine sportlich weil ihr

3 Write the correct word for 'his' or 'her' in each sentence.

1 ____________ Bruder lernt Hindi. (his)
2 ____________ Schwester ist Lehrerin. (her)
3 ____________ Hobby ist Gitarre spielen. (his)
4 ____________ Lieblingsfach ist Kunst. (her)
5 ____________ Schuluniform ist fantastisch. (his)
6 ____________ Bruder ist 19 Jahre alt. (her)

Grammatik
sein = his **ihr** = her (for masculine and neuter nouns)
seine = his **ihre** = her (for feminine nouns)
Check the gender of the noun if you are unsure.

4 Im Klassenzimmer (Seiten 82–83)

1 Draw a simple picture to show where each of these things is.

1 Der Musiklehrer ist im Klassenzimmer.
2 Das Buch ist neben dem Computer.
3 Das Poster ist an der Wand.
4 Der Stuhl ist auf dem Tisch und neben der Tür.

1	2	3	4

2 What is there in the classroom? Start each sentence with *Es gibt* (there is/there are). Write the numbers as words.

12  *Es gibt zwölf Tische im Klassenzimmer.*

6  ____________________

24  ____________________

2  ____________________

4 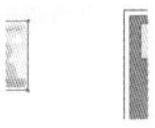 ____________________

5 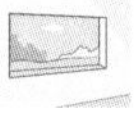 ____________________

! Look at the vocabulary on page 47 for the plurals of the nouns.

3 Answer the questions using the information in the pictures.

@peta_ush Darfst du dein Handy in der Schule benutzen?

____

@tara_winkel Darfst du im Klassenzimmer schnell laufen?

____

@e_atch Darfst du in der Pause Musik hören?

____

@janet_mc Darfst du dein Handy in der Mittagspause benutzen?

____

! ich darf du darfst er/sie/es darf

Mein Lieblingstag (Seiten 84–85)

1 Most of the verbs you've seen end in *–en* in the infinitive. Write the infinitive form of each verb in the table. Then try to work out its meaning from the context.

If the context doesn't help you, use a German–English dictionary.

verb	infinitive	meaning in English
Er **geht** in die Schule.	*gehen*	*to go, to walk*
Er **kauft** ein Auto.		
Er **steht** auf dem Tisch.		
Warum **redest** du so schnell?		
Ich **wasche** meinen Hund.		
Ich **nehme** das Buch.		

2 Guess the meaning of these compound nouns by separating out the words. Look up the compound nouns in a dictionary to find their gender and meaning.

The second word in each compound noun gives the gender.

compound noun	word 1	word 2	gender	meaning
Fußballfeld	*Fußball*		*das*	
Arbeitstag				
Sporthalle				
Klassenarbeit				
Lehrerzimmer				

3 Now write a short German sentence using each compound noun from exercise 2.

1 *Das Fußballfeld ist sehr grün und …*

2 ______________________

3 ______________________

4 ______________________

5 ______________________

Wiederholung 1

1 Mimi's description of her school day is in the wrong time order! Number the sentences 1–6 in the correct order of time.

- [ ] Ich habe um dreizehn Uhr fünfundzwanzig Musik.
- [ ] Die Pause beginnt um elf Uhr zehn.
- [ ] Die erste Stunde beginnt um acht Uhr vierzig.
- [ ] Der Bus kommt um fünfzehn Uhr siebenundvierzig.
- [ ] Ich komme um sechzehn Uhr dreißig nach Hause.
- [ ] Wir haben Mathe um elf Uhr fünfundzwanzig.

2 The school is running 20 minutes late today. Rewrite each of the six sentences in exercise 1 with the time that each activity begins today.

3 Complete the sentences by writing the correct possessive pronoun in each gap.

sein = his (for masculine and neuter nouns) **seine** = his (for feminine nouns)
ihr = her (for masculine and neuter nouns) **ihre** = her (for feminine nouns)

1 ________ Bruder heißt Pawel und ________ Schwester heißt Aga.
2 ________ Lieblingssport ist Eishockey.
3 ________ Katze ist braun, aber ________ Hund ist weiß.
4 ________ Schule ist in Hannover.

5 ________ Lieblingssport ist Reiten und ________ Lieblingsfach ist Mathe.
6 ________ Computer ist neu.
7 ________ Erdkundelehrerin ist sehr streng.
8 ________ Mutter wohnt in Salzburg, aber ________ Vater wohnt in Wien.

4 Describe where each of the items is located in the classroom.

1 Der Computer *ist auf dem Tisch.*
2 Das Poster ________
3 Das Whiteboard ________
4 Der Lehrer ________
5 Der Stuhl ________
6 Die Spinne ________

Wiederholung 2

1 Read the texts. Use your knowledge of vocabulary to help you to find these new phrases. Write each German phrase next to the English.

1 My name is ______________________
2 her favourite artist ______________________
3 unfortunately ______________________
4 My brother also goes ______________________
5 an indoor pool ______________________
6 a pot plant ______________________

Hallo! Mein Name ist **Maik** und ich wohne in München, in Deutschland. Meine Schule heißt Mathias Brauer Gymnasium und ich finde sie toll. An meiner Schule lerne ich sehr gern Englisch und Geschichte, aber mein Lieblingsfach ist Kunst. Ich mag Kunst, weil ich total kreativ bin. Ich finde meine Kunstlehrerin auch sehr nett. Sie heißt Frau Weber und ihr Lieblingskünstler ist Dürer.

Ich mag nicht Sport, weil ich nicht sehr sportlich bin. Leider habe ich am Montag und auch am Mittwoch Sport. Morgen spielen wir Tennis. Das finde ich nicht so schlecht.

lernen = to learn

Hallo Leute! Ich heiße **Sabine** und ich wohne in Zürich, in der Schweiz. Meine Schule ist sehr groß. Mein Bruder geht auch auf meine Schule.

Mein Lieblingsfach ist Musik und dieses Fach haben wir am Dienstag in der zweiten Stunde und auch am Donnerstag in der vierten Stunde. Sport mag ich auch, weil der Sportlehrer total lustig ist. Sein Lieblingssport ist Schwimmen und wir haben ein Hallenbad in der Schule. Wir haben Sport am Mittwoch in der fünften Stunde und auch am Freitag in der zweiten Stunde.

Mein Klassenzimmer ist sehr schön. Wir haben zehn Computer, ein Whiteboard neben der Tür, viele Poster an der Wand und eine Topfpflanze am Fenster!

2 Answer the questions about the texts in exercise 1. Write complete sentences in German for your answers.

1 Wie heißt Maiks Schule? ______________________
2 Was mag Maik? ______________________
3 Was lernt Maik nicht gern? ______________________
4 Wann hat Maik Sport? ______________________
5 Wo ist Zürich? ______________________
6 Was hat Sabine am Donnerstag in der vierten Stunde? ______________________
7 Warum mag Sabine Sport? ______________________
8 Wo ist die Topfpflanze? ______________________

Grammatik (Seiten 90–91)

1 Answer the questions in full sentences, using *weil* and the reason given.

1 Warum magst du Kunst? (it's creative)

Ich mag Kunst, weil es kreativ ist.

2 Warum magst du Englisch? (it's interesting)

______

3 Warum spielst du Tennis? (I'm sporty)

______

4 Warum hasst du Sport? (it's difficult)

______

5 Warum findest du Erdkunde toll? (it's easy)

______

2 Put the words in the right order to make sentences.

Remember the 'verb in second place' rule.

1 der in Geschichte dritten wir Stunde haben

______

2 habe Pause ich nach der Kunst ______

3 Fußball spiele heute ich ______

4 gibt Klassenzimmer Computer und viele einen es im Poster

______

5 Montag ich vierten Stunde habe in am der Mathe

______

3 Write the following school rules in sentences in German.

Example: Man darf am Montag ...

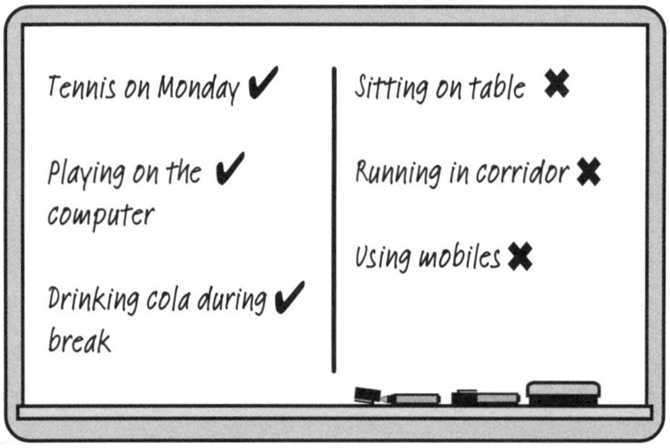

Man darf is often used to mean 'you/we are allowed to'.

Remember to use the correct preposition and the correct word for 'the' after it.

Mein Fortschritt

1 **Record your levels for *Kapitel* 4.**

2 **Look at the level descriptors on pages 59–60 and set your targets for *Kapitel* 5.**

3 **Fill in what you need to do to achieve these targets.**

Listening 	I have reached Level ______ in **Listening**. In *Kapitel* 5, I want to reach Level ______ I need to ________________________________ ________________________________ ________________________________ ________________________________
Speaking  	I have reached Level ______ in **Speaking**. In *Kapitel* 5, I want to reach Level ______ I need to ________________________________ ________________________________ ________________________________ ________________________________
Reading 	I have reached Level ______ in **Reading**. In *Kapitel* 5, I want to reach Level ______ I need to ________________________________ ________________________________ ________________________________ ________________________________
Writing 	I have reached Level ______ in **Writing**. In *Kapitel* 5, I want to reach Level ______ I need to ________________________________ ________________________________ ________________________________ ________________________________

Schulfächer • School subjects

Deutsch	*German*
Englisch	*English*
Erdkunde	*geography*
Geschichte	*history*
Informatik	*ICT*
Kunst	*art*
Mathe	*maths*
Musik	*music*
Naturwissenschaften	*science*
Sport	*sport, PE*
Technik	*technology*
Theater	*drama*

Meinungen • Opinions

mein Lieblingsfach ist ...	*my favourite subject is ...*
ich mag ... (sehr)	*I like ... (a lot)*
ich liebe	*I love*
ich mag ... nicht	*I don't like ...*
ich hasse	*I hate*
gut	*good*
toll	*great*
furchtbar	*awful*
einfach	*easy*
schwierig	*difficult*
interessant	*interesting*
langweilig	*boring*
nützlich	*useful*
nutzlos	*useless*
faszinierend	*fascinating*
nervig	*irritating*
supercool	*really cool*
stinklangweilig	*dead boring*

Die Wochentage • The days of the week

Montag (Mo.)	*Monday*
Dienstag (Di.)	*Tuesday*
Mittwoch (Mi.)	*Wednesday*
Donnerstag (Do.)	*Thursday*
Freitag (Fr.)	*Friday*
Samstag (Sa.)	*Saturday*
Sonntag (So.)	*Sunday*
Was hast du am Montag?	*What do you have on Monday?*
Am Dienstag habe ich ...	*I have ... on Tuesday*
Am Sonntag haben wir keine Schule.	*We have no school on Sunday.*

Die Zeit • Time

Wann?	*When?*
Um wie viel Uhr?	*At what time?*
Um 8:30 Uhr (acht Uhr dreißig).	*At 8:30.*
Wie viel Uhr ist es?	*What time is it?*
Es ist 9:50 Uhr (neun Uhr fünfzig).	*It's 9:50.*
in der ersten Stunde	*in the first lesson*
vor der Pause	*before break*
nach der Mittagspause	*after the lunch break*

Eigenschaften • Characteristics

Er/Sie ist ...	*He/She is ...*
alt	*old*
fair	*fair*
freundlich	*friendly*
jung	*young*
launisch	*moody*
lustig	*funny*
nervig	*annoying*
streng	*strict*
unpünktlich	*unpunctual*

In der Schule • In school

die Lehrerin(-nen)	*teacher (female)*
die Deutsch-lehrerin(-nen)	*German teacher (female)*
der Lehrer(–)	*teacher (male)*
der Sportlehrer(–)	*sports teacher (male)*
Was gibt es?	*What is there?*
Es gibt einen/eine/ein ...	*There is a ...*
Es gibt viele ...	*There are lots of ...*
das Klassenzimmer(–)	*classroom*
der Tisch(-e)	*table*
der Stuhl(¨-e)	*chair*
der Computer(–)	*computer*
das Whiteboard(-s)	*whiteboard*
das Poster(–)	*poster*
das Fenster(–)	*window*
die Wand(¨-e)	*wall*
die Tür(-en)	*door*
der Korridor(-e)	*corridor*

Wo ist das? • Where is it?

in der Schule	*in the school*
im Klassenzimmer	*in the classroom*
im Korridor	*in the corridor*
an der Wand	*on the wall*
am Fenster	*by the window*
am Tisch	*at the table*
auf dem Tisch	*on the table*
neben der Tür	*near/next to the door*

Oft benutzte Wörter • High-frequency words

weil	*because*
sein/seine	*his*
ihr/ihre	*her*
zu	*too*
sehr	*very*
ziemlich	*quite, fairly*
ein bisschen	*a bit*
nicht	*not*
haben	*to have*
sein	*to be*
in	*in*
an	*at, by, on (wall)*
auf	*on (top of)*
neben	*near, next to*
heute	*today*
morgen	*tomorrow*
vor	*before*
nach	*after*

1 In der Stadt (Seiten 98–99)

1 Write sentences to say what there is and isn't in the town.

1 Es gibt hier ______________________________. 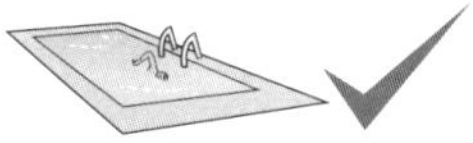

2 Hier gibt es ______________________________. 

3 In der Stadt gibt es ______________________________. 

4 Es gibt ______________________________ hier. 

Grammatik

der → einen/keinen **die** → eine/keine **das** → ein/kein

2 Read the texts. Tick the things there are in each person's town and cross the things there aren't.

Monika: *Ich wohne in Celle. Meine Stadt ist nicht sehr groß. Es gibt hier ein Schloss und auch einen Marktplatz. Leider gibt es kein Schwimmbad und auch keine Kegelbahn.*

leider = unfortunately

Erik: *Die Touristen kommen gern nach Verden, weil es eine Kirche und auch einen Marktplatz gibt. Ein Schloss gibt es auch, aber leider gibt es kein Schwimmbad und keine Imbissstube.*

Aisha: *Ich wohne in Neustadt, in der Nähe vom Titisee. Neustadt ist ganz klein, aber sehr schön. Es gibt hier kein Schloss, keine Kegelbahn und leider auch kein Kino. Wir haben aber einen Bahnhof, eine Kirche und auch einen alten Marktplatz. Wir haben kein Schwimmbad, aber man kann im Sommer im Titisee schwimmen!*

	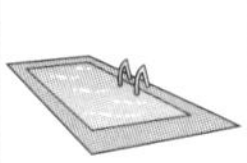		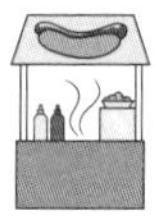	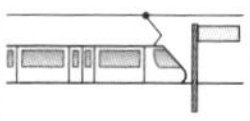	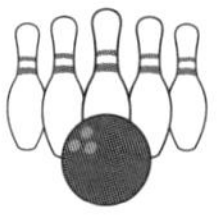	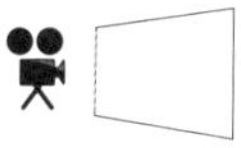		
Monika								
Erik								
Aisha								

3 Write two or three sentences about what there is to do where you live, as well as what there isn't. Use the texts in exercise 2 to help you.

2 Wir gehen einkaufen! (Seiten 100–101)

1 Write what the customers in the souvenir shop would like. Start your sentences with *Ich möchte*.

1 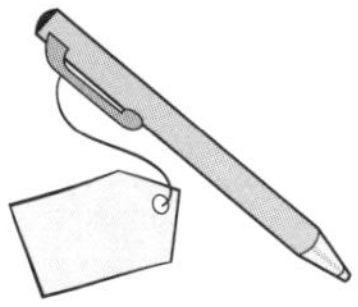

2 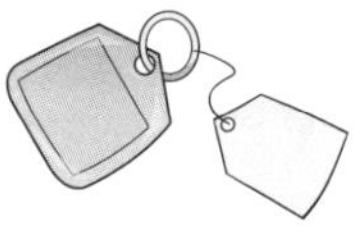

3 

4 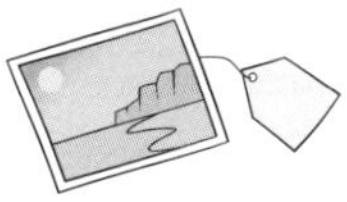

5 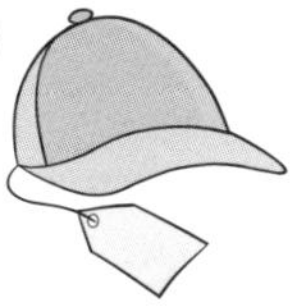

6 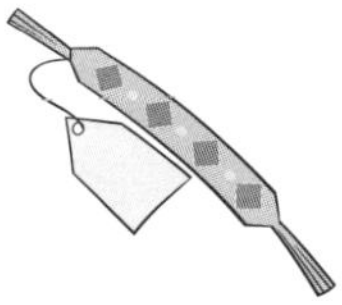

7 

8 

Look at the vocabulary on page 57 if you need to check which words to use.

1 *Ich möchte einen Kuli.*

2 ______________________

3 ______________________

4 ______________________

5 ______________________

6 ______________________

7 ______________________

8 ______________________

2 Complete the dialogue with words from the cloud below. Then number the lines of the conversation in the correct order 1–11.

- [ ] Guten Tag! ______________ ich dir helfen?
- [ ] Welche ______________ ? Wir haben blau, rot oder schwarz.
- [ ] Ja, klar! Dieser ______________ , zum Beispiel, kostet nur €18,95.
- [ ] Super!
- [ ] Danke. Auf ______________ .
- [ ] Sonst noch etwas?
- [ ] Alles ______________ kostet das €38,95.
- [ ] Guten Tag! Ich möchte ein Souvenir ______________ , vielleicht ein Kuscheltier. Haben Sie ______________ ?
- [ ] Bitte sehr.
- [ ] Ja. Ich möchte ein ______________ für meine Schwester.
- [ ] Schwarz, bitte. Wie viel ______________ das?

*zusammen   Elefant   Kuscheltiere
Wiedersehen   Kann
kostet   Fußballtrikot   kaufen
Farbe*

3 Mmm, lecker! (Seiten 102–103)

1 **Write four short conversations between hungry customers and the owner of the snack stand. The price of each individual item is shown: don't forget to add up the total price.**

1

× 1
drei Euro zehn

× 1
zwei Euro fünfunddreißig

2

× 2
zwei Euro sechzig

× 2
zwei Euro fünfundzwanzig

3

× 3
drei Euro zwanzig

× 1
ein Euro neunzig

4

× 4
drei Euro fünfundneunzig

× 1
zwei Euro zehn

Ich möchte .../Ich hätte gern ...	I'd like ...
Das kostet alles zusammen ...	All together that costs ...

1 *Guten Tag! Ich möchte einmal Hamburger und einmal Bratwurst, bitte.*

Das kostet alles zusammen € ...

2 ____________________

____

3 ____________________

____

4 ____________________

____

2 **Write a short review of the menu, saying what there is to eat and drink and what you do and don't like.**

Hamburger 
Bratwurst
Pommes 
Salat
Eis
Tee
Cola
Mineralwasser

Man kann ... trinken/essen.	You can eat/drink ...
Ich esse/trinke gern ...	I like eating/drinking ...
Ich esse/trinke nicht gern ...	I don't like eating/drinking ...
Ich mag ...	I like ....
Ich mag nicht ...	I don't like .....

____

____

____

4 In den Sommerferien (Seiten 104–105)

1 Circle the correct option to complete each sentence from the choices given. Then write the missing words in the gaps.

1 Ich ______________ im See baden.

a wirst **b** werden **c** werde

2 Wir werden im ______________ schwimmen.

a Meer **b** windsurfen **c** Bratwurst

3 ______________ du nach Innsbruck fahren?

a Wird **b** Wirst **c** Bist

4 Er ______________ nicht nach Hannover ______________ .

a werden; fahre **b** kann; fährt **c** wird; fahren

5 Tobi ______________ in den ______________ nach Portugal fahren.

a werde; Park **b** wird; Bahnhof **c** wird; Sommerferien

6 Wohin ______________ wir ______________ ?

a werden; gehen **b** kann; gehen **c** darf; fahren

2 Read the sentences and write the correct words from the cloud in the gaps. There are more words than you need.

1 Ich werde eine Kappe ______________ meinen Vater kaufen.
2 Ich ______________ ein Trikot kaufen.
3 In den ______________ fahren wir nach Rom.
4 Es ______________ ein Schwimmbad und ein Kino in Walsrode.
5 Wir ______________ nach Magdeburg fahren.
6 Ich möchte in den Bergen ______________ gehen.

für
gibt
möchte
nächste Woche
Sommerferien
wandern
werde
werden

3 Write about your plans for the summer holidays. Use the questions and illustrations to help you.

- Wohin wirst du fahren?

- Wer kommt mit?

- Was wirst du dort machen?

- Was wird dein Bruder / deine Schwester machen

- Wirst du Souvenirs kaufen?

1 **Rewrite each sentence. Swap the adjective in bold for an alternative adjective with a similar meaning.**

1 Das Mozart Museum ist **faszinierend**. ______

2 Der Marktplatz ist **historisch**. ______

3 Das Schwimmbad ist **modern**.

______

4 Die Kegelbahn ist **toll**. ______

2 **Join up the sentence halves to describe a trip to Vienna.**

1 In den Sommerferien werde	a Tage in Wien bleiben.
2 Dort gibt es einen	b ich nach Wien fahren.
3 Am Montag kann	c Wien fantastisch.
4 Ich finde	d Marktplatz, aber keinen See.
5 Wir werden vier	e man das Mozart Museum besuchen.

Now rewrite the sentences, varying the sentence structure. Remember that in German you always need the verb as the second idea.

Example: **1** Ich werde in den Sommerferien ...

3 **Read the text about Hahndorf. Try to work out what the words in bold mean from the context. If you can't work out the meanings, look them up in a dictionary.**

Hahndorf ist eine kleine Stadt in Südaustralien, in der Nähe von Adelaide. Es gibt dort deutsche **Einwanderer**. Die Stadt ist klein, aber **fein**! Hahndorf ist toll für Kinder und auch für **Erwachsene**. Dort gibt es viele deutsche Restaurants und Cafés. Am Mittwoch und am Sonntag gibt es immer einen Markt auf dem Marktplatz. Man kann hier Schokolade, **Kuchen** und **Kleidung** kaufen. **Wein** aus der Region kann man auch dort trinken. Ich werde **nächstes Jahr** mit meiner Schule nach Hahndorf fahren.

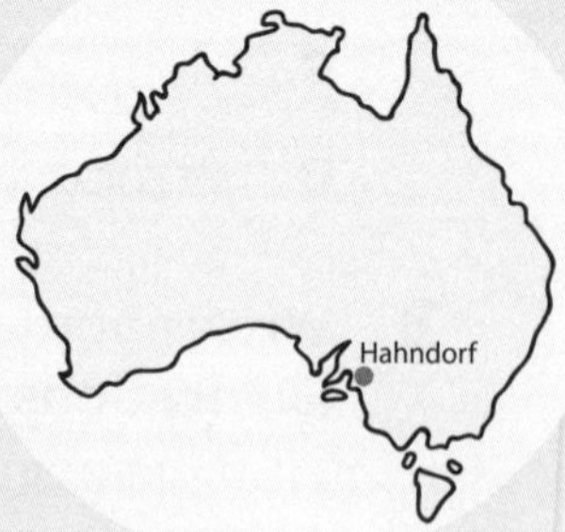

4 **Write about a city or town of your choice. Adapt some of the words and phrases from the text in exercise 3.**

Remember to include: the future tense, opinions, linking words, qualifiers, frequency expressions and inverted word order.

Wiederholung 1

1 **Decide which souvenir you would buy for each person and write the price in words.**

Grammatik
der → *er*   *die* → *sie*   *das* → *es*

Remember, *der* changes to *den* for masculine nouns.

1 Meine Mutter: Ich werde die Tasse für meine Mutter kaufen. Sie kostet sieben Euro fünfundfünfzig.

2 Onkel Karl: ______________________

3 Meine Schwester: ______________________

4 Meine Freundin: ______________________

5 Frau Roberts: ______________________

2 **Peter is in the tourist office in Munich. Read the dialogue, then answer the questions in full German sentences.**

Tourist guide: Guten Tag! Willkommen in München!

Peter: Guten Tag! Danke schön! Was gibt es hier in München?

Tourist guide: Hier gibt es viel zu tun! Man kann in München alles sehen!

Peter: Gibt es hier einen Marktplatz?

Tourist guide: Natürlich! Er heißt Marienplatz. Er ist sehr groß und total schön.

Peter: Wunderbar! Und kann man in München Ski fahren?

Tourist guide: Also ... nicht direkt in München, aber in der Nähe von hier kann man sehr gut Ski fahren.

Peter: Super. Und gibt es hier ein gutes Restaurant? Ich möchte gern Pizza essen.

Tourist guide: Ja, das gibt es! Es heißt *Robertos*. Dort kann man gut Pizza essen.

Peter: Vielen Dank. Ich werde im Restaurant *Robertos* essen. Auf Wiedersehen!

1 Was kann man in München machen?
2 Wie heißt der Marktplatz?
3 Wie ist er?
4 Wo kann man Ski fahren?
5 Was möchte Peter essen?
6 Was ist *Robertos*?

Wiederholung 2

1 Rewrite the sentences in the future tense. Identify the subject to help you change the form of *werden*.

1 Wir tauchen im Meer. Wir werden im Meer tauchen.

2 Wir baden im See. ____________________

3 Ich gehe an den Strand. ____________________

4 Lena und Michael klettern am Samstag in den Bergen.

____

5 Er kauft ein Kuscheltier für seine kleine Schwester.

____

6 Kaufst du eine Kappe als Souvenir? ____________________

7 Wir gehen am Wochenende mit meinen Freunden einkaufen.

____

2 Read the postcard and answer the questions in full German sentences.

Liebe Oma und Lieber Opa!

Hallo aus Mallorca in Spanien! Wir bleiben zwei Wochen hier, weil wir Sommerferien haben. Es gibt hier alles – einen Wasserpark, ein Schloss und auch einen Markt. Jeden Tag schwimmen wir im Meer. Im Hotel gibt es ein Schwimmbad und wir schwimmen auch hier. Man kann windsurfen und auch tauchen. Mallorca ist auch für das Essen sehr bekannt.

Nächste Woche werden wir in den Bergen klettern. Ich möchte auch segeln. Ich werde auch Souvenirs kaufen!

Alles Liebe,

Tamika

1 Warum ist Tamika in Spanien? ____________________

2 Was gibt es in Mallorca? ____________________

3 Was kann man machen? ____________________

4 Ist Mallorca bekannt für das Museum? ____________________

5 Was wird Tamika nächste Woche machen? ____________________

3 Write four true/false statements in English about the text in exercise 2. Then ask a friend to write 'True' or 'False' next to each statement.

Example: The postcard is to Tamika's parents. False

Grammatik (Seiten 112–113)

1 Rewrite the sentences to make them negative.

Use *keinen/keine/kein* to say what there is or isn't. Use *nicht* to say what you can't or don't like doing.

1 Es gibt in Düsseldorf einen Marktplatz.

____

2 Er mag Wasserball.

____

3 Beni kann Fußball spielen, weil er einen Ball hat.

____

4 In der Stadt gibt es ein Kino und auch eine Kirche.

____

5 Man darf hier schwimmen. _______________

2 Write the different forms of *möchten* in the table.

ich		wir	
du		ihr	
er/sie/es		Sie	
		sie	

möchten
möchte
möchten
möchtest
möchte
möchtet
möchten

Complete the sentences by writing the correct form of *möchten* in each gap. Then translate the sentences into English.

1 __________ du ein Schokoladeneis?

2 Nein, aber ich __________ gern ein Vanilleeis.

3 Anne __________ nach Kapstadt in Südafrika fahren.

4 __________ ihr auch nach Windhuk in Namibia fahren?

5 Wir __________ zweimal Salat und zweimal Mineralwasser, bitte.

6 Frau Winkelmann, __________ Sie eine Tasse Tee?

3 Fill in the gaps to complete the different forms of *werden*.

ich __e__de
du w__r__t
er/sie/es __ir__
wir we__ de__
ihr __er__e__
Sie/sie w__r__en

4 Write sentences about what you and your family/friends will do on your next holiday.

Example: Ich werde jeden Tag in Frankreich wandern. Mein Bruder … /Steffi …

Jahresbilanz

Record your levels for *Kapitel* 5.

Listening	I have reached Level ______ in **Listening**.
Speaking	I have reached Level ______ in **Speaking**.
Reading	I have reached Level ______ in **Reading**.
Writing	I have reached Level ______ in **Writing**.

Look back through your workbook and note down the level you achieved in each skill by the end of each *Kapitel*.

	Listening	**Speaking**	**Reading**	**Writing**
1 Meine Welt und ich				
2 Familie und Tiere				
3 Freizeit – juhu!				
4 Schule ist klasse!				
5 Gute Reise!				

You now have a record of your progress in German for the whole year.

In der Stadt • In town

Es gibt ...	*There is ... / There are ...*
Es gibt ein/eine/einen ...	*There is/are a ...*
Es gibt kein/keine/keinen ...	*There isn't/aren't ...*
in der Nähe von ...	*near to*
in der Nähe ...	*nearby*
der Bahnhof(-̈e)	*railway station(s)*
der Imbiss(-e)/die Imbissstube(-n)	*snack stand(s)*
die Kegelbahn(-en)	*bowling alley(s)*
das Kino(-s)	*cinema(s)*
die Kirche(-n)	*church(es)*
der Marktplatz(-̈e)	*market square(s)*
der Park(-s)	*park(s)*
das Schloss(-̈er)	*castle(s)*
das Schwimmbad(-̈er)	*swimming pool(s)*
die Eisbahn(-en)	*ice rink(s)*
der Fischmarkt(-̈e)	*fish market(s)*
das Kindertheater(-)	*children's theatre(s)*
der Radweg(-e)	*cycle path(s)*
das Sportzentrum (die Sportzentren)	*sports centre (sports centres)*
der Stadtpark(-s)	*city/town park(s)*
der Wasserpark(-s)	*water park(s)*

Verkaufsgespräch • Sales conversation

Ich gehe einkaufen.	*I am going shopping.*
Ich möchte ...	*I would like ...*
Ich möchte ... kaufen.	*I would like to buy ...*
Haben Sie ...?	*Do you have ...?*
Kann ich dir helfen?	*Can I help you?*
Sonst noch etwas?	*Anything else?*
alles zusammen	*all together*

Souvenirs • Souvenirs

der Aufkleber	*sticker*
das Freundschaftsband	*friendship bracelet*
die Kappe	*(baseball) cap*
der Kuli	*biro*
das Kuscheltier	*cuddly toy*
die Postkarte	*postcard*
der Schlüsselanhänger	*key ring*
die Tasse	*mug/cup*
das Trikot	*(football) shirt*
Wie viel kostet ...?	*How much does ... cost?*
Wie viel kostet das?	*How much does it cost?*
Es kostet €16.	*It costs 16 Euros.*

Snacks und Getränke kaufen • Buying snacks and drinks

die Bratwurst	*fried sausage*
der Hamburger	*hamburger*
die Pizza	*pizza*
die Pommes	*chips*
der Salat	*salad*
das Eis	*ice cream*
die Cola	*cola*
das Mineralwasser	*mineral water*
der Tee	*tea*
das Fleisch	*meat*
der Ketchup	*ketchup*
die Mayo(nnaise)/Majonäse	*mayo(nnaise)*
der Senf	*mustard*
Ich möchte einmal/zweimal/dreimal ...	*I would like one/two/three ...*
Ich hätte gern ...	*I would like ...*
Das macht €8.	*That's €8.*
Ich esse ... gern.	*I like eating ... .*
Ich trinke ... gern.	*I like drinking ... .*

Wörter

In den Sommerferien • During the summer holidays

Was wirst du machen?	*What will you do?*
Ich werde ...	*I will ...*
Wir werden ...	*We will ...*
klettern	*climb*
im Meer schwimmen	*swim in the sea*
rodeln	*toboggan*
im See baden	*bathe in the lake*
segeln	*sail*
an den Strand gehen	*go to the beach*
tauchen	*dive*
wandern	*hike*
windsurfen	*windsurf*
Was kann man dort machen?	*What can you do there?*
Man kann ... besuchen.	*'One'/People/ You can visit ...*
Die Stadt ist bekannt für ...	*The town is well known for ...*
Ich werde (eine Woche) bleiben.	*I will stay (for a week).*

Oft benutzte Wörter • High-frequency words

am Montag	*on Monday*
am Dienstag	*on Tuesday*
am Mittwoch	*on Wednesday*
am Donnerstag	*on Thursday*
am Freitag	*on Friday*
am Wochenende	*at the weekend*
sehr	*very*
nicht sehr	*not very*
ziemlich	*quite*
immer	*always*
nicht immer	*not always*
oft	*often*
nicht oft	*not often*
nie	*never*
alles	*everything*
dort	*there*
teuer	*expensive*

Level descriptors

Listening

Level 1	I can understand some familiar spoken words and phrases.
Level 2	I can understand a range of familiar spoken phrases.
Level 3	I can understand the main points of short spoken passages and note people's answers to questions.
Level 4	I can understand the main points of spoken passages and some of the detail.
Level 5	I can understand the main points and opinions in spoken passages about different topics. I can recognise if people are speaking about the future **OR** the past as well as the present.

Speaking

Level 1	I can say single words and short phrases.
Level 2	I can answer simple questions and use set phrases.
Level 3	I can ask questions and use short phrases to answer questions about myself.
Level 4	I can take part in conversations. I can express my opinions. I can use grammar to change phrases to say something new.
Level 5	I can give short talks, in which I express my opinions. I can take part in conversations giving information, opinions and reasons. I can speak about the future **OR** the past as well as the present.

Level descriptors

Reading

Level 1	I can understand familiar words and phrases.
Level 2	I can understand familiar phrases. I can read aloud familiar words and phrases. I can use a vocabulary list to check meanings.
Level 3	I can understand the main points and people's answers to questions in short written texts.
Level 4	I can understand the main points in short texts and some of the detail. Sometimes I can work out the meaning of new words.
Level 5	I can understand the main points and opinions in texts about different topics. I can recognise if the texts are about the future **OR** the past as well as the present.

Writing

Level 1	I can write or copy single words correctly.
Level 2	I can copy short sentences correctly and write some words from memory.
Level 3	I can answer questions about myself. I can write short phrases from memory. I can write short sentences with help.
Level 4	I can write short texts on familiar topics. I can use grammar to change phrases to write something new.
Level 5	I can write short texts on a range of familiar topics. I can write about the future **OR** the past as well as the present.

Notes

Notes

Published by Pearson Education Limited, Edinburgh Gate, Harlow, Essex, CM20 2JE.

www.pearsonschoolsandfecolleges.co.uk

Edited by Melanie Birdsall
Designed by Kamae Design

Illustrated by Caron at KJA Artists and Lisa Hunt

First published 2013

2022
17

British Library Cataloguing in Publication Data
A catalogue record for this book is available from the British Library

ISBN 978 1 447 94654 0

Printed in Great Britain by Bell and Bain Ltd, Glasgow

Acknowledgements

We would like to thank Melissa Weir, Angelika Libera, Janet Soame and Frances Reynolds for their invaluable help in the development of this course.

Every effort has been made to contact copyright holders of material reproduced in this book. Any omissions will be rectified in subsequent printings if notice is given to the publishers.

www.pearsonschools.co.uk
myorders@pearson.com

T 0845 630 33 33
F 0845 630 77 77

ISBN 978-1-4479-4654-0

Stimmt! 1

Übungsheft B

Malcolm Pacey

ALWAYS LEARNING

PEARSON

1 Hallo! (Seiten 8–9)

1 **Two of the words in each set have a sound that is the same. Circle the word with a different sound from the other two.**

1	*Schlange*	*Porsche*	*Buch*
2	*Bär*	*Löwe*	*Röntgenbild*
3	*Wildwassersport*	*Auf Wiedersehen*	*Tür*
4	*Biene*	*heiße*	*Eis*

2 **Join up the sentence halves.**

1 Gut, danke. Und
2 Auf
3 Ich heiße
4 Hallo! Wie heißt
5 Ich heiße Nadia. Wie
6 Nicht

a Wiedersehen.
b Ben. Wie heißt du?
c geht's, Ben?
d du?
e schlecht.
f dir?

3 **Write the sentences from exercise 2 in the correct order for the conversation. Then translate them into English.**

1 __________ __________
2 __________ __________
3 __________ __________
4 __________ __________
5 Nicht schlecht. Not bad.
6 __________ __________

4 **Unscramble the inventions. Look at the definite article (word for 'the') for each word. Then write each invention with the indefinite article (word for 'a').**

1 sad ngbönReltid das … ein …
2 erd reelmiDtoos
3 sda toF3rMmPa-
4 sad PeuAsotrcoh
5 ied sAMrkdadiae

2 Eins, zwei, drei ... (Seiten 10–11)

1 **The bank has sent texts to customers with their coded PIN numbers. Solve the maths problems in German to work out the PINs. Then write each customer's new PIN below the phone.**

1

Meine Bank

zehn – acht = zwei

vier + drei = sieben

zwei + drei = ______

fünf + eins = ______

2 7 _ _

2

Meine Bank

sechs + zwei = ______

zehn – neun = ______

sieben – drei = ______

eins + vier = ______

_ _ _ _

3

Meine Bank

sieben – vier = ______

acht + eins = ______

drei + sechs = ______

fünf + zwei = ______

_ _ _ _

2 **Write the winning lottery numbers in words.**

1 13 ______ **2** 11 ______ **3** 16 ______

4 18 ______ **5** 12 ______ **6** 17 ______

3 **Write two sentences for each speaker. Give the speaker's age and the age of his/her friend.**

er ist = he is
sie ist = she is

1

Ich bin dreizehn Jahre alt.
Sie ist zwölf Jahre alt.

2

______
______

3

______
______

3 Ich wohne in Deutschland (Seiten 12–13)

1 **Read the dialogue and complete the table with the correct forms of each verb.**

Melanie: Hallo! Ich heiße Melanie. Wie heißt du?
Marco: Ich heiße Marco. Ich wohne in Straubing. Wo wohnst du?
Melanie: Ich wohne in Braunschweig. Wie alt bist du?
Marco: Ich bin zwölf Jahre alt. Wer ist das?
Melanie: Sie heißt Jessie. Sie wohnt in Leipzig und ist dreizehn Jahre alt.

wer = who

	heißen (to be called)	**wohnen** (to live)	**sein** (to be)
ich (I)		*wohne*	
du (you)			*bist*
er/sie/es (he/she/it)	*heißt*		

2 **Write the missing word in each sentence and complete the crossword.**

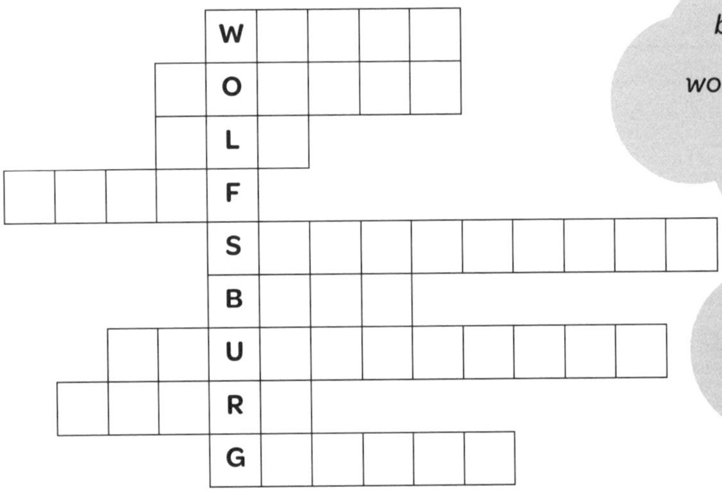

bist *zwölf* *wohne* *wohnst* *Jahre* *Schottland* *Deutschland* *geht's* *alt*

1 Ich __________ in Manchester.
2 Wo __________ du, Nick?
3 Wie __________ ist er?
4 Er ist __________ Jahre alt.
5 Glasgow ist in __________.
6 Wie alt __________ du?
7 Ich wohne in Berlin. Das ist in __________.
8 Ich bin elf __________ alt.
9 Wie __________?

3 **Research why the city of Wolfsburg is important to Germany.**

4 Meine Welt ist wunderbar! (Seiten 14–15)

1 The printer has made four mistakes labelling the illustrations. Write *richtig* or *falsch* under each caption.

1 
Ich bin musikalisch.
____

2 
Ich bin sehr launisch.
____

3 
Ich bin ziemlich freundlich.
____

4 
Ich bin kreativ.
____

5 
Ich bin laut.
____

6 
Ich bin lustig.
____

2 Rewrite the false captions from exercise 1, correcting them so that they are true.

____

____

____

____

faul
lustig
musikalisch
sportlich

3 Separate out the words to form three sentences.

meinelieblingsfußballmannschaftistbayernmünchen

meinlieblingssportisttennis

meinelieblingszahlistsieben

Remember that each sentence must start with a capital letter. Also, remember that nouns start with a capital letter.

1 ____

2 ____

3 ____

4 Write a sentence about your favourite …

1 football team: ________________________________

2 sport: ________________________________

3 number: ________________________________

5 Meine Sachen (Seiten 16–17)

1 Write the German question word under its English translation.

Who?	What?	How?	Where?	Where from?

Wie? *Was?* *Wo?* *Woher?* *Wer?*

2 Write the correct question word in each question. You may use each word more than once.

1 ______________ bist du? Sportlich?

2 ______________ wohnt Shiva?

3 ______________ heißt du?

4 ______________ kommst du?

5 ______________ ist das? Ist das Max?

6 ______________ alt ist Michael?

7 ______________ ist Hannover? *Hannover ist in Deutschland!*

8 ______________ ist deine Lieblingsmusik?

3 Read the paragraph below. Pretend that you're Gabi, and answer each question in a complete German sentence.

Hallo! Ich heiße Gabi und ich bin vierzehn Jahre alt. Ich wohne in Kiel, in Deutschland, aber ich komme aus Swansea. Das ist in Wales. Wie bin ich? Ich bin sportlich, lustig und auch sehr laut! Mein Lieblingsmonat ist Dezember und meine Lieblingssendung ist ‚Die Simpsons'. Ich habe ein iPad und auch einen Computer. Tschüs!

1 Wie heißt du? ______________________________

2 Wo wohnst du? ______________________________

3 Woher kommst du? ______________________________

4 Wie bist du? ______________________________

5 Wie heißt deine Lieblingssendung? ______________________________

6 Was hast du? ______________________________

6 Writing Skills Ich über mich (Seiten 18–19)

1 Complete the table with the correct words.

	the	a	my	your
masculine: Sport				
feminine: Musik				
neuter: Auto				

2 Write each sentence or question in German. Tick the boxes when you've checked each part of your work.

Part of writing accurately in any language is going back over your work to check that there aren't any mistakes. Get into the habit now and watch both your English and German improve!

1 I'm called Osman.

____

2 I live in Germany.

____

3 I'm quite friendly and also creative.

____

____

4 I have a mobile phone.

____

5 Where do you live?

____

- ☐ Spelling of key phonics sound 'ei'
- ☐ Name has a capital
- ☐ Spelling of key phonics sound 'eu'
- ☐ Full stop at the end
- ☐ Check the qualifier
- ☐ Check the connective
- ☐ Capital on the noun
- ☐ Right word for 'a'
- ☐ Correct question word
- ☐ Verb in second position

3 Write a short paragraph about yourself. Use the sentences in exercise 2 as prompts. Check your work against the checklist below.

☐ genders ☐ qualifiers ☐ connectives ☐ verbs
☐ capital letters ☐ spelling ☐ question words

____

____

Wiederholung 1

1 Fill in the gaps by writing the German for the words in brackets.

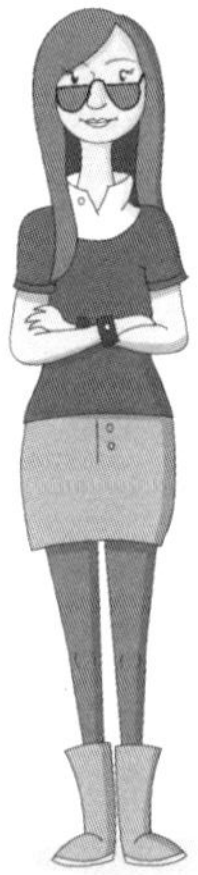

Hallo! Ich ________ (am called) Marie und ich ________ (live) in Walsrode. Das ist in ________ (Germany). Ich bin fünfzehn ________ (years) alt. Ich bin ________ (very) sportlich und ________ (quite) intelligent, ________ (but) ich bin ________ (also) faul. Mein ________ (favourite sport) ist Hockey und ________ (my) Lieblingsmusik ist Pop. Ich ________ (have) einen Vogel aus Amerika. Er ist ________ (very) freundlich, aber ________ (not) laut!

2 Crack the code and write the sentences correctly.

ä = 27 ü = 29
ö = 28 ß = 30

a 18/24/19 4/12/19/13/22 18/13 20/28/7/7/18/13/20/22/13

Ich wohne in Göttingen.

b 22/9 18/8/7 20/26/13/1 21/9/22/6/13/23/15/18/24/19

____

c 14/22/18/13/22 15/18/22/25/15/18/13/20/8/14/6/8/18/16 18/8/7 14/12/1/26/9/7

____

____

3 Make up a coded sentence in German for a classmate to solve. Don't forget to provide a key.

4 Write the questions you would ask to get these answers.

1 *Wie heißt du?*

Ich heiße Elaine.

2 ________

Mein Lieblingssport ist Tennis.

3 ________

Sami ist musikalisch und intelligent, aber sehr launisch.

4 ________

Alwin ist vierzehn Jahre alt.

Wiederholung 2

1 Read the website entries.

Ich heiße **Franzi** und suche Freunde aus England, Irland oder Nordirland. Ich habe eine Schlange zu Hause! Sie ist sechs Jahre alt. Ich wohne in Wien. Das ist in Österreich. Ich bin sehr kreativ und intelligent! Schreib mir bitte!

Hallo! Ich heiße **Hannah** und ich wohne in London, in England. Ich lerne Deutsch. Ich suche Freunde aus Deutschland, Österreich und auch aus der Schweiz. Ich bin sportlich und spiele Fußball und auch Tennis, aber ich bin sehr faul! Meine Lieblingsmusik ist Rock. Schreib mir!

Mein Name ist **Felix** und ich wohne in der Schweiz, aber ich komme aus Dortmund in Deutschland. Zu Hause habe ich eine Wii und mein Lieblingsspiel ist FIFA. Meine Lieblingsfußballmannschaft ist Bayern-München. Ich suche Freunde aus Schottland und Wales.

Hi! Ich bin **Muhammad** und ich wohne in Cardiff. Das ist in Wales. Ich bin sechzehn Jahre alt. Meine Lieblingssache ist Technologie. Ich habe zu Hause einen Computer, ein Handy und auch ein iPad. Ich bin nicht sehr sportlich, aber sehr freundlich. Mein Lieblingsland ist Deutschland und ich suche dort Freunde.

Write the name of the person who …

1. is looking for friends from Switzerland. Hannah
2. supports a football team. ________
3. has a pet. ________
4. is just looking for friends from Germany. ________
5. lives in a different place from where they were born. ________
6. does not particularly like sport. ________
7. lives in Switzerland. ________

suche = seek
Schreib mir (bitte)! = Write to me (please)!
dort = there

2 Write your own profile for the website. Use as much German as you can from *Kapitel 1* to describe yourself.

____

____

____

____

Grammatik (Seiten 22–23)

1 **Write a sentence using the correct German word for 'a' for each item.**

1  2  3  4  5  6  7  8 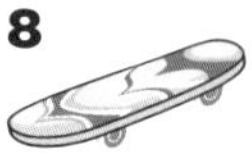

1 *Das ist ein Computer.*
2 ______________________
3 ______________________
4 ______________________
5 ______________________
6 ______________________
7 ______________________
8 ______________________

die Gitarre | *das Handy* | *der iPod* | *der Computer* | *das Skateboard* | *das Keyboard* | *der Fußball* | *die Wii*

Grammatik
masculine – *ein*
feminine – *eine*
neuter – *ein*

2 **Circle the correct verb form to complete each sentence.**

1 Lukas **habe / hat / hast** einen Computer.
2 Ich **heiße / habe / hat** einen Vogel zu Hause.
3 Wo **bist / ist / wohnst** er?
4 Er **ist / komme / bin** musikalisch und sportlich.
5 Julia **bin / ist / wohnt** fünfzehn Jahre alt.
6 Wie alt **wohnst / bist / bin** du?
7 Wo **hast / bist / bin** ich?

Grammatik
You can use the pronouns *er* ('he') or *sie* ('she') instead of writing someone's name. Both need the *er/sie/es* form of the verb.

3 **Complete the table with the correct forms of each regular verb.**

wohnen (to live)	**kommen** (to come)	**heißen** (to be called)
ich *wohne*	ich	ich
du	du *kommst*	du
er/sie/es	er/sie/es	er/sie/es *heißt*

Now use the table to write the correct verb in each gap.

1 Mein Handy ____________ aus China.
2 Meine Schlange ____________ Sissel.
3 Du ____________ Gabi.
4 ____________ du aus Berlin?
5 ____________ Monika in Hamburg?
6 Deine Lieblingssendung ____________ ,EastEnders'.
7 Ich ____________ Wolfgang.
8 Wo ____________ du?

Mein Fortschritt

1 Record your levels for *Kapitel* 1.

2 Look at the level descriptors on pages 59–60 and set your targets for *Kapitel* 2.

3 Fill in what you need to do to achieve these targets.

Listening 	I have reached Level ____ in **Listening**. In *Kapitel* 2, I want to reach Level ____ I need to ______________________ ______________________ ______________________ ______________________
Speaking 	I have reached Level ____ in **Speaking**. In *Kapitel* 2, I want to reach Level ____ I need to ______________________ ______________________ ______________________ ______________________
Reading 	I have reached Level ____ in **Reading**. In *Kapitel* 2, I want to reach Level ____ I need to ______________________ ______________________ ______________________ ______________________
Writing 	I have reached Level ____ in **Writing**. In *Kapitel* 2, I want to reach Level ____ I need to ______________________ ______________________ ______________________ ______________________

Wörter

Hallo! • Meeting and greeting

Wie heißt du?	*What's your name?*
Ich heiße ...	*My name is ...*
Hallo!	*Hello! / Hi!*
Guten Tag!	*Hello!*
Wie geht's?	*How are you?*
Gut, danke. Und dir?	*Fine, thanks. And you?*
Nicht schlecht.	*Not bad.*
Tschüs!	*Bye!*
Auf Wiedersehen!	*Goodbye!*

Die Zahlen 1–19 • Numbers 1–19

eins	*1*
zwei	*2*
drei	*3*
vier	*4*
fünf	*5*
sechs	*6*
sieben	*7*
acht	*8*
neun	*9*
zehn	*10*
elf	*11*
zwölf	*12*
dreizehn	*13*
vierzehn	*14*
fünfzehn	*15*
sechzehn	*16*
siebzehn	*17*
achtzehn	*18*
neunzehn	*19*
Wie alt bist du?	*How old are you?*
Ich bin ... Jahre alt.	*I am ... years old.*
Wie alt ist (Julia)?	*How old is (Julia)?*
(Julia) ist ... Jahre alt.	*(Julia) is ... years old.*

Wo wohnst du? • Where do you live?

Ich wohne in ...	*I live in ...*
Er/Sie/Es wohnt in ...	*He/She/It lives in ...*
... England	*England*
... Irland	*Ireland*
... Nordirland	*Northern Ireland*
... Schottland	*Scotland*
... Wales	*Wales*
... Deutschland	*Germany*
... Österreich	*Austria*
... der Schweiz	*Switzerland*

Wie bist du? • What are you like?

Ich bin ...	*I am ...*
Er/Sie ist ...	*He/She is ...*
faul	*lazy*
freundlich	*friendly*
intelligent	*intelligent*
kreativ	*creative*
launisch	*moody*
laut	*loud*
lustig	*funny*
musikalisch	*musical*
sportlich	*sporty*

Lieblingssachen • Favourite things

Mein Lieblingssport ist ...
My favourite sport is ...
Mein Lieblingsmonat ist ...
My favourite month is ...
Meine Lieblingsmusik ist ...
My favourite music is ...
Meine Lieblingszahl ist ...
My favourite number is ...
Meine Lieblingssendung ist ...
My favourite programme is ...
Meine Lieblingsfußballmannschaft ist ...
My favourite football team is ...
Mein Lieblingsspiel ist ...
My favourite game is ...
Mein Lieblingsland ist ...
My favourite country is ...
Mein Lieblingsauto ist ...
My favourite car is ...
Was ist dein Lieblingssport?
What's your favourite sport?
Was ist deine Lieblingszahl?
What's your favourite number?
Was ist dein Lieblingsland?
What's your favourite country?

Hast du einen Computer? • Have you got a computer?

Ich habe ...	*I have ...*
einen Computer	*a computer*
einen iPod	*an iPod*
einen Fußball	*a football*
eine Gitarre	*a guitar*
eine Wii	*a Wii*
eine Schlange	*a snake*
ein Handy	*a mobile phone*
ein Keyboard	*a keyboard*
ein Skateboard	*a skateboard*

Fragewörter • Question words

Wie?	*How?*
Was?	*What?*
Wo?	*Where?*
Woher?	*Where ... from?*
Wer?	*Who?*

Oft benutzte Wörter • High-frequency words

und	*and*
(und) auch	*(and) also*
aber	*but*
sehr	*very*
ziemlich	*quite*
nicht	*not*
Was denkst du?	*What do you think?*
Ich denke, ...	*I think ...*
Ich auch!	*Me too!*
Ich nicht!	*Not me!/That's not what I think!*
Was? Du spinnst!	*What? You're joking!*

1 **Complete the sentences about the pets. Write the correct words in the gaps. Remember to think about the gender of each animal.**

1 Ich habe ein Pferd. Es ist groß und heißt Romeo.
2 Ich habe ________ Kaninchen. ______ ist niedlich und heißt Timmo.
3 Ich habe ________ Katze. ______ ist intelligent und heißt Mieze.
4 Max hat ________ Schlange. ______ ist zwei Jahre alt.
5 Gabi hat ________ Pferd. ______ ist launish.
6 Ich habe ________ Hund. ______ ist freundlich und heißt Prinz.
7 Susi hat ________ Goldfisch. ______ heißt Nemo.

Grammatik
Remember: after *haben* the masculine word for 'a' changes from *ein* to *einen*.

Grammatik
m. der / ein → **er**
f. die / eine → **sie**
n. das / ein → **es**

2 **Tina Tierfan has lots of pets! Write Tina's answers to the interviewer's questions about how many of each animal she has.**

Grammatik
Hund (-e) Pferd (-e)
Katze (-n) Goldfisch (-e)
Schlange (-n) Maus (Mäuse)

1 Hast du einen Hund? Nein! Ich habe drei Hunde.
2 Hast du ein Pferd? ________________
3 Hast du eine Katze? ________________
4 Hast du einen Goldfisch? ________________
5 Hast du eine Schlange? ________________
6 Hast du eine Maus? ________________

2 Supertiere (Seiten 32–33)

1 Complete the sentences about the animals. Write the correct name in each gap.

Hermann 

Minnie 

Sisi 

Kizzi 

Moto 

Millie 

1 __________ ist schnell.

2 __________ ist süß.

3 __________ ist gemein.

4 __________ ist superintelligent.

5 __________ ist cool.

6 __________ ist kräftig.

2 Write a sentence to say what each of the *Supertiere* can do.

1 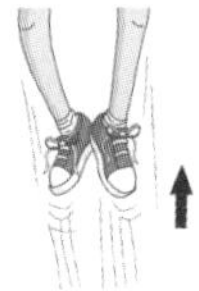
Hermann

2 
Sisi

3 
Minnie

4 

Kizzi

5 
Millie

6 
Moto

1 Hermann kann springen.

2 ______________________________

3 ______________________________

4 ______________________________

5 ______________________________

6 ______________________________

Grammatik
The verb *kann* is always followed by an infinitive verb.

3 Read the text below, then translate it into English.

Günther Goldfisch ist mein Lieblingstier. Er ist ein Jahr alt. Er ist sehr lustig und kräftig, aber auch ziemlich süß. Er kann schwimmen, springen und auch im Aquarium tanzen! Günther hat einen Freund: er ist sehr cool und schlau.

3 Meine Familie (Seiten 34–35)

1 **Find the numbers in the puzzle, and write them next to the correct numeral.**

v	i	e	r	u	n	d	s	e	c	h	z	i	g	m	e
b	a	l	c	o	e	z	n	f	w	i	r	d	s	k	s
s	e	c	h	s	u	n	d	d	r	e	i	ß	i	g	a
q	g	n	a	j	n	x	i	n	d	m	h	t	g	ü	o
h	a	c	h	t	u	n	d	f	ü	n	f	z	i	g	i
u	e	i	n	u	n	d	a	c	h	t	z	i	g	p	b
n	t	e	r	i	d	f	b	n	ß	e	d	z	g	d	s
d	r	e	i	u	n	d	v	i	e	r	z	i	g	w	e
e	v	h	f	r	e	a	m	ß	p	l	s	j	a	q	c
r	d	r	e	i	u	n	d	z	w	a	n	z	i	g	h
t	z	a	n	j	n	x	o	u	e	y	g	r	e	v	z
k	c	p	f	s	z	d	l	b	n	l	a	i	h	m	i
i	b	z	w	e	i	u	n	d	s	i	e	b	z	i	g
a	g	b	n	ü	g	y	i	a	z	o	m	e	d	h	e

100 ____________________

64 ____________________

99 ____________________

43 ____________________

72 ____________________

36 ____________________

58 ____________________

81 ____________________

60 ____________________

23 ____________________

2 **Describe each of the families. Fill in the gaps for the first family. Write the whole description for the second family.**

Ich heiße Tom. Ich bin vierzehn Jahre alt. Es gibt vier Personen in meiner Familie. Meine Mutter ist ____________________ Jahre alt. Ich habe einen Bruder. ____ ist ________ Jahre alt. Ich habe eine Schwester. ______ ist ____________ Jahre alt. Wir wohnen in ________ .

____

____

____

____

____

____

3 **Write about your family (real or imaginary). Use the descriptions in exercise 2 to help you.**

der Stiefbruder = stepbrother
die Halbschwester = half-sister
Ich bin Einzelkind. = I am an only child.

4 Die Farben der Welt (Seiten 36–37)

1 Describe each person's hair and eyes.

Grammatik
When you describe hair and eyes, the adjectives (colour, length) need an ***e*** on the end.

hell = light
dunkel = dark
hellbraun = light brown
dunkelblau = dark blue

1 Er heißt Niko. Er hat kurze, schwarze Haare und dunkelbraune Augen.

2 ____________________

3 ____________________

4 ____________________

5 ____________________

2 Complete the text by choosing the correct words from the cloud to fill the gaps. There are more words than you need.

Es gibt fünf __________ in meiner Familie. Wir __________ in Braunschweig. Das ist in __________. Meine __________ heißt Emma und sie ist neunundvierzig __________ alt. Sie ist sehr freundlich und hat __________, schwarze Haare. Mein Vater __________ auch neunundvierzig und er hat kurze, dunkelbraune Haare und braune __________.

Ich habe zwei __________: einen Bruder und eine Schwester. __________ Bruder heißt Mehmet und er ist __________ Jahre alt. Er ist launisch aber __________ lustig. __________ Schwester, Isla, hat grüne Augen und __________ Haare. Sie ist sechzehn Jahre alt, sehr klein und __________.

Deutschland alt Augen Personen braune wohnen sportlich Meine Mutter Jahre lange Geschwister zwölf auch Mein blau ist

Read the text for gist first. For each sentence, think about whether you need a noun, a verb, a connective or an adjective.

5 Alles Gute! (Seiten 38–39)

1 Reorder the words to make correct sentences. Don't forget the full stop!

1 am | Mai | Ich | Geburtstag | habe | neunzehnten

____

2 hat | Oktober | am | Oma | Geburtstag | elften | Meine

____

3 Geburtstag | Stiefbruder | Dezember | am | Dein | dritten | hat

____

4 hast | Geburtstag | einunddreißigsten | Juli | Du | am

____

5 und | Geburtstag | haben | achten | am | Michael | Juni | Monika

____

2 Complete each sentence by writing the date. Write each holiday in English.

01.01. Neujahr ist am *ersten Januar* ______________. *New Year*

01.05. Der Maifeiertag ist am ______________. ______________

03.10. Der Tag der Deutschen Einheit ist am ______________. *German Unity Day*

25.12. Weihnachten ist am ______________. ______________

31.12. Silvester ist am ______________. ______________

3 Read the short profile about Yannic and write a summary in the table.

Er heißt Yannic Spiller. Er ist dreizehn Jahre alt und kommt aus Trier. Trier ist in Deutschland. Yannic hat am siebten Januar Geburtstag. Er hat einen Bruder, Tim. Tim ist achtzehn Jahre alt. Yannic hat auch eine Schwester. Sie heißt Steffi und ist sechzehn Jahre alt. Die Familie Spiller hat zwei Haustiere: einen Hund und eine Katze.

Name:		Geschwister:	
Alter:			
Wohnt in:		Haustiere:	
Geburtstag:			

4 Now write a short profile about yourself.

6 Speaking Skills
Eine Superfamilie (Seiten 40–41)

1 Rescue the question words from the alphabet soup. Write each one on a line and use it to write a question.

Wie viele Brüder hast du?

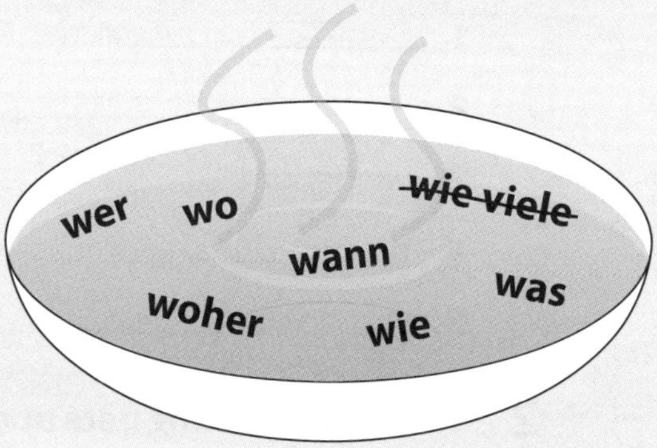

2 The police have written a summary about a crime suspect. Write six questions for a journalist to ask the suspect. The questions should cover all the information in the summary.

1 Wie heißt du?
2
3
4
5
6

Martin Kolwitz ist 24 Jahre alt. Er hat am achten November Geburtstag. Er wohnt in Hamburg, in Deutschland. Er hat einen Bruder. Er hat auch Haustiere: zwei Hunde.

Remember: the verb usually goes straight after the question word.

3 Use these notes to write questions to Martin about his accomplice, Sophie.

1 Wie heißt sie?
2
3
4
5

Sophie Meyer
19
Ebbingen, Deutschland
Haare – kurz, Augen – blau
Geb. 21.10.

Remember to use the correct part of the verb with the pronoun *sie*.

4 Write a summary about Sophie, like the one the police wrote about Martin in exercise 2.

Wiederholung 1

1 Complete the sentences. Choose the correct word from the cloud to fill in each gap.

1 ______________ Mutter ist sehr freundlich und intelligent.

2 Hast du ______________ Meerschweinchen?

3 Wir haben ______________ Haustier.

4 Wo ist ______________ Vogel?

5 Ich habe ______________ Bruder.

dein *kein*
ein *meine*
einen

2 You are describing pets at a pet show. Use the owners' notes to write what sort of pet they have, what the pet is like and what it can do.

Mareike

mouse
Pippa
cute, fast
fly, swim

Mareike hat ______________________________.

Sie heißt ______________________________.

Sie ist ______________________________.

Sie kann ______________________________.

Aaron

cat
Mieze
intelligent, cool,
mean
jump, play football

______________________________.

______________________________.

______________________________.

______________________________.

______________________________.

3 Decscribe the animal you'll be entering in the pet show by writing a similar description.

Example: Ich habe ...

Wiederholung 2

1 Read the texts below.

Hallo! Ich heiße **Anna** und ich bin fünfzehn Jahre alt. Ich habe am elften Februar Geburtstag. Ich wohne in Klagenfurt, in Österreich. Ich bin ziemlich groß und schlank und habe kurze, schwarze Haare und blaue Augen. Ich habe keine Geschwister – ich bin Einzelkind. Ich habe einen Goldfisch und einen Wellensittich. Ich kann Flöte spielen und Italienisch sprechen.

Hi! Ich bin **Noah** und ich komme aus Aachen. Das ist in Deutschland. Ich habe am zweiten November Geburtstag und bin vierzehn Jahre alt. Ich liebe Haustiere! Ich habe zwei Hunde, drei Katzen und eine Maus. Ich habe eine große Familie. Ich habe einen Halbbruder (er ist ein Baby) und zwei Schwestern. Mein Halbbruder ist sehr süß und klein. Er hat schwarze Haare und blaue Augen.

a Complete the sentences by writing *Anna* or *Noah*.

1 __________ lives in Austria.

2 __________ can play the flute.

3 __________'s birthday is on the 02.11.

4 __________ has a half-brother.

5 __________ is 15 years old.

6 __________ has cats.

b Write *richtig* or *falsch* next to each statement.

1 Anna hat einen Halbbruder. __________

2 Anna kann auch Englisch sprechen. __________

3 Noahs Halbbruder hat blaue Augen. __________

4 Klagenfurt ist nicht in Deutschland. __________

5 Anna hat am fünfzehnten Februar Geburtstag. __________

6 Anna hat keine Geschwister. __________

2 Translate these sentences into German.

1 My birthday is on the first of May. __________

2 She can speak German. __________

3 My guinea pig is very cute. __________

4 Your sister has light blue eyes. __________

5 My grandparents live in Southampton.

____

6 My brother can fly.

____

Grammatik (Seiten 44–45)

1 Complete the table by writing the correct form of *haben* for each pronoun.

haben *hast* *habt* *hat* *haben* *habe*

Words for 'you':
du (speaking to one family member or friend)
ihr (speaking to two or more family members or friends)
Sie (speaking to people you don't know or adults)

ich	du	er/sie/es	wir	ihr	Sie/sie

Now complete the sentences with the correct form of *haben*.

1 Katja, hast ________ du eine Katze?

2 Tom und Niko, ____________ ihr einen Hund?

3 ____________ Sie eine Schlange, Herr Brand?

4 Ich ____________ ein Pferd.

5 Frau Gerber, ____________ Sie eine Maus?

6 Herr Alexander ____________ ein Pferd.

2 Join each pronoun to a verb. There is more than one possible verb for some of the pronouns. Then write a question or a sentence with each pair.

1 ich	a macht	1 ____________
2 du	b heißen	2 ____________
3 er	c wohnst	3 ____________
4 wir	d heiße	4 ____________
5 ihr	e spielt	5 ____________
6 Sie	f spielen	6 ____________

3 Rewrite the sentences so they include the verb *kann*.

1 Mein Bruder fliegt. Mein Bruder kann fliegen.

2 Ich spiele Flöte. ____________

3 Meine Mutter schwimmt. ____________

4 Mein Vater springt. ____________

5 Ich tanze. ____________

6 Er singt gut. ____________

Mein Fortschritt

1 **Record your levels for *Kapitel* 2.**

2 **Look at the level descriptors on pages 59–60 and set your targets for *Kapitel* 3.**

3 **Fill in what you need to do to achieve these targets.**

Listening 	I have reached Level _____ in **Listening**. In *Kapitel* 3, I want to reach Level _____ I need to ______________________________ ______________________________ ______________________________ ______________________________
Speaking 	I have reached Level _____ in **Speaking**. In *Kapitel* 3, I want to reach Level _____ I need to ______________________________ ______________________________ ______________________________ ______________________________
Reading 	I have reached Level _____ in **Reading**. In *Kapitel* 3, I want to reach Level _____ I need to ______________________________ ______________________________ ______________________________ ______________________________
Writing 	I have reached Level _____ in **Writing**. In *Kapitel* 3, I want to reach Level _____ I need to ______________________________ ______________________________ ______________________________ ______________________________

Haustiere • Pets

Hast du ein Haustier?	*Have you got a pet?*
Ich habe ...	*I have ...*
einen Goldfisch	*a goldfish*
einen Hamster	*a hamster*
einen Hund	*a dog*
ein Kaninchen	*a rabbit*
eine Katze	*a cat*
eine Maus	*a mouse*
ein Meerschweinchen	*a guinea pig*
ein Pferd	*a horse*
eine Schlange	*a snake*
einen Wellensittich	*a budgie*
kein Haustier	*no pet*

Eigenschaften • Qualities

Wie ist er/sie/es?	*What is he/she/it like?*
Er/Sie/Es ist ...	*He/She/It is ...*
dick/schlank	*fat/thin*
frech/niedlich	*cheeky/cute*
gemein/süß	*mean/sweet*
groß/klein	*big/small*
kräftig	*strong*
schlau	*cunning*
(super)lustig	*(really) funny*
Er/Sie/Es kann ...	*He/She/It can ...*
Italienisch sprechen	*speak Italian*
fliegen	*fly*
Flöte/Fußball/Wii spielen	*play the flute/football/on the Wii*
(schnell) laufen	*run (fast)*
lesen	*read*
Rad fahren	*ride a bike*
schwimmen	*swim*
singen	*sing*
springen	*jump*
tanzen	*dance*

Die Zahlen 20–100 • Numbers 20–100

zwanzig	*twenty*
dreißig	*thirty*
vierzig	*forty*
fünfzig	*fifty*
sechzig	*sixty*
siebzig	*seventy*
achtzig	*eighty*
neunzig	*ninety*
hundert	*hundred*
einundzwanzig	*twenty-one*
zweiundzwanzig	*twenty-two*

Meine Familie • My family

Es gibt ... Personen in meiner Familie.	*There are ... people in my family.*
meine Mutter	*my mother*
mein Vater	*my father*
mein Bruder	*my brother*
mein Stiefbruder/Halbbruder	*my stepbrother/half-brother*
meine Schwester	*my sister*
meine Stiefschwester/Halbschwester	*my stepsister/half-sister*
meine Eltern	*my parents*
meine Großeltern	*my grandparents*
Hast du Geschwister?	*Have you any brothers and sisters?*
Ich habe zwei Brüder.	*I have two brothers.*
Ich habe drei Schwestern.	*I have three sisters.*
Ich bin Einzelkind.	*I'm an only child.*
Ich habe keine Geschwister.	*I have no brothers and sisters.*

Die Farben • Colours

schwarz	*black*
weiß	*white*
grau	*grey*
braun	*brown*
rot	*red*
orange	*orange*
gelb	*yellow*
grün	*green*
blau	*blue*
indigoblau	*indigo*
violett	*violet*
lila	*purple*
rosa	*pink*
bunt	*brightly coloured*
hellblau/dunkelblau	*light blue/dark blue*

Haare und Augen • Hair and eyes

Er/Sie hat ...	*He/She has ...*
schwarze/braune/ blonde/rote Haare	*black/brown/ blond/red hair*
kurze/lange/ mittellange Haare	*short/long/ mid length hair*
blaue/braune/grüne/ graue Augen	*blue/brown/green/ grey eyes*

Die Monate • The months

Januar	*January*
Februar	*February*
März	*March*
April	*April*
Mai	*May*
Juni	*June*
Juli	*July*
August	*August*
September	*September*
Oktober	*October*
November	*November*
Dezember	*December*

Das Datum • The date

Wann hast du Geburtstag?	*When is your birthday?*
am 1. (ersten) Januar	*on 1 January*
am 3. (dritten) Februar	*on 3 February*
am 7. (siebten) März	*on 7 March*
am 8. (achten) April	*on 8 April*
am 15. (fünfzehnten) Mai	*on 15 May*
am 29. (neunund-zwanzigsten) Juni	*on 29 June*
Ich habe (heute) Geburtstag.	*It's my birthday (today).*

Oft benutzte Wörter • High-frequency words

und	*and*
aber	*but*
oder	*or*
ziemlich	*fairly, quite*
sehr	*very*

1 Bist du sportlich? (Seiten 54–55)

1 **Look at the survey results in the table. Then answer the questions using full German sentences.**

Ahmed	🙂🙂			🙁			😐
Nicole		🙂🙂			🙁		
Christa	🙂		🙂🙂				😐
Torsten		🙁		🙂🙂		🙂	
Herr und Frau Meyer	🙂🙂			🙂	🙁	😐	

🙂🙂 = sehr gern 🙂 = gern 😐 = ziemlich gern 🙁 = nicht gern

1 Wer spielt sehr gern Fußball? *Nicole spielt sehr gern Fußball.*

2 Wer spielt gern Tischtennis? ______________________

3 Was spielt Christa sehr gern? ______________________

4 Was spielen Herr und Frau Meyer gern? ______________________

5 Wer spielt Basketball nicht gern? ______________________

6 Wer spielt ziemlich gern Handball? (2) ______________________

7 Und du? Was spielst du gern? ______________________

2 **Write three questions and three answers about the other people and sports in the table in exercise 1. Use the questions above as a model.**

____

____

____

____

____

____

2 Freizeit ist toll! (Seiten 56–57)

1 Write the words from the cloud in the grid. Translate the code word into English.

furchtbar
Eishockey
schlecht
spielst
irre
stinklangweilig
langweilig
Tischtennis
toll

2 Read about all the activities Hannes and Lola are involved in. Then write *richtig* or *falsch* next to each statement.

Hallo! Ich heiße **Hannes**. Ich finde Sport fantastisch. Ich spiele Tennis und schwimme. Schwimmen finde ich total super. Ich reite mit meiner Freundin, aber das finde ich langweilig. Fußball finde ich cool. Ich fahre auch gern Skateboard und lese sehr gern Sport- und Fitnessmagazine.

Meine Freundin heißt **Lola.** Sie findet Tischtennis toll. Lola fährt auch gern Rad – das ist sehr gesund! Sie findet schwimmen auch gut, aber Fußball findet sie nervig. Sie kann nicht Ski fahren. Im Winter spielt sie Eishockey und sie sieht sehr gern Eishockey im Fernsehen.

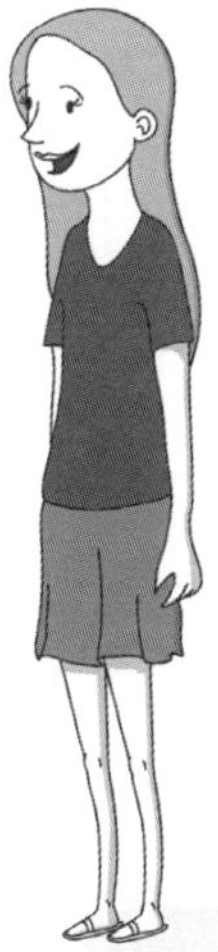

meine Freundin = my girlfriend
gesund = healthy
Fernsehen = television

1 Both Hannes and Lola participate in winter sports. ____________

2 Lola watches ice hockey on television. ____________

3 Hannes really likes swimming. ____________

4 Lola thinks skiing is fantastic. ____________

5 Lola plays ice hockey in winter. ____________

6 Hannes doesn't enjoying horse riding. ____________

7 Lola thinks football is exciting. ____________

8 Hannes watches sports programmes on television. ____________

3 In meiner Freizeit (Seiten 58–59)

1 **Separate the words to form five time phrases and write them below. Number the phrases in order of frequency, starting with 1 for the most frequent. Translate the phrases into English.**

jedenTagdreimalproWocheeinmalproMonatamWochenendesechsmalproMonat

☐ ______________________ ______________________
☐ ______________________ ______________________
☐ ______________________ ______________________
☐ ______________________ ______________________
☐ ______________________ ______________________

2 **Use the time phrases from exercise 1 to answer the questions about yourself. Write your answers in full sentences.**

1 Gehst du ins Kino? ______________________
2 Machst du Sport? ______________________
3 Gehst du einkaufen? ______________________
4 Hörst du Musik? ______________________
5 Spielst du Wii? ______________________
6 Chillst du mit deinen Freunden? ______________________

! **nie** = never

3 **Join up the sentence halves. Rewrite each sentence so that it starts with the time phrase.**

1 Ich höre am
2 Ich chille am
3 Ich spiele sehr
4 Ich mache jeden
5 Ich esse einmal
6 Ich gehe einmal pro

a Tag Sport.
b Abend Musik.
c pro Woche Pizza.
d Monat ins Kino.
e oft Xbox.
f Wochenende.

! Remember the 'verb in second place' rule.

4 Ich bin online (Seiten 60–61)

1 Unscramble and write down the time phrase in each sentence. Then translate the sentences into English.

Grammatik
You can use the present tense with a future time phrase to say what you are going to do – just as in English.

1 Wir machen ähnhcset eoWhc Filme. nächste Woche
We are going to make …

2 Ich suche ma Mtanog Infos im Internet. ______

______

3 Wir sehen ma eneneoWhcd Katzenvideos auf YouTube. ______

______

4 Ich chatte nejde denbA auf Facebook. ______

______

5 Stefan spielt ni iezw cnoWhe Wii Sport. ______

______

6 Ich lade gomrne Musik herunter. ______

______

2 Underline all the verbs in the text. Circle the words that are in first position in the sentences. Write a sentence about what you notice.

Hey du!
Franzi hier! Jetzt sind wir Freunde auf Facebook! Jeden Tag spiele ich Wii. Jede Woche schreibt mein Vater ein Blog, aber das finde ich langweilig. Am Abend lese ich gern E-Books. Morgen telefoniere ich mit Freunden in Kanada über Skype. Das finde ich cool! Im Sommer fahren wir nach Vancouver. Fantastisch! Was machst du am Computer und wie oft?

______

3 Reply to the question Franzi has asked you in his chat.

Use as many time phrases as you can in your reply.

Brieffreunde (Seiten 64–65)

1 What type of word is needed to fill the gap in each sentence? Complete each sentence by writing an appropriate German word or words in the gap.

verb *noun* *time/frequency phrase* *connective* *adjective*

		Type of word
1	Ich finde ________ Tennis toll.	verb
2	Meine Schwester findet Tischtennis ________ .	________
3	Wir sehen ________ fern.	________
4	Herr Peters spielt nächste Woche Tennis ________ Fußball.	________
5	Mein Bruder schreibt ein ________ .	________

2 Answer the questions about German grammar.

Use the sentences in exercise 1 to help you answer these questions.

1 Where in a sentence do verbs usually go? ________

2 What often goes after a verb? ________

3 What can you expect to go after *ein/eine*? ________

4 Which German verb suggests you're giving an opinion? ________

3 Replace the underlined word(s) with something else: a different noun, adjective or time phrase.

1 Ich finde Tischtennis <u>furchtbar</u>. Ich finde Tischtennis langweilig.

2 Ich spiele nicht gern <u>Fußball</u>. ________

3 Micha spielt gern <u>Wii</u>. ________

4 Er macht <u>einmal pro Monat</u> Judo. ________

5 Olli findet E-Books <u>fantastisch</u>. ________

6 Ich sehe <u>jede Woche</u> fern. Meine Schwester sieht <u>jeden Tag</u> Videos auf YouTube.

____

Remember that you'll keep the reader's interest if you use a variety of different words and phrases.

4 Write about your friends' hobbies.

Remember to include:
- opinions
- time/frequency phrases
- connectives
- 'verb in second place' rule

Wiederholung 1

1 **Put the words in the correct order to make sentences or questions. Don't forget to insert a full stop or question mark.**

1 fern | gern | sehr | Ich | sehe ______

2 einkaufen | er | Wochenende | geht | Am ______

3 Hausaufgaben | Ich | Infos | lese | die | für ______

4 in | Wie | Stadt | oft | du | fährst | die ______

5 Woche | Kai | Wasserball | Nächste | spielt ______

6 herunter | Videos | Ich | lade | Musik | und ______

2 **Rewrite each sentence, beginning with a time phrase. Then translate the sentences into English.**

1 Ich spiele Volleyball. (at the weekend) *Am Wochenende spiele ich Volleyball.*

At the weekend I am going to play volleyball.

2 Er spielt Basketball. (on Monday) ______

______

3 Du spielst Tischtennis. (every week) ______

______

4 Rosa spielt Fußball. (today) ______

______

5 Ich telefoniere mit Sam. (next week) ______

______

6 Sophie liest das Buch. (tomorrow) ______

______

3 **Underline the regular verbs and circle the irregular verbs.**

Ich spiele nicht gern Tennis. Ich finde Tennis langweilig. Fußball spiele ich dreimal pro Woche. Mein Bruder spielt sehr gern Tennis. Er fährt auch gern Rad. Radfahren findet er toll. Meine Schwester sieht ziemlich gern fern. Meine Mutter liest ziemlich gern. Oft liest sie Blogs im Internet. Ich lese auch oft. Mein Vater fährt gern Ski und spielt Gitarre.

Wiederholung 2

1 Read the email. Find the German for the following words and phrases in the text.

1 I think ______________________

2 about ______________________

3 but ______________________

4 New Zealand ______________________

5 comedies ______________________

6 Best wishes ______________________

Lieber Anish,

wie geht's? Danke für deine E-Mail.

Ich denke, Technologie ist toll. Ich bin sehr oft online. Ich chatte sehr gern mit Freunden auf Facebook. Facebook finde ich super und ich sehe oft Videos über Fußball auf YouTube.

Ich spiele Computerspiele nicht gern, aber ich suche ziemlich oft Infos für die Hausaufgaben. Meine Cousine, Connie, wohnt in Neuseeland und wir telefonieren ziemlich oft über Skype. Kannst du auch über Skype telefonieren?

Ich mache viel Sport mit meinen Freunden: Wir schwimmen zweimal pro Woche und wir spielen am Abend Basketball. Im Winter fahre ich auch Ski.

Ich esse manchmal am Wochenende mit meinen Freunden Pizza, und dann gehen wir ins Kino. Ich sehe gern Komödien. Nächste Woche sehen wir *Skyfall*.

Liebe Grüße,

Tibor

2 Answer the questions in complete German sentences.

1 Spielt Tibor gern Computerspiele? ______________________

2 Was macht Tibor auf Facebook? ______________________

3 Wer wohnt in Neuseeland? ______________________

4 Wie telefoniert Tibor mit seiner Cousine? ______________________

5 Wie oft schwimmt Tibor? ______________________

6 Was machen Tibor und seine Freunde am Wochenende?

____

3 Write a reply to Tibor's email about your hobbies and activities.

Grammatik (Seiten 68–69)

1 Complete the verb table.

	fahren (to go/travel)	**sehen** (to see)	**lesen** (to read)
ich			
du	fährst		liest
er/sie/es		sieht	
wir			
ihr			
Sie			
sie			

2 Complete the sentences by writing the correct form of the verb in brackets.

1 Ich ______________ das Auto. (waschen)

2 ______________ du gern Mangabücher? (lesen)

3 Er ______________ im Schlafzimmer. (schlafen)

4 Thomas ______________ nach Stockholm in Schweden. (fahren)

5 ______________ du morgen Torsten? (sehen)

6 ______________ du eine Schuluniform? (tragen)

Verbs like fahren:
tragen = to wear
schlafen = to sleep
waschen = to wash

die Schuluniform = school uniform

3 Write the question for each reply.

1 ______________________________ Ja, ich spiele Gitarre.

2 ______________________________ Nein, ich spiele nicht gern Wasserball.

3 ______________________________ Ja, Michael schläft im Bett.

4 ______________________________ Ja, ich fahre nach Bremen.

5 ______________________________ Ja, ich lese gern E-Books.

6 ______________________________ Nein, ich sehe nicht gern fern.

7 ______________________________ Ja, ich bin sportlich!

8 Was __________________________ Ich trage morgen Jeans und ein T-Shirt.

9 ______________________________ Michael trägt eine Schuluniform.

Remember, to form a question you put the verb before the subject:
Du spielst gern Tennis. → Spielst du gern Tennis?

Mein Fortschritt

1 Record your levels for *Kapitel* 3.

2 Look at the level descriptors on pages 59–60 and set your targets for *Kapitel* 4.

3 Fill in what you need to do to achieve these targets.

Listening 	I have reached Level ______ in **Listening**. In *Kapitel* 4, I want to reach Level ______ I need to ______________________________ ____ ____ ____
Speaking 	I have reached Level ______ in **Speaking**. In *Kapitel* 4, I want to reach Level ______ I need to ______________________________ ____ ____ ____
Reading 	I have reached Level ______ in **Reading**. In *Kapitel* 4, I want to reach Level ______ I need to ______________________________ ____ ____ ____
Writing 	I have reached Level ______ in **Writing**. In *Kapitel* 4, I want to reach Level ______ I need to ______________________________ ____ ____ ____

Wörter

Bist du sportlich? • Are you sporty?

Ich bin (sehr/ziemlich/ nicht sehr) sportlich.	*I am (very/quite/ not very) sporty.*
Was spielst du?	*What do you play?*
Ich spiele ...	*I play ...*
Ich spiele gern ...	*I like playing ...*
Ich spiele ziemlich gern ...	*I quite like playing ...*
Ich spiele nicht gern ...	*I don't like playing ... playing ...*
Badminton	*badminton*
Basketball	*basketball*
Eishockey	*ice hockey*
Fußball	*football*
Handball	*handball*
Tennis	*tennis*
Tischtennis	*table tennis*
Volleyball	*volleyball*
Wasserball	*water polo*

Was machst du gern? • What do you like doing?

Was machst du gern?	*What do you like doing?*
Ich fahre Rad.	*I ride my bike.*
Ich fahre Skateboard.	*I go skateboarding.*
Ich fahre Ski.	*I ski.*
Ich fahre Snowboard.	*I snowboard.*
Ich lese.	*I read.*
Ich mache Judo.	*I do judo.*
Ich mache Karate.	*I do karate.*
Ich reite.	*I go horse riding.*
Ich schwimme.	*I swim.*
Ich sehe fern.	*I watch TV.*
Ich spiele Gitarre.	*I play the guitar.*
Ich tanze.	*I dance.*

Wie findest du das? • What do you think of it?

Ich finde es ...	*I think it's ...*
Es ist ...	*It's ...*
irre	*amazing*
super	*super*
toll	*great*
cool	*cool*
gut	*good*
nicht schlecht	*not bad*
okay	*okay*
langweilig	*boring*
nervig	*annoying*
stinklangweilig	*deadly boring*
furchtbar	*awful*

Was machst du in deiner Freizeit? • What do you do in your free time?

Ich chille.	*I chill out.*
Ich esse Pizza oder Hamburger.	*I eat pizza or hamburgers.*
Ich gehe einkaufen.	*I go shopping.*
Ich gehe ins Kino.	*I go to the cinema.*
Ich gehe in den Park.	*I go to the park.*
Ich gehe in die Stadt.	*I go into town.*
Ich höre Musik.	*I listen to music.*
Ich mache Sport.	*I do sport.*
Ich spiele Xbox oder Wii.	*I play Xbox or on the Wii.*

Ich bin online • I'm online

Was machst du am Computer?	*What do you do on the computer?*
Was machst du auf deinem Handy?	*What do you do on your mobile?*
Ich chatte mit Freunden auf Facebook.	*I chat with friends on Facebook.*
Ich lade Musik herunter.	*I download music.*
Ich mache Fotos oder Filme.	*I take photos or make films.*
Ich sehe Videos.	*I watch videos.*
Ich simse.	*I text.*
Ich spiele Computerspiele.	*I play computer games.*
Ich suche und lese Infos für die Hausaufgaben.	*I look for and read information for my homework.*
Ich surfe im Internet.	*I surf the internet.*
Ich telefoniere mit Freunden.	*I call my friends.*
Ich mache ziemlich viel auf meinem Handy.	*I do quite a lot of things on my mobile.*

Oft benutzte Wörter • High-frequency words

Wie oft?	*How often?*
(sehr/ziemlich/ nicht so) oft	*(very/quite/not so) often*
einmal/zweimal/ dreimal pro Woche/ pro Monat	*once/twice/three times a week/ a month*
jeden Tag	*every day*
jeden Morgen	*every morning*
manchmal	*sometimes*
immer	*always*
nie	*never*
Wann?	*When?*
am Wochenende	*at the weekend*
am Abend	*in the evening*
heute	*today*
morgen	*tomorrow*
am Montag	*on Monday*
nächste Woche	*next week*
in zwei Wochen	*in two weeks*

1 Ich mag Deutsch! (Seiten 76–77)

1 Write a sentence for each illustration.

1 

2 

3 

4 

5 

6 

1 Ich mag ______
2 ______
3 ______
4 ______
5 ______
6 ______

> **!**
> **ich liebe** ☺☺
> **ich mag** ☺
> **ich mag ... nicht** ☹
> **ich hasse** ☹☹

2 Read the forum entries giving people's opinions about school subjects. Then answer the questions below.

Hallo Leute! Mein Lieblingsfach ist Englisch! Ich liebe Englisch, weil es total interessant ist. Ich lese sehr gern Bücher auf Spanisch und auf Deutsch. Mathe finde ich langweilig. **Pedro**
Hi Pedro! Ich mag Englisch nicht. Es ist sehr schwierig, aber ich mag Mathe und Naturwissenschaften. Ich finde Mathe supercool. **Nadine**
Grüezi aus der Schweiz! Ich liebe Theater und Kunst. Ich mag Kunst sehr gern, weil ich total kreativ bin. Informatik finde ich sehr langweilig, und Geschichte und Erdkunde sind nutzlos. **Marta**

Who ...

1 is very creative? ______
2 enjoys reading? ______
3 doesn't like English? ______
4 thinks ICT is boring? ______
5 likes maths? ______
6 can read Spanish? ______
7 loves art? ______
8 doesn't like geography? ______

3 Rewrite each sentence in exercise 1, adding *weil* and an opinion. Use the examples in exercise 2 to help you with word order.

2 Was und wann? (Seiten 78–79)

1 Look at the timetable. Write *richtig* or *falsch* next to each statement.

	Montag	Dienstag	Mittwoch	Donnerstag	Freitag
8.15	Mathe	Erdkunde	Englisch	Deutsch	Technik
9.15	Englisch	Informatik	Theater	Mathe	Deutsch
10.45	Kunst	Mathe	Deutsch	Kunst	Naturwissenschaften
11.45	Naturwissenschaften	Mathe	Naturwissenschaften	Geschichte	Theater
13.30	Deutsch	Sport	Technik	Musik	Englisch

vor = before **nach** = after **die Doppelstunde** = double period

1 Am Mittwoch habe ich Deutsch. ______________

2 Wir haben am Freitag nach der Pause Technik. ______________

3 Am Montag vor der Pause haben wir Englisch. ______________

4 Theater ist am Mittwoch und am Donnerstag. ______________

5 Ich habe am Donnerstag nach der Mittagspause Musik. ______________

6 Am Dienstag habe ich eine Doppelstunde Mathe. ______________

2 At what time do you have the following subjects? Write a sentence for each.

1 *Ich habe Englisch um neun Uhr zehn.*

2 ______________________________

3 ______________________________

4 ______________________________

5 ______________________________

6 ______________________________

um acht Uhr = at 8 o'clock

3 Look at the timetable in exercise 1 and describe one school day. Try to add interest to your sentences by giving opinions about some subjects.

Example: Am Montag um acht Uhr fünfzehn habe ich Mathe. Ich mag Mathe, weil es interessant ist.

Ich finde Mathe ...
= I find maths ...

1 **Write a description for each of the teachers.**

1 *Mein Sportlehrer heißt Herr Huber.*
Er ist cool, aber sehr unpünktlich.

2 ______________________________
____

3 ______________________________
____

4 ______________________________
____

Use some qualifiers in your descriptions: *sehr, zu, ziemlich, ein bisschen, nicht*

2 **Complete the text by writing the correct word from the cloud in each gap.**

Mein __________ an der Schule ist Geschichte, __________ meine Geschichtelehrerin sehr lustig ist! Sie __________ nur ein Haustier, aber ihr Haustier ist eine Schlange!

Am __________ und am Freitag haben wir Kunst. Ich finde Kunst ziemlich langweilg, weil es schwierig __________. Mein Kunstlehrer __________ Herr Ackermann. __________ Schwester ist auch Kunstlehrerin an meiner __________! Sie heißt Frau Ackermann! Meine Sportlehrerin ist __________ freundlich. Sie heißt Frau Krause und __________ Lieblingssport ist Volleyball. Ich mag Sport, weil ich sehr __________ bin.

heißt hat Mittwoch Lieblingsfach ist
sehr Schule Seine sportlich weil ihr

3 **Write the correct word for 'his' or 'her' in each sentence.**

1 __________ Bruder lernt Hindi. (his)
2 __________ Schwester ist Lehrerin. (her)
3 __________ Hobby ist Gitarre spielen. (his)
4 __________ Lieblingsfach ist Kunst. (her)
5 __________ Schuluniform ist fantastisch. (his)
6 __________ Bruder ist 19 Jahre alt. (her)

Grammatik
sein = his **ihr** = her (for masculine and neuter nouns)
seine = his **ihre** = her (for feminine nouns)
Check the gender of the noun if you are unsure.

4 Im Klassenzimmer (Seiten 82–83)

1 Draw a simple picture to show where each of these things is.

1 Der Musiklehrer ist im Klassenzimmer.
2 Das Buch ist neben dem Computer.
3 Das Poster ist an der Wand.
4 Der Stuhl ist auf dem Tisch und neben der Tür.

1	2	3	4

2 What is there in the classroom? Start each sentence with *Es gibt* (there is/there are). Write the numbers as words.

12  Es gibt zwölf Tische im Klassenzimmer.

6  ______________________

24  ______________________

2  ______________________

4  ______________________

5  ______________________

! Look at the vocabulary on page 47 for the plurals of the nouns.

3 Answer the questions using the information in the pictures.

@peta_ush Darfst du dein Handy in der Schule benutzen?

____

@tara_winkel Darfst du im Klassenzimmer schnell laufen?

____

@e_atch Darfst du in der Pause Musik hören?

____

@janet_mc Darfst du dein Handy in der Mittagspause benutzen?

____

! ich darf   du darfst   er/sie/es darf

Mein Lieblingstag (Seiten 84–85)

1 **Most of the verbs you've seen end in *-en* in the infinitive. Write the infinitive form of each verb in the table. Then try to work out its meaning from the context.**

If the context doesn't help you, use a German–English dictionary.

verb	**infinitive**	**meaning in English**
Er **geht** in die Schule.	*gehen*	*to go, to walk*
Er **kauft** ein Auto.		
Er **steht** auf dem Tisch.		
Warum **redest** du so schnell?		
Ich **wasche** meinen Hund.		
Ich **nehme** das Buch.		

2 **Guess the meaning of these compound nouns by separating out the words. Look up the compound nouns in a dictionary to find their gender and meaning.**

The second word in each compound noun gives the gender.

compound noun	**word 1**	**word 2**	**gender**	**meaning**
Fußballfeld	*Fußball*		*das*	
Arbeitstag				
Sporthalle				
Klassenarbeit				
Lehrerzimmer				

3 **Now write a short German sentence using each compound noun from exercise 2.**

1 *Das Fußballfeld ist sehr grün und …*

2 ______

3 ______

4 ______

5 ______

Wiederholung 1

1 Mimi's description of her school day is in the wrong time order! Number the sentences 1–6 in the correct order of time.

☐ Ich habe um dreizehn Uhr fünfundzwanzig Musik.
☐ Die Pause beginnt um elf Uhr zehn.
☐ Die erste Stunde beginnt um acht Uhr vierzig.
☐ Der Bus kommt um fünfzehn Uhr siebenundvierzig.
☐ Ich komme um sechzehn Uhr dreißig nach Hause.
☐ Wir haben Mathe um elf Uhr fünfundzwanzig.

2 The school is running 20 minutes late today. Rewrite each of the six sentences in exercise 1 with the time that each activity begins today.

3 Complete the sentences by writing the correct possessive pronoun in each gap.

sein = his (for masculine and neuter nouns) **seine** = his (for feminine nouns)
ihr = her (for masculine and neuter nouns) **ihre** = her (for feminine nouns)

1 ________ Bruder heißt Pawel und ________ Schwester heißt Aga.
2 ________ Lieblingssport ist Eishockey.
3 ________ Katze ist braun, aber ________ Hund ist weiß.
4 ________ Schule ist in Hannover.

5 ________ Lieblingssport ist Reiten und ________ Lieblingsfach ist Mathe.
6 ________ Computer ist neu.
7 ________ Erdkundelehrerin ist sehr streng.
8 ________ Mutter wohnt in Salzburg, aber ________ Vater wohnt in Wien.

4 Describe where each of the items is located in the classroom.

1 Der Computer ist auf dem Tisch.
2 Das Poster ________
3 Das Whiteboard ________
4 Der Lehrer ________
5 Der Stuhl ________
6 Die Spinne ________

Wiederholung 2

1 Read the texts. Use your knowledge of vocabulary to help you to find these new phrases. Write each German phrase next to the English.

1 My name is ______
2 her favourite artist ______
3 unfortunately ______
4 My brother also goes ______
5 an indoor pool ______
6 a pot plant ______

Hallo! Mein Name ist **Maik** und ich wohne in München, in Deutschland. Meine Schule heißt Mathias Brauer Gymnasium und ich finde sie toll. An meiner Schule lerne ich sehr gern Englisch und Geschichte, aber mein Lieblingsfach ist Kunst. Ich mag Kunst, weil ich total kreativ bin. Ich finde meine Kunstlehrerin auch sehr nett. Sie heißt Frau Weber und ihr Lieblingskünstler ist Dürer.

Ich mag nicht Sport, weil ich nicht sehr sportlich bin. Leider habe ich am Montag und auch am Mittwoch Sport. Morgen spielen wir Tennis. Das finde ich nicht so schlecht.

lernen = to learn

Hallo Leute! Ich heiße **Sabine** und ich wohne in Zürich, in der Schweiz. Meine Schule ist sehr groß. Mein Bruder geht auch auf meine Schule.

Mein Lieblingsfach ist Musik und dieses Fach haben wir am Dienstag in der zweiten Stunde und auch am Donnerstag in der vierten Stunde. Sport mag ich auch, weil der Sportlehrer total lustig ist. Sein Lieblingssport ist Schwimmen und wir haben ein Hallenbad in der Schule. Wir haben Sport am Mittwoch in der fünften Stunde und auch am Freitag in der zweiten Stunde.

Mein Klassenzimmer ist sehr schön. Wir haben zehn Computer, ein Whiteboard neben der Tür, viele Poster an der Wand und eine Topfpflanze am Fenster!

2 Answer the questions about the texts in exercise 1. Write complete sentences in German for your answers.

1 Wie heißt Maiks Schule? ______
2 Was mag Maik? ______
3 Was lernt Maik nicht gern? ______
4 Wann hat Maik Sport? ______
5 Wo ist Zürich? ______
6 Was hat Sabine am Donnerstag in der vierten Stunde? ______
7 Warum mag Sabine Sport? ______
8 Wo ist die Topfpflanze? ______

Grammatik (Seiten 90–91)

1 Answer the questions in full sentences, using *weil* and the reason given.

1 Warum magst du Kunst? (it's creative)

Ich mag Kunst, weil es kreativ ist.

2 Warum magst du Englisch? (it's interesting)

____

3 Warum spielst du Tennis? (I'm sporty)

____

4 Warum hasst du Sport? (it's difficult)

____

5 Warum findest du Erdkunde toll? (it's easy)

____

2 Put the words in the right order to make sentences.

Remember the 'verb in second place' rule.

1 der in Geschichte dritten wir Stunde haben

____

2 habe Pause ich nach der Kunst ______________________________

3 Fußball spiele heute ich ______________________________

4 gibt Klassenzimmer Computer und viele einen es im Poster

____

5 Montag ich vierten Stunde habe in am der Mathe

____

3 Write the following school rules in sentences in German.

Example: Man darf am Montag ...

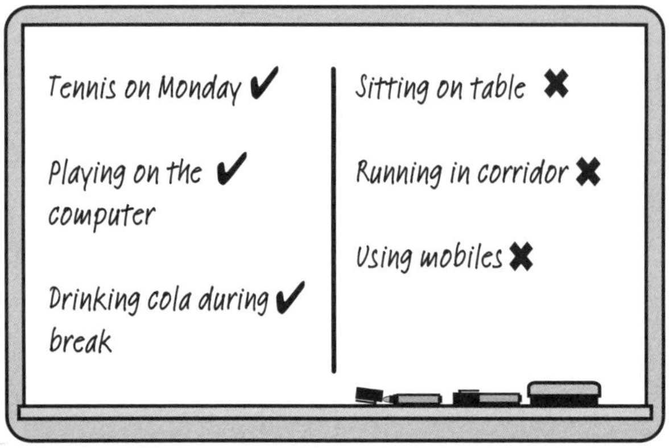

Man darf is often used to mean 'you/we are allowed to'.

Remember to use the correct preposition and the correct word for 'the' after it.

Mein Fortschritt

1 Record your levels for *Kapitel* 4.

2 Look at the level descriptors on pages 59–60 and set your targets for *Kapitel* 5.

3 Fill in what you need to do to achieve these targets.

Listening 	I have reached Level ______ in **Listening**. In *Kapitel* 5, I want to reach Level ______ I need to ______________________________
Speaking 	I have reached Level ______ in **Speaking**. In *Kapitel* 5, I want to reach Level ______ I need to ______________________________
Reading 	I have reached Level ______ in **Reading**. In *Kapitel* 5, I want to reach Level ______ I need to ______________________________
Writing 	I have reached Level ______ in **Writing**. In *Kapitel* 5, I want to reach Level ______ I need to ______________________________

Schulfächer • School subjects

Deutsch	*German*
Englisch	*English*
Erdkunde	*geography*
Geschichte	*history*
Informatik	*ICT*
Kunst	*art*
Mathe	*maths*
Musik	*music*
Naturwissenschaften	*science*
Sport	*sport, PE*
Technik	*technology*
Theater	*drama*

Meinungen • Opinions

mein Lieblingsfach ist ...	*my favourite subject is ...*
ich mag ... (sehr)	*I like ... (a lot)*
ich liebe	*I love*
ich mag ... nicht	*I don't like ...*
ich hasse	*I hate*
gut	*good*
toll	*great*
furchtbar	*awful*
einfach	*easy*
schwierig	*difficult*
interessant	*interesting*
langweilig	*boring*
nützlich	*useful*
nutzlos	*useless*
faszinierend	*fascinating*
nervig	*irritating*
supercool	*really cool*
stinklangweilig	*dead boring*

Die Wochentage • The days of the week

Montag (Mo.)	*Monday*
Dienstag (Di.)	*Tuesday*
Mittwoch (Mi.)	*Wednesday*
Donnerstag (Do.)	*Thursday*
Freitag (Fr.)	*Friday*
Samstag (Sa.)	*Saturday*
Sonntag (So.)	*Sunday*
Was hast du am Montag?	*What do you have on Monday?*
Am Dienstag habe ich ...	*I have ... on Tuesday*
Am Sonntag haben wir keine Schule.	*We have no school on Sunday.*

Die Zeit • Time

Wann?	*When?*
Um wie viel Uhr?	*At what time?*
Um 8:30 Uhr (acht Uhr dreißig).	*At 8:30.*
Wie viel Uhr ist es?	*What time is it?*
Es ist 9:50 Uhr (neun Uhr fünfzig).	*It's 9:50.*
in der ersten Stunde	*in the first lesson*
vor der Pause	*before break*
nach der Mittagspause	*after the lunch break*

Eigenschaften • Characteristics

Er/Sie ist ...	*He/She is ...*
alt	*old*
fair	*fair*
freundlich	*friendly*
jung	*young*
launisch	*moody*
lustig	*funny*
nervig	*annoying*
streng	*strict*
unpünktlich	*unpunctual*

In der Schule • In school

die Lehrerin(-nen)	*teacher (female)*
die Deutsch-lehrerin(-nen)	*German teacher (female)*
der Lehrer(–)	*teacher (male)*
der Sportlehrer(–)	*sports teacher (male)*
Was gibt es?	*What is there?*
Es gibt einen/eine/ein ...	*There is a ...*
Es gibt viele ...	*There are lots of ...*
das Klassenzimmer(–)	*classroom*
der Tisch(-e)	*table*
der Stuhl(¨-e)	*chair*
der Computer(–)	*computer*
das Whiteboard(-s)	*whiteboard*
das Poster(–)	*poster*
das Fenster(–)	*window*
die Wand(¨-e)	*wall*
die Tür(-en)	*door*
der Korridor(-e)	*corridor*

Wo ist das? • Where is it?

in der Schule	*in the school*
im Klassenzimmer	*in the classroom*
im Korridor	*in the corridor*
an der Wand	*on the wall*
am Fenster	*by the window*
am Tisch	*at the table*
auf dem Tisch	*on the table*
neben der Tür	*near/next to the door*

Oft benutzte Wörter • High-frequency words

weil	*because*
sein/seine	*his*
ihr/ihre	*her*
zu	*too*
sehr	*very*
ziemlich	*quite, fairly*
ein bisschen	*a bit*
nicht	*not*
haben	*to have*
sein	*to be*
in	*in*
an	*at, by, on (wall)*
auf	*on (top of)*
neben	*near, next to*
heute	*today*
morgen	*tomorrow*
vor	*before*
nach	*after*

1 In der Stadt (Seiten 98–99)

1 **Write sentences to say what there is and isn't in the town.**

1 Es gibt hier ____.

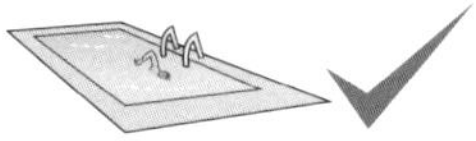

2 Hier gibt es ____.

3 In der Stadt gibt es ____.

4 Es gibt ____ hier.

Grammatik
der→einen/keinen **die**→eine/keine **das**→ein/kein

2 **Read the texts. Tick the things there are in each person's town and cross the things there aren't.**

Monika: *Ich wohne in Celle. Meine Stadt ist nicht sehr groß. Es gibt hier ein Schloss und auch einen Marktplatz. Leider gibt es kein Schwimmbad und auch keine Kegelbahn.*

leider = unfortunately

Erik: *Die Touristen kommen gern nach Verden, weil es eine Kirche und auch einen Marktplatz gibt. Ein Schloss gibt es auch, aber leider gibt es kein Schwimmbad und keine Imbissstube.*

Aisha: *Ich wohne in Neustadt, in der Nähe vom Titisee. Neustadt ist ganz klein, aber sehr schön. Es gibt hier kein Schloss, keine Kegelbahn und leider auch kein Kino. Wir haben aber einen Bahnhof, eine Kirche und auch einen alten Marktplatz. Wir haben kein Schwimmbad, aber man kann im Sommer im Titisee schwimmen!*

	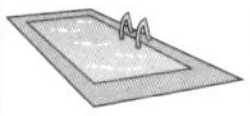		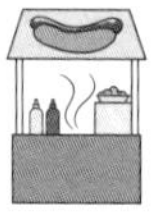	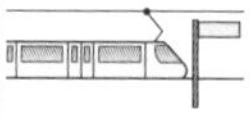				
Monika								
Erik								
Aisha								

3 **Write two or three sentences about what there is to do where you live, as well as what there isn't. Use the texts in exercise 2 to help you.**

2 Wir gehen einkaufen! (Seiten 100–101)

1 Write what the customers in the souvenir shop would like. Start your sentences with *Ich möchte*.

1 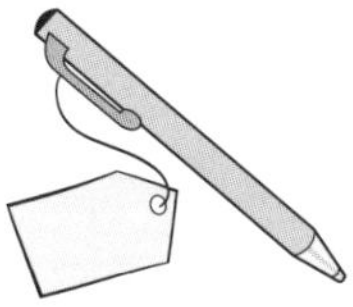
2 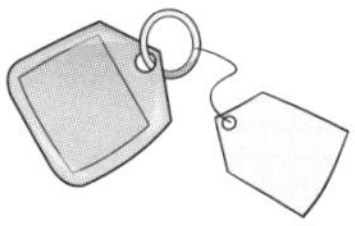
3 
4 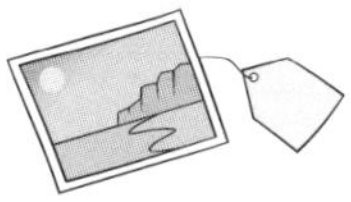
5 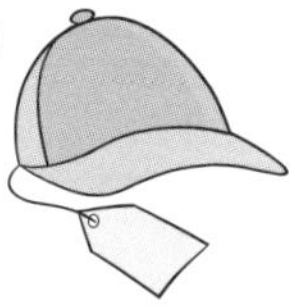
6 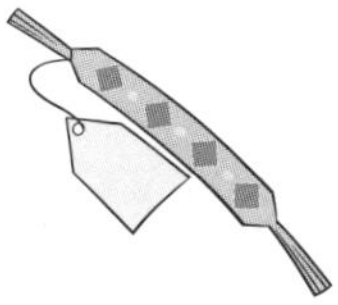
7 
8 

Look at the vocabulary on page 57 if you need to check which words to use.

1 Ich möchte einen Kuli.
2 ______________________
3 ______________________
4 ______________________
5 ______________________
6 ______________________
7 ______________________
8 ______________________

2 Complete the dialogue with words from the cloud below. Then number the lines of the conversation in the correct order 1–11.

☐ Guten Tag! ______________ ich dir helfen?

☐ Welche ______________? Wir haben blau, rot oder schwarz.

☐ Ja, klar! Dieser ______________, zum Beispiel, kostet nur €18,95.

☐ Super!

☐ Danke. Auf ______________.

☐ Sonst noch etwas?

☐ Alles ______________ kostet das €38,95.

☐ Guten Tag! Ich möchte ein Souvenir ______________, vielleicht ein Kuscheltier. Haben Sie ______________?

☐ Bitte sehr.

☐ Ja. Ich möchte ein ______________ für meine Schwester.

☐ Schwarz, bitte. Wie viel ______________ das?

zusammen Elefant Kuscheltiere Wiedersehen Kann kostet Fußballtrikot kaufen Farbe

3 Mmm, lecker! (Seiten 102–103)

1 **Write four short conversations between hungry customers and the owner of the snack stand. The price of each individual item is shown: don't forget to add up the total price.**

1

× 1
drei Euro zehn

× 1
zwei Euro fünfunddreißig

2

× 2
zwei Euro sechzig

× 2
zwei Euro fünfundzwanzig

3

× 3
drei Euro zwanzig

× 1
ein Euro neunzig

4

× 4
drei Euro fünfundneunzig

× 1
zwei Euro zehn

Ich möchte .../Ich hätte gern ...	I'd like ...
Das kostet alles zusammen ...	All together that costs ...

1 *Guten Tag! Ich möchte einmal Hamburger und einmal Bratwurst, bitte.*

Das kostet alles zusammen € ...

2 ______________________________

____

3 ______________________________

____

4 ______________________________

____

2 **Write a short review of the menu, saying what there is to eat and drink and what you do and don't like.**

Hamburger

Bratwurst
Pommes

Salat
Eis
Tee
Cola
Mineralwasser

Man kann ... trinken/essen.	You can eat/drink ...
Ich esse/trinke gern ...	I like eating/drinking ...
Ich esse/trinke nicht gern ...	I don't like eating/drinking ...
Ich mag ...	I like ....
Ich mag nicht ...	I don't like .....

____

____

____

4 In den Sommerferien (Seiten 104–105)

1 Circle the correct option to complete each sentence from the choices given. Then write the missing words in the gaps.

1 Ich ______________ im See baden.

a wirst　　b werden　　c werde

2 Wir werden im ______________ schwimmen.

a Meer　　b windsurfen　　c Bratwurst

3 ______________ du nach Innsbruck fahren?

a Wird　　b Wirst　　c Bist

4 Er ______________ nicht nach Hannover ______________ .

a werden; fahre　　b kann; fährt　　c wird; fahren

5 Tobi ______________ in den ______________ nach Portugal fahren.

a werde; Park　　b wird; Bahnhof　　c wird; Sommerferien

6 Wohin ______________ wir ______________ ?

a werden; gehen　　b kann; gehen　　c darf; fahren

2 Read the sentences and write the correct words from the cloud in the gaps. There are more words than you need.

1 Ich werde eine Kappe ______________ meinen Vater kaufen.

2 Ich ______________ ein Trikot kaufen.

3 In den ______________ fahren wir nach Rom.

4 Es ______________ ein Schwimmbad und ein Kino in Walsrode.

5 Wir ______________ nach Magdeburg fahren.

6 Ich möchte in den Bergen ______________ gehen.

für
gibt
möchte
nächste Woche
Sommerferien
wandern
werde
werden

3 Write about your plans for the summer holidays. Use the questions and illustrations to help you.

- Wohin wirst du fahren?

- Wer kommt mit?

- Was wirst du dort machen?

- Was wird dein Bruder / deine Schwester machen

- Wirst du Souvenirs kaufen?

1 **Rewrite each sentence. Swap the adjective in bold for an alternative adjective with a similar meaning.**

1. Das Mozart Museum ist **faszinierend**. ______________________________
2. Der Marktplatz ist **historisch**. ______________________________
3. Das Schwimmbad ist **modern**.
   ____
4. Die Kegelbahn ist **toll**. ______________________________

2 **Join up the sentence halves to describe a trip to Vienna.**

1	In den Sommerferien werde	**a**	Tage in Wien bleiben.
2	Dort gibt es einen	**b**	ich nach Wien fahren.
3	Am Montag kann	**c**	Wien fantastisch.
4	Ich finde	**d**	Marktplatz, aber keinen See.
5	Wir werden vier	**e**	man das Mozart Museum besuchen.

Now rewrite the sentences, varying the sentence structure. Remember that in German you always need the verb as the second idea.

Example: **1** Ich werde in den Sommerferien ...

3 **Read the text about Hahndorf. Try to work out what the words in bold mean from the context. If you can't work out the meanings, look them up in a dictionary.**

Hahndorf ist eine kleine Stadt in Südaustralien, in der Nähe von Adelaide. Es gibt dort deutsche **Einwanderer**. Die Stadt ist klein, aber **fein**! Hahndorf ist toll für Kinder und auch für **Erwachsene**. Dort gibt es viele deutsche Restaurants und Cafés. Am Mittwoch und am Sonntag gibt es immer einen Markt auf dem Marktplatz. Man kann hier Schokolade, **Kuchen** und **Kleidung** kaufen. **Wein** aus der Region kann man auch dort trinken. Ich werde **nächstes Jahr** mit meiner Schule nach Hahndorf fahren.

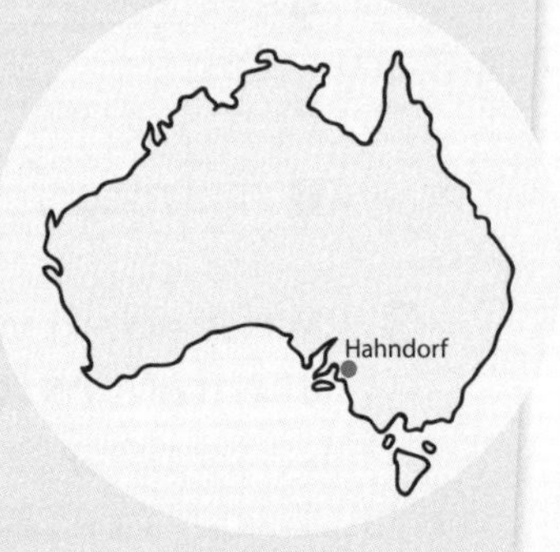

4 **Write about a city or town of your choice. Adapt some of the words and phrases from the text in exercise 3.**

Remember to include: the future tense, opinions, linking words, qualifiers, frequency expressions and inverted word order.

Wiederholung 1

1 **Decide which souvenir you would buy for each person and write the price in words.**

Grammatik

der → *er*   *die* → *sie*   *das* → *es*

Remember, *der* changes to *den* for masculine nouns.

1 Meine Mutter: *Ich werde die Tasse für meine Mutter kaufen. Sie kostet sieben Euro fünfundfünfzig.*

2 Onkel Karl: ____________________

3 Meine Schwester: ____________________

4 Meine Freundin: ____________________

5 Frau Roberts: ____________________

2 **Peter is in the tourist office in Munich. Read the dialogue, then answer the questions in full German sentences.**

Tourist guide: Guten Tag! Willkommen in München!

Peter: Guten Tag! Danke schön! Was gibt es hier in München?

Tourist guide: Hier gibt es viel zu tun! Man kann in München alles sehen!

Peter: Gibt es hier einen Marktplatz?

Tourist guide: Natürlich! Er heißt Marienplatz. Er ist sehr groß und total schön.

Peter: Wunderbar! Und kann man in München Ski fahren?

Tourist guide: Also ... nicht direkt in München, aber in der Nähe von hier kann man sehr gut Ski fahren.

Peter: Super. Und gibt es hier ein gutes Restaurant? Ich möchte gern Pizza essen.

Tourist guide: Ja, das gibt es! Es heißt *Robertos*. Dort kann man gut Pizza essen.

Peter: Vielen Dank. Ich werde im Restaurant *Robertos* essen. Auf Wiedersehen!

1 Was kann man in München machen?
2 Wie heißt der Marktplatz?
3 Wie ist er?
4 Wo kann man Ski fahren?
5 Was möchte Peter essen?
6 Was ist *Robertos*?

Wiederholung 2

1 Rewrite the sentences in the future tense. Identify the subject to help you change the form of *werden*.

1 Wir tauchen im Meer. Wir werden im Meer tauchen.

2 Wir baden im See. ______

3 Ich gehe an den Strand. ______

4 Lena und Michael klettern am Samstag in den Bergen.

______

5 Er kauft ein Kuscheltier für seine kleine Schwester.

______

6 Kaufst du eine Kappe als Souvenir? ______

7 Wir gehen am Wochenende mit meinen Freunden einkaufen.

______

2 Read the postcard and answer the questions in full German sentences.

Liebe Oma und Lieber Opa!

Hallo aus Mallorca in Spanien! Wir bleiben zwei Wochen hier, weil wir Sommerferien haben. Es gibt hier alles – einen Wasserpark, ein Schloss und auch einen Markt. Jeden Tag schwimmen wir im Meer. Im Hotel gibt es ein Schwimmbad und wir schwimmen auch hier. Man kann windsurfen und auch tauchen. Mallorca ist auch für das Essen sehr bekannt.

Nächste Woche werden wir in den Bergen klettern. Ich möchte auch segeln. Ich werde auch Souvenirs kaufen!

Alles Liebe,

Tamika

1 Warum ist Tamika in Spanien? ______

2 Was gibt es in Mallorca? ______

3 Was kann man machen? ______

4 Ist Mallorca bekannt für das Museum? ______

5 Was wird Tamika nächste Woche machen? ______

3 Write four true/false statements in English about the text in exercise 2. Then ask a friend to write 'True' or 'False' next to each statement.

Example: The postcard is to Tamika's parents. False

Grammatik (Seiten 112–113)

1 Rewrite the sentences to make them negative.

Use *keinen/keine/kein* to say what there is or isn't. Use *nicht* to say what you can't or don't like doing.

1 Es gibt in Düsseldorf einen Marktplatz.

____

2 Er mag Wasserball.

____

3 Beni kann Fußball spielen, weil er einen Ball hat.

____

4 In der Stadt gibt es ein Kino und auch eine Kirche.

____

5 Man darf hier schwimmen. _______________

2 Write the different forms of *möchten* in the table.

ich		wir	
du		ihr	
er/sie/es		Sie	
		sie	

möchten
möchte
möchten
möchtest
möchte
möchtet
möchten

Complete the sentences by writing the correct form of *möchten* in each gap. Then translate the sentences into English.

1 ______________ du ein Schokoladeneis?

2 Nein, aber ich ______________ gern ein Vanilleeis.

3 Anne ______________ nach Kapstadt in Südafrika fahren.

4 ______________ ihr auch nach Windhuk in Namibia fahren?

5 Wir ______________ zweimal Salat und zweimal Mineralwasser, bitte.

6 Frau Winkelmann, ______________ Sie eine Tasse Tee?

3 Fill in the gaps to complete the different forms of *werden*.

ich _e_de — wir we_de_

du w_r_t — ihr _er_e_

er/sie/es _ir_ — Sie/sie w_r_en

4 Write sentences about what you and your family/friends will do on your next holiday.

Example: Ich werde jeden Tag in Frankreich wandern. Mein Bruder ... /Steffi ...

Jahresbilanz

Record your levels for *Kapitel* 5.

Listening	I have reached Level ______ in **Listening**.
Speaking	I have reached Level ______ in **Speaking**.
Reading	I have reached Level ______ in **Reading**.
Writing	I have reached Level ______ in **Writing**.

Look back through your workbook and note down the level you achieved in each skill by the end of each *Kapitel*.

	Listening	**Speaking**	**Reading**	**Writing**
1 Meine Welt und ich				
2 Familie und Tiere				
3 Freizeit – juhu!				
4 Schule ist klasse!				
5 Gute Reise!				

You now have a record of your progress in German for the whole year.

In der Stadt • In town

Es gibt ...	*There is ... / There are ...*
Es gibt ein/eine/einen ...	*There is/are a ...*
Es gibt kein/keine/keinen ...	*There isn't/aren't ...*
in der Nähe von ...	*near to*
in der Nähe ...	*nearby*
der Bahnhof(¨-e)	*railway station(s)*
der Imbiss(-e)/die Imbissstube(-n)	*snack stand(s)*
die Kegelbahn(-en)	*bowling alley(s)*
das Kino(-s)	*cinema(s)*
die Kirche(-n)	*church(es)*
der Marktplatz(¨-e)	*market square(s)*
der Park(-s)	*park(s)*
das Schloss(¨-er)	*castle(s)*
das Schwimmbad(¨-er)	*swimming pool(s)*
die Eisbahn(-en)	*ice rink(s)*
der Fischmarkt(¨-e)	*fish market(s)*
das Kindertheater(-)	*children's theatre(s)*
der Radweg(-e)	*cycle path(s)*
das Sportzentrum (die Sportzentren)	*sports centre (sports centres)*
der Stadtpark(-s)	*city/town park(s)*
der Wasserpark(-s)	*water park(s)*

Verkaufsgespräch • Sales conversation

Ich gehe einkaufen.	*I am going shopping.*
Ich möchte ...	*I would like ...*
Ich möchte ... kaufen.	*I would like to buy ...*
Haben Sie ...?	*Do you have ...?*
Kann ich dir helfen?	*Can I help you?*
Sonst noch etwas?	*Anything else?*
alles zusammen	*all together*

Souvenirs • Souvenirs

der Aufkleber	*sticker*
das Freundschaftsband	*friendship bracelet*
die Kappe	*(baseball) cap*
der Kuli	*biro*
das Kuscheltier	*cuddly toy*
die Postkarte	*postcard*
der Schlüsselanhänger	*key ring*
die Tasse	*mug/cup*
das Trikot	*(football) shirt*
Wie viel kostet ...?	*How much does ... cost?*
Wie viel kostet das?	*How much does it cost?*
Es kostet €16.	*It costs 16 Euros.*

Snacks und Getränke kaufen • Buying snacks and drinks

die Bratwurst	*fried sausage*
der Hamburger	*hamburger*
die Pizza	*pizza*
die Pommes	*chips*
der Salat	*salad*
das Eis	*ice cream*
die Cola	*cola*
das Mineralwasser	*mineral water*
der Tee	*tea*
das Fleisch	*meat*
der Ketchup	*ketchup*
die Mayo(nnaise)/Majonäse	*mayo(nnaise)*
der Senf	*mustard*
Ich möchte einmal/zweimal/dreimal ...	*I would like one/two/three ...*
Ich hätte gern ...	*I would like ...*
Das macht €8.	*That's €8.*
Ich esse ... gern.	*I like eating ... .*
Ich trinke ... gern.	*I like drinking ... .*

Wörter

In den Sommerferien • During the summer holidays

Was wirst du machen?	*What will you do?*
Ich werde ...	*I will ...*
Wir werden ...	*We will ...*
klettern	*climb*
im Meer schwimmen	*swim in the sea*
rodeln	*toboggan*
im See baden	*bathe in the lake*
segeln	*sail*
an den Strand gehen	*go to the beach*
tauchen	*dive*
wandern	*hike*
windsurfen	*windsurf*
Was kann man dort machen?	*What can you do there?*
Man kann ... besuchen.	*'One'/People/ You can visit ...*
Die Stadt ist bekannt für ...	*The town is well known for ...*
Ich werde (eine Woche) bleiben.	*I will stay (for a week).*

Oft benutzte Wörter • High-frequency words

am Montag	*on Monday*
am Dienstag	*on Tuesday*
am Mittwoch	*on Wednesday*
am Donnerstag	*on Thursday*
am Freitag	*on Friday*
am Wochenende	*at the weekend*
sehr	*very*
nicht sehr	*not very*
ziemlich	*quite*
immer	*always*
nicht immer	*not always*
oft	*often*
nicht oft	*not often*
nie	*never*
alles	*everything*
dort	*there*
teuer	*expensive*

Listening

Level 1	I can understand some familiar spoken words and phrases.
Level 2	I can understand a range of familiar spoken phrases.
Level 3	I can understand the main points of short spoken passages and note people's answers to questions.
Level 4	I can understand the main points of spoken passages and some of the detail.
Level 5	I can understand the main points and opinions in spoken passages about different topics. I can recognise if people are speaking about the future **OR** the past as well as the present.

Speaking

Level 1	I can say single words and short phrases.
Level 2	I can answer simple questions and use set phrases.
Level 3	I can ask questions and use short phrases to answer questions about myself.
Level 4	I can take part in conversations. I can express my opinions. I can use grammar to change phrases to say something new.
Level 5	I can give short talks, in which I express my opinions. I can take part in conversations giving information, opinions and reasons. I can speak about the future **OR** the past as well as the present.

Level descriptors

Reading

Level 1	I can understand familiar words and phrases.
Level 2	I can understand familiar phrases. I can read aloud familiar words and phrases. I can use a vocabulary list to check meanings.
Level 3	I can understand the main points and people's answers to questions in short written texts.
Level 4	I can understand the main points in short texts and some of the detail. Sometimes I can work out the meaning of new words.
Level 5	I can understand the main points and opinions in texts about different topics. I can recognise if the texts are about the future **OR** the past as well as the present.

Writing

Level 1	I can write or copy single words correctly.
Level 2	I can copy short sentences correctly and write some words from memory.
Level 3	I can answer questions about myself. I can write short phrases from memory. I can write short sentences with help.
Level 4	I can write short texts on familiar topics. I can use grammar to change phrases to write something new.
Level 5	I can write short texts on a range of familiar topics. I can write about the future **OR** the past as well as the present.

Notes

Notes

Published by Pearson Education Limited, Edinburgh Gate, Harlow, Essex, CM20 2JE.

www.pearsonschoolsandfecolleges.co.uk

Edited by Melanie Birdsall
Designed by Kamae Design

Illustrated by Caron at KJA Artists and Lisa Hunt

First published 2013

2022
17

British Library Cataloguing in Publication Data
A catalogue record for this book is available from the British Library

ISBN 978 1 447 94654 0

Printed in Great Britain by Bell and Bain Ltd, Glasgow

Acknowledgements

We would like to thank Melissa Weir, Angelika Libera, Janet Soame and Frances Reynolds for their invaluable help in the development of this course.

Every effort has been made to contact copyright holders of material reproduced in this book. Any omissions will be rectified in subsequent printings if notice is given to the publishers.

www.pearsonschools.co.uk
myorders@pearson.com
T 0845 630 33 33
F 0845 630 77 77

ISBN 978-1-4479-4654-0

Stimmt! 1

Übungsheft B

Malcolm Pacey

ALWAYS LEARNING

PEARSON

1 Hallo! (Seiten 8–9)

1 **Two of the words in each set have a sound that is the same. Circle the word with a different sound from the other two.**

1	*Schlange*	*Porsche*	*Buch*
2	*Bär*	*Löwe*	*Röntgenbild*
3	*Wildwassersport*	*Auf Wiedersehen*	*Tür*
4	*Biene*	*heiße*	*Eis*

2 **Join up the sentence halves.**

1 Gut, danke. Und
2 Auf
3 Ich heiße
4 Hallo! Wie heißt
5 Ich heiße Nadia. Wie
6 Nicht

a Wiedersehen.
b Ben. Wie heißt du?
c geht's, Ben?
d du?
e schlecht.
f dir?

3 **Write the sentences from exercise 2 in the correct order for the conversation. Then translate them into English.**

1 ______ ______
2 ______ ______
3 ______ ______
4 ______ ______
5 *Nicht schlecht.* *Not bad.*
6 ______ ______

4 **Unscramble the inventions. Look at the definite article (word for 'the') for each word. Then write each invention with the indefinite article (word for 'a').**

1 sad ngbönReltid *das ...* *ein ...*
2 erd reelmiDtoos ______ ______
3 sda toF3rMmPa- ______ ______
4 sad PeuAsotrcoh ______ ______
5 ied sAMrkdadiae ______ ______

2 Eins, zwei, drei ... (Seiten 10–11)

1 The bank has sent texts to customers with their coded PIN numbers. Solve the maths problems in German to work out the PINs. Then write each customer's new PIN below the phone.

1

2 7 _ _

2

_ _ _ _

3

_ _ _ _

2 Write the winning lottery numbers in words.

1 

______

2 

______

3 

______

4 

______

5 

______

6 

______

3 Write two sentences for each speaker. Give the speaker's age and the age of his/her friend.

er ist = he is
sie ist = she is

1

Ich bin dreizehn Jahre alt.
Sie ist zwölf Jahre alt.

2
______
______

3

______
______

3 Ich wohne in Deutschland (Seiten 12–13)

1 **Read the dialogue and complete the table with the correct forms of each verb.**

Melanie: Hallo! Ich heiße Melanie. Wie heißt du?
Marco: Ich heiße Marco. Ich wohne in Straubing. Wo wohnst du?
Melanie: Ich wohne in Braunschweig. Wie alt bist du?
Marco: Ich bin zwölf Jahre alt. Wer ist das?
Melanie: Sie heißt Jessie. Sie wohnt in Leipzig und ist dreizehn Jahre alt.

wer = who

	heißen (to be called)	**wohnen** (to live)	**sein** (to be)
ich (I)		*wohne*	
du (you)			*bist*
er/sie/es (he/she/it)	*heißt*		

2 **Write the missing word in each sentence and complete the crossword.**

1					W	☐	☐	☐	☐					
2				☐	O	☐	☐	☐	☐					
3				☐	L	☐								
4	☐	☐	☐	☐	F									
5					S	☐	☐	☐	☐	☐	☐	☐	☐	☐
6					B	☐	☐	☐						
7			☐	☐	U	☐	☐	☐	☐	☐	☐	☐	☐	
8		☐	☐	☐	R	☐								
9					G	☐	☐	☐	☐	☐				

bist *zwölf* *wohne* *wohnst* *Jahre* *Schottland* *Deutschland* *geht's* *alt*

1 Ich ______________ in Manchester.
2 Wo ______________ du, Nick?
3 Wie ______________ ist er?
4 Er ist ______________ Jahre alt.
5 Glasgow ist in ______________.
6 Wie alt ______________ du?
7 Ich wohne in Berlin. Das ist in ______________.
8 Ich bin elf ______________ alt.
9 Wie ______________?

3 **Research why the city of Wolfsburg is important to Germany.**

4 Meine Welt ist wunderbar! (Seiten 14–15)

1 The printer has made four mistakes labelling the illustrations. Write *richtig* or *falsch* under each caption.

1 
Ich bin musikalisch.
____

2 
Ich bin sehr launisch.
____

3 
Ich bin ziemlich freundlich.
____

4 
Ich bin kreativ.
____

5 
Ich bin laut.
____

6 
Ich bin lustig.
____

2 Rewrite the false captions from exercise 1, correcting them so that they are true.

____
____
____
____

faul
lustig
musikalisch
sportlich

3 Separate out the words to form three sentences.

meinelieblingsfußballmannschaftistbayernmünchen

meinlieblingssportisttennis

meinelieblingszahlistsieben

! Remember that each sentence must start with a capital letter. Also, remember that nouns start with a capital letter.

1 ______________________________
2 ______________________________
3 ______________________________

4 Write a sentence about your favourite …

1 football team: ______________________________
2 sport: ______________________________
3 number: ______________________________

5 Meine Sachen (Seiten 16–17)

1 Write the German question word under its English translation.

Who?	What?	How?	Where?	Where from?

Wie? Was? Wo? Woher? Wer?

2 Write the correct question word in each question. You may use each word more than once.

1 ________________ bist du? Sportlich?

2 ________________ wohnt Shiva?

3 ________________ heißt du?

4 ________________ kommst du?

5 ________________ ist das? Ist das Max?

6 ________________ alt ist Michael?

7 ________________ ist Hannover? *Hannover ist in Deutschland!*

8 ________________ ist deine Lieblingsmusik?

3 Read the paragraph below. Pretend that you're Gabi, and answer each question in a complete German sentence.

Hallo! Ich heiße Gabi und ich bin vierzehn Jahre alt. Ich wohne in Kiel, in Deutschland, aber ich komme aus Swansea. Das ist in Wales. Wie bin ich? Ich bin sportlich, lustig und auch sehr laut! Mein Lieblingsmonat ist Dezember und meine Lieblingssendung ist ‚Die Simpsons'. Ich habe ein iPad und auch einen Computer. Tschüs!

1 Wie heißt du? ____

2 Wo wohnst du? ____

3 Woher kommst du? ____

4 Wie bist du? ____

5 Wie heißt deine Lieblingssendung? ____

6 Was hast du? ____

1 **Complete the table with the correct words.**

	the	a	my	your
masculine: Sport				
feminine: Musik				
neuter: Auto				

2 **Write each sentence or question in German. Tick the boxes when you've checked each part of your work.**

Part of writing accurately in any language is going back over your work to check that there aren't any mistakes. Get into the habit now and watch both your English and German improve!

1 I'm called Osman.

____

2 I live in Germany.

____

3 I'm quite friendly and also creative.

____

____

4 I have a mobile phone.

____

5 Where do you live?

____

☐ Spelling of key phonics sound 'ei'
☐ Name has a capital
☐ Spelling of key phonics sound 'eu'
☐ Full stop at the end
☐ Check the qualifier
☐ Check the connective
☐ Capital on the noun
☐ Right word for 'a'
☐ Correct question word
☐ Verb in second position

3 **Write a short paragraph about yourself. Use the sentences in exercise 2 as prompts. Check your work against the checklist below.**

☐ genders ☐ qualifiers ☐ connectives ☐ verbs
☐ capital letters ☐ spelling ☐ question words

____

____

Wiederholung 1

1 Fill in the gaps by writing the German for the words in brackets.

Hallo! Ich __________ (am called) Marie und ich __________ (live) in Walsrode. Das ist in __________ (Germany). Ich bin fünfzehn __________ (years) alt. Ich bin __________ (very) sportlich und __________ (quite) intelligent, __________ (but) ich bin __________ (also) faul. Mein __________ (favourite sport) ist Hockey und __________ (my) Lieblingsmusik ist Pop. Ich __________ (have) einen Vogel aus Amerika. Er ist __________ (very) freundlich, aber __________ (not) laut!

2 Crack the code and write the sentences correctly.

a 18/24/19 4/12/19/13/22 18/13 20/28/7/7/18/13/20/22/13

Ich wohne in Göttingen.

b 22/9 18/8/7 20/26/13/1 21/9/22/6/13/23/15/18/24/19

____

c 14/22/18/13/22 15/18/22/25/15/18/13/20/8/14/6/8/18/16 18/8/7 14/12/1/26/9/7

____

____

ä = 27 ü = 29
ö = 28 ß = 30

3 Make up a coded sentence in German for a classmate to solve. Don't forget to provide a key.

4 Write the questions you would ask to get these answers.

1 *Wie heißt du?*
Ich heiße Elaine.

2 __________
Mein Lieblingssport ist Tennis.

3 __________
Sami ist musikalisch und intelligent, aber sehr launisch.

4 __________
Alwin ist vierzehn Jahre alt.

Wiederholung 2

1 **Read the website entries.**

Ich heiße **Franzi** und suche Freunde aus England, Irland oder Nordirland. Ich habe eine Schlange zu Hause! Sie ist sechs Jahre alt. Ich wohne in Wien. Das ist in Österreich. Ich bin sehr kreativ und intelligent! Schreib mir bitte!

Hallo! Ich heiße **Hannah** und ich wohne in London, in England. Ich lerne Deutsch. Ich suche Freunde aus Deutschland, Österreich und auch aus der Schweiz. Ich bin sportlich und spiele Fußball und auch Tennis, aber ich bin sehr faul! Meine Lieblingsmusik ist Rock. Schreib mir!

Mein Name ist **Felix** und ich wohne in der Schweiz, aber ich komme aus Dortmund in Deutschland. Zu Hause habe ich eine Wii und mein Lieblingsspiel ist FIFA. Meine Lieblingsfußballmannschaft ist Bayern-München. Ich suche Freunde aus Schottland und Wales.

Hi! Ich bin **Muhammad** und ich wohne in Cardiff. Das ist in Wales. Ich bin sechzehn Jahre alt. Meine Lieblingssache ist Technologie. Ich habe zu Hause einen Computer, ein Handy und auch ein iPad. Ich bin nicht sehr sportlich, aber sehr freundlich. Mein Lieblingsland ist Deutschland und ich suche dort Freunde.

Write the name of the person who …

1 is looking for friends from Switzerland. Hannah

2 supports a football team. ____________

3 has a pet. ____________

4 is just looking for friends from Germany. ____________

5 lives in a different place from where they were born. ____________

6 does not particularly like sport. ____________

7 lives in Switzerland. ____________

suche = seek
Schreib mir (bitte)! = Write to me (please)!
dort = there

2 **Write your own profile for the website. Use as much German as you can from *Kapitel 1* to describe yourself.**

____

____

____

____

Grammatik (Seiten 22–23)

1 Write a sentence using the correct German word for 'a' for each item.

1  2  3  4  5 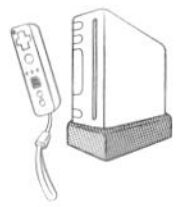 6  7  8 

1 *Das ist ein Computer.*
2 ______________________
3 ______________________
4 ______________________
5 ______________________
6 ______________________
7 ______________________
8 ______________________

die Gitarre · *das Handy*
der iPod · *der Computer*
das Skateboard · *das Keyboard*
der Fußball · *die Wii*

Grammatik
masculine – *ein*
feminine – *eine*
neuter – *ein*

2 Circle the correct verb form to complete each sentence.

1 Lukas **habe / hat / hast** einen Computer.
2 Ich **heiße / habe / hat** einen Vogel zu Hause.
3 Wo **bist / ist / wohnst** er?
4 Er **ist / komme / bin** musikalisch und sportlich.
5 Julia **bin / ist / wohnt** fünfzehn Jahre alt.
6 Wie alt **wohnst / bist / bin** du?
7 Wo **hast / bist / bin** ich?

Grammatik
You can use the pronouns *er* ('he') or *sie* ('she') instead of writing someone's name. Both need the *er/sie/es* form of the verb.

3 Complete the table with the correct forms of each regular verb.

wohnen (to live)	**kommen** (to come)	**heißen** (to be called)
ich *wohne*	ich	ich
du	du *kommst*	du
er/sie/es	er/sie/es	er/sie/es *heißt*

Now use the table to write the correct verb in each gap.

1 Mein Handy ____________ aus China.
2 Meine Schlange ____________ Sissel.
3 Du ____________ Gabi.
4 ____________ du aus Berlin?
5 ____________ Monika in Hamburg?
6 Deine Lieblingssendung ____________ ‚EastEnders'.
7 Ich ____________ Wolfgang.
8 Wo ____________ du?

Mein Fortschritt

1 **Record your levels for *Kapitel* 1.**

2 **Look at the level descriptors on pages 59–60 and set your targets for *Kapitel* 2.**

3 **Fill in what you need to do to achieve these targets.**

Listening 	I have reached Level ______ in **Listening**. In *Kapitel* 2, I want to reach Level ______ I need to ______________________________ ______________________________ ______________________________ ______________________________
Speaking 	I have reached Level ______ in **Speaking**. In *Kapitel* 2, I want to reach Level ______ I need to ______________________________ ______________________________ ______________________________ ______________________________
Reading 	I have reached Level ______ in **Reading**. In *Kapitel* 2, I want to reach Level ______ I need to ______________________________ ______________________________ ______________________________ ______________________________
Writing 	I have reached Level ______ in **Writing**. In *Kapitel* 2, I want to reach Level ______ I need to ______________________________ ______________________________ ______________________________ ______________________________

Wörter

Hallo! • Meeting and greeting

Wie heißt du?	*What's your name?*
Ich heiße ...	*My name is ...*
Hallo!	*Hello! / Hi!*
Guten Tag!	*Hello!*
Wie geht's?	*How are you?*
Gut, danke. Und dir?	*Fine, thanks. And you?*
Nicht schlecht.	*Not bad.*
Tschüs!	*Bye!*
Auf Wiedersehen!	*Goodbye!*

Die Zahlen 1–19 • Numbers 1–19

eins	*1*
zwei	*2*
drei	*3*
vier	*4*
fünf	*5*
sechs	*6*
sieben	*7*
acht	*8*
neun	*9*
zehn	*10*
elf	*11*
zwölf	*12*
dreizehn	*13*
vierzehn	*14*
fünfzehn	*15*
sechzehn	*16*
siebzehn	*17*
achtzehn	*18*
neunzehn	*19*
Wie alt bist du?	*How old are you?*
Ich bin ... Jahre alt.	*I am ... years old.*
Wie alt ist (Julia)?	*How old is (Julia)?*
(Julia) ist ... Jahre alt.	*(Julia) is ... years old.*

Wo wohnst du? • Where do you live?

Ich wohne in ...	*I live in ...*
Er/Sie/Es wohnt in ...	*He/She/It lives in ...*
... England	*England*
... Irland	*Ireland*
... Nordirland	*Northern Ireland*
... Schottland	*Scotland*
... Wales	*Wales*
... Deutschland	*Germany*
... Österreich	*Austria*
... der Schweiz	*Switzerland*

Wie bist du? • What are you like?

Ich bin ...	*I am ...*
Er/Sie ist ...	*He/She is ...*
faul	*lazy*
freundlich	*friendly*
intelligent	*intelligent*
kreativ	*creative*
launisch	*moody*
laut	*loud*
lustig	*funny*
musikalisch	*musical*
sportlich	*sporty*

Lieblingssachen • Favourite things

Mein Lieblingssport ist ...
My favourite sport is ...
Mein Lieblingsmonat ist ...
My favourite month is ...
Meine Lieblingsmusik ist ...
My favourite music is ...
Meine Lieblingszahl ist ...
My favourite number is ...
Meine Lieblingssendung ist ...
My favourite programme is ...
Meine Lieblingsfußballmannschaft ist ...
My favourite football team is ...
Mein Lieblingsspiel ist ...
My favourite game is ...
Mein Lieblingsland ist ...
My favourite country is ...
Mein Lieblingsauto ist ...
My favourite car is ...
Was ist dein Lieblingssport?
What's your favourite sport?
Was ist deine Lieblingszahl?
What's your favourite number?
Was ist dein Lieblingsland?
What's your favourite country?

Hast du einen Computer? • Have you got a computer?

Ich habe ...	*I have ...*
einen Computer	*a computer*
einen iPod	*an iPod*
einen Fußball	*a football*
eine Gitarre	*a guitar*
eine Wii	*a Wii*
eine Schlange	*a snake*
ein Handy	*a mobile phone*
ein Keyboard	*a keyboard*
ein Skateboard	*a skateboard*

Fragewörter • Question words

Wie?	*How?*
Was?	*What?*
Wo?	*Where?*
Woher?	*Where ... from?*
Wer?	*Who?*

Oft benutzte Wörter • High-frequency words

und	*and*
(und) auch	*(and) also*
aber	*but*
sehr	*very*
ziemlich	*quite*
nicht	*not*
Was denkst du?	*What do you think?*
Ich denke, ...	*I think ...*
Ich auch!	*Me too!*
Ich nicht!	*Not me!/That's not what I think!*
Was? Du spinnst!	*What? You're joking!*

1 Extreme Haustiere (Seiten 30–31)

1 Complete the sentences about the pets. Write the correct words in the gaps. Remember to think about the gender of each animal.

1 Ich habe _ein_______ Pferd. _Es___ ist groß und heißt Romeo.
2 Ich habe __________ Kaninchen. _____ ist niedlich und heißt Timmo.
3 Ich habe __________ Katze. _____ ist intelligent und heißt Mieze.
4 Max hat __________ Schlange. _____ ist zwei Jahre alt.
5 Gabi hat __________ Pferd. _____ ist launish.
6 Ich habe __________ Hund. _____ ist freundlich und heißt Prinz.
7 Susi hat __________ Goldfisch. _____ heißt Nemo.

Grammatik
Remember: after *haben* the masculine word for 'a' changes from *ein* to *einen*.

Grammatik
m. der / ein → **er**
f. die / eine → **sie**
n. das / ein → **es**

2 Tina Tierfan has lots of pets! Write Tina's answers to the interviewer's questions about how many of each animal she has.

Grammatik

Hund (-e)	Pferd (-e)
Katze (-n)	Goldfisch (-e)
Schlange (-n)	Maus (Mäuse)

1 Hast du einen Hund? _Nein! Ich habe drei Hunde._
2 Hast du ein Pferd? ______________________________
3 Hast du eine Katze? ______________________________
4 Hast du einen Goldfisch? ______________________________
5 Hast du eine Schlange? ______________________________
6 Hast du eine Maus? ______________________________

2 Supertiere (Seiten 32–33)

1 **Complete the sentences about the animals. Write the correct name in each gap.**

Hermann 

Minnie 

Sisi 

Kizzi 

Moto 

Millie 

1 __________ ist schnell.

2 __________ ist süß.

3 __________ ist gemein.

4 __________ ist superintelligent.

5 __________ ist cool.

6 __________ ist kräftig.

2 **Write a sentence to say what each of the *Supertiere* can do.**

1 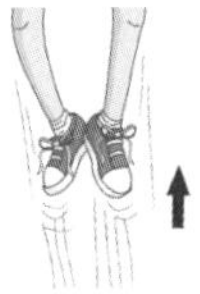
Hermann

2 
Sisi

3 
Minnie

4 

Kizzi

5 
Millie

6 
Moto

1 Hermann kann springen.

2 ______________________________

3 ______________________________

4 ______________________________

5 ______________________________

6 ______________________________

Grammatik
The verb *kann* is always followed by an infinitive verb.

3 **Read the text below, then translate it into English.**

Günther Goldfisch ist mein Lieblingstier. Er ist ein Jahr alt. Er ist sehr lustig und kräftig, aber auch ziemlich süß. Er kann schwimmen, springen und auch im Aquarium tanzen! Günther hat einen Freund: er ist sehr cool und schlau.

3 Meine Familie (Seiten 34–35)

1 Find the numbers in the puzzle, and write them next to the correct numeral.

v	i	e	r	u	n	d	s	e	c	h	z	i	g	m	e
b	a	l	c	o	e	z	n	f	w	i	r	d	s	k	s
s	e	c	h	s	u	n	d	d	r	e	i	ß	i	g	a
q	g	n	a	j	n	x	i	n	d	m	h	t	g	ü	o
h	a	c	h	t	u	n	d	f	ü	n	f	z	i	g	i
u	e	i	n	u	n	d	a	c	h	t	z	i	g	p	b
n	t	e	r	i	d	f	b	n	ß	e	d	z	g	d	s
d	r	e	i	u	n	d	v	i	e	r	z	i	g	w	e
e	v	h	f	r	e	a	m	ß	p	l	s	j	a	q	c
r	d	r	e	i	u	n	d	z	w	a	n	z	i	g	h
t	z	a	n	j	n	x	o	u	e	y	g	r	e	v	z
k	c	p	f	s	z	d	l	b	n	l	a	i	h	m	i
i	b	z	w	e	i	u	n	d	s	i	e	b	z	i	g
a	g	b	n	ü	g	y	i	a	z	o	m	e	d	h	e

100 ______________________

64 ______________________

99 ______________________

43 ______________________

72 ______________________

36 ______________________

58 ______________________

81 ______________________

60 ______________________

23 ______________________

2 Describe each of the families. Fill in the gaps for the first family. Write the whole description for the second family.

Oban

Ich heiße Tom. Ich bin vierzehn Jahre alt. Es gibt vier Personen in meiner Familie. Meine Mutter ist ______________________ Jahre alt. Ich habe einen Bruder. _____ ist __________ Jahre alt. Ich habe eine Schwester. ________ ist ______________ Jahre alt. Wir wohnen in __________.

Köln

____

____

____

____

____

____

3 Write about your family (real or imaginary). Use the descriptions in exercise 2 to help you.

der Stiefbruder = stepbrother
die Halbschwester = half-sister
Ich bin Einzelkind. = I am an only child.

4 Die Farben der Welt (Seiten 36–37)

1 Describe each person's hair and eyes.

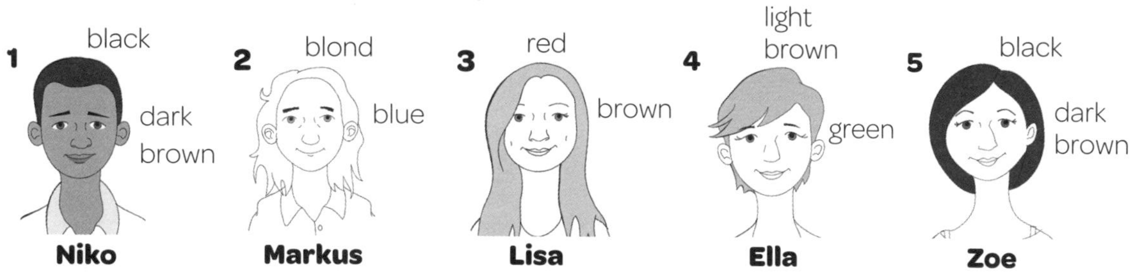

Grammatik
When you describe hair and eyes, the adjectives (colour, length) need an ***e*** on the end.

hell = light
dunkel = dark
hellbraun = light brown
dunkelblau = dark blue

1 Er heißt Niko. Er hat kurze, schwarze Haare und dunkelbraune Augen.
2 ______________________
3 ______________________
4 ______________________
5 ______________________

2 Complete the text by choosing the correct words from the cloud to fill the gaps. There are more words than you need.

Es gibt fünf __________ in meiner Familie. Wir __________ in Braunschweig. Das ist in __________. Meine __________ heißt Emma und sie ist neunundvierzig __________ alt. Sie ist sehr freundlich und hat __________, schwarze Haare. Mein Vater __________ auch neunundvierzig und er hat kurze, dunkelbraune Haare und braune __________.

Ich habe zwei __________: einen Bruder und eine Schwester. __________ Bruder heißt Mehmet und er ist __________ Jahre alt. Er ist launisch aber __________ lustig. __________ Schwester, Isla, hat grüne Augen und __________ Haare. Sie ist sechzehn Jahre alt, sehr klein und __________.

Deutschland alt Augen Personen braune wohnen sportlich Meine Mutter Jahre lange Geschwister zwölf auch Mein blau ist

Read the text for gist first. For each sentence, think about whether you need a noun, a verb, a connective or an adjective.

5 Alles Gute! (Seiten 38–39)

1 Reorder the words to make correct sentences. Don't forget the full stop!

1 am Mai Ich Geburtstag habe neunzehnten

____

2 hat Oktober am Oma Geburtstag elften Meine

____

3 Geburtstag Stiefbruder Dezember am Dein dritten hat

____

4 hast Geburtstag einunddreißigsten Juli Du am

____

5 und Geburtstag haben achten am Michael Juni Monika

____

2 Complete each sentence by writing the date. Write each holiday in English.

01.01. Neujahr ist am *ersten Januar*. *New Year*

01.05. Der Maifeiertag ist am ______________________. ______________

03.10. Der Tag der Deutschen Einheit ist am ______________________. *German Unity Day*

25.12. Weihnachten ist am ______________________. ______________

31.12. Silvester ist am ______________________. ______________

3 Read the short profile about Yannic and write a summary in the table.

Er heißt Yannic Spiller. Er ist dreizehn Jahre alt und kommt aus Trier. Trier ist in Deutschland. Yannic hat am siebten Januar Geburtstag. Er hat einen Bruder, Tim. Tim ist achtzehn Jahre alt. Yannic hat auch eine Schwester. Sie heißt Steffi und ist sechzehn Jahre alt. Die Familie Spiller hat zwei Haustiere: einen Hund und eine Katze.

Name:		Geschwister:	
Alter:			
Wohnt in:		Haustiere:	
Geburtstag:			

4 Now write a short profile about yourself.

6 Speaking Skills Eine Superfamilie (Seiten 40–41)

1 Rescue the question words from the alphabet soup. Write each one on a line and use it to write a question.

Wie viele Brüder hast du?

____

____

____

____

____

____

2 The police have written a summary about a crime suspect. Write six questions for a journalist to ask the suspect. The questions should cover all the information in the summary.

1 Wie heißt du?
2 ______________________________
3 ______________________________
4 ______________________________
5 ______________________________
6 ______________________________

Martin Kolwitz ist 24 Jahre alt. Er hat am achten November Geburtstag. Er wohnt in Hamburg, in Deutschland. Er hat einen Bruder. Er hat auch Haustiere: zwei Hunde.

Remember: the verb usually goes straight after the question word.

3 Use these notes to write questions to Martin about his accomplice, Sophie.

1 Wie heißt sie?
2 ______________________________
3 ______________________________
4 ______________________________
5 ______________________________

Sophie Meyer
19
Ebbingen, Deutschland
Haare – kurz, Augen – blau
Geb. 21.10.

Remember to use the correct part of the verb with the pronoun *sie*.

4 Write a summary about Sophie, like the one the police wrote about Martin in exercise 2.

Wiederholung 1

1 Complete the sentences. Choose the correct word from the cloud to fill in each gap.

1 ________________ Mutter ist sehr freundlich und intelligent.

2 Hast du ________________ Meerschweinchen?

3 Wir haben ________________ Haustier.

4 Wo ist ________________ Vogel?

5 Ich habe ________________ Bruder.

dein *kein*
ein *meine*
einen

2 You are describing pets at a pet show. Use the owners' notes to write what sort of pet they have, what the pet is like and what it can do.

Mareike

mouse
Pippa
cute, fast
fly, swim

Mareike hat ________________.

Sie heißt ________________.

Sie ist ________________.

Sie kann ________________.

Aaron

cat
Mieze
intelligent, cool, mean
jump, play football

________________.

________________.

________________.

________________.

________________.

3 Decscribe the animal you'll be entering in the pet show by writing a similar description.

Example: Ich habe ...

Wiederholung 2

1 Read the texts below.

Hallo! Ich heiße **Anna** und ich bin fünfzehn Jahre alt. Ich habe am elften Februar Geburtstag. Ich wohne in Klagenfurt, in Österreich. Ich bin ziemlich groß und schlank und habe kurze, schwarze Haare und blaue Augen. Ich habe keine Geschwister – ich bin Einzelkind. Ich habe einen Goldfisch und einen Wellensittich. Ich kann Flöte spielen und Italienisch sprechen.

Hi! Ich bin **Noah** und ich komme aus Aachen. Das ist in Deutschland. Ich habe am zweiten November Geburtstag und bin vierzehn Jahre alt. Ich liebe Haustiere! Ich habe zwei Hunde, drei Katzen und eine Maus. Ich habe eine große Familie. Ich habe einen Halbbruder (er ist ein Baby) und zwei Schwestern. Mein Halbbruder ist sehr süß und klein. Er hat schwarze Haare und blaue Augen.

a Complete the sentences by writing *Anna* or *Noah*.

1. ____________ lives in Austria.
2. ____________ can play the flute.
3. ____________ 's birthday is on the 02.11.
4. ____________ has a half-brother.
5. ____________ is 15 years old.
6. ____________ has cats.

b Write *richtig* or *falsch* next to each statement.

1. Anna hat einen Halbbruder. ____________
2. Anna kann auch Englisch sprechen. ____________
3. Noahs Halbbruder hat blaue Augen. ____________
4. Klagenfurt ist nicht in Deutschland. ____________
5. Anna hat am fünfzehnten Februar Geburtstag. ____________
6. Anna hat keine Geschwister. ____________

2 Translate these sentences into German.

1. My birthday is on the first of May. ______________________________
2. She can speak German. ______________________________
3. My guinea pig is very cute. ______________________________
4. Your sister has light blue eyes. ______________________________
5. My grandparents live in Southampton. ______________________________
6. My brother can fly. ______________________________

Grammatik (Seiten 44–45)

1 **Complete the table by writing the correct form of *haben* for each pronoun.**

haben *hast* *habt* *hat* *haben* *habe*

Words for 'you':
du (speaking to one family member or friend)
ihr (speaking to two or more family members or friends)
Sie (speaking to people you don't know or adults)

ich	du	er/sie/es	wir	ihr	Sie/sie

Now complete the sentences with the correct form of *haben*.

1 Katja, hast ________ du eine Katze?

2 Tom und Niko, ________ ihr einen Hund?

3 ________ Sie eine Schlange, Herr Brand?

4 Ich ________ ein Pferd.

5 Frau Gerber, ________ Sie eine Maus?

6 Herr Alexander ________ ein Pferd.

2 **Join each pronoun to a verb. There is more than one possible verb for some of the pronouns. Then write a question or a sentence with each pair.**

1 ich	**a** macht	**1**	________
2 du	**b** heißen	**2**	________
3 er	**c** wohnst	**3**	________
4 wir	**d** heiße	**4**	________
5 ihr	**e** spielt	**5**	________
6 Sie	**f** spielen	**6**	________

3 **Rewrite the sentences so they include the verb *kann*.**

1 Mein Bruder fliegt. Mein Bruder kann fliegen.

2 Ich spiele Flöte. ________

3 Meine Mutter schwimmt. ________

4 Mein Vater springt. ________

5 Ich tanze. ________

6 Er singt gut. ________

Mein Fortschritt

1 Record your levels for *Kapitel* 2.

2 Look at the level descriptors on pages 59–60 and set your targets for *Kapitel* 3.

3 Fill in what you need to do to achieve these targets.

Listening 	I have reached Level ____ in **Listening**. In *Kapitel* 3, I want to reach Level ____ I need to ______________________ ______________________ ______________________ ______________________
Speaking 	I have reached Level ____ in **Speaking**. In *Kapitel* 3, I want to reach Level ____ I need to ______________________ ______________________ ______________________ ______________________
Reading 	I have reached Level ____ in **Reading**. In *Kapitel* 3, I want to reach Level ____ I need to ______________________ ______________________ ______________________ ______________________
Writing 	I have reached Level ____ in **Writing**. In *Kapitel* 3, I want to reach Level ____ I need to ______________________ ______________________ ______________________ ______________________

Haustiere • Pets

Hast du ein Haustier?	*Have you got a pet?*
Ich habe ...	*I have ...*
einen Goldfisch	*a goldfish*
einen Hamster	*a hamster*
einen Hund	*a dog*
ein Kaninchen	*a rabbit*
eine Katze	*a cat*
eine Maus	*a mouse*
ein Meerschweinchen	*a guinea pig*
ein Pferd	*a horse*
eine Schlange	*a snake*
einen Wellensittich	*a budgie*
kein Haustier	*no pet*

Eigenschaften • Qualities

Wie ist er/sie/es?	*What is he/she/ it like?*
Er/Sie/Es ist ...	*He/She/It is ...*
dick/schlank	*fat/thin*
frech/niedlich	*cheeky/cute*
gemein/süß	*mean/sweet*
groß/klein	*big/small*
kräftig	*strong*
schlau	*cunning*
(super)lustig	*(really) funny*
Er/Sie/Es kann ...	*He/She/It can ...*
Italienisch sprechen	*speak Italian*
fliegen	*fly*
Flöte/Fußball/Wii spielen	*play the flute/ football/on the Wii*
(schnell) laufen	*run (fast)*
lesen	*read*
Rad fahren	*ride a bike*
schwimmen	*swim*
singen	*sing*
springen	*jump*
tanzen	*dance*

Die Zahlen 20–100 • Numbers 20–100

zwanzig	*twenty*
dreißig	*thirty*
vierzig	*forty*
fünfzig	*fifty*
sechzig	*sixty*
siebzig	*seventy*
achtzig	*eighty*
neunzig	*ninety*
hundert	*hundred*
einundzwanzig	*twenty-one*
zweiundzwanzig	*twenty-two*

Meine Familie • My family

Es gibt ... Personen in meiner Familie.	*There are ... people in my family.*
meine Mutter	*my mother*
mein Vater	*my father*
mein Bruder	*my brother*
mein Stiefbruder/ Halbbruder	*my stepbrother/ half-brother*
meine Schwester	*my sister*
meine Stiefschwester/ Halbschwester	*my stepsister/ half-sister*
meine Eltern	*my parents*
meine Großeltern	*my grandparents*
Hast du Geschwister?	*Have you any brothers and sisters?*
Ich habe zwei Brüder.	*I have two brothers.*
Ich habe drei Schwestern.	*I have three sisters.*
Ich bin Einzelkind.	*I'm an only child.*
Ich habe keine Geschwister.	*I have no brothers and sisters.*

Die Farben • Colours

schwarz	*black*
weiß	*white*
grau	*grey*
braun	*brown*
rot	*red*
orange	*orange*
gelb	*yellow*
grün	*green*
blau	*blue*
indigoblau	*indigo*
violett	*violet*
lila	*purple*
rosa	*pink*
bunt	*brightly coloured*
hellblau/dunkelblau	*light blue/dark blue*

Haare und Augen • Hair and eyes

Er/Sie hat ...	*He/She has ...*
schwarze/braune/ blonde/rote Haare	*black/brown/ blond/red hair*
kurze/lange/ mittellange Haare	*short/long/ mid length hair*
blaue/braune/grüne/ graue Augen	*blue/brown/green/ grey eyes*

Die Monate • The months

Januar	*January*
Februar	*February*
März	*March*
April	*April*
Mai	*May*
Juni	*June*
Juli	*July*
August	*August*
September	*September*
Oktober	*October*
November	*November*
Dezember	*December*

Das Datum • The date

Wann hast du Geburtstag?	*When is your birthday?*
am 1. (ersten) Januar	*on 1 January*
am 3. (dritten) Februar	*on 3 February*
am 7. (siebten) März	*on 7 March*
am 8. (achten) April	*on 8 April*
am 15. (fünfzehnten) Mai	*on 15 May*
am 29. (neunund-zwanzigsten) Juni	*on 29 June*
Ich habe (heute) Geburtstag.	*It's my birthday (today).*

Oft benutzte Wörter • High-frequency words

und	*and*
aber	*but*
oder	*or*
ziemlich	*fairly, quite*
sehr	*very*

1 Bist du sportlich? (Seiten 54–55)

1 **Look at the survey results in the table. Then answer the questions using full German sentences.**

Ahmed	🙂🙂			☹️			😐
Nicole		🙂🙂			☹️		
Christa	🙂		🙂🙂				😐
Torsten		☹️		🙂🙂		🙂	
Herr und Frau Meyer	🙂🙂			🙂	☹️	😐	

🙂🙂 = sehr gern 🙂 = gern 😐 = ziemlich gern ☹️ = nicht gern

1 Wer spielt sehr gern Fußball? Nicole spielt sehr gern Fußball.

2 Wer spielt gern Tischtennis? ____________

3 Was spielt Christa sehr gern? ____________

4 Was spielen Herr und Frau Meyer gern? ____________

5 Wer spielt Basketball nicht gern? ____________

6 Wer spielt ziemlich gern Handball? (2) ____________

7 Und du? Was spielst du gern? ____________

2 **Write three questions and three answers about the other people and sports in the table in exercise 1. Use the questions above as a model.**

____

____

____

____

____

____

2 Freizeit ist toll! (Seiten 56–57)

1 Write the words from the cloud in the grid. Translate the code word into English.

furchtbar
Eishockey
schlecht
spielst
irre
stinklangweilig
langweilig
Tischtennis
toll

2 Read about all the activities Hannes and Lola are involved in. Then write *richtig* or *falsch* next to each statement.

Hallo! Ich heiße **Hannes**. Ich finde Sport fantastisch. Ich spiele Tennis und schwimme. Schwimmen finde ich total super. Ich reite mit meiner Freundin, aber das finde ich langweilig. Fußball finde ich cool. Ich fahre auch gern Skateboard und lese sehr gern Sport- und Fitnessmagazine.

Meine Freundin heißt **Lola.** Sie findet Tischtennis toll. Lola fährt auch gern Rad – das ist sehr gesund! Sie findet schwimmen auch gut, aber Fußball findet sie nervig. Sie kann nicht Ski fahren. Im Winter spielt sie Eishockey und sie sieht sehr gern Eishockey im Fernsehen.

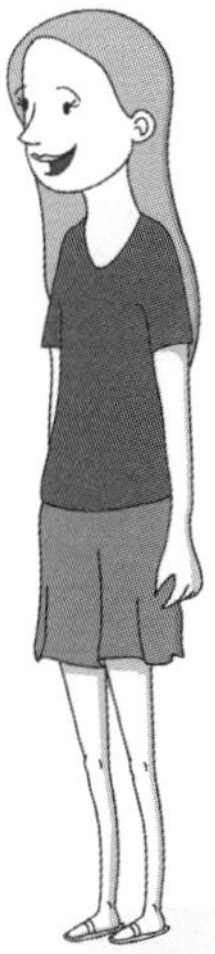

meine Freundin = my girlfriend
gesund = healthy
Fernsehen = television

1 Both Hannes and Lola participate in winter sports. ______________

2 Lola watches ice hockey on television. ______________

3 Hannes really likes swimming. ______________

4 Lola thinks skiing is fantastic. ______________

5 Lola plays ice hockey in winter. ______________

6 Hannes doesn't enjoying horse riding. ______________

7 Lola thinks football is exciting. ______________

8 Hannes watches sports programmes on television. ______________

3 In meiner Freizeit (Seiten 58–59)

1 **Separate the words to form five time phrases and write them below. Number the phrases in order of frequency, starting with 1 for the most frequent. Translate the phrases into English.**

Jeden TagdreimalproWocheeinmalproMonatamWochenendesechsmalproMonat

☐ ______________________ ______________________
☐ ______________________ ______________________
☐ ______________________ ______________________
☐ ______________________ ______________________
☐ ______________________ ______________________

2 **Use the time phrases from exercise 1 to answer the questions about yourself. Write your answers in full sentences.**

1 Gehst du ins Kino? ______________________
2 Machst du Sport? ______________________
3 Gehst du einkaufen? ______________________
4 Hörst du Musik? ______________________
5 Spielst du Wii? ______________________
6 Chillst du mit deinen Freunden? ______________________

! **nie** = never

3 **Join up the sentence halves. Rewrite each sentence so that it starts with the time phrase.**

1 Ich höre am	**a** Tag Sport.
2 Ich chille am	**b** Abend Musik.
3 Ich spiele sehr	**c** pro Woche Pizza.
4 Ich mache jeden	**d** Monat ins Kino.
5 Ich esse einmal	**e** oft Xbox.
6 Ich gehe einmal pro	**f** Wochenende.

! Remember the 'verb in second place' rule.

4 Ich bin online (Seiten 60–61)

1 Unscramble and write down the time phrase in each sentence. Then translate the sentences into English.

Grammatik
You can use the present tense with a future time phrase to say what you are going to do – just as in English.

1 Wir machen ähncset eoWhc Filme. *nächste Woche*

We are going to make …

2 Ich suche ma Mtanog Infos im Internet. ______

______

3 Wir sehen ma eneneoWhcd Katzenvideos auf YouTube. ______

______

4 Ich chatte nejde denbA auf Facebook. ______

______

5 Stefan spielt ni iezw cnoWhe Wii Sport. ______

______

6 Ich lade gomrne Musik herunter. ______

______

2 Underline all the verbs in the text. Circle the words that are in first position in the sentences. Write a sentence about what you notice.

Hey du!

Franzi hier! Jetzt sind wir Freunde auf Facebook! Jeden Tag spiele ich Wii. Jede Woche schreibt mein Vater ein Blog, aber das finde ich langweilig. Am Abend lese ich gern E-Books. Morgen telefoniere ich mit Freunden in Kanada über Skype. Das finde ich cool! Im Sommer fahren wir nach Vancouver. Fantastisch! Was machst du am Computer und wie oft?

______

3 Reply to the question Franzi has asked you in his chat.

Use as many time phrases as you can in your reply.

1 What type of word is needed to fill the gap in each sentence? Complete each sentence by writing an appropriate German word or words in the gap.

verb *noun* *time/frequency phrase* *connective* *adjective*

	Type of word
1 Ich finde ________ Tennis toll.	verb
2 Meine Schwester findet Tischtennis ________ .	________
3 Wir sehen ________ fern.	________
4 Herr Peters spielt nächste Woche Tennis ________ Fußball.	________
5 Mein Bruder schreibt ein ________ .	________

2 Answer the questions about German grammar.

Use the sentences in exercise 1 to help you answer these questions.

1 Where in a sentence do verbs usually go?
____

2 What often goes after a verb? ________

3 What can you expect to go after *ein/eine*? ________

4 Which German verb suggests you're giving an opinion? ________

3 Replace the underlined word(s) with something else: a different noun, adjective or time phrase.

1 Ich finde Tischtennis furchtbar. Ich finde Tischtennis langweilig.

2 Ich spiele nicht gern Fußball. ________

3 Micha spielt gern Wii. ________

4 Er macht einmal pro Monat Judo. ________

5 Olli findet E-Books fantastisch. ________

6 Ich sehe jede Woche fern. Meine Schwester sieht jeden Tag Videos auf YouTube.
____

Remember that you'll keep the reader's interest if you use a variety of different words and phrases.

4 Write about your friends' hobbies.

Remember to include:
- opinions
- time/frequency phrases
- connectives
- 'verb in second place' rule

Wiederholung 1

1 **Put the words in the correct order to make sentences or questions. Don't forget to insert a full stop or question mark.**

1 fern gern sehr Ich sehe ______

2 einkaufen er Wochenende geht Am ______

3 Hausaufgaben Ich Infos lese die für ______

4 in Wie Stadt oft du fährst die ______

5 Woche Kai Wasserball Nächste spielt ______

6 herunter Videos Ich lade Musik und ______

2 **Rewrite each sentence, beginning with a time phrase. Then translate the sentences into English.**

1 Ich spiele Volleyball. (at the weekend) *Am Wochenende spiele ich Volleyball.*

At the weekend I am going to play volleyball.

2 Er spielt Basketball. (on Monday) ______

______

3 Du spielst Tischtennis. (every week) ______

______

4 Rosa spielt Fußball. (today) ______

______

5 Ich telefoniere mit Sam. (next week) ______

______

6 Sophie liest das Buch. (tomorrow) ______

______

3 **Underline the regular verbs and circle the irregular verbs.**

Ich spiele nicht gern Tennis. Ich finde Tennis langweilig. Fußball spiele ich dreimal pro Woche. Mein Bruder spielt sehr gern Tennis. Er fährt auch gern Rad. Radfahren findet er toll. Meine Schwester sieht ziemlich gern fern. Meine Mutter liest ziemlich gern. Oft liest sie Blogs im Internet. Ich lese auch oft. Mein Vater fährt gern Ski und spielt Gitarre.

Wiederholung 2

1 Read the email. Find the German for the following words and phrases in the text.

1 I think ____________________
2 about ____________________
3 but ____________________
4 New Zealand ____________________
5 comedies ____________________
6 Best wishes ____________________

Lieber Anish,

wie geht's? Danke für deine E-Mail.

Ich denke, Technologie ist toll. Ich bin sehr oft online. Ich chatte sehr gern mit Freunden auf Facebook. Facebook finde ich super und ich sehe oft Videos über Fußball auf YouTube.

Ich spiele Computerspiele nicht gern, aber ich suche ziemlich oft Infos für die Hausaufgaben. Meine Cousine, Connie, wohnt in Neuseeland und wir telefonieren ziemlich oft über Skype. Kannst du auch über Skype telefonieren?

Ich mache viel Sport mit meinen Freunden: Wir schwimmen zweimal pro Woche und wir spielen am Abend Basketball. Im Winter fahre ich auch Ski.

Ich esse manchmal am Wochenende mit meinen Freunden Pizza, und dann gehen wir ins Kino. Ich sehe gern Komödien. Nächste Woche sehen wir *Skyfall*.

Liebe Grüße,

Tibor

2 Answer the questions in complete German sentences.

1 Spielt Tibor gern Computerspiele? ____________________
2 Was macht Tibor auf Facebook? ____________________
3 Wer wohnt in Neuseeland? ____________________
4 Wie telefoniert Tibor mit seiner Cousine? ____________________
5 Wie oft schwimmt Tibor? ____________________
6 Was machen Tibor und seine Freunde am Wochenende?

____

3 Write a reply to Tibor's email about your hobbies and activities.

Grammatik (Seiten 68–69)

1 Complete the verb table.

	fahren (to go/travel)	**sehen** (to see)	**lesen** (to read)
ich			
du	fährst		liest
er/sie/es		sieht	
wir			
ihr			
Sie			
sie			

2 Complete the sentences by writing the correct form of the verb in brackets.

1 Ich ________________ das Auto. (waschen)

2 ________________ du gern Mangabücher? (lesen)

3 Er ________________ im Schlafzimmer. (schlafen)

4 Thomas ________________ nach Stockholm in Schweden. (fahren)

5 ________________ du morgen Torsten? (sehen)

6 ________________ du eine Schuluniform? (tragen)

Verbs like fahren:
tragen = to wear
schlafen = to sleep
waschen = to wash

die Schuluniform = school uniform

3 Write the question for each reply.

1 ________________ Ja, ich spiele Gitarre.

2 ________________ Nein, ich spiele nicht gern Wasserball.

3 ________________ Ja, Michael schläft im Bett.

4 ________________ Ja, ich fahre nach Bremen.

5 ________________ Ja, ich lese gern E-Books.

6 ________________ Nein, ich sehe nicht gern fern.

7 ________________ Ja, ich bin sportlich!

8 Was ________________ Ich trage morgen Jeans und ein T-Shirt.

9 ________________ Michael trägt eine Schuluniform.

Remember, to form a question you put the verb before the subject:
Du spielst gern Tennis. → Spielst du gern Tennis?

Mein Fortschritt

1 Record your levels for *Kapitel* 3.

2 Look at the level descriptors on pages 59–60 and set your targets for *Kapitel* 4.

3 Fill in what you need to do to achieve these targets.

Listening 	I have reached Level _____ in **Listening**. In *Kapitel* 4, I want to reach Level _____ I need to ____ ____ ____ ____
Speaking 	I have reached Level _____ in **Speaking**. In *Kapitel* 4, I want to reach Level _____ I need to ____ ____ ____ ____
Reading 	I have reached Level _____ in **Reading**. In *Kapitel* 4, I want to reach Level _____ I need to ____ ____ ____ ____
Writing 	I have reached Level _____ in **Writing**. In *Kapitel* 4, I want to reach Level _____ I need to ____ ____ ____ ____

Bist du sportlich? • Are you sporty?

Ich bin (sehr/ziemlich/ nicht sehr) sportlich.	*I am (very/quite/ not very) sporty.*
Was spielst du?	*What do you play?*
Ich spiele ...	*I play ...*
Ich spiele gern ...	*I like playing ...*
Ich spiele ziemlich gern ...	*I quite like playing ...*
Ich spiele nicht gern ...	*I don't like playing ... playing ...*
Badminton	*badminton*
Basketball	*basketball*
Eishockey	*ice hockey*
Fußball	*football*
Handball	*handball*
Tennis	*tennis*
Tischtennis	*table tennis*
Volleyball	*volleyball*
Wasserball	*water polo*

Was machst du gern? • What do you like doing?

Was machst du gern?	*What do you like doing?*
Ich fahre Rad.	*I ride my bike.*
Ich fahre Skateboard.	*I go skateboarding.*
Ich fahre Ski.	*I ski.*
Ich fahre Snowboard.	*I snowboard.*
Ich lese.	*I read.*
Ich mache Judo.	*I do judo.*
Ich mache Karate.	*I do karate.*
Ich reite.	*I go horse riding.*
Ich schwimme.	*I swim.*
Ich sehe fern.	*I watch TV.*
Ich spiele Gitarre.	*I play the guitar.*
Ich tanze.	*I dance.*

Wie findest du das? • What do you think of it?

Ich finde es ...	*I think it's ...*
Es ist ...	*It's ...*
irre	*amazing*
super	*super*
toll	*great*
cool	*cool*
gut	*good*
nicht schlecht	*not bad*
okay	*okay*
langweilig	*boring*
nervig	*annoying*
stinklangweilig	*deadly boring*
furchtbar	*awful*

Was machst du in deiner Freizeit? • What do you do in your free time?

Ich chille.	*I chill out.*
Ich esse Pizza oder Hamburger.	*I eat pizza or hamburgers.*
Ich gehe einkaufen.	*I go shopping.*
Ich gehe ins Kino.	*I go to the cinema.*
Ich gehe in den Park.	*I go to the park.*
Ich gehe in die Stadt.	*I go into town.*
Ich höre Musik.	*I listen to music.*
Ich mache Sport.	*I do sport.*
Ich spiele Xbox oder Wii.	*I play Xbox or on the Wii.*

Ich bin online • I'm online

Was machst du am Computer?	*What do you do on the computer?*
Was machst du auf deinem Handy?	*What do you do on your mobile?*
Ich chatte mit Freunden auf Facebook.	*I chat with friends on Facebook.*
Ich lade Musik herunter.	*I download music.*
Ich mache Fotos oder Filme.	*I take photos or make films.*
Ich sehe Videos.	*I watch videos.*
Ich simse.	*I text.*
Ich spiele Computerspiele.	*I play computer games.*
Ich suche und lese Infos für die Hausaufgaben.	*I look for and read information for my homework.*
Ich surfe im Internet.	*I surf the internet.*
Ich telefoniere mit Freunden.	*I call my friends.*
Ich mache ziemlich viel auf meinem Handy.	*I do quite a lot of things on my mobile.*

Oft benutzte Wörter • High-frequency words

Wie oft?	*How often?*
(sehr/ziemlich/nicht so) oft	*(very/quite/not so) often*
einmal/zweimal/dreimal pro Woche/pro Monat	*once/twice/three times a week/a month*
jeden Tag	*every day*
jeden Morgen	*every morning*
manchmal	*sometimes*
immer	*always*
nie	*never*
Wann?	*When?*
am Wochenende	*at the weekend*
am Abend	*in the evening*
heute	*today*
morgen	*tomorrow*
am Montag	*on Monday*
nächste Woche	*next week*
in zwei Wochen	*in two weeks*

1 Ich mag Deutsch! (Seiten 76–77)

1 Write a sentence for each illustration.

1

2

3

4

5

6

1 Ich mag ______________________________

2 ______________________________

3 ______________________________

4 ______________________________

5 ______________________________

6 ______________________________

> **ich liebe** ☺☺
> **ich mag** ☺
> **ich mag … nicht** ☹
> **ich hasse** ☹☹

2 Read the forum entries giving people's opinions about school subjects. Then answer the questions below.

Hallo Leute! Mein Lieblingsfach ist Englisch! Ich liebe Englisch, weil es total interessant ist. Ich lese sehr gern Bücher auf Spanisch und auf Deutsch. Mathe finde ich langweilig. **Pedro**

Hi Pedro! Ich mag Englisch nicht. Es ist sehr schwierig, aber ich mag Mathe und Naturwissenschaften. Ich finde Mathe supercool. **Nadine**

Grüezi aus der Schweiz! Ich liebe Theater und Kunst. Ich mag Kunst sehr gern, weil ich total kreativ bin. Informatik finde ich sehr langweilig, und Geschichte und Erdkunde sind nutzlos. **Marta**

Who …

1 is very creative? ______________

2 enjoys reading? ______________

3 doesn't like English? ______________

4 thinks ICT is boring? ______________

5 likes maths? ______________

6 can read Spanish? ______________

7 loves art? ______________

8 doesn't like geography? ______________

3 Rewrite each sentence in exercise 1, adding *weil* and an opinion. Use the examples in exercise 2 to help you with word order.

2 Was und wann? (Seiten 78–79)

1 Look at the timetable. Write *richtig* or *falsch* next to each statement.

	Montag	**Dienstag**	**Mittwoch**	**Donnerstag**	**Freitag**
8.15	Mathe	Erdkunde	Englisch	Deutsch	Technik
9.15	Englisch	Informatik	Theater	Mathe	Deutsch
10.45	Kunst	Mathe	Deutsch	Kunst	Naturwissenschaften
11.45	Naturwissenschaften	Mathe	Naturwissenschaften	Geschichte	Theater
13.30	Deutsch	Sport	Technik	Musik	Englisch

vor = before **nach** = after **die Doppelstunde** = double period

1 Am Mittwoch habe ich Deutsch. ____________

2 Wir haben am Freitag nach der Pause Technik. ____________

3 Am Montag vor der Pause haben wir Englisch. ____________

4 Theater ist am Mittwoch und am Donnerstag. ____________

5 Ich habe am Donnerstag nach der Mittagspause Musik. ____________

6 Am Dienstag habe ich eine Doppelstunde Mathe. ____________

2 At what time do you have the following subjects? Write a sentence for each.

1 *Ich habe Englisch um neun Uhr zehn.*  09:10

2 ______________________  10:05

3 ______________________  11:15

4 ______________________  12:10

5 ______________________  13:20

6 ______________________  14:15

um acht Uhr = at 8 o'clock

3 Look at the timetable in exercise 1 and describe one school day. Try to add interest to your sentences by giving opinions about some subjects.

Example: Am Montag um acht Uhr fünfzehn habe ich Mathe. Ich mag Mathe, weil es interessant ist.

Ich finde Mathe ...
= I find maths ...

3 Lehrer und Lehrerinnen (Seiten 80–81)

1 Write a description for each of the teachers.

1 Mein Sportlehrer heißt Herr Huber.
Er ist cool, aber sehr unpünktlich.

2 ______________________________
____

3 ______________________________
____

4 ______________________________
____

! Use some qualifiers in your descriptions: *sehr, zu, ziemlich, ein bisschen, nicht*

2 Complete the text by writing the correct word from the cloud in each gap.

Mein ______________ an der Schule ist Geschichte, ______________ meine Geschichtelehrerin sehr lustig ist! Sie ______________ nur ein Haustier, aber ihr Haustier ist eine Schlange!

Am ______________ und am Freitag haben wir Kunst. Ich finde Kunst ziemlich langweilg, weil es schwierig ______________. Mein Kunstlehrer ______________ Herr Ackermann. ______________ Schwester ist auch Kunstlehrerin an meiner ______________! Sie heißt Frau Ackermann! Meine Sportlehrerin ist ______________ freundlich. Sie heißt Frau Krause und ______________ Lieblingssport ist Volleyball. Ich mag Sport, weil ich sehr ______________ bin.

heißt   hat   Mittwoch   Lieblingsfach   ist
sehr   Schule   Seine   sportlich   weil   ihr

3 Write the correct word for 'his' or 'her' in each sentence.

1 ______________ Bruder lernt Hindi. (his)

2 ______________ Schwester ist Lehrerin. (her)

3 ______________ Hobby ist Gitarre spielen. (his)

4 ______________ Lieblingsfach ist Kunst. (her)

5 ______________ Schuluniform ist fantastisch. (his)

6 ______________ Bruder ist 19 Jahre alt. (her)

Grammatik

sein = his **ihr** = her (for masculine and neuter nouns)

seine = his **ihre** = her (for feminine nouns)

Check the gender of the noun if you are unsure.

4 Im Klassenzimmer (Seiten 82–83)

1 Draw a simple picture to show where each of these things is.

1 Der Musiklehrer ist im Klassenzimmer.
2 Das Buch ist neben dem Computer.
3 Das Poster ist an der Wand.
4 Der Stuhl ist auf dem Tisch und neben der Tür.

1	2	3	4

2 What is there in the classroom? Start each sentence with *Es gibt* (there is/there are). Write the numbers as words.

12  Es gibt zwölf Tische im Klassenzimmer.

6  ______________________________

24  ______________________________

2  ______________________________

4 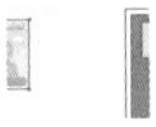 ______________________________

5  ______________________________

Look at the vocabulary on page 47 for the plurals of the nouns.

3 Answer the questions using the information in the pictures.

@peta_ush Darfst du dein Handy in der Schule benutzen?

____

@tara_winkel Darfst du im Klassenzimmer schnell laufen?

____

@e_atch Darfst du in der Pause Musik hören?

____

@janet_mc Darfst du dein Handy in der Mittagspause benutzen?

____

ich darf du darfst er/sie/es darf

1 **Most of the verbs you've seen end in *–en* in the infinitive. Write the infinitive form of each verb in the table. Then try to work out its meaning from the context.**

If the context doesn't help you, use a German–English dictionary.

verb	**infinitive**	**meaning in English**
Er **geht** in die Schule.	*gehen*	*to go, to walk*
Er **kauft** ein Auto.		
Er **steht** auf dem Tisch.		
Warum **redest** du so schnell?		
Ich **wasche** meinen Hund.		
Ich **nehme** das Buch.		

2 **Guess the meaning of these compound nouns by separating out the words. Look up the compound nouns in a dictionary to find their gender and meaning.**

The second word in each compound noun gives the gender.

compound noun	**word 1**	**word 2**	**gender**	**meaning**
Fußballfeld	*Fußball*		*das*	
Arbeitstag				
Sporthalle				
Klassenarbeit				
Lehrerzimmer				

3 **Now write a short German sentence using each compound noun from exercise 2.**

1 *Das Fußballfeld ist sehr grün und …* __________

2 __________

3 __________

4 __________

5 __________

Wiederholung 1

1 Mimi's description of her school day is in the wrong time order! Number the sentences 1–6 in the correct order of time.

☐ Ich habe um dreizehn Uhr fünfundzwanzig Musik.

☐ Die Pause beginnt um elf Uhr zehn.

☐ Die erste Stunde beginnt um acht Uhr vierzig.

☐ Der Bus kommt um fünfzehn Uhr siebenundvierzig.

☐ Ich komme um sechzehn Uhr dreißig nach Hause.

☐ Wir haben Mathe um elf Uhr fünfundzwanzig.

2 The school is running 20 minutes late today. Rewrite each of the six sentences in exercise 1 with the time that each activity begins today.

3 Complete the sentences by writing the correct possessive pronoun in each gap.

sein = his (for masculine and neuter nouns) **seine** = his (for feminine nouns)
ihr = her (for masculine and neuter nouns) **ihre** = her (for feminine nouns)

1 ________ Bruder heißt Pawel und ________ Schwester heißt Aga.

2 ________ Lieblingssport ist Eishockey.

3 ________ Katze ist braun, aber ________ Hund ist weiß.

4 ________ Schule ist in Hannover.

5 ________ Lieblingssport ist Reiten und ________ Lieblingsfach ist Mathe.

6 ________ Computer ist neu.

7 ________ Erdkundelehrerin ist sehr streng.

8 ________ Mutter wohnt in Salzburg, aber ________ Vater wohnt in Wien.

4 Describe where each of the items is located in the classroom.

1 Der Computer *ist auf dem Tisch.*

2 Das Poster ________

3 Das Whiteboard ________

4 Der Lehrer ________

5 Der Stuhl ________

6 Die Spinne ________

Wiederholung 2

1 Read the texts. Use your knowledge of vocabulary to help you to find these new phrases. Write each German phrase next to the English.

1 My name is ____________________
2 her favourite artist ____________________
3 unfortunately ____________________
4 My brother also goes ____________________
5 an indoor pool ____________________
6 a pot plant ____________________

Hallo! Mein Name ist **Maik** und ich wohne in München, in Deutschland. Meine Schule heißt Mathias Brauer Gymnasium und ich finde sie toll. An meiner Schule lerne ich sehr gern Englisch und Geschichte, aber mein Lieblingsfach ist Kunst. Ich mag Kunst, weil ich total kreativ bin. Ich finde meine Kunstlehrerin auch sehr nett. Sie heißt Frau Weber und ihr Lieblingskünstler ist Dürer.

Ich mag nicht Sport, weil ich nicht sehr sportlich bin. Leider habe ich am Montag und auch am Mittwoch Sport. Morgen spielen wir Tennis. Das finde ich nicht so schlecht.

lernen = to learn

Hallo Leute! Ich heiße **Sabine** und ich wohne in Zürich, in der Schweiz. Meine Schule ist sehr groß. Mein Bruder geht auch auf meine Schule.

Mein Lieblingsfach ist Musik und dieses Fach haben wir am Dienstag in der zweiten Stunde und auch am Donnerstag in der vierten Stunde. Sport mag ich auch, weil der Sportlehrer total lustig ist. Sein Lieblingssport ist Schwimmen und wir haben ein Hallenbad in der Schule. Wir haben Sport am Mittwoch in der fünften Stunde und auch am Freitag in der zweiten Stunde.

Mein Klassenzimmer ist sehr schön. Wir haben zehn Computer, ein Whiteboard neben der Tür, viele Poster an der Wand und eine Topfpflanze am Fenster!

2 Answer the questions about the texts in exercise 1. Write complete sentences in German for your answers.

1 Wie heißt Maiks Schule? ____________________
2 Was mag Maik? ____________________
3 Was lernt Maik nicht gern? ____________________
4 Wann hat Maik Sport? ____________________
5 Wo ist Zürich? ____________________
6 Was hat Sabine am Donnerstag in der vierten Stunde? ____________________
7 Warum mag Sabine Sport? ____________________
8 Wo ist die Topfpflanze? ____________________

Grammatik (Seiten 90–91)

1 Answer the questions in full sentences, using *weil* and the reason given.

1 Warum magst du Kunst? (it's creative)

Ich mag Kunst, weil es kreativ ist.

2 Warum magst du Englisch? (it's interesting)

____

3 Warum spielst du Tennis? (I'm sporty)

____

4 Warum hasst du Sport? (it's difficult)

____

5 Warum findest du Erdkunde toll? (it's easy)

____

2 Put the words in the right order to make sentences.

Remember the 'verb in second place' rule.

1 der in Geschichte dritten wir Stunde haben

____

2 habe Pause ich nach der Kunst ____________________

3 Fußball spiele heute ich ____________________

4 gibt Klassenzimmer Computer und viele einen es im Poster

____

5 Montag ich vierten Stunde habe in am der Mathe

____

3 Write the following school rules in sentences in German.

Example: Man darf am Montag ...

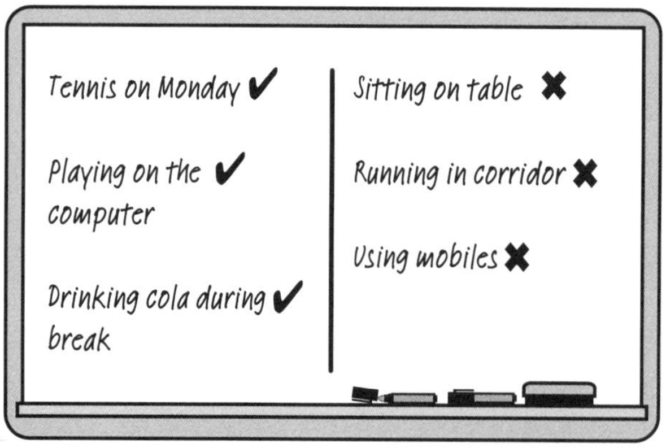

Man darf is often used to mean 'you/we are allowed to'.

Remember to use the correct preposition and the correct word for 'the' after it.

Mein Fortschritt

1 **Record your levels for *Kapitel* 4.**

2 **Look at the level descriptors on pages 59–60 and set your targets for *Kapitel* 5.**

3 **Fill in what you need to do to achieve these targets.**

Listening 	I have reached Level ______ in **Listening**. In *Kapitel* 5, I want to reach Level ______ I need to ______________________________ ______________________________ ______________________________ ______________________________
Speaking 	I have reached Level ______ in **Speaking**. In *Kapitel* 5, I want to reach Level ______ I need to ______________________________ ______________________________ ______________________________ ______________________________
Reading 	I have reached Level ______ in **Reading**. In *Kapitel* 5, I want to reach Level ______ I need to ______________________________ ______________________________ ______________________________ ______________________________
Writing 	I have reached Level ______ in **Writing**. In *Kapitel* 5, I want to reach Level ______ I need to ______________________________ ______________________________ ______________________________ ______________________________

Schulfächer • School subjects

Deutsch	*German*
Englisch	*English*
Erdkunde	*geography*
Geschichte	*history*
Informatik	*ICT*
Kunst	*art*
Mathe	*maths*
Musik	*music*
Naturwissenschaften	*science*
Sport	*sport, PE*
Technik	*technology*
Theater	*drama*

Meinungen • Opinions

mein Lieblingsfach ist …	*my favourite subject is …*
ich mag … (sehr)	*I like … (a lot)*
ich liebe	*I love*
ich mag … nicht	*I don't like …*
ich hasse	*I hate*
gut	*good*
toll	*great*
furchtbar	*awful*
einfach	*easy*
schwierig	*difficult*
interessant	*interesting*
langweilig	*boring*
nützlich	*useful*
nutzlos	*useless*
faszinierend	*fascinating*
nervig	*irritating*
supercool	*really cool*
stinklangweilig	*dead boring*

Die Wochentage • The days of the week

Montag (Mo.)	*Monday*
Dienstag (Di.)	*Tuesday*
Mittwoch (Mi.)	*Wednesday*
Donnerstag (Do.)	*Thursday*
Freitag (Fr.)	*Friday*
Samstag (Sa.)	*Saturday*
Sonntag (So.)	*Sunday*
Was hast du am Montag?	*What do you have on Monday?*
Am Dienstag habe ich …	*I have … on Tuesday*
Am Sonntag haben wir keine Schule.	*We have no school on Sunday.*

Die Zeit • Time

Wann?	*When?*
Um wie viel Uhr?	*At what time?*
Um 8:30 Uhr (acht Uhr dreißig).	*At 8:30.*
Wie viel Uhr ist es?	*What time is it?*
Es ist 9:50 Uhr (neun Uhr fünfzig).	*It's 9:50.*
in der ersten Stunde	*in the first lesson*
vor der Pause	*before break*
nach der Mittagspause	*after the lunch break*

Eigenschaften • Characteristics

Er/Sie ist ...	*He/She is ...*
alt	*old*
fair	*fair*
freundlich	*friendly*
jung	*young*
launisch	*moody*
lustig	*funny*
nervig	*annoying*
streng	*strict*
unpünktlich	*unpunctual*

In der Schule • In school

die Lehrerin(-nen)	*teacher (female)*
die Deutsch-lehrerin(-nen)	*German teacher (female)*
der Lehrer(–)	*teacher (male)*
der Sportlehrer(–)	*sports teacher (male)*
Was gibt es?	*What is there?*
Es gibt einen/eine/ein ...	*There is a ...*
Es gibt viele ...	*There are lots of ...*
das Klassenzimmer(–)	*classroom*
der Tisch(-e)	*table*
der Stuhl(¨-e)	*chair*
der Computer(–)	*computer*
das Whiteboard(-s)	*whiteboard*
das Poster(–)	*poster*
das Fenster(–)	*window*
die Wand(¨-e)	*wall*
die Tür(-en)	*door*
der Korridor(-e)	*corridor*

Wo ist das? • Where is it?

in der Schule	*in the school*
im Klassenzimmer	*in the classroom*
im Korridor	*in the corridor*
an der Wand	*on the wall*
am Fenster	*by the window*
am Tisch	*at the table*
auf dem Tisch	*on the table*
neben der Tür	*near/next to the door*

Oft benutzte Wörter • High-frequency words

weil	*because*
sein/seine	*his*
ihr/ihre	*her*
zu	*too*
sehr	*very*
ziemlich	*quite, fairly*
ein bisschen	*a bit*
nicht	*not*
haben	*to have*
sein	*to be*
in	*in*
an	*at, by, on (wall)*
auf	*on (top of)*
neben	*near, next to*
heute	*today*
morgen	*tomorrow*
vor	*before*
nach	*after*

1 In der Stadt (Seiten 98–99)

1 Write sentences to say what there is and isn't in the town.

1 Es gibt hier ______________________________ .

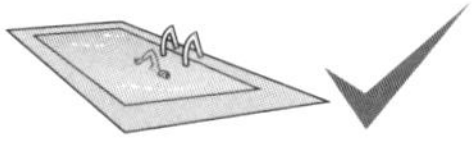

2 Hier gibt es ______________________________ .

3 In der Stadt gibt es ______________________________ .

4 Es gibt ______________________________ hier.

Grammatik

der→einen/keinen **die**→eine/keine **das**→ein/kein

2 Read the texts. Tick the things there are in each person's town and cross the things there aren't.

Monika: *Ich wohne in Celle. Meine Stadt ist nicht sehr groß. Es gibt hier ein Schloss und auch einen Marktplatz. Leider gibt es kein Schwimmbad und auch keine Kegelbahn.*

leider = unfortunately

Erik: *Die Touristen kommen gern nach Verden, weil es eine Kirche und auch einen Marktplatz gibt. Ein Schloss gibt es auch, aber leider gibt es kein Schwimmbad und keine Imbissstube.*

Aisha: *Ich wohne in Neustadt, in der Nähe vom Titisee. Neustadt ist ganz klein, aber sehr schön. Es gibt hier kein Schloss, keine Kegelbahn und leider auch kein Kino. Wir haben aber einen Bahnhof, eine Kirche und auch einen alten Marktplatz. Wir haben kein Schwimmbad, aber man kann im Sommer im Titisee schwimmen!*

	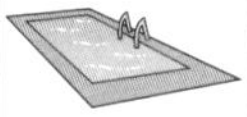			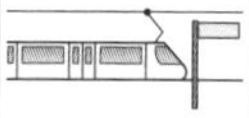				
Monika								
Erik								
Aisha								

3 Write two or three sentences about what there is to do where you live, as well as what there isn't. Use the texts in exercise 2 to help you.

2 Wir gehen einkaufen! (Seiten 100–101)

1 Write what the customers in the souvenir shop would like. Start your sentences with *Ich möchte*.

1 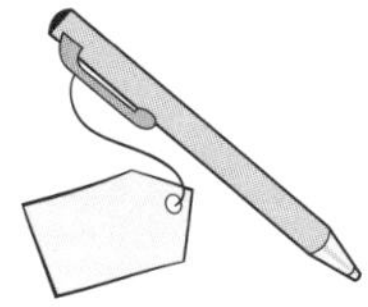
2 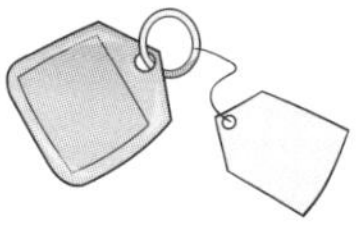
3 
4 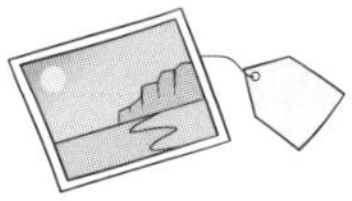
5 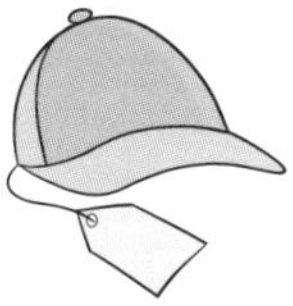
6 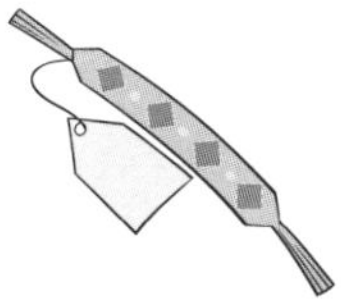
7 
8 

Look at the vocabulary on page 57 if you need to check which words to use.

1 Ich möchte einen Kuli.
2 ____________
3 ____________
4 ____________
5 ____________
6 ____________
7 ____________
8 ____________

2 Complete the dialogue with words from the cloud below. Then number the lines of the conversation in the correct order 1–11.

☐ Guten Tag! ____________ ich dir helfen?
☐ Welche ____________? Wir haben blau, rot oder schwarz.
☐ Ja, klar! Dieser ____________, zum Beispiel, kostet nur €18,95.
☐ Super!
☐ Danke. Auf ____________.
☐ Sonst noch etwas?
☐ Alles ____________ kostet das €38,95.
☐ Guten Tag! Ich möchte ein Souvenir ____________, vielleicht ein Kuscheltier. Haben Sie ____________?
☐ Bitte sehr.
☐ Ja. Ich möchte ein ____________ für meine Schwester.
☐ Schwarz, bitte. Wie viel ____________ das?

zusammen Elefant Kuscheltiere Wiedersehen Kann kostet Fußballtrikot kaufen Farbe

3 Mmm, lecker! (Seiten 102–103)

1 Write four short conversations between hungry customers and the owner of the snack stand. The price of each individual item is shown: don't forget to add up the total price.

1

× 1
drei Euro zehn

× 1
zwei Euro fünfunddreißig

2

× 2
zwei Euro sechzig

× 2
zwei Euro funfundzwanzig

3

× 3
drei Euro zwanzig

× 1
ein Euro neunzig

4

× 4
drei Euro fünfundneunzig

× 1
zwei Euro zehn

Ich möchte .../Ich hätte gern ...	I'd like ...
Das kostet alles zusammen ...	All together that costs ...

1 *Guten Tag! Ich möchte einmal Hamburger und einmal Bratwurst, bitte.*
Das kostet alles zusammen € ...

2 ______________________

3 ______________________

4 ______________________

2 Write a short review of the menu, saying what there is to eat and drink and what you do and don't like.

Hamburger

Bratwurst
Pommes

Salat
Eis
Tee
Cola
Mineralwasser

Man kann ... trinken/essen.	You can eat/drink ...
Ich esse/trinke gern ...	I like eating/drinking ...
Ich esse/trinke nicht gern ...	I don't like eating/drinking ...
Ich mag ...	I like ....
Ich mag nicht ...	I don't like .....

____

4 In den Sommerferien (Seiten 104–105)

1 Circle the correct option to complete each sentence from the choices given. Then write the missing words in the gaps.

1 Ich ______________ im See baden.

a wirst **b** werden **c** werde

2 Wir werden im ______________ schwimmen.

a Meer **b** windsurfen **c** Bratwurst

3 ______________ du nach Innsbruck fahren?

a Wird **b** Wirst **c** Bist

4 Er ______________ nicht nach Hannover ______________ .

a werden; fahre **b** kann; fährt **c** wird; fahren

5 Tobi ______________ in den ______________ nach Portugal fahren.

a werde; Park **b** wird; Bahnhof **c** wird; Sommerferien

6 Wohin ______________ wir ______________ ?

a werden; gehen **b** kann; gehen **c** darf; fahren

2 Read the sentences and write the correct words from the cloud in the gaps. There are more words than you need.

1 Ich werde eine Kappe ______________ meinen Vater kaufen.

2 Ich ______________ ein Trikot kaufen.

3 In den ______________ fahren wir nach Rom.

4 Es ______________ ein Schwimmbad und ein Kino in Walsrode.

5 Wir ______________ nach Magdeburg fahren.

6 Ich möchte in den Bergen ______________ gehen.

für
gibt
möchte
nächste Woche
Sommerferien
wandern
werde
werden

3 Write about your plans for the summer holidays. Use the questions and illustrations to help you.

- Wohin wirst du fahren?

- Wer kommt mit?

- Was wirst du dort machen?

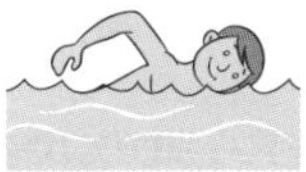

- Was wird dein Bruder / deine Schwester machen

- Wirst du Souvenirs kaufen?

1 Rewrite each sentence. Swap the adjective in bold for an alternative adjective with a similar meaning.

1 Das Mozart Museum ist **faszinierend**. ____________________

2 Der Marktplatz ist **historisch**. ____________________

3 Das Schwimmbad ist **modern**.

____

4 Die Kegelbahn ist **toll**. ____________________

2 Join up the sentence halves to describe a trip to Vienna.

1 In den Sommerferien werde	**a** Tage in Wien bleiben.
2 Dort gibt es einen	**b** ich nach Wien fahren.
3 Am Montag kann	**c** Wien fantastisch.
4 Ich finde	**d** Marktplatz, aber keinen See.
5 Wir werden vier	**e** man das Mozart Museum besuchen.

Now rewrite the sentences, varying the sentence structure. Remember that in German you always need the verb as the second idea.

Example: **1** Ich werde in den Sommerferien …

3 Read the text about Hahndorf. Try to work out what the words in bold mean from the context. If you can't work out the meanings, look them up in a dictionary.

Hahndorf ist eine kleine Stadt in Südaustralien, in der Nähe von Adelaide. Es gibt dort deutsche **Einwanderer**. Die Stadt ist klein, aber **fein**! Hahndorf ist toll für Kinder und auch für **Erwachsene**. Dort gibt es viele deutsche Restaurants und Cafés. Am Mittwoch und am Sonntag gibt es immer einen Markt auf dem Marktplatz. Man kann hier Schokolade, **Kuchen** und **Kleidung** kaufen. **Wein** aus der Region kann man auch dort trinken. Ich werde **nächstes Jahr** mit meiner Schule nach Hahndorf fahren.

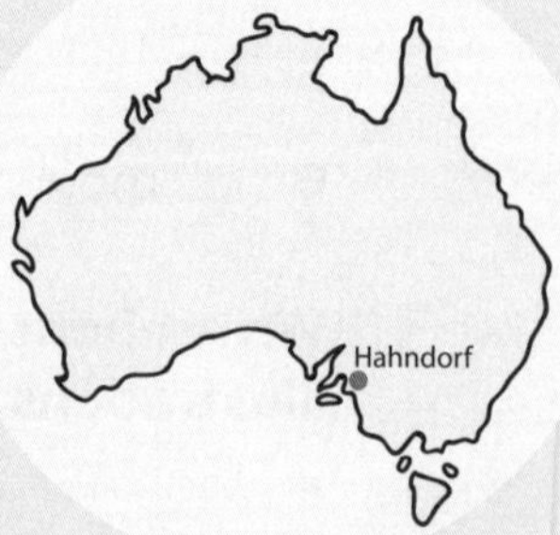

4 Write about a city or town of your choice. Adapt some of the words and phrases from the text in exercise 3.

Remember to include: the future tense, opinions, linking words, qualifiers, frequency expressions and inverted word order.

Wiederholung 1

1 **Decide which souvenir you would buy for each person and write the price in words.**

Grammatik
der → *er*   *die* → *sie*   *das* → *es*

Remember, *der* changes to *den* for masculine nouns.

1 Meine Mutter: Ich werde die Tasse für meine Mutter kaufen. Sie kostet sieben Euro fünfundfünfzig.

2 Onkel Karl: ______________________

3 Meine Schwester: ______________________

4 Meine Freundin: ______________________

5 Frau Roberts: ______________________

2 **Peter is in the tourist office in Munich. Read the dialogue, then answer the questions in full German sentences.**

Tourist guide: Guten Tag! Willkommen in München!

Peter: Guten Tag! Danke schön! Was gibt es hier in München?

Tourist guide: Hier gibt es viel zu tun! Man kann in München alles sehen!

Peter: Gibt es hier einen Marktplatz?

Tourist guide: Natürlich! Er heißt Marienplatz. Er ist sehr groß und total schön.

Peter: Wunderbar! Und kann man in München Ski fahren?

Tourist guide: Also ... nicht direkt in München, aber in der Nähe von hier kann man sehr gut Ski fahren.

Peter: Super. Und gibt es hier ein gutes Restaurant? Ich möchte gern Pizza essen.

Tourist guide: Ja, das gibt es! Es heißt *Robertos*. Dort kann man gut Pizza essen.

Peter: Vielen Dank. Ich werde im Restaurant *Robertos* essen. Auf Wiedersehen!

1 Was kann man in München machen?
2 Wie heißt der Marktplatz?
3 Wie ist er?
4 Wo kann man Ski fahren?
5 Was möchte Peter essen?
6 Was ist *Robertos*?

Wiederholung 2

1 Rewrite the sentences in the future tense. Identify the subject to help you change the form of *werden*.

1 Wir tauchen im Meer. *Wir werden im Meer tauchen.*

2 Wir baden im See. ____________________

3 Ich gehe an den Strand. ____________________

4 Lena und Michael klettern am Samstag in den Bergen.

____

5 Er kauft ein Kuscheltier für seine kleine Schwester.

____

6 Kaufst du eine Kappe als Souvenir? ____________________

7 Wir gehen am Wochenende mit meinen Freunden einkaufen.

____

2 Read the postcard and answer the questions in full German sentences.

Liebe Oma und Lieber Opa!

Hallo aus Mallorca in Spanien! Wir bleiben zwei Wochen hier, weil wir Sommerferien haben. Es gibt hier alles – einen Wasserpark, ein Schloss und auch einen Markt. Jeden Tag schwimmen wir im Meer. Im Hotel gibt es ein Schwimmbad und wir schwimmen auch hier. Man kann windsurfen und auch tauchen. Mallorca ist auch für das Essen sehr bekannt.

Nächste Woche werden wir in den Bergen klettern. Ich möchte auch segeln. Ich werde auch Souvenirs kaufen!

Alles Liebe,

Tamika

1 Warum ist Tamika in Spanien? ____________________

2 Was gibt es in Mallorca? ____________________

3 Was kann man machen? ____________________

4 Ist Mallorca bekannt für das Museum? ____________________

5 Was wird Tamika nächste Woche machen? ____________________

3 Write four true/false statements in English about the text in exercise 2. Then ask a friend to write 'True' or 'False' next to each statement.

Example: The postcard is to Tamika's parents. False

Grammatik (Seiten 112–113)

1 Rewrite the sentences to make them negative.

> Use *keinen/keine/kein* to say what there is or isn't. Use *nicht* to say what you can't or don't like doing.

1 Es gibt in Düsseldorf einen Marktplatz.

____

2 Er mag Wasserball.

____

3 Beni kann Fußball spielen, weil er einen Ball hat.

____

4 In der Stadt gibt es ein Kino und auch eine Kirche.

____

5 Man darf hier schwimmen. ______________________________

2 Write the different forms of *möchten* in the table.

möchten
möchte
möchten
möchtest
möchte
möchtet
möchten

ich		wir	
du		ihr	
er/sie/es		Sie	
		sie	

Complete the sentences by writing the correct form of *möchten* in each gap. Then translate the sentences into English.

1 ______________ du ein Schokoladeneis?

2 Nein, aber ich ______________ gern ein Vanilleeis.

3 Anne ______________ nach Kapstadt in Südafrika fahren.

4 ______________ ihr auch nach Windhuk in Namibia fahren?

5 Wir ______________ zweimal Salat und zweimal Mineralwasser, bitte.

6 Frau Winkelmann, ______________ Sie eine Tasse Tee?

3 Fill in the gaps to complete the different forms of *werden*.

ich __e__de	wir we__de__
du w__r__t	ihr __er__e__
er/sie/es __ir__	Sie/sie w__r__en

4 Write sentences about what you and your family/friends will do on your next holiday.

Example: Ich werde jeden Tag in Frankreich wandern. Mein Bruder ... /Steffi ...

Jahresbilanz

Record your levels for *Kapitel* 5.

Listening	I have reached Level ______ in **Listening**.
Speaking	I have reached Level ______ in **Speaking**.
Reading	I have reached Level ______ in **Reading**.
Writing	I have reached Level ______ in **Writing**.

Look back through your workbook and note down the level you achieved in each skill by the end of each *Kapitel*.

	Listening	**Speaking**	**Reading**	**Writing**
1 Meine Welt und ich				
2 Familie und Tiere				
3 Freizeit – juhu!				
4 Schule ist klasse!				
5 Gute Reise!				

You now have a record of your progress in German for the whole year.

In der Stadt • In town

Es gibt …	*There is … / There are …*
Es gibt ein/eine/einen …	*There is/are a …*
Es gibt kein/keine/keinen …	*There isn't/aren't …*
in der Nähe von …	*near to*
in der Nähe …	*nearby*
der Bahnhof(¨-e)	*railway station(s)*
der Imbiss(-e)/die Imbissstube(-n)	*snack stand(s)*
die Kegelbahn(-en)	*bowling alley(s)*
das Kino(-s)	*cinema(s)*
die Kirche(-n)	*church(es)*
der Marktplatz(¨-e)	*market square(s)*
der Park(-s)	*park(s)*
das Schloss(¨-er)	*castle(s)*
das Schwimmbad(¨-er)	*swimming pool(s)*
die Eisbahn(-en)	*ice rink(s)*
der Fischmarkt(¨-e)	*fish market(s)*
das Kindertheater(-)	*children's theatre(s)*
der Radweg(-e)	*cycle path(s)*
das Sportzentrum (die Sportzentren)	*sports centre (sports centres)*
der Stadtpark(-s)	*city/town park(s)*
der Wasserpark(-s)	*water park(s)*

Verkaufsgespräch • Sales conversation

Ich gehe einkaufen.	*I am going shopping.*
Ich möchte …	*I would like …*
Ich möchte … kaufen.	*I would like to buy …*
Haben Sie …?	*Do you have …?*
Kann ich dir helfen?	*Can I help you?*
Sonst noch etwas?	*Anything else?*
alles zusammen	*all together*

Souvenirs • Souvenirs

der Aufkleber	*sticker*
das Freundschaftsband	*friendship bracelet*
die Kappe	*(baseball) cap*
der Kuli	*biro*
das Kuscheltier	*cuddly toy*
die Postkarte	*postcard*
der Schlüsselanhänger	*key ring*
die Tasse	*mug/cup*
das Trikot	*(football) shirt*
Wie viel kostet …?	*How much does … cost?*
Wie viel kostet das?	*How much does it cost?*
Es kostet €16.	*It costs 16 Euros.*

Snacks und Getränke kaufen • Buying snacks and drinks

die Bratwurst	*fried sausage*
der Hamburger	*hamburger*
die Pizza	*pizza*
die Pommes	*chips*
der Salat	*salad*
das Eis	*ice cream*
die Cola	*cola*
das Mineralwasser	*mineral water*
der Tee	*tea*
das Fleisch	*meat*
der Ketchup	*ketchup*
die Mayo(nnaise)/Majonäse	*mayo(nnaise)*
der Senf	*mustard*
Ich möchte einmal/zweimal/dreimal …	*I would like one/two/three …*
Ich hätte gern …	*I would like …*
Das macht €8.	*That's €8.*
Ich esse … gern.	*I like eating … .*
Ich trinke … gern.	*I like drinking … .*

Wörter

In den Sommerferien • During the summer holidays

Was wirst du machen?	*What will you do?*
Ich werde ...	*I will ...*
Wir werden ...	*We will ...*
klettern	*climb*
im Meer schwimmen	*swim in the sea*
rodeln	*toboggan*
im See baden	*bathe in the lake*
segeln	*sail*
an den Strand gehen	*go to the beach*
tauchen	*dive*
wandern	*hike*
windsurfen	*windsurf*
Was kann man dort machen?	*What can you do there?*
Man kann ... besuchen.	*'One'/People/ You can visit ...*
Die Stadt ist bekannt für ...	*The town is well known for ...*
Ich werde (eine Woche) bleiben.	*I will stay (for a week).*

Oft benutzte Wörter • High-frequency words

am Montag	*on Monday*
am Dienstag	*on Tuesday*
am Mittwoch	*on Wednesday*
am Donnerstag	*on Thursday*
am Freitag	*on Friday*
am Wochenende	*at the weekend*
sehr	*very*
nicht sehr	*not very*
ziemlich	*quite*
immer	*always*
nicht immer	*not always*
oft	*often*
nicht oft	*not often*
nie	*never*
alles	*everything*
dort	*there*
teuer	*expensive*

Level descriptors

Listening

Level 1	I can understand some familiar spoken words and phrases.
Level 2	I can understand a range of familiar spoken phrases.
Level 3	I can understand the main points of short spoken passages and note people's answers to questions.
Level 4	I can understand the main points of spoken passages and some of the detail.
Level 5	I can understand the main points and opinions in spoken passages about different topics. I can recognise if people are speaking about the future **OR** the past as well as the present.

Speaking

Level 1	I can say single words and short phrases.
Level 2	I can answer simple questions and use set phrases.
Level 3	I can ask questions and use short phrases to answer questions about myself.
Level 4	I can take part in conversations. I can express my opinions. I can use grammar to change phrases to say something new.
Level 5	I can give short talks, in which I express my opinions. I can take part in conversations giving information, opinions and reasons. I can speak about the future **OR** the past as well as the present.

Level descriptors

Reading

Level 1	I can understand familiar words and phrases.
Level 2	I can understand familiar phrases. I can read aloud familiar words and phrases. I can use a vocabulary list to check meanings.
Level 3	I can understand the main points and people's answers to questions in short written texts.
Level 4	I can understand the main points in short texts and some of the detail. Sometimes I can work out the meaning of new words.
Level 5	I can understand the main points and opinions in texts about different topics. I can recognise if the texts are about the future **OR** the past as well as the present.

Writing

Level 1	I can write or copy single words correctly.
Level 2	I can copy short sentences correctly and write some words from memory.
Level 3	I can answer questions about myself. I can write short phrases from memory. I can write short sentences with help.
Level 4	I can write short texts on familiar topics. I can use grammar to change phrases to write something new.
Level 5	I can write short texts on a range of familiar topics. I can write about the future **OR** the past as well as the present.

Notes

Notes

Published by Pearson Education Limited, Edinburgh Gate, Harlow, Essex, CM20 2JE.

www.pearsonschoolsandfecolleges.co.uk

Edited by Melanie Birdsall
Designed by Kamae Design

Illustrated by Caron at KJA Artists and Lisa Hunt

First published 2013

2022
17

British Library Cataloguing in Publication Data
A catalogue record for this book is available from the British Library

ISBN 978 1 447 94654 0

Printed in Great Britain by Bell and Bain Ltd, Glasgow

Acknowledgements

We would like to thank Melissa Weir, Angelika Libera, Janet Soame and Frances Reynolds for their invaluable help in the development of this course.

Every effort has been made to contact copyright holders of material reproduced in this book. Any omissions will be rectified in subsequent printings if notice is given to the publishers.

www.pearsonschools.co.uk
myorders@pearson.com

T 0845 630 33 33
F 0845 630 77 77

ISBN 978-1-4479-4654-0

Stimmt! 1

Übungsheft B

Malcolm Pacey

ALWAYS LEARNING

PEARSON

1 Hallo! (Seiten 8–9)

1 **Two of the words in each set have a sound that is the same. Circle the word with a different sound from the other two.**

1	*Schlange*	*Porsche*	*Buch*
2	*Bär*	*Löwe*	*Röntgenbild*
3	*Wildwassersport*	*Auf Wiedersehen*	*Tür*
4	*Biene*	*heiße*	*Eis*

2 **Join up the sentence halves.**

1	Gut, danke. Und	**a**	Wiedersehen.
2	Auf	**b**	Ben. Wie heißt du?
3	Ich heiße	**c**	geht's, Ben?
4	Hallo! Wie heißt	**d**	du?
5	Ich heiße Nadia. Wie	**e**	schlecht.
6	Nicht	**f**	dir?

3 **Write the sentences from exercise 2 in the correct order for the conversation. Then translate them into English.**

1 ______________________ ______________________

2 ______________________ ______________________

3 ______________________ ______________________

4 ______________________ ______________________

5 Nicht schlecht. Not bad.

6 ______________________ ______________________

4 **Unscramble the inventions. Look at the definite article (word for 'the') for each word. Then write each invention with the indefinite article (word for 'a').**

1 sad ngbönReltid das … ein …

2 erd reelmiDtoos ______________________ ______________________

3 sda toF3rMmPa- ______________________ ______________________

4 sad PeuAsotrcoh ______________________ ______________________

5 ied sAMrkdadiae ______________________ ______________________

2 Eins, zwei, drei ... (Seiten 10–11)

1 **The bank has sent texts to customers with their coded PIN numbers. Solve the maths problems in German to work out the PINs. Then write each customer's new PIN below the phone.**

1

Meine Bank

zehn – acht = zwei

vier + drei = sieben

zwei + drei = ______

fünf + eins = ______

2 7 _ _

2

Meine Bank

sechs + zwei = ______

zehn – neun = ______

sieben – drei = ______

eins + vier = ______

_ _ _ _

3

Meine Bank

sieben – vier = ______

acht + eins = ______

drei + sechs = ______

fünf + zwei = ______

_ _ _ _

2 **Write the winning lottery numbers in words.**

1 13 ______

2 11 ______

3 16 ______

4 18 ______

5 12 ______

6 17 ______

3 **Write two sentences for each speaker. Give the speaker's age and the age of his/her friend.**

er ist = he is
sie ist = she is

1

Ich bin dreizehn Jahre alt.

Sie ist zwölf Jahre alt.

2

______

______

3

______

______

3 Ich wohne in Deutschland (Seiten 12–13)

1 Read the dialogue and complete the table with the correct forms of each verb.

Melanie: Hallo! Ich heiße Melanie. Wie heißt du?
Marco: Ich heiße Marco. Ich wohne in Straubing. Wo wohnst du?
Melanie: Ich wohne in Braunschweig. Wie alt bist du?
Marco: Ich bin zwölf Jahre alt. Wer ist das?
Melanie: Sie heißt Jessie. Sie wohnt in Leipzig und ist dreizehn Jahre alt.

wer = who

	heißen (to be called)	**wohnen** (to live)	**sein** (to be)
ich (I)		*wohne*	
du (you)			*bist*
er/sie/es (he/she/it)	*heißt*		

2 Write the missing word in each sentence and complete the crossword.

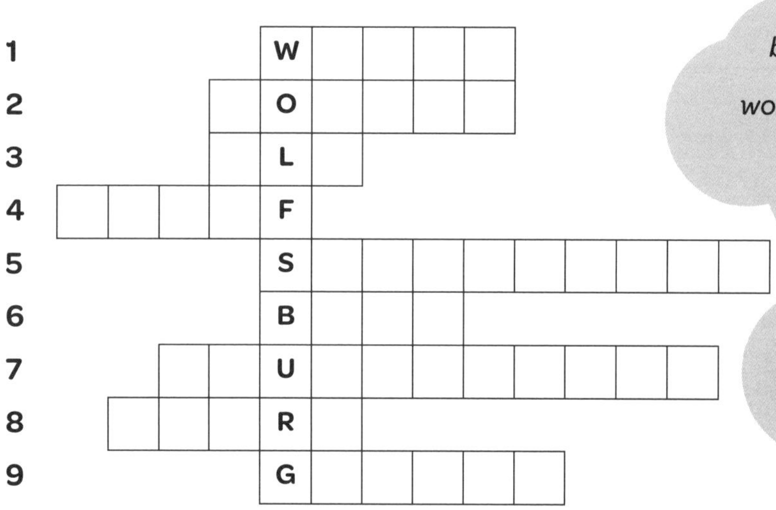

bist *zwölf* *wohne* *wohnst* *Jahre* *Schottland* *Deutschland* *geht's* *alt*

1 Ich ______________ in Manchester.
2 Wo ______________ du, Nick?
3 Wie ______________ ist er?
4 Er ist ______________ Jahre alt.
5 Glasgow ist in ______________.
6 Wie alt ______________ du?
7 Ich wohne in Berlin. Das ist in ______________.
8 Ich bin elf ______________ alt.
9 Wie ______________?

3 Research why the city of Wolfsburg is important to Germany.

4 Meine Welt ist wunderbar! (Seiten 14–15)

1 The printer has made four mistakes labelling the illustrations. Write *richtig* or *falsch* under each caption.

1  Ich bin musikalisch.

____

2  Ich bin sehr launisch.

____

3  Ich bin ziemlich freundlich.

____

4  Ich bin kreativ.

____

5  Ich bin laut.

____

6  Ich bin lustig.

____

2 Rewrite the false captions from exercise 1, correcting them so that they are true.

____

____

____

____

faul
lustig
musikalisch
sportlich

3 Separate out the words to form three sentences.

meinelieblingsfußballmannschaftistbayernmünchen

meinlieblingssportisttennis

meinelieblingszahlistsieben

Remember that each sentence must start with a capital letter. Also, remember that nouns start with a capital letter.

1 ______________________________

2 ______________________________

3 ______________________________

4 Write a sentence about your favourite …

1 football team: ______________________________

2 sport: ______________________________

3 number: ______________________________

5 Meine Sachen (Seiten 16–17)

1 **Write the German question word under its English translation.**

Who?	What?	How?	Where?	Where from?

Wie? *Was?*
Wo? *Woher?*
Wer?

2 **Write the correct question word in each question. You may use each word more than once.**

1 ______________ bist du? Sportlich?

2 ______________ wohnt Shiva?

3 ______________ heißt du?

4 ______________ kommst du?

5 ______________ ist das? Ist das Max?

6 ______________ alt ist Michael?

7 ______________ ist Hannover? *Hannover ist in Deutschland!*

8 ______________ ist deine Lieblingsmusik?

3 **Read the paragraph below. Pretend that you're Gabi, and answer each question in a complete German sentence.**

Hallo! Ich heiße Gabi und ich bin vierzehn Jahre alt. Ich wohne in Kiel, in Deutschland, aber ich komme aus Swansea. Das ist in Wales. Wie bin ich? Ich bin sportlich, lustig und auch sehr laut! Mein Lieblingsmonat ist Dezember und meine Lieblingssendung ist ‚Die Simpsons'. Ich habe ein iPad und auch einen Computer. Tschüs!

1 Wie heißt du? ______________________________

2 Wo wohnst du? ______________________________

3 Woher kommst du? ______________________________

4 Wie bist du? ______________________________

5 Wie heißt deine Lieblingssendung? ______________________________

6 Was hast du? ______________________________

Ich über mich (Seiten 18–19)

1 Complete the table with the correct words.

	the	a	my	your
masculine: Sport				
feminine: Musik				
neuter: Auto				

2 Write each sentence or question in German. Tick the boxes when you've checked each part of your work.

Part of writing accurately in any language is going back over your work to check that there aren't any mistakes. Get into the habit now and watch both your English and German improve!

1 I'm called Osman.

____

2 I live in Germany.

____

3 I'm quite friendly and also creative.

____

____

4 I have a mobile phone.

____

5 Where do you live?

____

- ☐ Spelling of key phonics sound 'ei'
- ☐ Name has a capital
- ☐ Spelling of key phonics sound 'eu'
- ☐ Full stop at the end
- ☐ Check the qualifier
- ☐ Check the connective
- ☐ Capital on the noun
- ☐ Right word for 'a'
- ☐ Correct question word
- ☐ Verb in second position

3 Write a short paragraph about yourself. Use the sentences in exercise 2 as prompts. Check your work against the checklist below.

☐ genders ☐ qualifiers ☐ connectives ☐ verbs
☐ capital letters ☐ spelling ☐ question words

____

____

Wiederholung 1

1 Fill in the gaps by writing the German for the words in brackets.

Hallo! Ich __________ (am called) Marie und ich __________ (live) in Walsrode. Das ist in __________ (Germany). Ich bin fünfzehn __________ (years) alt. Ich bin __________ (very) sportlich und __________ (quite) intelligent, __________ (but) ich bin __________ (also) faul. Mein __________ (favourite sport) ist Hockey und __________ (my) Lieblingsmusik ist Pop. Ich __________ (have) einen Vogel aus Amerika. Er ist __________ (very) freundlich, aber __________ (not) laut!

2 Crack the code and write the sentences correctly.

a 18/24/19 4/12/19/13/22 18/13 20/28/7/7/18/13/20/22/13

Ich wohne in Göttingen.

ä = 27 ü = 29
ö = 28 ß = 30

b 22/9 18/8/7 20/26/13/1 21/9/22/6/13/23/15/18/24/19

____

c 14/22/18/13/22 15/18/22/25/15/18/13/20/8/14/6/8/18/16 18/8/7 14/12/1/26/9/7

____

____

3 Make up a coded sentence in German for a classmate to solve. Don't forget to provide a key.

4 Write the questions you would ask to get these answers.

1 *Wie heißt du?*

Ich heiße Elaine.

2 __________

Mein Lieblingssport ist Tennis.

3 __________

Sami ist musikalisch und intelligent, aber sehr launisch.

4 __________

Alwin ist vierzehn Jahre alt.

Wiederholung 2

1 **Read the website entries.**

Ich heiße **Franzi** und suche Freunde aus England, Irland oder Nordirland. Ich habe eine Schlange zu Hause! Sie ist sechs Jahre alt. Ich wohne in Wien. Das ist in Österreich. Ich bin sehr kreativ und intelligent! Schreib mir bitte!

Hallo! Ich heiße **Hannah** und ich wohne in London, in England. Ich lerne Deutsch. Ich suche Freunde aus Deutschland, Österreich und auch aus der Schweiz. Ich bin sportlich und spiele Fußball und auch Tennis, aber ich bin sehr faul! Meine Lieblingsmusik ist Rock. Schreib mir!

Mein Name ist **Felix** und ich wohne in der Schweiz, aber ich komme aus Dortmund in Deutschland. Zu Hause habe ich eine Wii und mein Lieblingsspiel ist FIFA. Meine Lieblingsfußballmannschaft ist Bayern-München. Ich suche Freunde aus Schottland und Wales.

Hi! Ich bin **Muhammad** und ich wohne in Cardiff. Das ist in Wales. Ich bin sechzehn Jahre alt. Meine Lieblingssache ist Technologie. Ich habe zu Hause einen Computer, ein Handy und auch ein iPad. Ich bin nicht sehr sportlich, aber sehr freundlich. Mein Lieblingsland ist Deutschland und ich suche dort Freunde.

Write the name of the person who ...

1 is looking for friends from Switzerland. Hannah

2 supports a football team. ____________

3 has a pet. ____________

4 is just looking for friends from Germany. ____________

5 lives in a different place from where they were born. ____________

6 does not particularly like sport. ____________

7 lives in Switzerland. ____________

suche = seek
Schreib mir (bitte)! = Write to me (please)!
dort = there

2 **Write your own profile for the website. Use as much German as you can from *Kapitel 1* to describe yourself.**

____

____

____

____

Grammatik (Seiten 22–23)

1 Write a sentence using the correct German word for 'a' for each item.

1  2  3  4  5 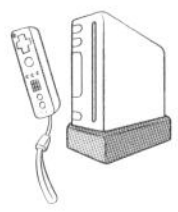 6  7  8 

1 *Das ist ein Computer.*
2 ____________________
3 ____________________
4 ____________________
5 ____________________
6 ____________________
7 ____________________
8 ____________________

die Gitarre *das Handy*
der iPod *der Computer*
das Skateboard *das Keyboard*
der Fußball *die Wii*

Grammatik
masculine – *ein*
feminine – *eine*
neuter – *ein*

2 Circle the correct verb form to complete each sentence.

1 Lukas **habe / hat / hast** einen Computer.
2 Ich **heiße / habe / hat** einen Vogel zu Hause.
3 Wo **bist / ist / wohnst** er?
4 Er **ist / komme / bin** musikalisch und sportlich.
5 Julia **bin / ist / wohnt** fünfzehn Jahre alt.
6 Wie alt **wohnst / bist / bin** du?
7 Wo **hast / bist / bin** ich?

Grammatik
You can use the pronouns *er* ('he') or *sie* ('she') instead of writing someone's name. Both need the *er*/*sie*/*es* form of the verb.

3 Complete the table with the correct forms of each regular verb.

wohnen (to live)	**kommen** (to come)	**heißen** (to be called)
ich *wohne*	ich	ich
du	du *kommst*	du
er/sie/es	er/sie/es	er/sie/es *heißt*

Now use the table to write the correct verb in each gap.

1 Mein Handy ____________ aus China.
2 Meine Schlange ____________ Sissel.
3 Du ____________ Gabi.
4 ____________ du aus Berlin?
5 ____________ Monika in Hamburg?
6 Deine Lieblingssendung ____________ 'EastEnders'.
7 Ich ____________ Wolfgang.
8 Wo ____________ du?

Mein Fortschritt

1 **Record your levels for *Kapitel* 1.**

2 **Look at the level descriptors on pages 59–60 and set your targets for *Kapitel* 2.**

3 **Fill in what you need to do to achieve these targets.**

Listening 	I have reached Level ______ in **Listening**. In *Kapitel* 2, I want to reach Level ______ I need to ______________________________ ______________________________ ______________________________ ______________________________
Speaking 	I have reached Level ______ in **Speaking**. In *Kapitel* 2, I want to reach Level ______ I need to ______________________________ ______________________________ ______________________________ ______________________________
Reading 	I have reached Level ______ in **Reading**. In *Kapitel* 2, I want to reach Level ______ I need to ______________________________ ______________________________ ______________________________ ______________________________
Writing 	I have reached Level ______ in **Writing**. In *Kapitel* 2, I want to reach Level ______ I need to ______________________________ ______________________________ ______________________________ ______________________________

Hallo! • Meeting and greeting

Wie heißt du?	*What's your name?*
Ich heiße ...	*My name is ...*
Hallo!	*Hello! / Hi!*
Guten Tag!	*Hello!*
Wie geht's?	*How are you?*
Gut, danke. Und dir?	*Fine, thanks. And you?*
Nicht schlecht.	*Not bad.*
Tschüs!	*Bye!*
Auf Wiedersehen!	*Goodbye!*

Die Zahlen 1–19 • Numbers 1–19

eins	*1*
zwei	*2*
drei	*3*
vier	*4*
fünf	*5*
sechs	*6*
sieben	*7*
acht	*8*
neun	*9*
zehn	*10*
elf	*11*
zwölf	*12*
dreizehn	*13*
vierzehn	*14*
fünfzehn	*15*
sechzehn	*16*
siebzehn	*17*
achtzehn	*18*
neunzehn	*19*
Wie alt bist du?	*How old are you?*
Ich bin ... Jahre alt.	*I am ... years old.*
Wie alt ist (Julia)?	*How old is (Julia)?*
(Julia) ist ... Jahre alt.	*(Julia) is ... years old.*

Wo wohnst du? • Where do you live?

Ich wohne in ...	*I live in ...*
Er/Sie/Es wohnt in ...	*He/She/It lives in ...*
... England	*England*
... Irland	*Ireland*
... Nordirland	*Northern Ireland*
... Schottland	*Scotland*
... Wales	*Wales*
... Deutschland	*Germany*
... Österreich	*Austria*
... der Schweiz	*Switzerland*

Wie bist du? • What are you like?

Ich bin ...	*I am ...*
Er/Sie ist ...	*He/She is ...*
faul	*lazy*
freundlich	*friendly*
intelligent	*intelligent*
kreativ	*creative*
launisch	*moody*
laut	*loud*
lustig	*funny*
musikalisch	*musical*
sportlich	*sporty*

Lieblingssachen • Favourite things

Mein Lieblingssport ist ...
My favourite sport is ...

Mein Lieblingsmonat ist ...
My favourite month is ...

Meine Lieblingsmusik ist ...
My favourite music is ...

Meine Lieblingszahl ist ...
My favourite number is ...

Meine Lieblingssendung ist ...
My favourite programme is ...

Meine Lieblingsfußballmannschaft ist ...
My favourite football team is ...

Mein Lieblingsspiel ist ...
My favourite game is ...

Mein Lieblingsland ist ...
My favourite country is ...

Mein Lieblingsauto ist ...
My favourite car is ...

Was ist dein Lieblingssport?
What's your favourite sport?

Was ist deine Lieblingszahl?
What's your favourite number?

Was ist dein Lieblingsland?
What's your favourite country?

Hast du einen Computer? • Have you got a computer?

Ich habe ...	*I have ...*
einen Computer	*a computer*
einen iPod	*an iPod*
einen Fußball	*a football*
eine Gitarre	*a guitar*
eine Wii	*a Wii*
eine Schlange	*a snake*
ein Handy	*a mobile phone*
ein Keyboard	*a keyboard*
ein Skateboard	*a skateboard*

Fragewörter • Question words

Wie?	*How?*
Was?	*What?*
Wo?	*Where?*
Woher?	*Where ... from?*
Wer?	*Who?*

Oft benutzte Wörter • High-frequency words

und	*and*
(und) auch	*(and) also*
aber	*but*
sehr	*very*
ziemlich	*quite*
nicht	*not*
Was denkst du?	*What do you think?*
Ich denke, ...	*I think ...*
Ich auch!	*Me too!*
Ich nicht!	*Not me!/That's not what I think!*
Was? Du spinnst!	*What? You're joking!*

1 Extreme Haustiere (Seiten 30–31)

1 Complete the sentences about the pets. Write the correct words in the gaps. Remember to think about the gender of each animal.

1. Ich habe _ein_ Pferd. _Es_ ist groß und heißt Romeo.
2. Ich habe ______ Kaninchen. ______ ist niedlich und heißt Timmo.
3. Ich habe ______ Katze. ______ ist intelligent und heißt Mieze.
4. Max hat ______ Schlange. ______ ist zwei Jahre alt.
5. Gabi hat ______ Pferd. ______ ist launish.
6. Ich habe ______ Hund. ______ ist freundlich und heißt Prinz.
7. Susi hat ______ Goldfisch. ______ heißt Nemo.

Grammatik
Remember: after *haben* the masculine word for 'a' changes from *ein* to *einen*.

Grammatik
m. der / ein → **er**
f. die / eine → **sie**
n. das / ein → **es**

2 Tina Tierfan has lots of pets! Write Tina's answers to the interviewer's questions about how many of each animal she has.

Grammatik

Hund (-e)	Pferd (-e)
Katze (-n)	Goldfisch (-e)
Schlange (-n)	Maus (Mäuse)

1. Hast du einen Hund? _Nein! Ich habe drei Hunde._
2. Hast du ein Pferd? ______
3. Hast du eine Katze? ______
4. Hast du einen Goldfisch? ______
5. Hast du eine Schlange? ______
6. Hast du eine Maus? ______

2 Supertiere (Seiten 32–33)

1 **Complete the sentences about the animals. Write the correct name in each gap.**

Hermann 
Minnie 
Sisi 

Kizzi 
Moto 
Millie 

1 ____________ ist schnell.
2 ____________ ist süß.
3 ____________ ist gemein.
4 ____________ ist superintelligent.
5 ____________ ist cool.
6 ____________ ist kräftig.

2 **Write a sentence to say what each of the *Supertiere* can do.**

1 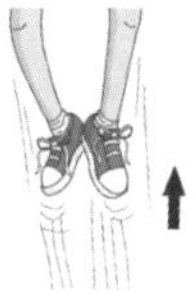
Hermann

2 
Sisi

3 
Minnie

4 

Kizzi

5 
Millie

6 
Moto

1 Hermann kann springen.
2 ______________________________
3 ______________________________
4 ______________________________
5 ______________________________
6 ______________________________

Grammatik
The verb *kann* is always followed by an infinitive verb.

3 **Read the text below, then translate it into English.**

Günther Goldfisch ist mein Lieblingstier. Er ist ein Jahr alt. Er ist sehr lustig und kräftig, aber auch ziemlich süß. Er kann schwimmen, springen und auch im Aquarium tanzen! Günther hat einen Freund: er ist sehr cool und schlau.

3 Meine Familie (Seiten 34–35)

1 Find the numbers in the puzzle, and write them next to the correct numeral.

v	i	e	r	u	n	d	s	e	c	h	z	i	g	m	e
b	a	l	c	o	e	z	n	f	w	i	r	d	s	k	s
s	e	c	h	s	u	n	d	d	r	e	i	ß	i	g	a
q	g	n	a	j	n	x	i	n	d	m	h	t	g	ü	o
h	a	c	h	t	u	n	d	f	ü	n	f	z	i	g	i
u	e	i	n	u	n	d	a	c	h	t	z	i	g	p	b
n	t	e	r	i	d	f	b	n	ß	e	d	z	g	d	s
d	r	e	i	u	n	d	v	i	e	r	z	i	g	w	e
e	v	h	f	r	e	a	m	ß	p	l	s	j	a	q	c
r	d	r	e	i	u	n	d	z	w	a	n	z	i	g	h
t	z	a	n	j	n	x	o	u	e	y	g	r	e	v	z
k	c	p	f	s	z	d	l	b	n	l	a	i	h	m	i
i	b	z	w	e	i	u	n	d	s	i	e	b	z	i	g
a	g	b	n	ü	g	y	i	a	z	o	m	e	d	h	e

100 ____________________

64 ____________________

99 ____________________

43 ____________________

72 ____________________

36 ____________________

58 ____________________

81 ____________________

60 ____________________

23 ____________________

2 Describe each of the families. Fill in the gaps for the first family. Write the whole description for the second family.

Ich heiße Tom. Ich bin vierzehn Jahre alt. Es gibt vier Personen in meiner Familie. Meine Mutter ist ____________________ Jahre alt. Ich habe einen Bruder. ____ ist ________ Jahre alt. Ich habe eine Schwester. ________ ist ____________ Jahre alt. Wir wohnen in ________ .

____

____

____

____

____

____

3 Write about your family (real or imaginary). Use the descriptions in exercise 2 to help you.

der Stiefbruder = stepbrother
die Halbschwester = half-sister
Ich bin Einzelkind. = I am an only child.

4 Die Farben der Welt (Seiten 36–37)

1 Describe each person's hair and eyes.

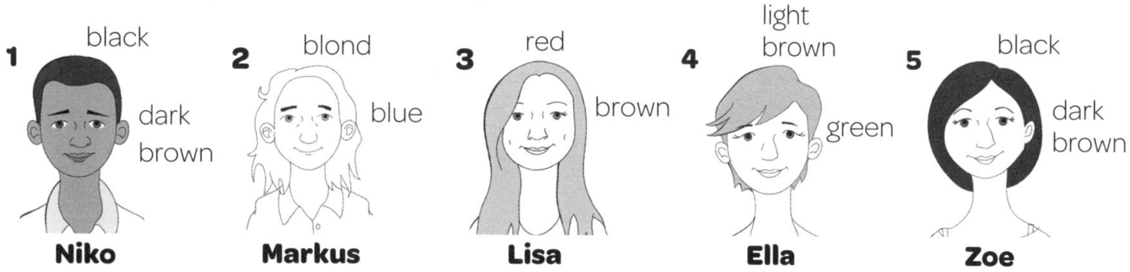

Grammatik
When you describe hair and eyes, the adjectives (colour, length) need an ***e*** on the end.

hell = light | **hellbraun** = light brown
dunkel = dark | **dunkelblau** = dark blue

1 Er heißt Niko. Er hat kurze, schwarze Haare und dunkelbraune Augen.

2 ______________________________

3 ______________________________

4 ______________________________

5 ______________________________

2 Complete the text by choosing the correct words from the cloud to fill the gaps. There are more words than you need.

Es gibt fünf __________ in meiner Familie. Wir __________ in Braunschweig. Das ist in __________. Meine __________ heißt Emma und sie ist neunundvierzig __________ alt. Sie ist sehr freundlich und hat __________, schwarze Haare. Mein Vater __________ auch neunundvierzig und er hat kurze, dunkelbraune Haare und braune __________.

Ich habe zwei __________: einen Bruder und eine Schwester. __________ Bruder heißt Mehmet und er ist __________ Jahre alt. Er ist launisch aber __________ lustig. __________ Schwester, Isla, hat grüne Augen und __________ Haare. Sie ist sechzehn Jahre alt, sehr klein und __________.

Deutschland alt Augen Personen braune wohnen sportlich Meine Mutter Jahre lange Geschwister zwölf auch Mein blau ist

Read the text for gist first. For each sentence, think about whether you need a noun, a verb, a connective or an adjective.

5 Alles Gute! (Seiten 38–39)

1 Reorder the words to make correct sentences. Don't forget the full stop!

1 am | Mai | Ich | Geburtstag | habe | neunzehnten

____

2 hat | Oktober | am | Oma | Geburtstag | elften | Meine

____

3 Geburtstag | Stiefbruder | Dezember | am | Dein | dritten | hat

____

4 hast | Geburtstag | einunddreißigsten | Juli | Du | am

____

5 und | Geburtstag | haben | achten | am | Michael | Juni | Monika

____

2 Complete each sentence by writing the date. Write each holiday in English.

Neujahr ist am *ersten Januar*. *New Year*

Der Maifeiertag ist am ______________________. ______________

Der Tag der Deutschen Einheit ist am ______________________. *German Unity Day*

Weihnachten ist am ______________________. ______________

Silvester ist am ______________________. ______________

3 Read the short profile about Yannic and write a summary in the table.

Er heißt Yannic Spiller. Er ist dreizehn Jahre alt und kommt aus Trier. Trier ist in Deutschland. Yannic hat am siebten Januar Geburtstag. Er hat einen Bruder, Tim. Tim ist achtzehn Jahre alt. Yannic hat auch eine Schwester. Sie heißt Steffi und ist sechzehn Jahre alt. Die Familie Spiller hat zwei Haustiere: einen Hund und eine Katze.

Name:		Geschwister:	
Alter:			
Wohnt in:		Haustiere:	
Geburtstag:			

4 Now write a short profile about yourself.

6 Speaking Skills Eine Superfamilie (Seiten 40–41)

1 Rescue the question words from the alphabet soup. Write each one on a line and use it to write a question.

Wie viele Brüder hast du?

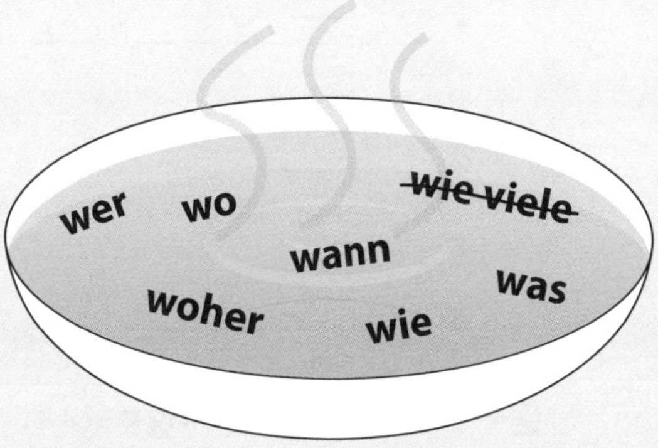

2 The police have written a summary about a crime suspect. Write six questions for a journalist to ask the suspect. The questions should cover all the information in the summary.

1 Wie heißt du?
2
3
4
5
6

Martin Kolwitz ist 24 Jahre alt. Er hat am achten November Geburtstag. Er wohnt in Hamburg, in Deutschland. Er hat einen Bruder. Er hat auch Haustiere: zwei Hunde.

Remember: the verb usually goes straight after the question word.

3 Use these notes to write questions to Martin about his accomplice, Sophie.

1 Wie heißt sie?
2
3
4
5

Sophie Meyer
19
Ebbingen, Deutschland
Haare – kurz, Augen – blau
Geb. 21.10.

Remember to use the correct part of the verb with the pronoun *sie*.

4 Write a summary about Sophie, like the one the police wrote about Martin in exercise 2.

Wiederholung 1

1 **Complete the sentences. Choose the correct word from the cloud to fill in each gap.**

1 ______________ Mutter ist sehr freundlich und intelligent.

2 Hast du ______________ Meerschweinchen?

3 Wir haben ______________ Haustier.

4 Wo ist ______________ Vogel?

5 Ich habe ______________ Bruder.

dein *kein*
ein *meine*
einen

2 **You are describing pets at a pet show. Use the owners' notes to write what sort of pet they have, what the pet is like and what it can do.**

Mareike

mouse
Pippa
cute, fast
fly, swim

Mareike hat ______________.

Sie heißt ______________.

Sie ist ______________.

Sie kann ______________.

Aaron

cat
Mieze
intelligent, cool, mean
jump, play football

______________.

______________.

______________.

______________.

______________.

3 **Decscribe the animal you'll be entering in the pet show by writing a similar description.**

Example: Ich habe ...

Wiederholung 2

1 Read the texts below.

Hallo! Ich heiße **Anna** und ich bin fünfzehn Jahre alt. Ich habe am elften Februar Geburtstag. Ich wohne in Klagenfurt, in Österreich. Ich bin ziemlich groß und schlank und habe kurze, schwarze Haare und blaue Augen. Ich habe keine Geschwister – ich bin Einzelkind. Ich habe einen Goldfisch und einen Wellensittich. Ich kann Flöte spielen und Italienisch sprechen.

Hi! Ich bin **Noah** und ich komme aus Aachen. Das ist in Deutschland. Ich habe am zweiten November Geburtstag und bin vierzehn Jahre alt. Ich liebe Haustiere! Ich habe zwei Hunde, drei Katzen und eine Maus. Ich habe eine große Familie. Ich habe einen Halbbruder (er ist ein Baby) und zwei Schwestern. Mein Halbbruder ist sehr süß und klein. Er hat schwarze Haare und blaue Augen.

a Complete the sentences by writing *Anna* or *Noah*.

1. __________ lives in Austria.
2. __________ can play the flute.
3. __________'s birthday is on the 02.11.
4. __________ has a half-brother.
5. __________ is 15 years old.
6. __________ has cats.

b Write *richtig* or *falsch* next to each statement.

1. Anna hat einen Halbbruder. __________
2. Anna kann auch Englisch sprechen. __________
3. Noahs Halbbruder hat blaue Augen. __________
4. Klagenfurt ist nicht in Deutschland. __________
5. Anna hat am fünfzehnten Februar Geburtstag. __________
6. Anna hat keine Geschwister. __________

2 Translate these sentences into German.

1. My birthday is on the first of May. __________
2. She can speak German. __________
3. My guinea pig is very cute. __________
4. Your sister has light blue eyes. __________
5. My grandparents live in Southampton. __________
6. My brother can fly. __________

Grammatik (Seiten 44–45)

1 **Complete the table by writing the correct form of *haben* for each pronoun.**

haben *hast* *habt* *hat* *habe* *haben*

Words for 'you':
du (speaking to one family member or friend)
ihr (speaking to two or more family members or friends)
Sie (speaking to people you don't know or adults)

ich	du	er/sie/es	wir	ihr	Sie/sie

Now complete the sentences with the correct form of *haben*.

1 Katja, hast ______ du eine Katze?

2 Tom und Niko, ______ ihr einen Hund?

3 ______ Sie eine Schlange, Herr Brand?

4 Ich ______ ein Pferd.

5 Frau Gerber, ______ Sie eine Maus?

6 Herr Alexander ______ ein Pferd.

2 **Join each pronoun to a verb. There is more than one possible verb for some of the pronouns. Then write a question or a sentence with each pair.**

1 ich	**a** macht	**1** ______
2 du	**b** heißen	**2** ______
3 er	**c** wohnst	**3** ______
4 wir	**d** heiße	**4** ______
5 ihr	**e** spielt	**5** ______
6 Sie	**f** spielen	**6** ______

3 **Rewrite the sentences so they include the verb *kann*.**

1 Mein Bruder fliegt. Mein Bruder kann fliegen.

2 Ich spiele Flöte. ______

3 Meine Mutter schwimmt. ______

4 Mein Vater springt. ______

5 Ich tanze. ______

6 Er singt gut. ______

Mein Fortschritt

1 **Record your levels for *Kapitel* 2.**

2 **Look at the level descriptors on pages 59–60 and set your targets for *Kapitel* 3.**

3 **Fill in what you need to do to achieve these targets.**

Listening 	I have reached Level _____ in **Listening**. In *Kapitel* 3, I want to reach Level _____ I need to ______________________________ ______________________________ ______________________________ ______________________________
Speaking 	I have reached Level _____ in **Speaking**. In *Kapitel* 3, I want to reach Level _____ I need to ______________________________ ______________________________ ______________________________ ______________________________
Reading 	I have reached Level _____ in **Reading**. In *Kapitel* 3, I want to reach Level _____ I need to ______________________________ ______________________________ ______________________________ ______________________________
Writing 	I have reached Level _____ in **Writing**. In *Kapitel* 3, I want to reach Level _____ I need to ______________________________ ______________________________ ______________________________ ______________________________

Haustiere • Pets

Hast du ein Haustier?	*Have you got a pet?*
Ich habe ...	*I have ...*
einen Goldfisch	*a goldfish*
einen Hamster	*a hamster*
einen Hund	*a dog*
ein Kaninchen	*a rabbit*
eine Katze	*a cat*
eine Maus	*a mouse*
ein Meerschweinchen	*a guinea pig*
ein Pferd	*a horse*
eine Schlange	*a snake*
einen Wellensittich	*a budgie*
kein Haustier	*no pet*

Eigenschaften • Qualities

Wie ist er/sie/es?	*What is he/she/ it like?*
Er/Sie/Es ist ...	*He/She/It is ...*
dick/schlank	*fat/thin*
frech/niedlich	*cheeky/cute*
gemein/süß	*mean/sweet*
groß/klein	*big/small*
kräftig	*strong*
schlau	*cunning*
(super)lustig	*(really) funny*
Er/Sie/Es kann ...	*He/She/It can ...*
Italienisch sprechen	*speak Italian*
fliegen	*fly*
Flöte/Fußball/Wii spielen	*play the flute/ football/on the Wii*
(schnell) laufen	*run (fast)*
lesen	*read*
Rad fahren	*ride a bike*
schwimmen	*swim*
singen	*sing*
springen	*jump*
tanzen	*dance*

Die Zahlen 20–100 • Numbers 20–100

zwanzig	*twenty*
dreißig	*thirty*
vierzig	*forty*
fünfzig	*fifty*
sechzig	*sixty*
siebzig	*seventy*
achtzig	*eighty*
neunzig	*ninety*
hundert	*hundred*
einundzwanzig	*twenty-one*
zweiundzwanzig	*twenty-two*

Meine Familie • My family

Es gibt ... Personen in meiner Familie.	*There are ... people in my family.*
meine Mutter	*my mother*
mein Vater	*my father*
mein Bruder	*my brother*
mein Stiefbruder/ Halbbruder	*my stepbrother/ half-brother*
meine Schwester	*my sister*
meine Stiefschwester/ Halbschwester	*my stepsister/ half-sister*
meine Eltern	*my parents*
meine Großeltern	*my grandparents*
Hast du Geschwister?	*Have you any brothers and sisters?*
Ich habe zwei Brüder.	*I have two brothers.*
Ich habe drei Schwestern.	*I have three sisters.*
Ich bin Einzelkind.	*I'm an only child.*
Ich habe keine Geschwister.	*I have no brothers and sisters.*

Die Farben • Colours

schwarz	*black*
weiß	*white*
grau	*grey*
braun	*brown*
rot	*red*
orange	*orange*
gelb	*yellow*
grün	*green*
blau	*blue*
indigoblau	*indigo*
violett	*violet*
lila	*purple*
rosa	*pink*
bunt	*brightly coloured*
hellblau/dunkelblau	*light blue/dark blue*

Haare und Augen • Hair and eyes

Er/Sie hat ...	*He/She has ...*
schwarze/braune/ blonde/rote Haare	*black/brown/ blond/red hair*
kurze/lange/ mittellange Haare	*short/long/ mid length hair*
blaue/braune/grüne/ graue Augen	*blue/brown/green/ grey eyes*

Die Monate • The months

Januar	*January*
Februar	*February*
März	*March*
April	*April*
Mai	*May*
Juni	*June*
Juli	*July*
August	*August*
September	*September*
Oktober	*October*
November	*November*
Dezember	*December*

Das Datum • The date

Wann hast du Geburtstag?	*When is your birthday?*
am 1. (ersten) Januar	*on 1 January*
am 3. (dritten) Februar	*on 3 February*
am 7. (siebten) März	*on 7 March*
am 8. (achten) April	*on 8 April*
am 15. (fünfzehnten) Mai	*on 15 May*
am 29. (neunund-zwanzigsten) Juni	*on 29 June*
Ich habe (heute) Geburtstag.	*It's my birthday (today).*

Oft benutzte Wörter • High-frequency words

und	*and*
aber	*but*
oder	*or*
ziemlich	*fairly, quite*
sehr	*very*

1 **Look at the survey results in the table. Then answer the questions using full German sentences.**

Ahmed	☺☺			☹			😐
Nicole		☺☺			☹		
Christa	☺		☺☺				😐
Torsten		☹		☺☺		☺	
Herr und Frau Meyer	☺☺			☺	☹	😐	

☺☺ = sehr gern ☺ = gern 😐 = ziemlich gern ☹ = nicht gern

1 Wer spielt sehr gern Fußball? Nicole spielt sehr gern Fußball.
2 Wer spielt gern Tischtennis? ______
3 Was spielt Christa sehr gern? ______
4 Was spielen Herr und Frau Meyer gern? ______
5 Wer spielt Basketball nicht gern? ______
6 Wer spielt ziemlich gern Handball? (2) ______
7 Und du? Was spielst du gern? ______

2 **Write three questions and three answers about the other people and sports in the table in exercise 1. Use the questions above as a model.**

______
______
______
______
______
______

2 Freizeit ist toll! (Seiten 56–57)

1 **Write the words from the cloud in the grid. Translate the code word into English.**

furchtbar
Eishockey
schlecht
spielst
irre
stinklangweilig
langweilig
Tischtennis
toll

2 **Read about all the activities Hannes and Lola are involved in.
Then write *richtig* or *falsch* next to each statement.**

Hallo! Ich heiße **Hannes**. Ich finde Sport fantastisch. Ich spiele Tennis und schwimme. Schwimmen finde ich total super. Ich reite mit meiner Freundin, aber das finde ich langweilig. Fußball finde ich cool. Ich fahre auch gern Skateboard und lese sehr gern Sport- und Fitnessmagazine.

Meine Freundin heißt **Lola.** Sie findet Tischtennis toll. Lola fährt auch gern Rad – das ist sehr gesund! Sie findet schwimmen auch gut, aber Fußball findet sie nervig. Sie kann nicht Ski fahren. Im Winter spielt sie Eishockey und sie sieht sehr gern Eishockey im Fernsehen.

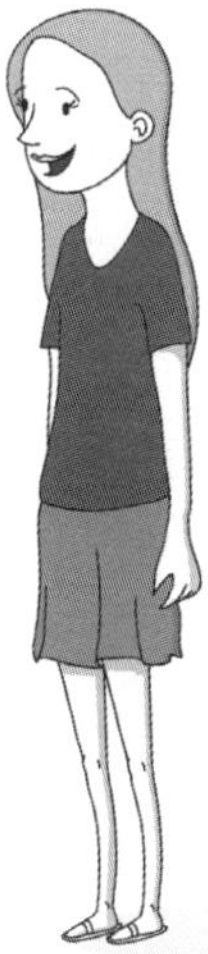

meine Freundin = my girlfriend
gesund = healthy
Fernsehen = television

1 Both Hannes and Lola participate in winter sports. ______________

2 Lola watches ice hockey on television. ______________

3 Hannes really likes swimming. ______________

4 Lola thinks skiing is fantastic. ______________

5 Lola plays ice hockey in winter. ______________

6 Hannes doesn’t enjoying horse riding. ______________

7 Lola thinks football is exciting. ______________

8 Hannes watches sports programmes on television. ______________

3 In meiner Freizeit (Seiten 58–59)

1 **Separate the words to form five time phrases and write them below. Number the phrases in order of frequency, starting with 1 for the most frequent. Translate the phrases into English.**

JedenTagdreimalproWocheeinmalproMonatamWochenendesechsmalproMonat

☐ ______________________ ______________________
☐ ______________________ ______________________
☐ ______________________ ______________________
☐ ______________________ ______________________
☐ ______________________ ______________________

2 **Use the time phrases from exercise 1 to answer the questions about yourself. Write your answers in full sentences.**

1 Gehst du ins Kino? ______________________

2 Machst du Sport? ______________________

3 Gehst du einkaufen? ______________________

4 Hörst du Musik? ______________________

5 Spielst du Wii? ______________________

6 Chillst du mit deinen Freunden? ______________________

nie = never

3 **Join up the sentence halves. Rewrite each sentence so that it starts with the time phrase.**

1 Ich höre am

2 Ich chille am

3 Ich spiele sehr

4 Ich mache jeden

5 Ich esse einmal

6 Ich gehe einmal pro

a Tag Sport.

b Abend Musik.

c pro Woche Pizza.

d Monat ins Kino.

e oft Xbox.

f Wochenende.

Remember the 'verb in second place' rule.

4 Ich bin online (Seiten 60–61)

1 Unscramble and write down the time phrase in each sentence. Then translate the sentences into English.

Grammatik
You can use the present tense with a future time phrase to say what you are going to do – just as in English.

1 Wir machen ähnhcset eoWhc Filme. *nächste Woche*

We are going to make …

2 Ich suche ma Mtanog Infos im Internet. ____________________

____

3 Wir sehen ma eneneoWhcd Katzenvideos auf YouTube. ____________________

____

4 Ich chatte nejde denbA auf Facebook. ____________________

____

5 Stefan spielt ni iezw cnoWhe Wii Sport. ____________________

____

6 Ich lade gomrne Musik herunter. ____________________

____

2 Underline all the verbs in the text. Circle the words that are in first position in the sentences. Write a sentence about what you notice.

Hey du!

Franzi hier! Jetzt sind wir Freunde auf Facebook! Jeden Tag spiele ich Wii. Jede Woche schreibt mein Vater ein Blog, aber das finde ich langweilig. Am Abend lese ich gern E-Books. Morgen telefoniere ich mit Freunden in Kanada über Skype. Das finde ich cool! Im Sommer fahren wir nach Vancouver. Fantastisch! Was machst du am Computer und wie oft?

____

3 Reply to the question Franzi has asked you in his chat.

Use as many time phrases as you can in your reply.

Brieffreunde (Seiten 64–65)

1 What type of word is needed to fill the gap in each sentence? Complete each sentence by writing an appropriate German word or words in the gap.

verb *noun* *time/frequency phrase* *connective* *adjective*

		Type of word
1	Ich *finde* Tennis toll.	*verb*
2	Meine Schwester findet Tischtennis ______.	______
3	Wir sehen ______ fern.	______
4	Herr Peters spielt nächste Woche Tennis ______ Fußball.	______
5	Mein Bruder schreibt ein ______.	______

2 Answer the questions about German grammar.

Use the sentences in exercise 1 to help you answer these questions.

1 Where in a sentence do verbs usually go? ______

2 What often goes after a verb? ______

3 What can you expect to go after *ein/eine*? ______

4 Which German verb suggests you're giving an opinion? ______

3 Replace the underlined word(s) with something else: a different noun, adjective or time phrase.

1 Ich finde Tischtennis furchtbar. *Ich finde Tischtennis langweilig.*

2 Ich spiele nicht gern Fußball. ______

3 Micha spielt gern Wii. ______

4 Er macht einmal pro Monat Judo. ______

5 Olli findet E-Books fantastisch. ______

6 Ich sehe jede Woche fern. Meine Schwester sieht jeden Tag Videos auf YouTube.

______

Remember that you'll keep the reader's interest if you use a variety of different words and phrases.

4 Write about your friends' hobbies.

Remember to include:
- opinions
- connectives
- time/frequency phrases
- 'verb in second place' rule

Wiederholung 1

1 Put the words in the correct order to make sentences or questions. Don't forget to insert a full stop or question mark.

1 fern | gern | sehr | Ich | sehe ______

2 einkaufen | er | Wochenende | geht | Am ______

3 Hausaufgaben | Ich | Infos | lese | die | für ______

4 in | Wie | Stadt | oft | du | fährst | die ______

5 Woche | Kai | Wasserball | Nächste | spielt ______

6 herunter | Videos | Ich | lade | Musik | und ______

2 Rewrite each sentence, beginning with a time phrase. Then translate the sentences into English.

1 Ich spiele Volleyball. (at the weekend) *Am Wochenende spiele ich Volleyball.*

At the weekend I am going to play volleyball.

2 Er spielt Basketball. (on Monday) ______

______

3 Du spielst Tischtennis. (every week) ______

______

4 Rosa spielt Fußball. (today) ______

______

5 Ich telefoniere mit Sam. (next week) ______

______

6 Sophie liest das Buch. (tomorrow) ______

______

3 Underline the regular verbs and circle the irregular verbs.

Ich spiele nicht gern Tennis. Ich finde Tennis langweilig. Fußball spiele ich dreimal pro Woche. Mein Bruder spielt sehr gern Tennis. Er fährt auch gern Rad. Radfahren findet er toll. Meine Schwester sieht ziemlich gern fern. Meine Mutter liest ziemlich gern. Oft liest sie Blogs im Internet. Ich lese auch oft. Mein Vater fährt gern Ski und spielt Gitarre.

Wiederholung 2

1 Read the email. Find the German for the following words and phrases in the text.

1 I think ______________________

2 about ______________________

3 but ______________________

4 New Zealand ______________________

5 comedies ______________________

6 Best wishes ______________________

Lieber Anish,

wie geht's? Danke für deine E-Mail.

Ich denke, Technologie ist toll. Ich bin sehr oft online. Ich chatte sehr gern mit Freunden auf Facebook. Facebook finde ich super und ich sehe oft Videos über Fußball auf YouTube.

Ich spiele Computerspiele nicht gern, aber ich suche ziemlich oft Infos für die Hausaufgaben. Meine Cousine, Connie, wohnt in Neuseeland und wir telefonieren ziemlich oft über Skype. Kannst du auch über Skype telefonieren?

Ich mache viel Sport mit meinen Freunden: Wir schwimmen zweimal pro Woche und wir spielen am Abend Basketball. Im Winter fahre ich auch Ski.

Ich esse manchmal am Wochenende mit meinen Freunden Pizza, und dann gehen wir ins Kino. Ich sehe gern Komödien. Nächste Woche sehen wir *Skyfall*.

Liebe Grüße,

Tibor

2 Answer the questions in complete German sentences.

1 Spielt Tibor gern Computerspiele? ______________________

2 Was macht Tibor auf Facebook? ______________________

3 Wer wohnt in Neuseeland? ______________________

4 Wie telefoniert Tibor mit seiner Cousine? ______________________

5 Wie oft schwimmt Tibor? ______________________

6 Was machen Tibor und seine Freunde am Wochenende?

____

3 Write a reply to Tibor's email about your hobbies and activities.

Grammatik (Seiten 68–69)

1 Complete the verb table.

	fahren (to go/travel)	**sehen** (to see)	**lesen** (to read)
ich			
du	fährst		liest
er/sie/es		sieht	
wir			
ihr			
Sie			
sie			

2 Complete the sentences by writing the correct form of the verb in brackets.

1 Ich ________________ das Auto. (waschen)
2 ________________ du gern Mangabücher? (lesen)
3 Er ________________ im Schlafzimmer. (schlafen)
4 Thomas ________________ nach Stockholm in Schweden. (fahren)
5 ________________ du morgen Torsten? (sehen)
6 ________________ du eine Schuluniform? (tragen)

Verbs like fahren:
tragen = to wear
schlafen = to sleep
waschen = to wash

die Schuluniform = school uniform

3 Write the question for each reply.

1 ________________ Ja, ich spiele Gitarre.
2 ________________ Nein, ich spiele nicht gern Wasserball.
3 ________________ Ja, Michael schläft im Bett.
4 ________________ Ja, ich fahre nach Bremen.
5 ________________ Ja, ich lese gern E-Books.
6 ________________ Nein, ich sehe nicht gern fern.
7 ________________ Ja, ich bin sportlich!
8 Was ________________ Ich trage morgen Jeans und ein T-Shirt.
9 ________________ Michael trägt eine Schuluniform.

Remember, to form a question you put the verb before the subject:
Du spielst gern Tennis. → Spielst du gern Tennis?

Mein Fortschritt

1 Record your levels for *Kapitel* 3.

2 Look at the level descriptors on pages 59–60 and set your targets for *Kapitel* 4.

3 Fill in what you need to do to achieve these targets.

Listening 	I have reached Level ______ in **Listening**. In *Kapitel* 4, I want to reach Level ______ I need to ______________________ ______________________ ______________________ ______________________
Speaking 	I have reached Level ______ in **Speaking**. In *Kapitel* 4, I want to reach Level ______ I need to ______________________ ______________________ ______________________ ______________________
Reading 	I have reached Level ______ in **Reading**. In *Kapitel* 4, I want to reach Level ______ I need to ______________________ ______________________ ______________________ ______________________
Writing 	I have reached Level ______ in **Writing**. In *Kapitel* 4, I want to reach Level ______ I need to ______________________ ______________________ ______________________ ______________________

Bist du sportlich? • Are you sporty?

Ich bin (sehr/ziemlich/ nicht sehr) sportlich.	*I am (very/quite/ not very) sporty.*
Was spielst du?	*What do you play?*
Ich spiele ...	*I play ...*
Ich spiele gern ...	*I like playing ...*
Ich spiele ziemlich gern ...	*I quite like playing ...*
Ich spiele nicht gern ...	*I don't like playing ... playing ...*
Badminton	*badminton*
Basketball	*basketball*
Eishockey	*ice hockey*
Fußball	*football*
Handball	*handball*
Tennis	*tennis*
Tischtennis	*table tennis*
Volleyball	*volleyball*
Wasserball	*water polo*

Was machst du gern? • What do you like doing?

Was machst du gern?	*What do you like doing?*
Ich fahre Rad.	*I ride my bike.*
Ich fahre Skateboard.	*I go skateboarding.*
Ich fahre Ski.	*I ski.*
Ich fahre Snowboard.	*I snowboard.*
Ich lese.	*I read.*
Ich mache Judo.	*I do judo.*
Ich mache Karate.	*I do karate.*
Ich reite.	*I go horse riding.*
Ich schwimme.	*I swim.*
Ich sehe fern.	*I watch TV.*
Ich spiele Gitarre.	*I play the guitar.*
Ich tanze.	*I dance.*

Wie findest du das? • What do you think of it?

Ich finde es ...	*I think it's ...*
Es ist ...	*It's ...*
irre	*amazing*
super	*super*
toll	*great*
cool	*cool*
gut	*good*
nicht schlecht	*not bad*
okay	*okay*
langweilig	*boring*
nervig	*annoying*
stinklangweilig	*deadly boring*
furchtbar	*awful*

Was machst du in deiner Freizeit? • What do you do in your free time?

Ich chille.	*I chill out.*
Ich esse Pizza oder Hamburger.	*I eat pizza or hamburgers.*
Ich gehe einkaufen.	*I go shopping.*
Ich gehe ins Kino.	*I go to the cinema.*
Ich gehe in den Park.	*I go to the park.*
Ich gehe in die Stadt.	*I go into town.*
Ich höre Musik.	*I listen to music.*
Ich mache Sport.	*I do sport.*
Ich spiele Xbox oder Wii.	*I play Xbox or on the Wii.*

Ich bin online • I'm online

Was machst du am Computer?	*What do you do on the computer?*
Was machst du auf deinem Handy?	*What do you do on your mobile?*
Ich chatte mit Freunden auf Facebook.	*I chat with friends on Facebook.*
Ich lade Musik herunter.	*I download music.*
Ich mache Fotos oder Filme.	*I take photos or make films.*
Ich sehe Videos.	*I watch videos.*
Ich simse.	*I text.*
Ich spiele Computerspiele.	*I play computer games.*
Ich suche und lese Infos für die Hausaufgaben.	*I look for and read information for my homework.*
Ich surfe im Internet.	*I surf the internet.*
Ich telefoniere mit Freunden.	*I call my friends.*
Ich mache ziemlich viel auf meinem Handy.	*I do quite a lot of things on my mobile.*

Oft benutzte Wörter • High-frequency words

Wie oft?	*How often?*
(sehr/ziemlich/nicht so) oft	*(very/quite/not so) often*
einmal/zweimal/dreimal pro Woche/pro Monat	*once/twice/three times a week/a month*
jeden Tag	*every day*
jeden Morgen	*every morning*
manchmal	*sometimes*
immer	*always*
nie	*never*
Wann?	*When?*
am Wochenende	*at the weekend*
am Abend	*in the evening*
heute	*today*
morgen	*tomorrow*
am Montag	*on Monday*
nächste Woche	*next week*
in zwei Wochen	*in two weeks*

1 Ich mag Deutsch! (Seiten 76–77)

1 Write a sentence for each illustration.

1

2

3

4

5

6

1 Ich mag ____________________
2 ____________________
3 ____________________
4 ____________________
5 ____________________
6 ____________________

!
ich liebe 🙂🙂
ich mag 🙂
ich mag ... nicht 🙁
ich hasse 🙁🙁

2 Read the forum entries giving people's opinions about school subjects. Then answer the questions below.

Hallo Leute! Mein Lieblingsfach ist Englisch! Ich liebe Englisch, weil es total interessant ist. Ich lese sehr gern Bücher auf Spanisch und auf Deutsch. Mathe finde ich langweilig. **Pedro**

Hi Pedro! Ich mag Englisch nicht. Es ist sehr schwierig, aber ich mag Mathe und Naturwissenschaften. Ich finde Mathe supercool. **Nadine**

Grüezi aus der Schweiz! Ich liebe Theater und Kunst. Ich mag Kunst sehr gern, weil ich total kreativ bin. Informatik finde ich sehr langweilig, und Geschichte und Erdkunde sind nutzlos. **Marta**

Who ...

1 is very creative? ____________
2 enjoys reading? ____________
3 doesn't like English? ____________
4 thinks ICT is boring? ____________
5 likes maths? ____________
6 can read Spanish? ____________
7 loves art? ____________
8 doesn't like geography? ____________

3 Rewrite each sentence in exercise 1, adding *weil* and an opinion. Use the examples in exercise 2 to help you with word order.

2 Was und wann? (Seiten 78–79)

1 Look at the timetable. Write *richtig* or *falsch* next to each statement.

	Montag	Dienstag	Mittwoch	Donnerstag	Freitag
8.15	Mathe	Erdkunde	Englisch	Deutsch	Technik
9.15	Englisch	Informatik	Theater	Mathe	Deutsch
10.45	Kunst	Mathe	Deutsch	Kunst	Naturwissenschaften
11.45	Naturwissenschaften	Mathe	Naturwissenschaften	Geschichte	Theater
13.30	Deutsch	Sport	Technik	Musik	Englisch

vor = before **nach** = after **die Doppelstunde** = double period

1 Am Mittwoch habe ich Deutsch. ____________

2 Wir haben am Freitag nach der Pause Technik. ____________

3 Am Montag vor der Pause haben wir Englisch. ____________

4 Theater ist am Mittwoch und am Donnerstag. ____________

5 Ich habe am Donnerstag nach der Mittagspause Musik. ____________

6 Am Dienstag habe ich eine Doppelstunde Mathe. ____________

2 At what time do you have the following subjects? Write a sentence for each.

1 Ich habe Englisch um neun Uhr zehn.  09:10

2 ____________  10:05

3 ____________  11:15

4 ____________  12:10

5 ____________  13:20

6 ____________  14:15

um acht Uhr = at 8 o'clock

3 Look at the timetable in exercise 1 and describe one school day. Try to add interest to your sentences by giving opinions about some subjects.

Example: Am Montag um acht Uhr fünfzehn habe ich Mathe. Ich mag Mathe, weil es interessant ist.

Ich finde Mathe ...
= I find maths ...

3 Lehrer und Lehrerinnen (Seiten 80–81)

1 Write a description for each of the teachers.

1 Mein Sportlehrer heißt Herr Huber.
Er ist cool, aber sehr unpünktlich.

2 ______________________________
____

3 ______________________________
____

4 ______________________________
____

Use some qualifiers in your descriptions: *sehr, zu, ziemlich, ein bisschen, nicht*

2 Complete the text by writing the correct word from the cloud in each gap.

Mein ____________ an der Schule ist Geschichte, ____________ meine Geschichtelehrerin sehr lustig ist! Sie ____________ nur ein Haustier, aber ihr Haustier ist eine Schlange!

Am ____________ und am Freitag haben wir Kunst. Ich finde Kunst ziemlich langweilg, weil es schwierig ____________. Mein Kunstlehrer ____________ Herr Ackermann. ____________ Schwester ist auch Kunstlehrerin an meiner ____________! Sie heißt Frau Ackermann! Meine Sportlehrerin ist ____________ freundlich. Sie heißt Frau Krause und ____________ Lieblingssport ist Volleyball. Ich mag Sport, weil ich sehr ____________ bin.

heißt hat Mittwoch Lieblingsfach ist sehr Schule Seine sportlich weil ihr

3 Write the correct word for 'his' or 'her' in each sentence.

1 ____________ Bruder lernt Hindi. (his)
2 ____________ Schwester ist Lehrerin. (her)
3 ____________ Hobby ist Gitarre spielen. (his)
4 ____________ Lieblingsfach ist Kunst. (her)
5 ____________ Schuluniform ist fantastisch. (his)
6 ____________ Bruder ist 19 Jahre alt. (her)

Grammatik
sein = his **ihr** = her (for masculine and neuter nouns)
seine = his **ihre** = her (for feminine nouns)
Check the gender of the noun if you are unsure.

4 Im Klassenzimmer (Seiten 82–83)

1 **Draw a simple picture to show where each of these things is.**

1 Der Musiklehrer ist im Klassenzimmer.
2 Das Buch ist neben dem Computer.
3 Das Poster ist an der Wand.
4 Der Stuhl ist auf dem Tisch und neben der Tür.

1	2	3	4

2 **What is there in the classroom? Start each sentence with *Es gibt* (there is/there are). Write the numbers as words.**

12  Es gibt zwölf Tische im Klassenzimmer.

6  ____________________

24  ____________________

2 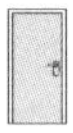 ____________________

4 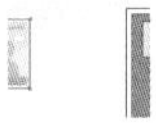 ____________________

5  ____________________

! Look at the vocabulary on page 47 for the plurals of the nouns.

3 **Answer the questions using the information in the pictures.**

@peta_ush Darfst du dein Handy in der Schule benutzen?

____

@tara_winkel Darfst du im Klassenzimmer schnell laufen?

____

@e_atch Darfst du in der Pause Musik hören?

____

@janet_mc Darfst du dein Handy in der Mittagspause benutzen?

____

! ich darf du darfst er/sie/es darf

Mein Lieblingstag (Seiten 84–85)

1 Most of the verbs you've seen end in *–en* in the infinitive. Write the infinitive form of each verb in the table. Then try to work out its meaning from the context.

If the context doesn't help you, use a German–English dictionary.

verb	infinitive	meaning in English
Er **geht** in die Schule.	*gehen*	*to go, to walk*
Er **kauft** ein Auto.		
Er **steht** auf dem Tisch.		
Warum **redest** du so schnell?		
Ich **wasche** meinen Hund.		
Ich **nehme** das Buch.		

2 Guess the meaning of these compound nouns by separating out the words. Look up the compound nouns in a dictionary to find their gender and meaning.

The second word in each compound noun gives the gender.

compound noun	word 1	word 2	gender	meaning
Fußballfeld	*Fußball*		*das*	
Arbeitstag				
Sporthalle				
Klassenarbeit				
Lehrerzimmer				

3 Now write a short German sentence using each compound noun from exercise 2.

1 *Das Fußballfeld ist sehr grün und …* ______

2 ______

3 ______

4 ______

5 ______

Wiederholung 1

1 Mimi's description of her school day is in the wrong time order! Number the sentences 1–6 in the correct order of time.

- ☐ Ich habe um dreizehn Uhr fünfundzwanzig Musik.
- ☐ Die Pause beginnt um elf Uhr zehn.
- ☐ Die erste Stunde beginnt um acht Uhr vierzig.
- ☐ Der Bus kommt um fünfzehn Uhr siebenundvierzig.
- ☐ Ich komme um sechzehn Uhr dreißig nach Hause.
- ☐ Wir haben Mathe um elf Uhr fünfundzwanzig.

2 The school is running 20 minutes late today. Rewrite each of the six sentences in exercise 1 with the time that each activity begins today.

3 Complete the sentences by writing the correct possessive pronoun in each gap.

> **!** **sein** = his (for masculine and neuter nouns) **seine** = his (for feminine nouns)
> **ihr** = her (for masculine and neuter nouns) **ihre** = her (for feminine nouns)

1. ________ Bruder heißt Pawel und ________ Schwester heißt Aga.
2. ________ Lieblingssport ist Eishockey.
3. ________ Katze ist braun, aber ________ Hund ist weiß.
4. ________ Schule ist in Hannover.

5. ________ Lieblingssport ist Reiten und ________ Lieblingsfach ist Mathe.
6. ________ Computer ist neu.
7. ________ Erdkundelehrerin ist sehr streng.
8. ________ Mutter wohnt in Salzburg, aber ________ Vater wohnt in Wien.

4 Describe where each of the items is located in the classroom.

1. Der Computer *ist auf dem Tisch.*
2. Das Poster ________
3. Das Whiteboard ________
4. Der Lehrer ________
5. Der Stuhl ________
6. Die Spinne ________

Wiederholung 2

1 Read the texts. Use your knowledge of vocabulary to help you to find these new phrases. Write each German phrase next to the English.

1 My name is ____________________
2 her favourite artist ____________________
3 unfortunately ____________________
4 My brother also goes ____________________
5 an indoor pool ____________________
6 a pot plant ____________________

Hallo! Mein Name ist **Maik** und ich wohne in München, in Deutschland. Meine Schule heißt Mathias Brauer Gymnasium und ich finde sie toll. An meiner Schule lerne ich sehr gern Englisch und Geschichte, aber mein Lieblingsfach ist Kunst. Ich mag Kunst, weil ich total kreativ bin. Ich finde meine Kunstlehrerin auch sehr nett. Sie heißt Frau Weber und ihr Lieblingskünstler ist Dürer.

Ich mag nicht Sport, weil ich nicht sehr sportlich bin. Leider habe ich am Montag und auch am Mittwoch Sport. Morgen spielen wir Tennis. Das finde ich nicht so schlecht.

lernen = to learn

Hallo Leute! Ich heiße **Sabine** und ich wohne in Zürich, in der Schweiz. Meine Schule ist sehr groß. Mein Bruder geht auch auf meine Schule.

Mein Lieblingsfach ist Musik und dieses Fach haben wir am Dienstag in der zweiten Stunde und auch am Donnerstag in der vierten Stunde. Sport mag ich auch, weil der Sportlehrer total lustig ist. Sein Lieblingssport ist Schwimmen und wir haben ein Hallenbad in der Schule. Wir haben Sport am Mittwoch in der fünften Stunde und auch am Freitag in der zweiten Stunde.

Mein Klassenzimmer ist sehr schön. Wir haben zehn Computer, ein Whiteboard neben der Tür, viele Poster an der Wand und eine Topfpflanze am Fenster!

2 Answer the questions about the texts in exercise 1. Write complete sentences in German for your answers.

1 Wie heißt Maiks Schule? ____________________
2 Was mag Maik? ____________________
3 Was lernt Maik nicht gern? ____________________
4 Wann hat Maik Sport? ____________________
5 Wo ist Zürich? ____________________
6 Was hat Sabine am Donnerstag in der vierten Stunde? ____________________
7 Warum mag Sabine Sport? ____________________
8 Wo ist die Topfpflanze? ____________________

Grammatik (Seiten 90–91)

1 Answer the questions in full sentences, using *weil* and the reason given.

1 Warum magst du Kunst? (it's creative)

Ich mag Kunst, weil es kreativ ist.

2 Warum magst du Englisch? (it's interesting)

______

3 Warum spielst du Tennis? (I'm sporty)

______

4 Warum hasst du Sport? (it's difficult)

______

5 Warum findest du Erdkunde toll? (it's easy)

______

2 Put the words in the right order to make sentences.

Remember the 'verb in second place' rule.

1 der in Geschichte dritten wir Stunde haben

______

2 habe Pause ich nach der Kunst ______

3 Fußball spiele heute ich ______

4 gibt Klassenzimmer Computer und viele einen es im Poster

______

5 Montag ich vierten Stunde habe in am der Mathe

______

3 Write the following school rules in sentences in German.

Example: Man darf am Montag …

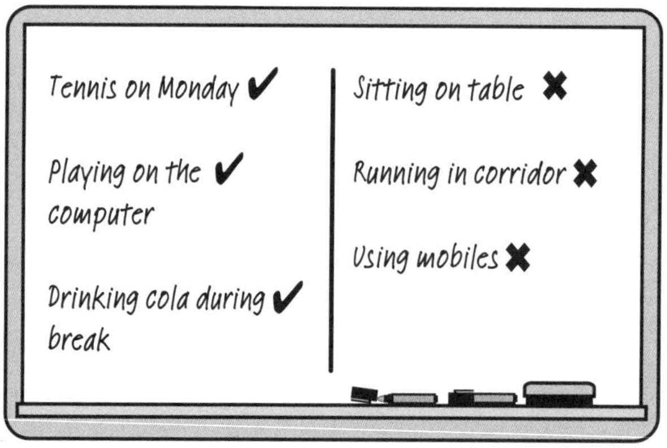

Man darf is often used to mean 'you/we are allowed to'.

Remember to use the correct preposition and the correct word for 'the' after it.

Mein Fortschritt

1 Record your levels for *Kapitel* 4.

2 Look at the level descriptors on pages 59–60 and set your targets for *Kapitel* 5.

3 Fill in what you need to do to achieve these targets.

Listening 	I have reached Level _____ in **Listening**. In *Kapitel* 5, I want to reach Level _____ I need to ____________________ ____________________ ____________________ ____________________
Speaking  	I have reached Level _____ in **Speaking**. In *Kapitel* 5, I want to reach Level _____ I need to ____________________ ____________________ ____________________ ____________________
Reading 	I have reached Level _____ in **Reading**. In *Kapitel* 5, I want to reach Level _____ I need to ____________________ ____________________ ____________________ ____________________
Writing 	I have reached Level _____ in **Writing**. In *Kapitel* 5, I want to reach Level _____ I need to ____________________ ____________________ ____________________ ____________________

Schulfächer • School subjects

Deutsch	*German*
Englisch	*English*
Erdkunde	*geography*
Geschichte	*history*
Informatik	*ICT*
Kunst	*art*
Mathe	*maths*
Musik	*music*
Naturwissenschaften	*science*
Sport	*sport, PE*
Technik	*technology*
Theater	*drama*

Meinungen • Opinions

mein Lieblingsfach ist ...	*my favourite subject is ...*
ich mag ... (sehr)	*I like ... (a lot)*
ich liebe	*I love*
ich mag ... nicht	*I don't like ...*
ich hasse	*I hate*
gut	*good*
toll	*great*
furchtbar	*awful*
einfach	*easy*
schwierig	*difficult*
interessant	*interesting*
langweilig	*boring*
nützlich	*useful*
nutzlos	*useless*
faszinierend	*fascinating*
nervig	*irritating*
supercool	*really cool*
stinklangweilig	*dead boring*

Die Wochentage • The days of the week

Montag (Mo.)	*Monday*
Dienstag (Di.)	*Tuesday*
Mittwoch (Mi.)	*Wednesday*
Donnerstag (Do.)	*Thursday*
Freitag (Fr.)	*Friday*
Samstag (Sa.)	*Saturday*
Sonntag (So.)	*Sunday*
Was hast du am Montag?	*What do you have on Monday?*
Am Dienstag habe ich ...	*I have ... on Tuesday*
Am Sonntag haben wir keine Schule.	*We have no school on Sunday.*

Die Zeit • Time

Wann?	*When?*
Um wie viel Uhr?	*At what time?*
Um 8:30 Uhr (acht Uhr dreißig).	*At 8:30.*
Wie viel Uhr ist es?	*What time is it?*
Es ist 9:50 Uhr (neun Uhr fünfzig).	*It's 9:50.*
in der ersten Stunde	*in the first lesson*
vor der Pause	*before break*
nach der Mittagspause	*after the lunch break*

Eigenschaften • Characteristics

Er/Sie ist ...	*He/She is ...*
alt	*old*
fair	*fair*
freundlich	*friendly*
jung	*young*
launisch	*moody*
lustig	*funny*
nervig	*annoying*
streng	*strict*
unpünktlich	*unpunctual*

In der Schule • In school

die Lehrerin(-nen)	*teacher (female)*
die Deutsch-lehrerin(-nen)	*German teacher (female)*
der Lehrer(–)	*teacher (male)*
der Sportlehrer(–)	*sports teacher (male)*
Was gibt es?	*What is there?*
Es gibt einen/eine/ein ...	*There is a ...*
Es gibt viele ...	*There are lots of ...*
das Klassenzimmer(–)	*classroom*
der Tisch(-e)	*table*
der Stuhl(¨-e)	*chair*
der Computer(–)	*computer*
das Whiteboard(-s)	*whiteboard*
das Poster(–)	*poster*
das Fenster(–)	*window*
die Wand(¨-e)	*wall*
die Tür(-en)	*door*
der Korridor(-e)	*corridor*

Wo ist das? • Where is it?

in der Schule	*in the school*
im Klassenzimmer	*in the classroom*
im Korridor	*in the corridor*
an der Wand	*on the wall*
am Fenster	*by the window*
am Tisch	*at the table*
auf dem Tisch	*on the table*
neben der Tür	*near/next to the door*

Oft benutzte Wörter • High-frequency words

weil	*because*
sein/seine	*his*
ihr/ihre	*her*
zu	*too*
sehr	*very*
ziemlich	*quite, fairly*
ein bisschen	*a bit*
nicht	*not*
haben	*to have*
sein	*to be*
in	*in*
an	*at, by, on (wall)*
auf	*on (top of)*
neben	*near, next to*
heute	*today*
morgen	*tomorrow*
vor	*before*
nach	*after*

1 In der Stadt (Seiten 98–99)

1 Write sentences to say what there is and isn't in the town.

1 Es gibt hier ______________________________.
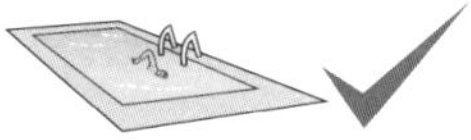

2 Hier gibt es ______________________________.
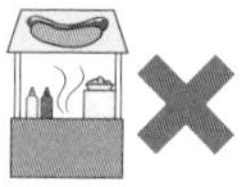

3 In der Stadt gibt es ______________________________.

4 Es gibt ______________________________ hier.

Grammatik
der→einen/keinen **die**→eine/keine **das**→ein/kein

2 Read the texts. Tick the things there are in each person's town and cross the things there aren't.

Monika: *Ich wohne in Celle. Meine Stadt ist nicht sehr groß. Es gibt hier ein Schloss und auch einen Marktplatz. Leider gibt es kein Schwimmbad und auch keine Kegelbahn.*

leider = unfortunately

Erik: *Die Touristen kommen gern nach Verden, weil es eine Kirche und auch einen Marktplatz gibt. Ein Schloss gibt es auch, aber leider gibt es kein Schwimmbad und keine Imbissstube.*

Aisha: *Ich wohne in Neustadt, in der Nähe vom Titisee. Neustadt ist ganz klein, aber sehr schön. Es gibt hier kein Schloss, keine Kegelbahn und leider auch kein Kino. Wir haben aber einen Bahnhof, eine Kirche und auch einen alten Marktplatz. Wir haben kein Schwimmbad, aber man kann im Sommer im Titisee schwimmen!*

	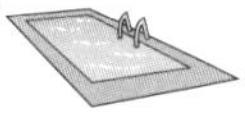		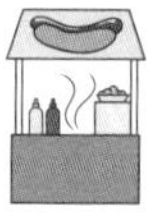	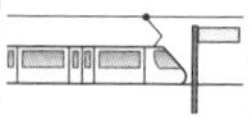				
Monika								
Erik								
Aisha								

3 Write two or three sentences about what there is to do where you live, as well as what there isn't. Use the texts in exercise 2 to help you.

2 Wir gehen einkaufen! (Seiten 100–101)

1 Write what the customers in the souvenir shop would like. Start your sentences with *Ich möchte*.

1 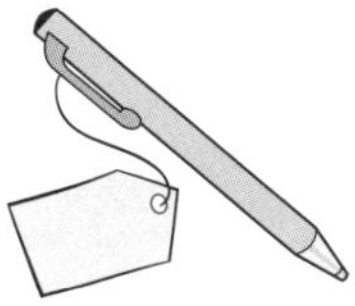
2 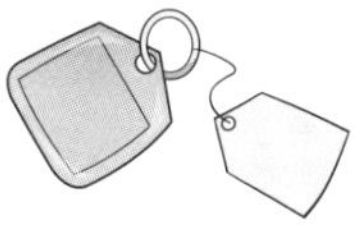
3 
4 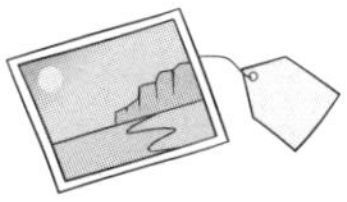
5 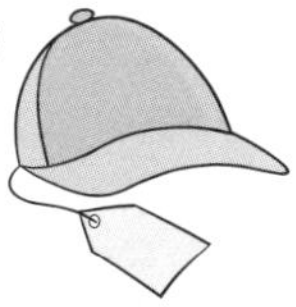
6 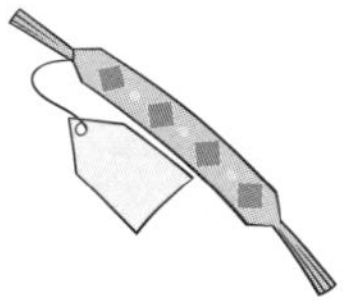
7 
8 

Look at the vocabulary on page 57 if you need to check which words to use.

1 *Ich möchte einen Kuli.*
2 ______________________
3 ______________________
4 ______________________
5 ______________________
6 ______________________
7 ______________________
8 ______________________

2 Complete the dialogue with words from the cloud below. Then number the lines of the conversation in the correct order 1–11.

☐ Guten Tag! ______________ ich dir helfen?
☐ Welche ______________ ? Wir haben blau, rot oder schwarz.
☐ Ja, klar! Dieser ______________ , zum Beispiel, kostet nur €18,95.
☐ Super!
☐ Danke. Auf ______________ .
☐ Sonst noch etwas?
☐ Alles ______________ kostet das €38,95.
☐ Guten Tag! Ich möchte ein Souvenir ______________ , vielleicht ein Kuscheltier. Haben Sie ______________ ?
☐ Bitte sehr.
☐ Ja. Ich möchte ein ______________ für meine Schwester.
☐ Schwarz, bitte. Wie viel ______________ das?

zusammen Elefant Kuscheltiere Wiedersehen Kann kostet Fußballtrikot kaufen Farbe

3 Mmm, lecker! (Seiten 102–103)

1 Write four short conversations between hungry customers and the owner of the snack stand. The price of each individual item is shown: don't forget to add up the total price.

1

× 1
drei Euro zehn

× 1
zwei Euro fünfunddreißig

2

× 2
zwei Euro sechzig

× 2
zwei Euro fünfundzwanzig

3

× 3
drei Euro zwanzig

× 1
ein Euro neunzig

4

× 4
drei Euro fünfundneunzig

× 1
zwei Euro zehn

Ich möchte .../Ich hätte gern ...	I'd like ...
Das kostet alles zusammen ...	All together that costs ...

1 *Guten Tag! Ich möchte einmal Hamburger und einmal Bratwurst, bitte.*
Das kostet alles zusammen € ...

2 ______________________________

____

3 ______________________________

____

4 ______________________________

____

2 Write a short review of the menu, saying what there is to eat and drink and what you do and don't like.

Hamburger

Bratwurst

Pommes
Salat
Eis
Tee
Cola
Mineralwasser

Man kann ... trinken/essen.	You can eat/drink ...
Ich esse/trinke gern ...	I like eating/drinking ...
Ich esse/trinke nicht gern ...	I don't like eating/drinking ...
Ich mag ...	I like ....
Ich mag nicht ...	I don't like .....

____

____

____

4 In den Sommerferien (Seiten 104–105)

1 **Circle the correct option to complete each sentence from the choices given. Then write the missing words in the gaps.**

1 Ich ______________ im See baden.

a wirst **b** werden **c** werde

2 Wir werden im ______________ schwimmen.

a Meer **b** windsurfen **c** Bratwurst

3 ______________ du nach Innsbruck fahren?

a Wird **b** Wirst **c** Bist

4 Er ______________ nicht nach Hannover ______________ .

a werden; fahre **b** kann; fährt **c** wird; fahren

5 Tobi ______________ in den ______________ nach Portugal fahren.

a werde; Park **b** wird; Bahnhof **c** wird; Sommerferien

6 Wohin ______________ wir ______________ ?

a werden; gehen **b** kann; gehen **c** darf; fahren

2 **Read the sentences and write the correct words from the cloud in the gaps. There are more words than you need.**

1 Ich werde eine Kappe ______________ meinen Vater kaufen.

2 Ich ______________ ein Trikot kaufen.

3 In den ______________ fahren wir nach Rom.

4 Es ______________ ein Schwimmbad und ein Kino in Walsrode.

5 Wir ______________ nach Magdeburg fahren.

6 Ich möchte in den Bergen ______________ gehen.

für
gibt
möchte
nächste Woche
Sommerferien
wandern
werde
werden

3 **Write about your plans for the summer holidays. Use the questions and illustrations to help you.**

- Wohin wirst du fahren?

- Wer kommt mit?

- Was wirst du dort machen?

- Was wird dein Bruder / deine Schwester machen

- Wirst du Souvenirs kaufen?

1 **Rewrite each sentence. Swap the adjective in bold for an alternative adjective with a similar meaning.**

1 Das Mozart Museum ist **faszinierend**. ______

2 Der Marktplatz ist **historisch**. ______

3 Das Schwimmbad ist **modern**.

______

4 Die Kegelbahn ist **toll**. ______

2 **Join up the sentence halves to describe a trip to Vienna.**

1	In den Sommerferien werde	a	Tage in Wien bleiben.
2	Dort gibt es einen	b	ich nach Wien fahren.
3	Am Montag kann	c	Wien fantastisch.
4	Ich finde	d	Marktplatz, aber keinen See.
5	Wir werden vier	e	man das Mozart Museum besuchen.

Now rewrite the sentences, varying the sentence structure. Remember that in German you always need the verb as the second idea.

Example: **1** Ich werde in den Sommerferien ...

3 **Read the text about Hahndorf. Try to work out what the words in bold mean from the context. If you can't work out the meanings, look them up in a dictionary.**

Hahndorf ist eine kleine Stadt in Südaustralien, in der Nähe von Adelaide. Es gibt dort deutsche **Einwanderer**. Die Stadt ist klein, aber **fein**! Hahndorf ist toll für Kinder und auch für **Erwachsene**. Dort gibt es viele deutsche Restaurants und Cafés. Am Mittwoch und am Sonntag gibt es immer einen Markt auf dem Marktplatz. Man kann hier Schokolade, **Kuchen** und **Kleidung** kaufen. **Wein** aus der Region kann man auch dort trinken. Ich werde **nächstes Jahr** mit meiner Schule nach Hahndorf fahren.

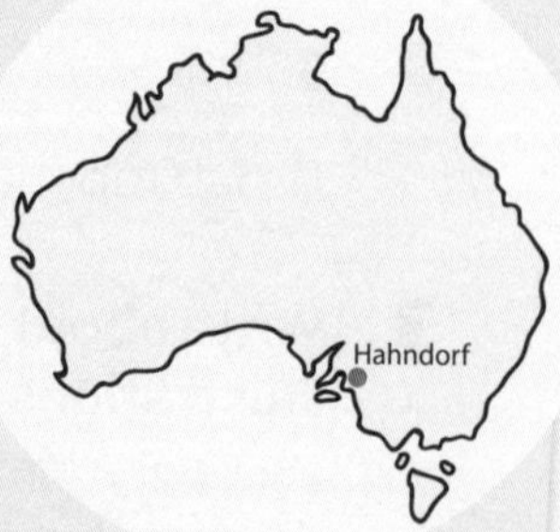

4 **Write about a city or town of your choice. Adapt some of the words and phrases from the text in exercise 3.**

Remember to include: the future tense, opinions, linking words, qualifiers, frequency expressions and inverted word order.

Wiederholung 1

1 Decide which souvenir you would buy for each person and write the price in words.

Grammatik

der → er　　*die → sie*　　*das → es*

Remember, *der* changes to *den* for masculine nouns.

1 MeineMutter: *Ich werde die Tasse für meine Mutter kaufen. Sie kostet sieben Euro fünfundfünfzig.*

2 Onkel Karl: ______________________

3 Meine Schwester: ______________________

4 Meine Freundin: ______________________

5 Frau Roberts: ______________________

2 Peter is in the tourist office in Munich. Read the dialogue, then answer the questions in full German sentences.

Tourist guide: Guten Tag! Willkommen in München!

Peter: Guten Tag! Danke schön! Was gibt es hier in München?

Tourist guide: Hier gibt es viel zu tun! Man kann in München alles sehen!

Peter: Gibt es hier einen Marktplatz?

Tourist guide: Natürlich! Er heißt Marienplatz. Er ist sehr groß und total schön.

Peter: Wunderbar! Und kann man in München Ski fahren?

Tourist guide: Also ... nicht direkt in München, aber in der Nähe von hier kann man sehr gut Ski fahren.

Peter: Super. Und gibt es hier ein gutes Restaurant? Ich möchte gern Pizza essen.

Tourist guide: Ja, das gibt es! Es heißt *Robertos*. Dort kann man gut Pizza essen.

Peter: Vielen Dank. Ich werde im Restaurant *Robertos* essen. Auf Wiedersehen!

1 Was kann man in München machen?
2 Wie heißt der Marktplatz?
3 Wie ist er?
4 Wo kann man Ski fahren?
5 Was möchte Peter essen?
6 Was ist *Robertos*?

Wiederholung 2

1 **Rewrite the sentences in the future tense. Identify the subject to help you change the form of *werden*.**

1 Wir tauchen im Meer. Wir werden im Meer tauchen.

2 Wir baden im See. ____________________

3 Ich gehe an den Strand. ____________________

4 Lena und Michael klettern am Samstag in den Bergen.

____

5 Er kauft ein Kuscheltier für seine kleine Schwester.

____

6 Kaufst du eine Kappe als Souvenir? ____________________

7 Wir gehen am Wochenende mit meinen Freunden einkaufen.

____

2 **Read the postcard and answer the questions in full German sentences.**

Liebe Oma und Lieber Opa!

Hallo aus Mallorca in Spanien! Wir bleiben zwei Wochen hier, weil wir Sommerferien haben. Es gibt hier alles – einen Wasserpark, ein Schloss und auch einen Markt. Jeden Tag schwimmen wir im Meer. Im Hotel gibt es ein Schwimmbad und wir schwimmen auch hier. Man kann windsurfen und auch tauchen. Mallorca ist auch für das Essen sehr bekannt.

Nächste Woche werden wir in den Bergen klettern. Ich möchte auch segeln. Ich werde auch Souvenirs kaufen!

Alles Liebe,

Tamika

1 Warum ist Tamika in Spanien? ____________________

2 Was gibt es in Mallorca? ____________________

3 Was kann man machen? ____________________

4 Ist Mallorca bekannt für das Museum? ____________________

5 Was wird Tamika nächste Woche machen? ____________________

3 **Write four true/false statements in English about the text in exercise 2. Then ask a friend to write 'True' or 'False' next to each statement.**

Example: The postcard is to Tamika's parents. False

Grammatik (Seiten 112–113)

1 Rewrite the sentences to make them negative.

Use *keinen/keine/kein* to say what there is or isn't. Use *nicht* to say what you can't or don't like doing.

1 Es gibt in Düsseldorf einen Marktplatz.

____

2 Er mag Wasserball.

____

3 Beni kann Fußball spielen, weil er einen Ball hat.

____

4 In der Stadt gibt es ein Kino und auch eine Kirche.

____

5 Man darf hier schwimmen. ______________________________

2 Write the different forms of *möchten* in the table.

ich		wir	
du		ihr	
er/sie/es		Sie	
		sie	

möchten
möchte
möchten
möchtest
möchte
möchtet
möchten

Complete the sentences by writing the correct form of *möchten* in each gap. Then translate the sentences into English.

1 ______________ du ein Schokoladeneis?

2 Nein, aber ich ______________ gern ein Vanilleeis.

3 Anne ______________ nach Kapstadt in Südafrika fahren.

4 ______________ ihr auch nach Windhuk in Namibia fahren?

5 Wir ______________ zweimal Salat und zweimal Mineralwasser, bitte.

6 Frau Winkelmann, ______________ Sie eine Tasse Tee?

3 Fill in the gaps to complete the different forms of *werden*.

ich __e__de

du w__r__t

er/sie/es __ir__

wir we__ de__

ihr __er__e__

Sie/sie w__r__en

4 Write sentences about what you and your family/friends will do on your next holiday.

Example: Ich werde jeden Tag in Frankreich wandern. Mein Bruder ... /Steffi ...

Jahresbilanz

Record your levels for *Kapitel* 5.

Listening	I have reached Level ______ in **Listening**.
Speaking	I have reached Level ______ in **Speaking**.
Reading	I have reached Level ______ in **Reading**.
Writing	I have reached Level ______ in **Writing**.

Look back through your workbook and note down the level you achieved in each skill by the end of each *Kapitel*.

	Listening	**Speaking**	**Reading**	**Writing**
1 Meine Welt und ich				
2 Familie und Tiere				
3 Freizeit – juhu!				
4 Schule ist klasse!				
5 Gute Reise!				

You now have a record of your progress in German for the whole year.

In der Stadt • In town

Es gibt ...	*There is ... / There are ...*
Es gibt ein/eine/einen ...	*There is/are a ...*
Es gibt kein/keine/keinen ...	*There isn't/aren't ...*
in der Nähe von ...	*near to*
in der Nähe ...	*nearby*
der Bahnhof(¨-e)	*railway station(s)*
der Imbiss(-e)/die Imbissstube(-n)	*snack stand(s)*
die Kegelbahn(-en)	*bowling alley(s)*
das Kino(-s)	*cinema(s)*
die Kirche(-n)	*church(es)*
der Marktplatz(¨-e)	*market square(s)*
der Park(-s)	*park(s)*
das Schloss(¨-er)	*castle(s)*
das Schwimmbad(¨-er)	*swimming pool(s)*
die Eisbahn(-en)	*ice rink(s)*
der Fischmarkt(¨-e)	*fish market(s)*
das Kindertheater(-)	*children's theatre(s)*
der Radweg(-e)	*cycle path(s)*
das Sportzentrum (die Sportzentren)	*sports centre (sports centres)*
der Stadtpark(-s)	*city/town park(s)*
der Wasserpark(-s)	*water park(s)*

Verkaufsgespräch • Sales conversation

Ich gehe einkaufen.	*I am going shopping.*
Ich möchte ...	*I would like ...*
Ich möchte ... kaufen.	*I would like to buy ...*
Haben Sie ...?	*Do you have ...?*
Kann ich dir helfen?	*Can I help you?*
Sonst noch etwas?	*Anything else?*
alles zusammen	*all together*

Souvenirs • Souvenirs

der Aufkleber	*sticker*
das Freundschaftsband	*friendship bracelet*
die Kappe	*(baseball) cap*
der Kuli	*biro*
das Kuscheltier	*cuddly toy*
die Postkarte	*postcard*
der Schlüsselanhänger	*key ring*
die Tasse	*mug/cup*
das Trikot	*(football) shirt*
Wie viel kostet ...?	*How much does ... cost?*
Wie viel kostet das?	*How much does it cost?*
Es kostet €16.	*It costs 16 Euros.*

Snacks und Getränke kaufen • Buying snacks and drinks

die Bratwurst	*fried sausage*
der Hamburger	*hamburger*
die Pizza	*pizza*
die Pommes	*chips*
der Salat	*salad*
das Eis	*ice cream*
die Cola	*cola*
das Mineralwasser	*mineral water*
der Tee	*tea*
das Fleisch	*meat*
der Ketchup	*ketchup*
die Mayo(nnaise)/Majonäse	*mayo(nnaise)*
der Senf	*mustard*
Ich möchte einmal/zweimal/dreimal ...	*I would like one/two/three ...*
Ich hätte gern ...	*I would like ...*
Das macht €8.	*That's €8.*
Ich esse ... gern.	*I like eating ... .*
Ich trinke ... gern.	*I like drinking ... .*

Wörter

In den Sommerferien • *During the summer holidays*

Was wirst du machen?	*What will you do?*
Ich werde ...	*I will ...*
Wir werden ...	*We will ...*
klettern	*climb*
im Meer schwimmen	*swim in the sea*
rodeln	*toboggan*
im See baden	*bathe in the lake*
segeln	*sail*
an den Strand gehen	*go to the beach*
tauchen	*dive*
wandern	*hike*
windsurfen	*windsurf*
Was kann man dort machen?	*What can you do there?*
Man kann ... besuchen.	*'One'/People/ You can visit ...*
Die Stadt ist bekannt für ...	*The town is well known for ...*
Ich werde (eine Woche) bleiben.	*I will stay (for a week).*

Oft benutzte Wörter • *High-frequency words*

am Montag	*on Monday*
am Dienstag	*on Tuesday*
am Mittwoch	*on Wednesday*
am Donnerstag	*on Thursday*
am Freitag	*on Friday*
am Wochenende	*at the weekend*
sehr	*very*
nicht sehr	*not very*
ziemlich	*quite*
immer	*always*
nicht immer	*not always*
oft	*often*
nicht oft	*not often*
nie	*never*
alles	*everything*
dort	*there*
teuer	*expensive*

Listening

Level 1	I can understand some familiar spoken words and phrases.
Level 2	I can understand a range of familiar spoken phrases.
Level 3	I can understand the main points of short spoken passages and note people's answers to questions.
Level 4	I can understand the main points of spoken passages and some of the detail.
Level 5	I can understand the main points and opinions in spoken passages about different topics. I can recognise if people are speaking about the future **OR** the past as well as the present.

Speaking

Level 1	I can say single words and short phrases.
Level 2	I can answer simple questions and use set phrases.
Level 3	I can ask questions and use short phrases to answer questions about myself.
Level 4	I can take part in conversations. I can express my opinions. I can use grammar to change phrases to say something new.
Level 5	I can give short talks, in which I express my opinions. I can take part in conversations giving information, opinions and reasons. I can speak about the future **OR** the past as well as the present.

Level descriptors

Reading

Level 1	I can understand familiar words and phrases.
Level 2	I can understand familiar phrases. I can read aloud familiar words and phrases. I can use a vocabulary list to check meanings.
Level 3	I can understand the main points and people's answers to questions in short written texts.
Level 4	I can understand the main points in short texts and some of the detail. Sometimes I can work out the meaning of new words.
Level 5	I can understand the main points and opinions in texts about different topics. I can recognise if the texts are about the future **OR** the past as well as the present.

Writing

Level 1	I can write or copy single words correctly.
Level 2	I can copy short sentences correctly and write some words from memory.
Level 3	I can answer questions about myself. I can write short phrases from memory. I can write short sentences with help.
Level 4	I can write short texts on familiar topics. I can use grammar to change phrases to write something new.
Level 5	I can write short texts on a range of familiar topics. I can write about the future **OR** the past as well as the present.

Notes

Notes

Published by Pearson Education Limited, Edinburgh Gate, Harlow, Essex, CM20 2JE.

www.pearsonschoolsandfecolleges.co.uk

Edited by Melanie Birdsall
Designed by Kamae Design

Illustrated by Caron at KJA Artists and Lisa Hunt

First published 2013

2022
17

British Library Cataloguing in Publication Data
A catalogue record for this book is available from the British Library

ISBN 978 1 447 94654 0

Printed in Great Britain by Bell and Bain Ltd, Glasgow

Acknowledgements

We would like to thank Melissa Weir, Angelika Libera, Janet Soame and Frances Reynolds for their invaluable help in the development of this course.

Every effort has been made to contact copyright holders of material reproduced in this book. Any omissions will be rectified in subsequent printings if notice is given to the publishers.

www.pearsonschools.co.uk
myorders@pearson.com

T 0845 630 33 33
F 0845 630 77 77

ISBN 978-1-4479-4654-0

Stimmt! 1

Übungsheft B

Malcolm Pacey

1 Hallo! (Seiten 8–9)

1 **Two of the words in each set have a sound that is the same. Circle the word with a different sound from the other two.**

1	*Schlange*	*Porsche*	*Buch*
2	*Bär*	*Löwe*	*Röntgenbild*
3	*Wildwassersport*	*Auf Wiedersehen*	*Tür*
4	*Biene*	*heiße*	*Eis*

2 **Join up the sentence halves.**

1 Gut, danke. Und
2 Auf
3 Ich heiße
4 Hallo! Wie heißt
5 Ich heiße Nadia. Wie
6 Nicht

a Wiedersehen.
b Ben. Wie heißt du?
c geht's, Ben?
d du?
e schlecht.
f dir?

3 **Write the sentences from exercise 2 in the correct order for the conversation. Then translate them into English.**

1 ______________________ ______________________
2 ______________________ ______________________
3 ______________________ ______________________
4 ______________________ ______________________
5 Nicht schlecht. ______________________ Not bad. ______________________
6 ______________________ ______________________

4 **Unscramble the inventions. Look at the definite article (word for 'the') for each word. Then write each invention with the indefinite article (word for 'a').**

1 sad ngbönReltid das … ______________________ ein … ______________________
2 erd reelmiDtoos ______________________ ______________________
3 sda toF3rMmPa- ______________________ ______________________
4 sad PeuAsotrcoh ______________________ ______________________
5 ied sAMrkdadiae ______________________ ______________________

2 Eins, zwei, drei … (Seiten 10–11)

1 **The bank has sent texts to customers with their coded PIN numbers. Solve the maths problems in German to work out the PINs. Then write each customer's new PIN below the phone.**

1

Meine Bank

zehn – acht = zwei
vier + drei = sieben
zwei + drei = ______
fünf + eins = ______

2 7 _ _

2

Meine Bank

sechs + zwei = ______
zehn – neun = ______
sieben – drei = ______
eins + vier = ______

_ _ _ _

3

Meine Bank

sieben – vier = ______
acht + eins = ______
drei + sechs = ______
fünf + zwei = ______

_ _ _ _

2 **Write the winning lottery numbers in words.**

1 13 ______
2 11 ______
3 16 ______
4 18 ______
5 12 ______
6 17 ______

3 **Write two sentences for each speaker. Give the speaker's age and the age of his/her friend.**

er ist = he is
sie ist = she is

1

Ich bin dreizehn Jahre alt.
Sie ist zwölf Jahre alt.

2

______
______

3

______
______

3 Ich wohne in Deutschland (Seiten 12–13)

1 Read the dialogue and complete the table with the correct forms of each verb.

Melanie: Hallo! Ich heiße Melanie. Wie heißt du?
Marco: Ich heiße Marco. Ich wohne in Straubing. Wo wohnst du?
Melanie: Ich wohne in Braunschweig. Wie alt bist du?
Marco: Ich bin zwölf Jahre alt. Wer ist das?
Melanie: Sie heißt Jessie. Sie wohnt in Leipzig und ist dreizehn Jahre alt.

wer = who

	heißen (to be called)	**wohnen** (to live)	**sein** (to be)
ich (I)		*wohne*	
du (you)			*bist*
er/sie/es (he/she/it)	*heißt*		

2 Write the missing word in each sentence and complete the crossword.

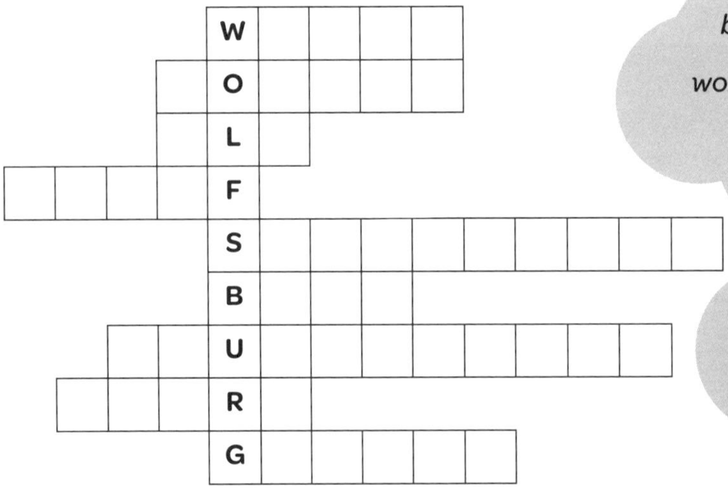

bist *zwölf* *wohne* *wohnst* *Jahre* *Schottland* *Deutschland* *geht's* *alt*

1 Ich __________ in Manchester.
2 Wo __________ du, Nick?
3 Wie __________ ist er?
4 Er ist __________ Jahre alt.
5 Glasgow ist in __________ .
6 Wie alt __________ du?
7 Ich wohne in Berlin. Das ist in __________ .
8 Ich bin elf __________ alt.
9 Wie __________ ?

3 Research why the city of Wolfsburg is important to Germany.

4 Meine Welt ist wunderbar! (Seiten 14–15)

1 The printer has made four mistakes labelling the illustrations. Write *richtig* or *falsch* under each caption.

1 
Ich bin musikalisch.

____

2 
Ich bin sehr launisch.

____

3 
Ich bin ziemlich freundlich.

____

4 
Ich bin kreativ.

____

5 
Ich bin laut.

____

6 
Ich bin lustig.

____

2 Rewrite the false captions from exercise 1, correcting them so that they are true.

____

____

____

____

faul
lustig
musikalisch
sportlich

3 Separate out the words to form three sentences.

meinelieblingsfußballmannschaftistbayernmünchen

meinlieblingssportisttennis

meinelieblingszahlistsieben

Remember that each sentence must start with a capital letter. Also, remember that nouns start with a capital letter.

1 ______________________________

2 ______________________________

3 ______________________________

4 Write a sentence about your favourite …

1 football team: ______________________________

2 sport: ______________________________

3 number: ______________________________

5 Meine Sachen (Seiten 16–17)

1 **Write the German question word under its English translation.**

Who?	What?	How?	Where?	Where from?

Wie? Was? Wo? Woher? Wer?

2 **Write the correct question word in each question. You may use each word more than once.**

1 ______________ bist du? Sportlich?

2 ______________ wohnt Shiva?

3 ______________ heißt du?

4 ______________ kommst du?

5 ______________ ist das? Ist das Max?

6 ______________ alt ist Michael?

7 ______________ ist Hannover? *Hannover ist in Deutschland!*

8 ______________ ist deine Lieblingsmusik?

3 **Read the paragraph below. Pretend that you're Gabi, and answer each question in a complete German sentence.**

Hallo! Ich heiße Gabi und ich bin vierzehn Jahre alt. Ich wohne in Kiel, in Deutschland, aber ich komme aus Swansea. Das ist in Wales. Wie bin ich? Ich bin sportlich, lustig und auch sehr laut! Mein Lieblingsmonat ist Dezember und meine Lieblingssendung ist ‚Die Simpsons'. Ich habe ein iPad und auch einen Computer. Tschüs!

1 Wie heißt du? ______________________________

2 Wo wohnst du? ______________________________

3 Woher kommst du? ______________________________

4 Wie bist du? ______________________________

5 Wie heißt deine Lieblingssendung? ______________________________

6 Was hast du? ______________________________

1 Complete the table with the correct words.

	the	a	my	your
masculine: Sport				
feminine: Musik				
neuter: Auto				

2 Write each sentence or question in German. Tick the boxes when you've checked each part of your work.

Part of writing accurately in any language is going back over your work to check that there aren't any mistakes. Get into the habit now and watch both your English and German improve!

1 I'm called Osman.

____

2 I live in Germany.

____

3 I'm quite friendly and also creative.

____

____

4 I have a mobile phone.

____

5 Where do you live?

____

- ☐ Spelling of key phonics sound 'ei'
- ☐ Name has a capital
- ☐ Spelling of key phonics sound 'eu'
- ☐ Full stop at the end
- ☐ Check the qualifier
- ☐ Check the connective
- ☐ Capital on the noun
- ☐ Right word for 'a'
- ☐ Correct question word
- ☐ Verb in second position

3 Write a short paragraph about yourself. Use the sentences in exercise 2 as prompts. Check your work against the checklist below.

☐ genders ☐ qualifiers ☐ connectives ☐ verbs
☐ capital letters ☐ spelling ☐ question words

____

____

Wiederholung 1

1 Fill in the gaps by writing the German for the words in brackets.

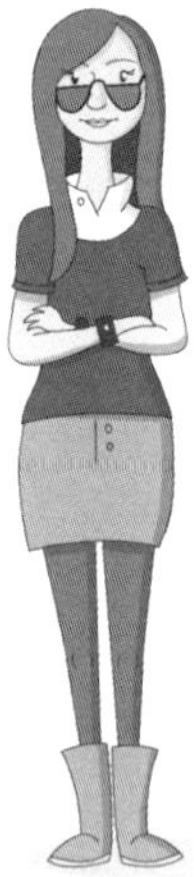

Hallo! Ich __________ (am called) Marie und ich __________ (live) in Walsrode. Das ist in __________ (Germany). Ich bin fünfzehn __________ (years) alt. Ich bin __________ (very) sportlich und __________ (quite) intelligent, __________ (but) ich bin __________ (also) faul. Mein __________ (favourite sport) ist Hockey und __________ (my) Lieblingsmusik ist Pop. Ich __________ (have) einen Vogel aus Amerika. Er ist __________ (very) freundlich, aber __________ (not) laut!

2 Crack the code and write the sentences correctly.

a 18/24/19 4/12/19/13/22 18/13 20/28/7/7/18/13/20/22/13

Ich wohne in Göttingen.

b 22/9 18/8/7 20/26/13/1 21/9/22/6/13/23/15/18/24/19

____

ä = 27 ü = 29
ö = 28 ß = 30

c 14/22/18/13/22 15/18/22/25/15/18/13/20/8/14/6/8/18/16 18/8/7 14/12/1/26/9/7

____

____

3 Make up a coded sentence in German for a classmate to solve. Don't forget to provide a key.

4 Write the questions you would ask to get these answers.

1 *Wie heißt du?*

Ich heiße Elaine.

2 __________

Mein Lieblingssport ist Tennis.

3 __________

Sami ist musikalisch und intelligent, aber sehr launisch.

4 __________

Alwin ist vierzehn Jahre alt.

Wiederholung 2

1 **Read the website entries.**

Ich heiße **Franzi** und suche Freunde aus England, Irland oder Nordirland. Ich habe eine Schlange zu Hause! Sie ist sechs Jahre alt. Ich wohne in Wien. Das ist in Österreich. Ich bin sehr kreativ und intelligent! Schreib mir bitte!

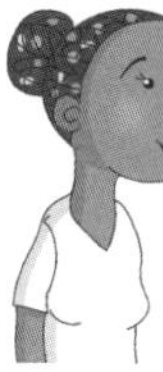

Hallo! Ich heiße **Hannah** und ich wohne in London, in England. Ich lerne Deutsch. Ich suche Freunde aus Deutschland, Österreich und auch aus der Schweiz. Ich bin sportlich und spiele Fußball und auch Tennis, aber ich bin sehr faul! Meine Lieblingsmusik ist Rock. Schreib mir!

Mein Name ist **Felix** und ich wohne in der Schweiz, aber ich komme aus Dortmund in Deutschland. Zu Hause habe ich eine Wii und mein Lieblingsspiel ist FIFA. Meine Lieblingsfußballmannschaft ist Bayern-München. Ich suche Freunde aus Schottland und Wales.

Hi! Ich bin **Muhammad** und ich wohne in Cardiff. Das ist in Wales. Ich bin sechzehn Jahre alt. Meine Lieblingssache ist Technologie. Ich habe zu Hause einen Computer, ein Handy und auch ein iPad. Ich bin nicht sehr sportlich, aber sehr freundlich. Mein Lieblingsland ist Deutschland und ich suche dort Freunde.

Write the name of the person who ...

1 is looking for friends from Switzerland. Hannah

2 supports a football team. ____________

3 has a pet. ____________

4 is just looking for friends from Germany. ____________

5 lives in a different place from where they were born. ____________

6 does not particularly like sport. ____________

7 lives in Switzerland. ____________

suche = seek
Schreib mir (bitte)! = Write to me (please)!
dort = there

2 **Write your own profile for the website. Use as much German as you can from *Kapitel 1* to describe yourself.**

____

____

____

____

Grammatik (Seiten 22–23)

1 **Write a sentence using the correct German word for 'a' for each item.**

1  2  3  4  5 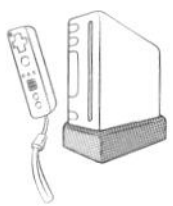 6  7  8 

1 Das ist ein Computer.
2 ____________________
3 ____________________
4 ____________________
5 ____________________
6 ____________________
7 ____________________
8 ____________________

die Gitarre | *das Handy*
der iPod | *der Computer*
das Skateboard | *das Keyboard*
der Fußball | *die Wii*

Grammatik
masculine – *ein*
feminine – *eine*
neuter – *ein*

2 **Circle the correct verb form to complete each sentence.**

1 Lukas **habe / hat / hast** einen Computer.
2 Ich **heiße / habe / hat** einen Vogel zu Hause.
3 Wo **bist / ist / wohnst** er?
4 Er **ist / komme / bin** musikalisch und sportlich.
5 Julia **bin / ist / wohnt** fünfzehn Jahre alt.
6 Wie alt **wohnst / bist / bin** du?
7 Wo **hast / bist / bin** ich?

Grammatik
You can use the pronouns *er* ('he') or *sie* ('she') instead of writing someone's name. Both need the *er/sie/es* form of the verb.

3 **Complete the table with the correct forms of each regular verb.**

wohnen (to live)	**kommen** (to come)	**heißen** (to be called)
ich *wohne*	ich	ich
du	du *kommst*	du
er/sie/es	er/sie/es	er/sie/es *heißt*

Now use the table to write the correct verb in each gap.

1 Mein Handy __________ aus China.
2 Meine Schlange __________ Sissel.
3 Du __________ Gabi.
4 __________ du aus Berlin?
5 __________ Monika in Hamburg?
6 Deine Lieblingssendung __________ ‚EastEnders'.
7 Ich __________ Wolfgang.
8 Wo __________ du?

Mein Fortschritt

1 **Record your levels for *Kapitel* 1.**

2 **Look at the level descriptors on pages 59–60 and set your targets for *Kapitel* 2.**

3 **Fill in what you need to do to achieve these targets.**

Listening 	I have reached Level ____ in **Listening**. In *Kapitel* 2, I want to reach Level ____ I need to ________________________________ ________________________________ ________________________________ ________________________________
Speaking 	I have reached Level ____ in **Speaking**. In *Kapitel* 2, I want to reach Level ____ I need to ________________________________ ________________________________ ________________________________ ________________________________
Reading 	I have reached Level ____ in **Reading**. In *Kapitel* 2, I want to reach Level ____ I need to ________________________________ ________________________________ ________________________________ ________________________________
Writing 	I have reached Level ____ in **Writing**. In *Kapitel* 2, I want to reach Level ____ I need to ________________________________ ________________________________ ________________________________ ________________________________

Wörter

Hallo! • Meeting and greeting

Wie heißt du?	*What's your name?*
Ich heiße ...	*My name is ...*
Hallo!	*Hello! / Hi!*
Guten Tag!	*Hello!*
Wie geht's?	*How are you?*
Gut, danke. Und dir?	*Fine, thanks. And you?*
Nicht schlecht.	*Not bad.*
Tschüs!	*Bye!*
Auf Wiedersehen!	*Goodbye!*

Die Zahlen 1–19 • Numbers 1–19

eins	*1*
zwei	*2*
drei	*3*
vier	*4*
fünf	*5*
sechs	*6*
sieben	*7*
acht	*8*
neun	*9*
zehn	*10*
elf	*11*
zwölf	*12*
dreizehn	*13*
vierzehn	*14*
fünfzehn	*15*
sechzehn	*16*
siebzehn	*17*
achtzehn	*18*
neunzehn	*19*
Wie alt bist du?	*How old are you?*
Ich bin ... Jahre alt.	*I am ... years old.*
Wie alt ist (Julia)?	*How old is (Julia)?*
(Julia) ist ... Jahre alt.	*(Julia) is ... years old.*

Wo wohnst du? • Where do you live?

Ich wohne in ...	*I live in ...*
Er/Sie/Es wohnt in ...	*He/She/It lives in ...*
... England	*England*
... Irland	*Ireland*
... Nordirland	*Northern Ireland*
... Schottland	*Scotland*
... Wales	*Wales*
... Deutschland	*Germany*
... Österreich	*Austria*
... der Schweiz	*Switzerland*

Wie bist du? • What are you like?

Ich bin ...	*I am ...*
Er/Sie ist ...	*He/She is ...*
faul	*lazy*
freundlich	*friendly*
intelligent	*intelligent*
kreativ	*creative*
launisch	*moody*
laut	*loud*
lustig	*funny*
musikalisch	*musical*
sportlich	*sporty*

Lieblingssachen • Favourite things

Mein Lieblingssport ist ...
My favourite sport is ...

Mein Lieblingsmonat ist ...
My favourite month is ...

Meine Lieblingsmusik ist ...
My favourite music is ...

Meine Lieblingszahl ist ...
My favourite number is ...

Meine Lieblingssendung ist ...
My favourite programme is ...

Meine Lieblingsfußballmannschaft ist ...
My favourite football team is ...

Mein Lieblingsspiel ist ...
My favourite game is ...

Mein Lieblingsland ist ...
My favourite country is ...

Mein Lieblingsauto ist ...
My favourite car is ...

Was ist dein Lieblingssport?
What's your favourite sport?

Was ist deine Lieblingszahl?
What's your favourite number?

Was ist dein Lieblingsland?
What's your favourite country?

Hast du einen Computer? • Have you got a computer?

Ich habe ...	*I have ...*
einen Computer	*a computer*
einen iPod	*an iPod*
einen Fußball	*a football*
eine Gitarre	*a guitar*
eine Wii	*a Wii*
eine Schlange	*a snake*
ein Handy	*a mobile phone*
ein Keyboard	*a keyboard*
ein Skateboard	*a skateboard*

Fragewörter • Question words

Wie?	*How?*
Was?	*What?*
Wo?	*Where?*
Woher?	*Where ... from?*
Wer?	*Who?*

Oft benutzte Wörter • High-frequency words

und	*and*
(und) auch	*(and) also*
aber	*but*
sehr	*very*
ziemlich	*quite*
nicht	*not*
Was denkst du?	*What do you think?*
Ich denke, ...	*I think ...*
Ich auch!	*Me too!*
Ich nicht!	*Not me!/That's not what I think!*
Was? Du spinnst!	*What? You're joking!*

1 Extreme Haustiere (Seiten 30–31)

1 Complete the sentences about the pets. Write the correct words in the gaps. Remember to think about the gender of each animal.

1 Ich habe _ein_ ______ Pferd. _Es_ ___ ist groß und heißt Romeo.
2 Ich habe __________ Kaninchen. _____ ist niedlich und heißt Timmo.
3 Ich habe __________ Katze. _____ ist intelligent und heißt Mieze.
4 Max hat __________ Schlange. _____ ist zwei Jahre alt.
5 Gabi hat __________ Pferd. _____ ist launish.
6 Ich habe __________ Hund. _____ ist freundlich und heißt Prinz.
7 Susi hat __________ Goldfisch. _____ heißt Nemo.

Grammatik
Remember: after *haben* the masculine word for 'a' changes from *ein* to *einen*.

Grammatik
m. der / ein → **er**
f. die / eine → **sie**
n. das / ein → **es**

2 Tina Tierfan has lots of pets! Write Tina's answers to the interviewer's questions about how many of each animal she has.

Grammatik

Hund (-e)	Pferd (-e)
Katze (-n)	Goldfisch (-e)
Schlange (-n)	Maus (Mäuse)

1 Hast du einen Hund? _Nein! Ich habe drei Hunde._
2 Hast du ein Pferd? ______________________
3 Hast du eine Katze? ______________________
4 Hast du einen Goldfisch? ______________________
5 Hast du eine Schlange? ______________________
6 Hast du eine Maus? ______________________

2 Supertiere (Seiten 32–33)

1 Complete the sentences about the animals. Write the correct name in each gap.

Hermann

Minnie

Sisi

Kizzi

Moto

Millie

1 ____________ ist schnell.
2 ____________ ist süß.
3 ____________ ist gemein.
4 ____________ ist superintelligent.
5 ____________ ist cool.
6 ____________ ist kräftig.

2 Write a sentence to say what each of the *Supertiere* can do.

1 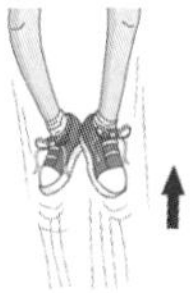
Hermann

2 
Sisi

3 
Minnie

4 

Kizzi

5 
Millie

6 
Moto

1 Hermann kann springen.
2 ______________________________
3 ______________________________
4 ______________________________
5 ______________________________
6 ______________________________

Grammatik
The verb *kann* is always followed by an infinitive verb.

3 Read the text below, then translate it into English.

Günther Goldfisch ist mein Lieblingstier. Er ist ein Jahr alt. Er ist sehr lustig und kräftig, aber auch ziemlich süß. Er kann schwimmen, springen und auch im Aquarium tanzen! Günther hat einen Freund: er ist sehr cool und schlau.

1 **Find the numbers in the puzzle, and write them next to the correct numeral.**

v	i	e	r	u	n	d	s	e	c	h	z	i	g	m	e
b	a	l	c	o	e	z	n	f	w	i	r	d	s	k	s
s	e	c	h	s	u	n	d	d	r	e	i	ß	i	g	a
q	g	n	a	j	n	x	i	n	d	m	h	t	g	ü	o
h	a	c	h	t	u	n	d	f	ü	n	f	z	i	g	i
u	e	i	n	u	n	d	a	c	h	t	z	i	g	p	b
n	t	e	r	i	d	f	b	n	ß	e	d	z	g	d	s
d	r	e	i	u	n	d	v	i	e	r	z	i	g	w	e
e	v	h	f	r	e	a	m	ß	p	l	s	j	a	q	c
r	d	r	e	i	u	n	d	z	w	a	n	z	i	g	h
t	z	a	n	j	n	x	o	u	e	y	g	r	e	v	z
k	c	p	f	s	z	d	l	b	n	l	a	i	h	m	i
i	b	z	w	e	i	u	n	d	s	i	e	b	z	i	g
a	g	b	n	ü	g	y	i	a	z	o	m	e	d	h	e

100 ______________

64 ______________

99 ______________

43 ______________

72 ______________

36 ______________

58 ______________

81 ______________

60 ______________

23 ______________

2 **Describe each of the families. Fill in the gaps for the first family. Write the whole description for the second family.**

Ich heiße Tom. Ich bin vierzehn Jahre alt. Es gibt vier Personen in meiner Familie. Meine Mutter ist ______________ Jahre alt. Ich habe einen Bruder. ____ ist ________ Jahre alt. Ich habe eine Schwester. ______ ist __________ Jahre alt. Wir wohnen in ________ .

____

____

____

____

____

____

3 **Write about your family (real or imaginary). Use the descriptions in exercise 2 to help you.**

der Stiefbruder = stepbrother
die Halbschwester = half-sister
Ich bin Einzelkind. = I am an only child.

4 Die Farben der Welt (Seiten 36–37)

1 Describe each person's hair and eyes.

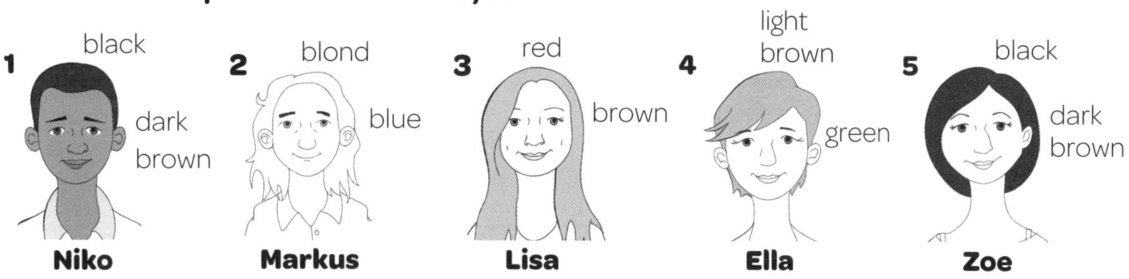

Grammatik
When you describe hair and eyes, the adjectives (colour, length) need an ***e*** on the end.

hell = light	**hellbraun** = light brown
dunkel = dark	**dunkelblau** = dark blue

1 *Er heißt Niko. Er hat kurze, schwarze Haare und dunkelbraune Augen.*

2 ______________________________

3 ______________________________

4 ______________________________

5 ______________________________

2 Complete the text by choosing the correct words from the cloud to fill the gaps. There are more words than you need.

Es gibt fünf __________ in meiner Familie. Wir __________ in Braunschweig. Das ist in __________________. Meine __________ heißt Emma und sie ist neunundvierzig __________ alt. Sie ist sehr freundlich und hat __________, schwarze Haare. Mein Vater __________ auch neunundvierzig und er hat kurze, dunkelbraune Haare und braune __________.

Ich habe zwei __________: einen Bruder und eine Schwester. __________ Bruder heißt Mehmet und er ist __________ Jahre alt. Er ist launisch aber __________ lustig. __________ Schwester, Isla, hat grüne Augen und __________ Haare. Sie ist sechzehn Jahre alt, sehr klein und __________________.

Deutschland alt Augen Personen
braune wohnen sportlich Meine
Mutter Jahre lange Geschwister
zwölf auch Mein blau ist

Read the text for gist first. For each sentence, think about whether you need a noun, a verb, a connective or an adjective.

1 Reorder the words to make correct sentences. Don't forget the full stop!

1. am | Mai | Ich | Geburtstag | habe | neunzehnten

   ____

2. hat | Oktober | am | Oma | Geburtstag | elften | Meine

   ____

3. Geburtstag | Stiefbruder | Dezember | am | Dein | dritten | hat

   ____

4. hast | Geburtstag | einunddreißigsten | Juli | Du | am

   ____

5. und | Geburtstag | haben | achten | am | Michael | Juni | Monika

   ____

2 Complete each sentence by writing the date. Write each holiday in English.

01.01. Neujahr ist am *ersten Januar* ______________. *New Year*

01.05. Der Maifeiertag ist am ______________. ______________

03.10. Der Tag der Deutschen Einheit ist am ______________. *German Unity Day*

25.12. Weihnachten ist am ______________. ______________

31.12. Silvester ist am ______________. ______________

3 Read the short profile about Yannic and write a summary in the table.

Er heißt Yannic Spiller. Er ist dreizehn Jahre alt und kommt aus Trier. Trier ist in Deutschland. Yannic hat am siebten Januar Geburtstag. Er hat einen Bruder, Tim. Tim ist achtzehn Jahre alt. Yannic hat auch eine Schwester. Sie heißt Steffi und ist sechzehn Jahre alt. Die Familie Spiller hat zwei Haustiere: einen Hund und eine Katze.

Name:		Geschwister:	
Alter:			
Wohnt in:		Haustiere:	
Geburtstag:			

4 Now write a short profile about yourself.

1 **Rescue the question words from the alphabet soup. Write each one on a line and use it to write a question.**

Wie viele Brüder hast du?

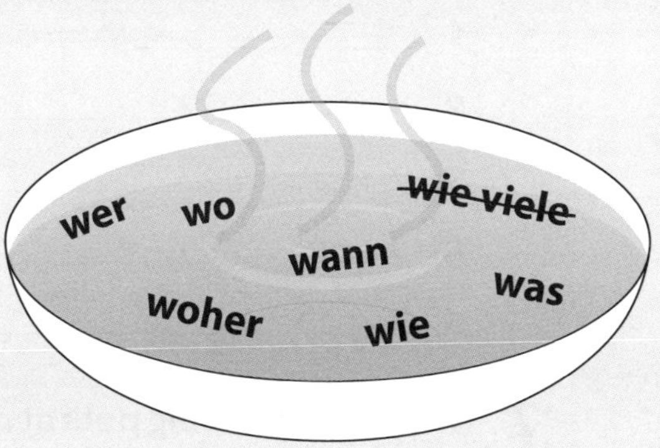

2 **The police have written a summary about a crime suspect. Write six questions for a journalist to ask the suspect. The questions should cover all the information in the summary.**

1 Wie heißt du?
2
3
4
5
6

Martin Kolwitz ist 24 Jahre alt. Er hat am achten November Geburtstag. Er wohnt in Hamburg, in Deutschland. Er hat einen Bruder. Er hat auch Haustiere: zwei Hunde.

Remember: the verb usually goes straight after the question word.

3 **Use these notes to write questions to Martin about his accomplice, Sophie.**

1 Wie heißt sie?
2
3
4
5

Sophie Meyer
19
Ebbingen, Deutschland
Haare – kurz, Augen – blau
Geb. 21.10.

Remember to use the correct part of the verb with the pronoun *sie*.

4 **Write a summary about Sophie, like the one the police wrote about Martin in exercise 2.**

Wiederholung 1

1 **Complete the sentences. Choose the correct word from the cloud to fill in each gap.**

1 ______________ Mutter ist sehr freundlich und intelligent.

2 Hast du ______________ Meerschweinchen?

3 Wir haben ______________ Haustier.

4 Wo ist ______________ Vogel?

5 Ich habe ______________ Bruder.

dein *kein* *ein* *meine* *einen*

2 **You are describing pets at a pet show. Use the owners' notes to write what sort of pet they have, what the pet is like and what it can do.**

Mareike

mouse
Pippa
cute, fast
fly, swim

Mareike hat ______________.

Sie heißt ______________.

Sie ist ______________.

Sie kann ______________.

Aaron

cat
Mieze
intelligent, cool, mean
jump, play football

______________.

______________.

______________.

______________.

______________.

3 **Decscribe the animal you'll be entering in the pet show by writing a similar description.**

Example: Ich habe ...

Wiederholung 2

1 Read the texts below.

Hallo! Ich heiße **Anna** und ich bin fünfzehn Jahre alt. Ich habe am elften Februar Geburtstag. Ich wohne in Klagenfurt, in Österreich. Ich bin ziemlich groß und schlank und habe kurze, schwarze Haare und blaue Augen. Ich habe keine Geschwister – ich bin Einzelkind. Ich habe einen Goldfisch und einen Wellensittich. Ich kann Flöte spielen und Italienisch sprechen.

Hi! Ich bin **Noah** und ich komme aus Aachen. Das ist in Deutschland. Ich habe am zweiten November Geburtstag und bin vierzehn Jahre alt. Ich liebe Haustiere! Ich habe zwei Hunde, drei Katzen und eine Maus. Ich habe eine große Familie. Ich habe einen Halbbruder (er ist ein Baby) und zwei Schwestern. Mein Halbbruder ist sehr süß und klein. Er hat schwarze Haare und blaue Augen.

a Complete the sentences by writing *Anna* or *Noah*.

1 __________ lives in Austria.
2 __________ can play the flute.
3 __________'s birthday is on the 02.11.
4 __________ has a half-brother.
5 __________ is 15 years old.
6 __________ has cats.

b Write *richtig* or *falsch* next to each statement.

1 Anna hat einen Halbbruder. __________
2 Anna kann auch Englisch sprechen. __________
3 Noahs Halbbruder hat blaue Augen. __________
4 Klagenfurt ist nicht in Deutschland. __________
5 Anna hat am fünfzehnten Februar Geburtstag. __________
6 Anna hat keine Geschwister. __________

2 Translate these sentences into German.

1 My birthday is on the first of May. ____________________
2 She can speak German. ____________________
3 My guinea pig is very cute. ____________________
4 Your sister has light blue eyes. ____________________
5 My grandparents live in Southampton. ____________________
6 My brother can fly. ____________________

Grammatik (Seiten 44–45)

1 Complete the table by writing the correct form of *haben* for each pronoun.

haben *hast* *habt* *hat* *haben* *habe*

Words for 'you':
du (speaking to one family member or friend)
ihr (speaking to two or more family members or friends)
Sie (speaking to people you don't know or adults)

ich	du	er/sie/es	wir	ihr	Sie/sie

Now complete the sentences with the correct form of *haben*.

1 Katja, hast ______ du eine Katze?
2 Tom und Niko, ______ ihr einen Hund?
3 ______ Sie eine Schlange, Herr Brand?
4 Ich ______ ein Pferd.
5 Frau Gerber, ______ Sie eine Maus?
6 Herr Alexander ______ ein Pferd.

2 Join each pronoun to a verb. There is more than one possible verb for some of the pronouns. Then write a question or a sentence with each pair.

1 ich	a macht	1 ______
2 du	b heißen	2 ______
3 er	c wohnst	3 ______
4 wir	d heiße	4 ______
5 ihr	e spielt	5 ______
6 Sie	f spielen	6 ______

3 Rewrite the sentences so they include the verb *kann*.

1 Mein Bruder fliegt. Mein Bruder kann fliegen.
2 Ich spiele Flöte. ______
3 Meine Mutter schwimmt. ______
4 Mein Vater springt. ______
5 Ich tanze. ______
6 Er singt gut. ______

Mein Fortschritt

1 **Record your levels for *Kapitel* 2.**

2 **Look at the level descriptors on pages 59–60 and set your targets for *Kapitel* 3.**

3 **Fill in what you need to do to achieve these targets.**

Listening 	I have reached Level ____ in **Listening**. In *Kapitel* 3, I want to reach Level ____ I need to ______________________________ ______________________________ ______________________________ ______________________________
Speaking 	I have reached Level ____ in **Speaking**. In *Kapitel* 3, I want to reach Level ____ I need to ______________________________ ______________________________ ______________________________ ______________________________
Reading 	I have reached Level ____ in **Reading**. In *Kapitel* 3, I want to reach Level ____ I need to ______________________________ ______________________________ ______________________________ ______________________________
Writing 	I have reached Level ____ in **Writing**. In *Kapitel* 3, I want to reach Level ____ I need to ______________________________ ______________________________ ______________________________ ______________________________

Haustiere • Pets

Hast du ein Haustier?	*Have you got a pet?*
Ich habe ...	*I have ...*
einen Goldfisch	*a goldfish*
einen Hamster	*a hamster*
einen Hund	*a dog*
ein Kaninchen	*a rabbit*
eine Katze	*a cat*
eine Maus	*a mouse*
ein Meerschweinchen	*a guinea pig*
ein Pferd	*a horse*
eine Schlange	*a snake*
einen Wellensittich	*a budgie*
kein Haustier	*no pet*

Eigenschaften • Qualities

Wie ist er/sie/es?	*What is he/she/it like?*
Er/Sie/Es ist ...	*He/She/It is ...*
dick/schlank	*fat/thin*
frech/niedlich	*cheeky/cute*
gemein/süß	*mean/sweet*
groß/klein	*big/small*
kräftig	*strong*
schlau	*cunning*
(super)lustig	*(really) funny*
Er/Sie/Es kann ...	*He/She/It can ...*
Italienisch sprechen	*speak Italian*
fliegen	*fly*
Flöte/Fußball/Wii spielen	*play the flute/football/on the Wii*
(schnell) laufen	*run (fast)*
lesen	*read*
Rad fahren	*ride a bike*
schwimmen	*swim*
singen	*sing*
springen	*jump*
tanzen	*dance*

Die Zahlen 20–100 • Numbers 20–100

zwanzig	*twenty*
dreißig	*thirty*
vierzig	*forty*
fünfzig	*fifty*
sechzig	*sixty*
siebzig	*seventy*
achtzig	*eighty*
neunzig	*ninety*
hundert	*hundred*
einundzwanzig	*twenty-one*
zweiundzwanzig	*twenty-two*

Meine Familie • My family

Es gibt ... Personen in meiner Familie.	*There are ... people in my family.*
meine Mutter	*my mother*
mein Vater	*my father*
mein Bruder	*my brother*
mein Stiefbruder/Halbbruder	*my stepbrother/half-brother*
meine Schwester	*my sister*
meine Stiefschwester/Halbschwester	*my stepsister/half-sister*
meine Eltern	*my parents*
meine Großeltern	*my grandparents*
Hast du Geschwister?	*Have you any brothers and sisters?*
Ich habe zwei Brüder.	*I have two brothers.*
Ich habe drei Schwestern.	*I have three sisters.*
Ich bin Einzelkind.	*I'm an only child.*
Ich habe keine Geschwister.	*I have no brothers and sisters.*

Wörter

Die Farben • Colours

schwarz	*black*
weiß	*white*
grau	*grey*
braun	*brown*
rot	*red*
orange	*orange*
gelb	*yellow*
grün	*green*
blau	*blue*
indigoblau	*indigo*
violett	*violet*
lila	*purple*
rosa	*pink*
bunt	*brightly coloured*
hellblau/dunkelblau	*light blue/dark blue*

Haare und Augen • Hair and eyes

Er/Sie hat ...	*He/She has ...*
schwarze/braune/ blonde/rote Haare	*black/brown/ blond/red hair*
kurze/lange/ mittellange Haare	*short/long/ mid length hair*
blaue/braune/grüne/ graue Augen	*blue/brown/green/ grey eyes*

Die Monate • The months

Januar	*January*
Februar	*February*
März	*March*
April	*April*
Mai	*May*
Juni	*June*
Juli	*July*
August	*August*
September	*September*
Oktober	*October*
November	*November*
Dezember	*December*

Das Datum • The date

Wann hast du Geburtstag?	*When is your birthday?*
am 1. (ersten) Januar	*on 1 January*
am 3. (dritten) Februar	*on 3 February*
am 7. (siebten) März	*on 7 March*
am 8. (achten) April	*on 8 April*
am 15. (fünfzehnten) Mai	*on 15 May*
am 29. (neunund-zwanzigsten) Juni	*on 29 June*
Ich habe (heute) Geburtstag.	*It's my birthday (today).*

Oft benutzte Wörter • High-frequency words

und	*and*
aber	*but*
oder	*or*
ziemlich	*fairly, quite*
sehr	*very*

1 Bist du sportlich? (Seiten 54–55)

1 **Look at the survey results in the table. Then answer the questions using full German sentences.**

Ahmed	☺☺			☹			😐
Nicole		☺☺			☹		
Christa	☺		☺☺				😐
Torsten		☹		☺☺		☺	
Herr und Frau Meyer	☺☺			☺	☹	😐	

☺☺ = sehr gern ☺ = gern 😐 = ziemlich gern ☹ = nicht gern

1 Wer spielt sehr gern Fußball? Nicole spielt sehr gern Fußball.
2 Wer spielt gern Tischtennis? ______
3 Was spielt Christa sehr gern? ______
4 Was spielen Herr und Frau Meyer gern? ______
5 Wer spielt Basketball nicht gern? ______
6 Wer spielt ziemlich gern Handball? (2) ______
7 Und du? Was spielst du gern? ______

2 **Write three questions and three answers about the other people and sports in the table in exercise 1. Use the questions above as a model.**

______
______
______
______
______
______

2 Freizeit ist toll! (Seiten 56–57)

1 Write the words from the cloud in the grid. Translate the code word into English.

furchtbar
Eishockey
schlecht
spielst
irre
stinklangweilig
langweilig
Tischtennis
toll

2 Read about all the activities Hannes and Lola are involved in. Then write *richtig* or *falsch* next to each statement.

Hallo! Ich heiße **Hannes**. Ich finde Sport fantastisch. Ich spiele Tennis und schwimme. Schwimmen finde ich total super. Ich reite mit meiner Freundin, aber das finde ich langweilig. Fußball finde ich cool. Ich fahre auch gern Skateboard und lese sehr gern Sport- und Fitnessmagazine.

Meine Freundin heißt **Lola.** Sie findet Tischtennis toll. Lola fährt auch gern Rad – das ist sehr gesund! Sie findet schwimmen auch gut, aber Fußball findet sie nervig. Sie kann nicht Ski fahren. Im Winter spielt sie Eishockey und sie sieht sehr gern Eishockey im Fernsehen.

meine Freundin = my girlfriend
gesund = healthy
Fernsehen = television

1 Both Hannes and Lola participate in winter sports. ______________
2 Lola watches ice hockey on television. ______________
3 Hannes really likes swimming. ______________
4 Lola thinks skiing is fantastic. ______________
5 Lola plays ice hockey in winter. ______________
6 Hannes doesn't enjoying horse riding. ______________
7 Lola thinks football is exciting. ______________
8 Hannes watches sports programmes on television. ______________

1 **Separate the words to form five time phrases and write them below. Number the phrases in order of frequency, starting with 1 for the most frequent. Translate the phrases into English.**

jedenTagdreimalproWocheeinmalproMonatamWochenendesechsmalproMonat

☐ ______________________ ______________________

☐ ______________________ ______________________

☐ ______________________ ______________________

☐ ______________________ ______________________

☐ ______________________ ______________________

2 **Use the time phrases from exercise 1 to answer the questions about yourself. Write your answers in full sentences.**

1 Gehst du ins Kino? ______________________

2 Machst du Sport? ______________________

3 Gehst du einkaufen? ______________________

4 Hörst du Musik? ______________________

5 Spielst du Wii? ______________________

6 Chillst du mit deinen Freunden? ______________________

nie = never

3 **Join up the sentence halves. Rewrite each sentence so that it starts with the time phrase.**

1 Ich höre am	**a** Tag Sport.
2 Ich chille am	**b** Abend Musik.
3 Ich spiele sehr	**c** pro Woche Pizza.
4 Ich mache jeden	**d** Monat ins Kino.
5 Ich esse einmal	**e** oft Xbox.
6 Ich gehe einmal pro	**f** Wochenende.

Remember the 'verb in second place' rule.

4 Ich bin online (Seiten 60–61)

1 Unscramble and write down the time phrase in each sentence. Then translate the sentences into English.

Grammatik
You can use the present tense with a future time phrase to say what you are going to do – just as in English.

1 Wir machen ähncset eoWhc Filme. *nächste Woche*
We are going to make …

2 Ich suche ma Mtanog Infos im Internet. ______

3 Wir sehen ma eneneoWhcd Katzenvideos auf YouTube. ______

4 Ich chatte nejde denbA auf Facebook. ______

5 Stefan spielt ni iezw cnoWhe Wii Sport. ______

6 Ich lade gomrne Musik herunter. ______

2 Underline all the verbs in the text. Circle the words that are in first position in the sentences. Write a sentence about what you notice.

Hey du!
Franzi hier! Jetzt sind wir Freunde auf Facebook! Jeden Tag spiele ich Wii. Jede Woche schreibt mein Vater ein Blog, aber das finde ich langweilig. Am Abend lese ich gern E-Books. Morgen telefoniere ich mit Freunden in Kanada über Skype. Das finde ich cool! Im Sommer fahren wir nach Vancouver. Fantastisch! Was machst du am Computer und wie oft?

______

3 Reply to the question Franzi has asked you in his chat.

Use as many time phrases as you can in your reply.

1 **What type of word is needed to fill the gap in each sentence? Complete each sentence by writing an appropriate German word or words in the gap.**

verb
noun
time/frequency phrase
connective
adjective

		Type of word
1	Ich *finde* ______ Tennis toll.	*verb*
2	Meine Schwester findet Tischtennis __________.	__________
3	Wir sehen ____________ fern.	__________
4	Herr Peters spielt nächste Woche Tennis __________ Fußball.	__________
5	Mein Bruder schreibt ein __________.	__________

2 **Answer the questions about German grammar.**

Use the sentences in exercise 1 to help you answer these questions.

1 Where in a sentence do verbs usually go?

____

2 What often goes after a verb? ____________________

3 What can you expect to go after *ein/eine*? ____________________

4 Which German verb suggests you're giving an opinion? ____________________

3 **Replace the underlined word(s) with something else: a different noun, adjective or time phrase.**

1 Ich finde Tischtennis <u>furchtbar</u>. *Ich finde Tischtennis langweilig.*

2 Ich spiele nicht gern <u>Fußball</u>. ____________________

3 Micha spielt gern <u>Wii</u>. ____________________

4 Er macht <u>einmal pro Monat</u> Judo. ____________________

5 Olli findet E-Books <u>fantastisch</u>. ____________________

6 Ich sehe <u>jede Woche</u> fern. Meine Schwester sieht <u>jeden Tag</u> Videos auf YouTube.

____

Remember that you'll keep the reader's interest if you use a variety of different words and phrases.

4 **Write about your friends' hobbies.**

Remember to include:

- opinions
- time/frequency phrases
- connectives
- 'verb in second place' rule

Wiederholung 1

1 Put the words in the correct order to make sentences or questions. Don't forget to insert a full stop or question mark.

1 fern gern sehr Ich sehe ____________________

2 einkaufen er Wochenende geht Am ____________________

3 Hausaufgaben Ich Infos lese die für ____________________

4 in Wie Stadt oft du fährst die ____________________

5 Woche Kai Wasserball Nächste spielt ____________________

6 herunter Videos Ich lade Musik und ____________________

2 Rewrite each sentence, beginning with a time phrase. Then translate the sentences into English.

1 Ich spiele Volleyball. (at the weekend) *Am Wochenende spiele ich Volleyball.*

At the weekend I am going to play volleyball.

2 Er spielt Basketball. (on Monday) ____________________

____

3 Du spielst Tischtennis. (every week) ____________________

____

4 Rosa spielt Fußball. (today) ____________________

____

5 Ich telefoniere mit Sam. (next week) ____________________

____

6 Sophie liest das Buch. (tomorrow) ____________________

____

3 Underline the regular verbs and circle the irregular verbs.

Ich spiele nicht gern Tennis. Ich finde Tennis langweilig. Fußball spiele ich dreimal pro Woche. Mein Bruder spielt sehr gern Tennis. Er fährt auch gern Rad. Radfahren findet er toll. Meine Schwester sieht ziemlich gern fern. Meine Mutter liest ziemlich gern. Oft liest sie Blogs im Internet. Ich lese auch oft. Mein Vater fährt gern Ski und spielt Gitarre.

Wiederholung 2

1 Read the email. Find the German for the following words and phrases in the text.

1 I think ______________________
2 about ______________________
3 but ______________________
4 New Zealand ______________________
5 comedies ______________________
6 Best wishes ______________________

Lieber Anish,

wie geht's? Danke für deine E-Mail.

Ich denke, Technologie ist toll. Ich bin sehr oft online. Ich chatte sehr gern mit Freunden auf Facebook. Facebook finde ich super und ich sehe oft Videos über Fußball auf YouTube.

Ich spiele Computerspiele nicht gern, aber ich suche ziemlich oft Infos für die Hausaufgaben. Meine Cousine, Connie, wohnt in Neuseeland und wir telefonieren ziemlich oft über Skype. Kannst du auch über Skype telefonieren?

Ich mache viel Sport mit meinen Freunden: Wir schwimmen zweimal pro Woche und wir spielen am Abend Basketball. Im Winter fahre ich auch Ski.

Ich esse manchmal am Wochenende mit meinen Freunden Pizza, und dann gehen wir ins Kino. Ich sehe gern Komödien. Nächste Woche sehen wir *Skyfall*.

Liebe Grüße,

Tibor

2 Answer the questions in complete German sentences.

1 Spielt Tibor gern Computerspiele? ______________________
2 Was macht Tibor auf Facebook? ______________________
3 Wer wohnt in Neuseeland? ______________________
4 Wie telefoniert Tibor mit seiner Cousine? ______________________
5 Wie oft schwimmt Tibor? ______________________
6 Was machen Tibor und seine Freunde am Wochenende?

____

3 Write a reply to Tibor's email about your hobbies and activities.

Grammatik (Seiten 68–69)

1 Complete the verb table.

	fahren (to go/travel)	**sehen** (to see)	**lesen** (to read)
ich			
du	fährst		liest
er/sie/es		sieht	
wir			
ihr			
Sie			
sie			

2 Complete the sentences by writing the correct form of the verb in brackets.

1 Ich __________ das Auto. (waschen)

2 __________ du gern Mangabücher? (lesen)

3 Er __________ im Schlafzimmer. (schlafen)

4 Thomas __________ nach Stockholm in Schweden. (fahren)

5 __________ du morgen Torsten? (sehen)

6 __________ du eine Schuluniform? (tragen)

Verbs like fahren:
tragen = to wear
schlafen = to sleep
waschen = to wash

die Schuluniform = school uniform

3 Write the question for each reply.

1 __________ Ja, ich spiele Gitarre.

2 __________ Nein, ich spiele nicht gern Wasserball.

3 __________ Ja, Michael schläft im Bett.

4 __________ Ja, ich fahre nach Bremen.

5 __________ Ja, ich lese gern E-Books.

6 __________ Nein, ich sehe nicht gern fern.

7 __________ Ja, ich bin sportlich!

8 Was __________ Ich trage morgen Jeans und ein T-Shirt.

9 __________ Michael trägt eine Schuluniform.

Remember, to form a question you put the verb before the subject:
Du spielst gern Tennis. → Spielst du gern Tennis?

Mein Fortschritt

1 Record your levels for *Kapitel* 3.

2 Look at the level descriptors on pages 59–60 and set your targets for *Kapitel* 4.

3 Fill in what you need to do to achieve these targets.

Listening 	I have reached Level ____ in **Listening**. In *Kapitel* 4, I want to reach Level ____ I need to ________________ ________________ ________________ ________________
Speaking 	I have reached Level ____ in **Speaking**. In *Kapitel* 4, I want to reach Level ____ I need to ________________ ________________ ________________ ________________
Reading 	I have reached Level ____ in **Reading**. In *Kapitel* 4, I want to reach Level ____ I need to ________________ ________________ ________________ ________________
Writing 	I have reached Level ____ in **Writing**. In *Kapitel* 4, I want to reach Level ____ I need to ________________ ________________ ________________ ________________

Bist du sportlich? • Are you sporty?

Ich bin (sehr/ziemlich/ nicht sehr) sportlich.	*I am (very/quite/ not very) sporty.*
Was spielst du?	*What do you play?*
Ich spiele ...	*I play ...*
Ich spiele gern ...	*I like playing ...*
Ich spiele ziemlich gern ...	*I quite like playing ...*
Ich spiele nicht gern ...	*I don't like playing ... playing ...*
Badminton	*badminton*
Basketball	*basketball*
Eishockey	*ice hockey*
Fußball	*football*
Handball	*handball*
Tennis	*tennis*
Tischtennis	*table tennis*
Volleyball	*volleyball*
Wasserball	*water polo*

Was machst du gern? • What do you like doing?

Was machst du gern?	*What do you like doing?*
Ich fahre Rad.	*I ride my bike.*
Ich fahre Skateboard.	*I go skateboarding.*
Ich fahre Ski.	*I ski.*
Ich fahre Snowboard.	*I snowboard.*
Ich lese.	*I read.*
Ich mache Judo.	*I do judo.*
Ich mache Karate.	*I do karate.*
Ich reite.	*I go horse riding.*
Ich schwimme.	*I swim.*
Ich sehe fern.	*I watch TV.*
Ich spiele Gitarre.	*I play the guitar.*
Ich tanze.	*I dance.*

Wie findest du das? • What do you think of it?

Ich finde es ...	*I think it's ...*
Es ist ...	*It's ...*
irre	*amazing*
super	*super*
toll	*great*
cool	*cool*
gut	*good*
nicht schlecht	*not bad*
okay	*okay*
langweilig	*boring*
nervig	*annoying*
stinklangweilig	*deadly boring*
furchtbar	*awful*

Was machst du in deiner Freizeit? • What do you do in your free time?

Ich chille.	*I chill out.*
Ich esse Pizza oder Hamburger.	*I eat pizza or hamburgers.*
Ich gehe einkaufen.	*I go shopping.*
Ich gehe ins Kino.	*I go to the cinema.*
Ich gehe in den Park.	*I go to the park.*
Ich gehe in die Stadt.	*I go into town.*
Ich höre Musik.	*I listen to music.*
Ich mache Sport.	*I do sport.*
Ich spiele Xbox oder Wii.	*I play Xbox or on the Wii.*

Wörter

Ich bin online • I'm online

Was machst du am Computer?	*What do you do on the computer?*
Was machst du auf deinem Handy?	*What do you do on your mobile?*
Ich chatte mit Freunden auf Facebook.	*I chat with friends on Facebook.*
Ich lade Musik herunter.	*I download music.*
Ich mache Fotos oder Filme.	*I take photos or make films.*
Ich sehe Videos.	*I watch videos.*
Ich simse.	*I text.*
Ich spiele Computerspiele.	*I play computer games.*
Ich suche und lese Infos für die Hausaufgaben.	*I look for and read information for my homework.*
Ich surfe im Internet.	*I surf the internet.*
Ich telefoniere mit Freunden.	*I call my friends.*
Ich mache ziemlich viel auf meinem Handy.	*I do quite a lot of things on my mobile.*

Oft benutzte Wörter • High-frequency words

Wie oft?	*How often?*
(sehr/ziemlich/nicht so) oft	*(very/quite/not so) often*
einmal/zweimal/dreimal pro Woche/pro Monat	*once/twice/three times a week/a month*
jeden Tag	*every day*
jeden Morgen	*every morning*
manchmal	*sometimes*
immer	*always*
nie	*never*
Wann?	*When?*
am Wochenende	*at the weekend*
am Abend	*in the evening*
heute	*today*
morgen	*tomorrow*
am Montag	*on Monday*
nächste Woche	*next week*
in zwei Wochen	*in two weeks*

1 Ich mag Deutsch! (Seiten 76–77)

1 Write a sentence for each illustration.

1

2

3

4

5

6

1 Ich mag ______
2 ______
3 ______
4 ______
5 ______
6 ______

ich liebe ☺☺
ich mag ☺
ich mag ... nicht ☹
ich hasse ☹☹

2 Read the forum entries giving people's opinions about school subjects. Then answer the questions below.

Hallo Leute! Mein Lieblingsfach ist Englisch! Ich liebe Englisch, weil es total interessant ist. Ich lese sehr gern Bücher auf Spanisch und auf Deutsch. Mathe finde ich langweilig. **Pedro**

Hi Pedro! Ich mag Englisch nicht. Es ist sehr schwierig, aber ich mag Mathe und Naturwissenschaften. Ich finde Mathe supercool. **Nadine**

Grüezi aus der Schweiz! Ich liebe Theater und Kunst. Ich mag Kunst sehr gern, weil ich total kreativ bin. Informatik finde ich sehr langweilig, und Geschichte und Erdkunde sind nutzlos. **Marta**

Who ...

1 is very creative? ______
2 enjoys reading? ______
3 doesn't like English? ______
4 thinks ICT is boring? ______
5 likes maths? ______
6 can read Spanish? ______
7 loves art? ______
8 doesn't like geography? ______

3 Rewrite each sentence in exercise 1, adding *weil* and an opinion. Use the examples in exercise 2 to help you with word order.

2 Was und wann? (Seiten 78–79)

1 Look at the timetable. Write *richtig* or *falsch* next to each statement.

	Montag	Dienstag	Mittwoch	Donnerstag	Freitag
8.15	Mathe	Erdkunde	Englisch	Deutsch	Technik
9.15	Englisch	Informatik	Theater	Mathe	Deutsch
10.45	Kunst	Mathe	Deutsch	Kunst	Naturwissenschaften
11.45	Naturwissenschaften	Mathe	Naturwissenschaften	Geschichte	Theater
13.30	Deutsch	Sport	Technik	Musik	Englisch

vor = before **nach** = after **die Doppelstunde** = double period

1 Am Mittwoch habe ich Deutsch. ______

2 Wir haben am Freitag nach der Pause Technik. ______

3 Am Montag vor der Pause haben wir Englisch. ______

4 Theater ist am Mittwoch und am Donnerstag. ______

5 Ich habe am Donnerstag nach der Mittagspause Musik. ______

6 Am Dienstag habe ich eine Doppelstunde Mathe. ______

2 At what time do you have the following subjects? Write a sentence for each.

1 Ich habe Englisch um neun Uhr zehn.

2 ______

3 ______

4 ______

5 ______

6 ______

um acht Uhr = at 8 o'clock

3 Look at the timetable in exercise 1 and describe one school day. Try to add interest to your sentences by giving opinions about some subjects.

Example: Am Montag um acht Uhr fünfzehn habe ich Mathe. Ich mag Mathe, weil es interessant ist.

Ich finde Mathe ...
= I find maths ...

3 Lehrer und Lehrerinnen (Seiten 80–81)

1 Write a description for each of the teachers.

1 Mein Sportlehrer heißt Herr Huber.
Er ist cool, aber sehr unpünktlich.

2 ______________________________
____

3 ______________________________
____

4 ______________________________
____

Use some qualifiers in your descriptions: *sehr, zu, ziemlich, ein bisschen, nicht*

2 Complete the text by writing the correct word from the cloud in each gap.

Mein ______________ an der Schule ist Geschichte, ______________ meine Geschichtelehrerin sehr lustig ist! Sie ______________ nur ein Haustier, aber ihr Haustier ist eine Schlange!

Am ______________ und am Freitag haben wir Kunst. Ich finde Kunst ziemlich langweilg, weil es schwierig ______________. Mein Kunstlehrer ______________ Herr Ackermann. ______________ Schwester ist auch Kunstlehrerin an meiner ______________! Sie heißt Frau Ackermann! Meine Sportlehrerin ist ______________ freundlich. Sie heißt Frau Krause und ______________ Lieblingssport ist Volleyball. Ich mag Sport, weil ich sehr ______________ bin.

heißt hat Mittwoch Lieblingsfach ist sehr Schule Seine sportlich weil ihr

3 Write the correct word for 'his' or 'her' in each sentence.

1 ______________ Bruder lernt Hindi. (his)
2 ______________ Schwester ist Lehrerin. (her)
3 ______________ Hobby ist Gitarre spielen. (his)
4 ______________ Lieblingsfach ist Kunst. (her)
5 ______________ Schuluniform ist fantastisch. (his)
6 ______________ Bruder ist 19 Jahre alt. (her)

Grammatik
sein = his **ihr** = her (for masculine and neuter nouns)
seine = his **ihre** = her (for feminine nouns)
Check the gender of the noun if you are unsure.

4 Im Klassenzimmer (Seiten 82–83)

1 Draw a simple picture to show where each of these things is.

1 Der Musiklehrer ist im Klassenzimmer.
2 Das Buch ist neben dem Computer.
3 Das Poster ist an der Wand.
4 Der Stuhl ist auf dem Tisch und neben der Tür.

1	2	3	4

2 What is there in the classroom? Start each sentence with *Es gibt* (there is/there are). Write the numbers as words.

12  Es gibt zwölf Tische im Klassenzimmer.

6  ______________________________

24  ______________________________

2  ______________________________

4 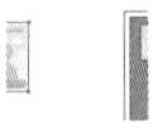 ______________________________

5  ______________________________

! Look at the vocabulary on page 47 for the plurals of the nouns.

3 Answer the questions using the information in the pictures.

@peta_ush Darfst du dein Handy in der Schule benutzen?

____

@tara_winkel Darfst du im Klassenzimmer schnell laufen?

____

@e_atch Darfst du in der Pause Musik hören?

____

@janet_mc Darfst du dein Handy in der Mittagspause benutzen?

____

! ich darf   du darfst   er/sie/es darf

5 Mein Lieblingstag (Seiten 84–85)

1 **Most of the verbs you've seen end in *–en* in the infinitive. Write the infinitive form of each verb in the table. Then try to work out its meaning from the context.**

If the context doesn't help you, use a German–English dictionary.

verb	infinitive	meaning in English
Er **geht** in die Schule.	*gehen*	*to go, to walk*
Er **kauft** ein Auto.		
Er **steht** auf dem Tisch.		
Warum **redest** du so schnell?		
Ich **wasche** meinen Hund.		
Ich **nehme** das Buch.		

2 **Guess the meaning of these compound nouns by separating out the words. Look up the compound nouns in a dictionary to find their gender and meaning.**

The second word in each compound noun gives the gender.

compound noun	word 1	word 2	gender	meaning
Fußballfeld	*Fußball*		*das*	
Arbeitstag				
Sporthalle				
Klassenarbeit				
Lehrerzimmer				

3 **Now write a short German sentence using each compound noun from exercise 2.**

1 *Das Fußballfeld ist sehr grün und …* ______

2 ______

3 ______

4 ______

5 ______

Wiederholung 1

1 **Mimi's description of her school day is in the wrong time order! Number the sentences 1–6 in the correct order of time.**

☐ Ich habe um dreizehn Uhr fünfundzwanzig Musik.
☐ Die Pause beginnt um elf Uhr zehn.
☐ Die erste Stunde beginnt um acht Uhr vierzig.
☐ Der Bus kommt um fünfzehn Uhr siebenundvierzig
☐ Ich komme um sechzehn Uhr dreißig nach Hause.
☐ Wir haben Mathe um elf Uhr fünfundzwanzig.

2 **The school is running 20 minutes late today. Rewrite each of the six sentences in exercise 1 with the time that each activity begins today.**

3 **Complete the sentences by writing the correct possessive pronoun in each gap.**

sein = his (for masculine and neuter nouns) **seine** = his (for feminine nouns)
ihr = her (for masculine and neuter nouns) **ihre** = her (for feminine nouns)

1 ________ Bruder heißt Pawel und ________ Schwester heißt Aga.
2 ________ Lieblingssport ist Eishockey.
3 ________ Katze ist braun, aber ________ Hund ist weiß.
4 ________ Schule ist in Hannover.

5 ________ Lieblingssport ist Reiten und ________ Lieblingsfach ist Mathe.
6 ________ Computer ist neu.
7 ________ Erdkundelehrerin ist sehr streng.
8 ________ Mutter wohnt in Salzburg, aber ________ Vater wohnt in Wien.

4 **Describe where each of the items is located in the classroom.**

1 Der Computer ist auf dem Tisch.
2 Das Poster ________
3 Das Whiteboard ________
4 Der Lehrer ________
5 Der Stuhl ________
6 Die Spinne ________

Wiederholung 2

1 Read the texts. Use your knowledge of vocabulary to help you to find these new phrases. Write each German phrase next to the English.

1 My name is ____________

2 her favourite artist ____________

3 unfortunately ____________

4 My brother also goes ____________

5 an indoor pool ____________

6 a pot plant ____________

Hallo! Mein Name ist **Maik** und ich wohne in München, in Deutschland. Meine Schule heißt Mathias Brauer Gymnasium und ich finde sie toll. An meiner Schule lerne ich sehr gern Englisch und Geschichte, aber mein Lieblingsfach ist Kunst. Ich mag Kunst, weil ich total kreativ bin. Ich finde meine Kunstlehrerin auch sehr nett. Sie heißt Frau Weber und ihr Lieblingskünstler ist Dürer.

Ich mag nicht Sport, weil ich nicht sehr sportlich bin. Leider habe ich am Montag und auch am Mittwoch Sport. Morgen spielen wir Tennis. Das finde ich nicht so schlecht.

lernen = to learn

Hallo Leute! Ich heiße **Sabine** und ich wohne in Zürich, in der Schweiz. Meine Schule ist sehr groß. Mein Bruder geht auch auf meine Schule.

Mein Lieblingsfach ist Musik und dieses Fach haben wir am Dienstag in der zweiten Stunde und auch am Donnerstag in der vierten Stunde. Sport mag ich auch, weil der Sportlehrer total lustig ist. Sein Lieblingssport ist Schwimmen und wir haben ein Hallenbad in der Schule. Wir haben Sport am Mittwoch in der fünften Stunde und auch am Freitag in der zweiten Stunde.

Mein Klassenzimmer ist sehr schön. Wir haben zehn Computer, ein Whiteboard neben der Tür, viele Poster an der Wand und eine Topfpflanze am Fenster!

2 Answer the questions about the texts in exercise 1. Write complete sentences in German for your answers.

1 Wie heißt Maiks Schule? ____________

2 Was mag Maik? ____________

3 Was lernt Maik nicht gern? ____________

4 Wann hat Maik Sport? ____________

5 Wo ist Zürich? ____________

6 Was hat Sabine am Donnerstag in der vierten Stunde?

____

7 Warum mag Sabine Sport? ____________

8 Wo ist die Topfpflanze? ____________

Grammatik (Seiten 90–91)

1 **Answer the questions in full sentences, using *weil* and the reason given.**

1 Warum magst du Kunst? (it's creative)

Ich mag Kunst, weil es kreativ ist.

2 Warum magst du Englisch? (it's interesting)

____

3 Warum spielst du Tennis? (I'm sporty)

____

4 Warum hasst du Sport? (it's difficult)

____

5 Warum findest du Erdkunde toll? (it's easy)

____

2 **Put the words in the right order to make sentences.**

Remember the 'verb in second place' rule.

1 der in Geschichte dritten wir Stunde haben

____

2 habe Pause ich nach der Kunst ____________________

3 Fußball spiele heute ich ____________________

4 gibt Klassenzimmer Computer und viele einen es im Poster

____

5 Montag ich vierten Stunde habe in am der Mathe

____

3 **Write the following school rules in sentences in German.**

Example: Man darf am Montag ...

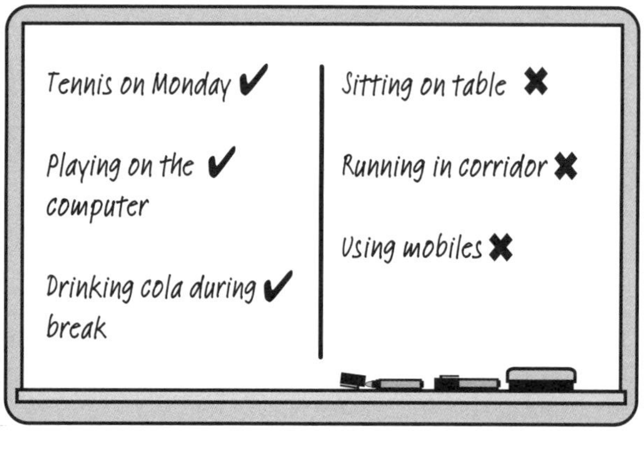

Man darf is often used to mean 'you/we are allowed to'.

Remember to use the correct preposition and the correct word for 'the' after it.

Mein Fortschritt

1 **Record your levels for *Kapitel* 4.**

2 **Look at the level descriptors on pages 59–60 and set your targets for *Kapitel* 5.**

3 **Fill in what you need to do to achieve these targets.**

Listening 	I have reached Level ______ in **Listening**. In *Kapitel* 5, I want to reach Level ______ I need to ________________________________ ________________________________ ________________________________ ________________________________
Speaking 	I have reached Level ______ in **Speaking**. In *Kapitel* 5, I want to reach Level ______ I need to ________________________________ ________________________________ ________________________________ ________________________________
Reading 	I have reached Level ______ in **Reading**. In *Kapitel* 5, I want to reach Level ______ I need to ________________________________ ________________________________ ________________________________ ________________________________
Writing 	I have reached Level ______ in **Writing**. In *Kapitel* 5, I want to reach Level ______ I need to ________________________________ ________________________________ ________________________________ ________________________________

Schulfächer • School subjects

Deutsch	*German*
Englisch	*English*
Erdkunde	*geography*
Geschichte	*history*
Informatik	*ICT*
Kunst	*art*
Mathe	*maths*
Musik	*music*
Naturwissenschaften	*science*
Sport	*sport, PE*
Technik	*technology*
Theater	*drama*

Meinungen • Opinions

mein Lieblingsfach ist ...	*my favourite subject is ...*
ich mag ... (sehr)	*I like ... (a lot)*
ich liebe	*I love*
ich mag ... nicht	*I don't like ...*
ich hasse	*I hate*
gut	*good*
toll	*great*
furchtbar	*awful*
einfach	*easy*
schwierig	*difficult*
interessant	*interesting*
langweilig	*boring*
nützlich	*useful*
nutzlos	*useless*
faszinierend	*fascinating*
nervig	*irritating*
supercool	*really cool*
stinklangweilig	*dead boring*

Die Wochentage • The days of the week

Montag (Mo.)	*Monday*
Dienstag (Di.)	*Tuesday*
Mittwoch (Mi.)	*Wednesday*
Donnerstag (Do.)	*Thursday*
Freitag (Fr.)	*Friday*
Samstag (Sa.)	*Saturday*
Sonntag (So.)	*Sunday*
Was hast du am Montag?	*What do you have on Monday?*
Am Dienstag habe ich ...	*I have ... on Tuesday*
Am Sonntag haben wir keine Schule.	*We have no school on Sunday.*

Die Zeit • Time

Wann?	*When?*
Um wie viel Uhr?	*At what time?*
Um 8:30 Uhr (acht Uhr dreißig).	*At 8:30.*
Wie viel Uhr ist es?	*What time is it?*
Es ist 9:50 Uhr (neun Uhr fünfzig).	*It's 9:50.*
in der ersten Stunde	*in the first lesson*
vor der Pause	*before break*
nach der Mittagspause	*after the lunch break*

Eigenschaften • Characteristics

Er/Sie ist ...	*He/She is ...*
alt	*old*
fair	*fair*
freundlich	*friendly*
jung	*young*
launisch	*moody*
lustig	*funny*
nervig	*annoying*
streng	*strict*
unpünktlich	*unpunctual*

In der Schule • In school

die Lehrerin(-nen)	*teacher (female)*
die Deutsch-lehrerin(-nen)	*German teacher (female)*
der Lehrer(–)	*teacher (male)*
der Sportlehrer(–)	*sports teacher (male)*
Was gibt es?	*What is there?*
Es gibt einen/eine/ein ...	*There is a ...*
Es gibt viele ...	*There are lots of ...*
das Klassenzimmer(–)	*classroom*
der Tisch(-e)	*table*
der Stuhl(¨-e)	*chair*
der Computer(–)	*computer*
das Whiteboard(-s)	*whiteboard*
das Poster(–)	*poster*
das Fenster(–)	*window*
die Wand(¨-e)	*wall*
die Tür(-en)	*door*
der Korridor(-e)	*corridor*

Wo ist das? • Where is it?

in der Schule	*in the school*
im Klassenzimmer	*in the classroom*
im Korridor	*in the corridor*
an der Wand	*on the wall*
am Fenster	*by the window*
am Tisch	*at the table*
auf dem Tisch	*on the table*
neben der Tür	*near/next to the door*

Oft benutzte Wörter • High-frequency words

weil	*because*
sein/seine	*his*
ihr/ihre	*her*
zu	*too*
sehr	*very*
ziemlich	*quite, fairly*
ein bisschen	*a bit*
nicht	*not*
haben	*to have*
sein	*to be*
in	*in*
an	*at, by, on (wall)*
auf	*on (top of)*
neben	*near, next to*
heute	*today*
morgen	*tomorrow*
vor	*before*
nach	*after*

1 In der Stadt (Seiten 98–99)

1 Write sentences to say what there is and isn't in the town.

1 Es gibt hier ______________________. 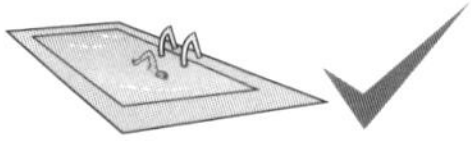

2 Hier gibt es ______________________. 

3 In der Stadt gibt es ______________________. 

4 Es gibt ______________________ hier. 

Grammatik

der→einen/keinen **die**→eine/keine **das**→ein/kein

2 Read the texts. Tick the things there are in each person's town and cross the things there aren't.

Monika: *Ich wohne in Celle. Meine Stadt ist nicht sehr groß. Es gibt hier ein Schloss und auch einen Marktplatz. Leider gibt es kein Schwimmbad und auch keine Kegelbahn.*

leider = unfortunately

Erik: *Die Touristen kommen gern nach Verden, weil es eine Kirche und auch einen Marktplatz gibt. Ein Schloss gibt es auch, aber leider gibt es kein Schwimmbad und keine Imbissstube.*

Aisha: *Ich wohne in Neustadt, in der Nähe vom Titisee. Neustadt ist ganz klein, aber sehr schön. Es gibt hier kein Schloss, keine Kegelbahn und leider auch kein Kino. Wir haben aber einen Bahnhof, eine Kirche und auch einen alten Marktplatz. Wir haben kein Schwimmbad, aber man kann im Sommer im Titisee schwimmen!*

	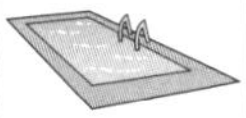			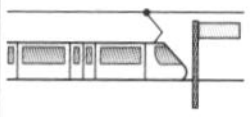				
Monika								
Erik								
Aisha								

3 Write two or three sentences about what there is to do where you live, as well as what there isn't. Use the texts in exercise 2 to help you.

2 Wir gehen einkaufen! (Seiten 100–101)

1 Write what the customers in the souvenir shop would like. Start your sentences with *Ich möchte*.

1 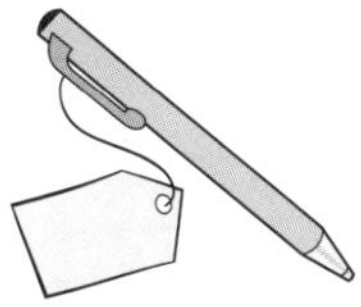
2 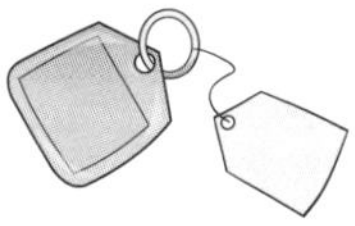
3 
4 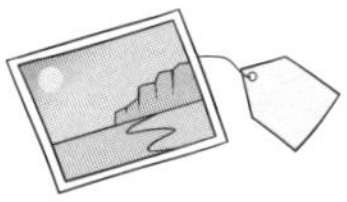
5 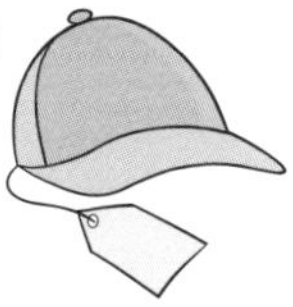
6 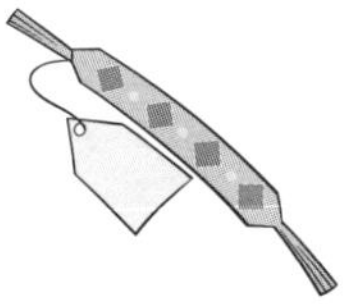
7 
8 

Look at the vocabulary on page 57 if you need to check which words to use.

1 Ich möchte einen Kuli.
2 ______________________
3 ______________________
4 ______________________
5 ______________________
6 ______________________
7 ______________________
8 ______________________

2 Complete the dialogue with words from the cloud below. Then number the lines of the conversation in the correct order 1–11.

☐ Guten Tag! ______________ ich dir helfen?
☐ Welche ______________ ? Wir haben blau, rot oder schwarz.
☐ Ja, klar! Dieser ______________ , zum Beispiel, kostet nur €18,95.
☐ Super!
☐ Danke. Auf ______________ .
☐ Sonst noch etwas?
☐ Alles ______________ kostet das €38,95.
☐ Guten Tag! Ich möchte ein Souvenir ______________ , vielleicht ein Kuscheltier. Haben Sie ______________ ?
☐ Bitte sehr.
☐ Ja. Ich möchte ein ______________ für meine Schwester.
☐ Schwarz, bitte. Wie viel ______________ das?

zusammen *Elefant* *Kuscheltiere* *Wiedersehen* *Kann* *kostet* *Fußballtrikot* *kaufen* *Farbe*

3 Mmm, lecker! (Seiten 102–103)

1 Write four short conversations between hungry customers and the owner of the snack stand. The price of each individual item is shown: don't forget to add up the total price.

1

× 1
drei Euro zehn

× 1
zwei Euro fünfunddreißig

2

× 2
zwei Euro sechzig

× 2
zwei Euro fünfundzwanzig

3

× 3
drei Euro zwanzig

× 1
ein Euro neunzig

4

× 4
drei Euro fünfundneunzig

× 1
zwei Euro zehn

Ich möchte …/Ich hätte gern …	I'd like …
Das kostet alles zusammen …	All together that costs …

1 *Guten Tag! Ich möchte einmal Hamburger und einmal Bratwurst, bitte.*

Das kostet alles zusammen € …

2 ______________________________

____

3 ______________________________

____

4 ______________________________

____

2 Write a short review of the menu, saying what there is to eat and drink and what you do and don't like.

Hamburger

Bratwurst
Pommes

Salat
Eis
Tee
Cola
Mineralwasser

Man kann … trinken/essen.	You can eat/drink …
Ich esse/trinke gern …	I like eating/drinking …
Ich esse/trinke nicht gern …	I don't like eating/drinking …
Ich mag …	I like ….
Ich mag nicht …	I don't like …..

____

____

____

4 In den Sommerferien (Seiten 104–105)

1 Circle the correct option to complete each sentence from the choices given. Then write the missing words in the gaps.

1 Ich ______________ im See baden.

a wirst **b** werden **c** werde

2 Wir werden im ______________ schwimmen.

a Meer **b** windsurfen **c** Bratwurst

3 ______________ du nach Innsbruck fahren?

a Wird **b** Wirst **c** Bist

4 Er ______________ nicht nach Hannover ______________ .

a werden; fahre **b** kann; fährt **c** wird; fahren

5 Tobi ______________ in den ______________ nach Portugal fahren.

a werde; Park **b** wird; Bahnhof **c** wird; Sommerferien

6 Wohin ______________ wir ______________ ?

a werden; gehen **b** kann; gehen **c** darf; fahren

2 Read the sentences and write the correct words from the cloud in the gaps. There are more words than you need.

1 Ich werde eine Kappe ______________ meinen Vater kaufen.

2 Ich ______________ ein Trikot kaufen.

3 In den ______________ fahren wir nach Rom.

4 Es ______________ ein Schwimmbad und ein Kino in Walsrode.

5 Wir ______________ nach Magdeburg fahren.

6 Ich möchte in den Bergen ______________ gehen.

für
gibt
möchte
nächste Woche
Sommerferien
wandern
werde
werden

3 Write about your plans for the summer holidays. Use the questions and illustrations to help you.

- Wohin wirst du fahren?

- Wer kommt mit?

- Was wirst du dort machen?

- Was wird dein Bruder / deine Schwester machen

- Wirst du Souvenirs kaufen?

Willkommen! (Seiten 108–109)

1 Rewrite each sentence. Swap the adjective in bold for an alternative adjective with a similar meaning.

1 Das Mozart Museum ist **faszinierend**. ______________________

2 Der Marktplatz ist **historisch**. ______________________

3 Das Schwimmbad ist **modern**.

____

4 Die Kegelbahn ist **toll**. ______________________

2 Join up the sentence halves to describe a trip to Vienna.

1 In den Sommerferien werde	**a** Tage in Wien bleiben.
2 Dort gibt es einen	**b** ich nach Wien fahren.
3 Am Montag kann	**c** Wien fantastisch.
4 Ich finde	**d** Marktplatz, aber keinen See.
5 Wir werden vier	**e** man das Mozart Museum besuchen.

Now rewrite the sentences, varying the sentence structure. Remember that in German you always need the verb as the second idea.

Example: **1** Ich werde in den Sommerferien ...

3 Read the text about Hahndorf. Try to work out what the words in bold mean from the context. If you can't work out the meanings, look them up in a dictionary.

Hahndorf ist eine kleine Stadt in Südaustralien, in der Nähe von Adelaide. Es gibt dort deutsche **Einwanderer**. Die Stadt ist klein, aber **fein**! Hahndorf ist toll für Kinder und auch für **Erwachsene**. Dort gibt es viele deutsche Restaurants und Cafés. Am Mittwoch und am Sonntag gibt es immer einen Markt auf dem Marktplatz. Man kann hier Schokolade, **Kuchen** und **Kleidung** kaufen. **Wein** aus der Region kann man auch dort trinken. Ich werde **nächstes Jahr** mit meiner Schule nach Hahndorf fahren.

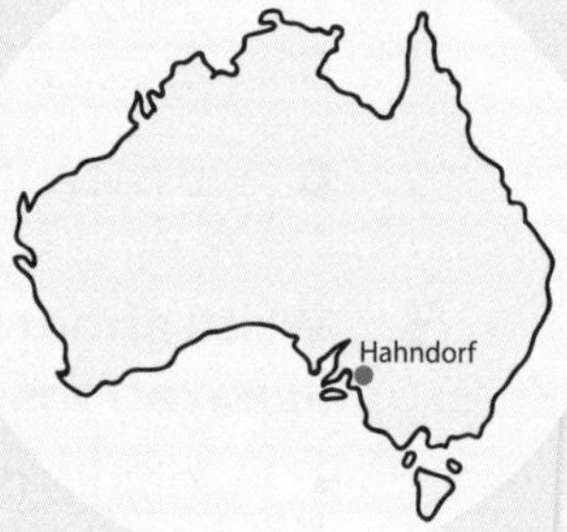

4 Write about a city or town of your choice. Adapt some of the words and phrases from the text in exercise 3.

Remember to include: the future tense, opinions, linking words, qualifiers, frequency expressions and inverted word order.

Wiederholung 1

1 Decide which souvenir you would buy for each person and write the price in words.

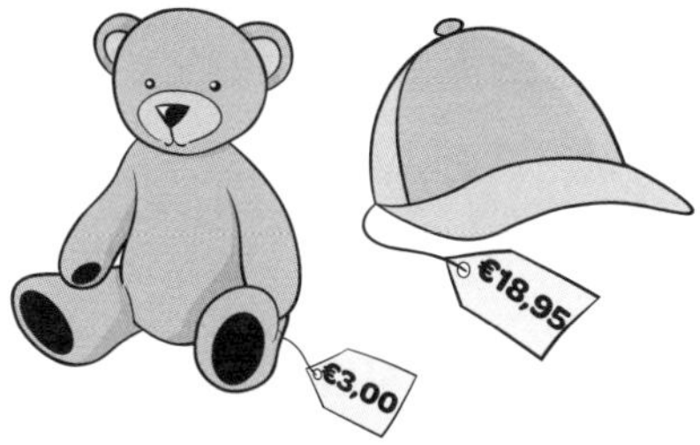

Grammatik

der → *er*   *die* → *sie*   *das* → *es*

Remember, *der* changes to *den* for masculine nouns.

1 Meine Mutter: Ich werde die Tasse für meine Mutter kaufen. Sie kostet sieben Euro fünfundfünfzig.

2 Onkel Karl: ______

3 Meine Schwester: ______

4 Meine Freundin: ______

5 Frau Roberts: ______

2 Peter is in the tourist office in Munich. Read the dialogue, then answer the questions in full German sentences.

Tourist guide: Guten Tag! Willkommen in München!

Peter: Guten Tag! Danke schön! Was gibt es hier in München?

Tourist guide: Hier gibt es viel zu tun! Man kann in München alles sehen!

Peter: Gibt es hier einen Marktplatz?

Tourist guide: Natürlich! Er heißt Marienplatz. Er ist sehr groß und total schön.

Peter: Wunderbar! Und kann man in München Ski fahren?

Tourist guide: Also ... nicht direkt in München, aber in der Nähe von hier kann man sehr gut Ski fahren.

Peter: Super. Und gibt es hier ein gutes Restaurant? Ich möchte gern Pizza essen.

Tourist guide: Ja, das gibt es! Es heißt *Robertos*. Dort kann man gut Pizza essen.

Peter: Vielen Dank. Ich werde im Restaurant *Robertos* essen. Auf Wiedersehen!

1 Was kann man in München machen?
2 Wie heißt der Marktplatz?
3 Wie ist er?
4 Wo kann man Ski fahren?
5 Was möchte Peter essen?
6 Was ist *Robertos*?

Wiederholung 2

1 Rewrite the sentences in the future tense. Identify the subject to help you change the form of *werden*.

1 Wir tauchen im Meer. *Wir werden im Meer tauchen.*

2 Wir baden im See. ______________________

3 Ich gehe an den Strand. ______________________

4 Lena und Michael klettern am Samstag in den Bergen.

____

5 Er kauft ein Kuscheltier für seine kleine Schwester.

____

6 Kaufst du eine Kappe als Souvenir? ______________________

7 Wir gehen am Wochenende mit meinen Freunden einkaufen.

____

2 Read the postcard and answer the questions in full German sentences.

Liebe Oma und Lieber Opa!

Hallo aus Mallorca in Spanien! Wir bleiben zwei Wochen hier, weil wir Sommerferien haben. Es gibt hier alles – einen Wasserpark, ein Schloss und auch einen Markt. Jeden Tag schwimmen wir im Meer. Im Hotel gibt es ein Schwimmbad und wir schwimmen auch hier. Man kann windsurfen und auch tauchen. Mallorca ist auch für das Essen sehr bekannt.

Nächste Woche werden wir in den Bergen klettern. Ich möchte auch segeln. Ich werde auch Souvenirs kaufen!

Alles Liebe,

Tamika

1 Warum ist Tamika in Spanien? ______________________

2 Was gibt es in Mallorca? ______________________

3 Was kann man machen? ______________________

4 Ist Mallorca bekannt für das Museum? ______________________

5 Was wird Tamika nächste Woche machen? ______________________

3 Write four true/false statements in English about the text in exercise 2. Then ask a friend to write 'True' or 'False' next to each statement.

Example: The postcard is to Tamika's parents. False

Grammatik (Seiten 112–113)

1 Rewrite the sentences to make them negative.

Use *keinen/keine/kein* to say what there is or isn't. Use *nicht* to say what you can't or don't like doing.

1 Es gibt in Düsseldorf einen Marktplatz.

____

2 Er mag Wasserball.

____

3 Beni kann Fußball spielen, weil er einen Ball hat.

____

4 In der Stadt gibt es ein Kino und auch eine Kirche.

____

5 Man darf hier schwimmen. ______________________________

2 Write the different forms of *möchten* in the table.

möchten
möchte
möchten
möchtest
möchte
möchtet
möchten

ich		wir	
du		ihr	
er/sie/es		Sie	
		sie	

Complete the sentences by writing the correct form of *möchten* in each gap. Then translate the sentences into English.

1 ______________ du ein Schokoladeneis?

2 Nein, aber ich ______________ gern ein Vanilleeis.

3 Anne ______________ nach Kapstadt in Südafrika fahren.

4 ______________ ihr auch nach Windhuk in Namibia fahren?

5 Wir ______________ zweimal Salat und zweimal Mineralwasser, bitte.

6 Frau Winkelmann, ______________ Sie eine Tasse Tee?

3 Fill in the gaps to complete the different forms of *werden*.

ich __e__de	wir we__ de__
du w__r__t	ihr __er__e__
er/sie/es __ir__	Sie/sie w__r__en

4 Write sentences about what you and your family/friends will do on your next holiday.

Example: Ich werde jeden Tag in Frankreich wandern. Mein Bruder ... /Steffi ...

Jahresbilanz

Record your levels for *Kapitel* 5.

Listening	I have reached Level ______ in **Listening**.
Speaking	I have reached Level ______ in **Speaking**.
Reading	I have reached Level ______ in **Reading**.
Writing	I have reached Level ______ in **Writing**.

Look back through your workbook and note down the level you achieved in each skill by the end of each *Kapitel*.

	Listening	**Speaking**	**Reading**	**Writing**
1 Meine Welt und ich				
2 Familie und Tiere				
3 Freizeit – juhu!				
4 Schule ist klasse!				
5 Gute Reise!				

You now have a record of your progress in German for the whole year.

In der Stadt • In town

Es gibt ...	*There is ... / There are ...*
Es gibt ein/eine/einen ...	*There is/are a ...*
Es gibt kein/keine/keinen ...	*There isn't/aren't ...*
in der Nähe von ...	*near to*
in der Nähe ...	*nearby*
der Bahnhof(¨-e)	*railway station(s)*
der Imbiss(-e)/die Imbissstube(-n)	*snack stand(s)*
die Kegelbahn(-en)	*bowling alley(s)*
das Kino(-s)	*cinema(s)*
die Kirche(-n)	*church(es)*
der Marktplatz(¨-e)	*market square(s)*
der Park(-s)	*park(s)*
das Schloss(¨-er)	*castle(s)*
das Schwimmbad(¨-er)	*swimming pool(s)*
die Eisbahn(-en)	*ice rink(s)*
der Fischmarkt(¨-e)	*fish market(s)*
das Kindertheater(-)	*children's theatre(s)*
der Radweg(-e)	*cycle path(s)*
das Sportzentrum (die Sportzentren)	*sports centre (sports centres)*
der Stadtpark(-s)	*city/town park(s)*
der Wasserpark(-s)	*water park(s)*

Verkaufsgespräch • Sales conversation

Ich gehe einkaufen.	*I am going shopping.*
Ich möchte ...	*I would like ...*
Ich möchte ... kaufen.	*I would like to buy ...*
Haben Sie ...?	*Do you have ...?*
Kann ich dir helfen?	*Can I help you?*
Sonst noch etwas?	*Anything else?*
alles zusammen	*all together*

Souvenirs • Souvenirs

der Aufkleber	*sticker*
das Freundschaftsband	*friendship bracelet*
die Kappe	*(baseball) cap*
der Kuli	*biro*
das Kuscheltier	*cuddly toy*
die Postkarte	*postcard*
der Schlüsselanhänger	*key ring*
die Tasse	*mug/cup*
das Trikot	*(football) shirt*
Wie viel kostet ...?	*How much does ... cost?*
Wie viel kostet das?	*How much does it cost?*
Es kostet €16.	*It costs 16 Euros.*

Snacks und Getränke kaufen • Buying snacks and drinks

die Bratwurst	*fried sausage*
der Hamburger	*hamburger*
die Pizza	*pizza*
die Pommes	*chips*
der Salat	*salad*
das Eis	*ice cream*
die Cola	*cola*
das Mineralwasser	*mineral water*
der Tee	*tea*
das Fleisch	*meat*
der Ketchup	*ketchup*
die Mayo(nnaise)/Majonäse	*mayo(nnaise)*
der Senf	*mustard*
Ich möchte einmal/zweimal/dreimal ...	*I would like one/two/three ...*
Ich hätte gern ...	*I would like ...*
Das macht €8.	*That's €8.*
Ich esse ... gern.	*I like eating ... .*
Ich trinke ... gern.	*I like drinking ... .*

Wörter

In den Sommerferien • During the summer holidays

Was wirst du machen?	*What will you do?*
Ich werde ...	*I will ...*
Wir werden ...	*We will ...*
klettern	*climb*
im Meer schwimmen	*swim in the sea*
rodeln	*toboggan*
im See baden	*bathe in the lake*
segeln	*sail*
an den Strand gehen	*go to the beach*
tauchen	*dive*
wandern	*hike*
windsurfen	*windsurf*
Was kann man dort machen?	*What can you do there?*
Man kann ... besuchen.	*'One'/People/ You can visit ...*
Die Stadt ist bekannt für ...	*The town is well known for ...*
Ich werde (eine Woche) bleiben.	*I will stay (for a week).*

Oft benutzte Wörter • High-frequency words

am Montag	*on Monday*
am Dienstag	*on Tuesday*
am Mittwoch	*on Wednesday*
am Donnerstag	*on Thursday*
am Freitag	*on Friday*
am Wochenende	*at the weekend*
sehr	*very*
nicht sehr	*not very*
ziemlich	*quite*
immer	*always*
nicht immer	*not always*
oft	*often*
nicht oft	*not often*
nie	*never*
alles	*everything*
dort	*there*
teuer	*expensive*

Level descriptors

Listening

Level 1	I can understand some familiar spoken words and phrases.
Level 2	I can understand a range of familiar spoken phrases.
Level 3	I can understand the main points of short spoken passages and note people's answers to questions.
Level 4	I can understand the main points of spoken passages and some of the detail.
Level 5	I can understand the main points and opinions in spoken passages about different topics. I can recognise if people are speaking about the future **OR** the past as well as the present.

Speaking

Level 1	I can say single words and short phrases.
Level 2	I can answer simple questions and use set phrases.
Level 3	I can ask questions and use short phrases to answer questions about myself.
Level 4	I can take part in conversations. I can express my opinions. I can use grammar to change phrases to say something new.
Level 5	I can give short talks, in which I express my opinions. I can take part in conversations giving information, opinions and reasons. I can speak about the future **OR** the past as well as the present.

Level descriptors

Reading

Level 1	I can understand familiar words and phrases.
Level 2	I can understand familiar phrases. I can read aloud familiar words and phrases. I can use a vocabulary list to check meanings.
Level 3	I can understand the main points and people's answers to questions in short written texts.
Level 4	I can understand the main points in short texts and some of the detail. Sometimes I can work out the meaning of new words.
Level 5	I can understand the main points and opinions in texts about different topics. I can recognise if the texts are about the future **OR** the past as well as the present.

Writing

Level 1	I can write or copy single words correctly.
Level 2	I can copy short sentences correctly and write some words from memory.
Level 3	I can answer questions about myself. I can write short phrases from memory. I can write short sentences with help.
Level 4	I can write short texts on familiar topics. I can use grammar to change phrases to write something new.
Level 5	I can write short texts on a range of familiar topics. I can write about the future **OR** the past as well as the present.

Notes

Notes

Published by Pearson Education Limited, Edinburgh Gate, Harlow, Essex, CM20 2JE.

www.pearsonschoolsandfecolleges.co.uk

Edited by Melanie Birdsall
Designed by Kamae Design

Illustrated by Caron at KJA Artists and Lisa Hunt

First published 2013

2022
17

British Library Cataloguing in Publication Data
A catalogue record for this book is available from the British Library

ISBN 978 1 447 94654 0

Printed in Great Britain by Bell and Bain Ltd, Glasgow

Acknowledgements

We would like to thank Melissa Weir, Angelika Libera, Janet Soame and Frances Reynolds for their invaluable help in the development of this course.

Every effort has been made to contact copyright holders of material reproduced in this book. Any omissions will be rectified in subsequent printings if notice is given to the publishers.

www.pearsonschools.co.uk
myorders@pearson.com
T 0845 630 33 33
F 0845 630 77 77

ISBN 978-1-4479-4654-0

Stimmt! 1

Übungsheft B

Malcolm Pacey

ALWAYS LEARNING

PEARSON

1 Hallo! (Seiten 8–9)

1 **Two of the words in each set have a sound that is the same. Circle the word with a different sound from the other two.**

1	*Schlange*	*Porsche*	*Buch*
2	*Bär*	*Löwe*	*Röntgenbild*
3	*Wildwassersport*	*Auf Wiedersehen*	*Tür*
4	*Biene*	*heiße*	*Eis*

2 **Join up the sentence halves.**

1	Gut, danke. Und	**a**	Wiedersehen.
2	Auf	**b**	Ben. Wie heißt du?
3	Ich heiße	**c**	geht's, Ben?
4	Hallo! Wie heißt	**d**	du?
5	Ich heiße Nadia. Wie	**e**	schlecht.
6	Nicht	**f**	dir?

3 **Write the sentences from exercise 2 in the correct order for the conversation. Then translate them into English.**

1 ______ ______
2 ______ ______
3 ______ ______
4 ______ ______
5 Nicht schlecht. Not bad.
6 ______ ______

4 **Unscramble the inventions. Look at the definite article (word for 'the') for each word. Then write each invention with the indefinite article (word for 'a').**

1	sad ngbönReltid	das …	ein …
2	erd reelmiDtoos		
3	sda toF3rMmPa-		
4	sad PeuAsotrcoh		
5	ied sAMrkdadiae		

2 Eins, zwei, drei … (Seiten 10–11)

1 **The bank has sent texts to customers with their coded PIN numbers. Solve the maths problems in German to work out the PINs. Then write each customer's new PIN below the phone.**

1
Meine Bank
zehn – acht = zwei
vier + drei = sieben
zwei + drei = ______
fünf + eins = ______

2 7 _ _

2
Meine Bank
sechs + zwei = ______
zehn – neun = ______
sieben – drei = ______
eins + vier = ______

_ _ _ _

3
Meine Bank
sieben – vier = ______
acht + eins = ______
drei + sechs = ______
fünf + zwei = ______

_ _ _ _

2 **Write the winning lottery numbers in words.**

1 13 ______
2 11 ______
3 16 ______
4 18 ______
5 12 ______
6 17 ______

3 **Write two sentences for each speaker. Give the speaker's age and the age of his/her friend.**

er ist = he is
sie ist = she is

1

Ich bin dreizehn Jahre alt.
Sie ist zwölf Jahre alt.

2
______
______

3

______
______

3 Ich wohne in Deutschland (Seiten 12–13)

1 Read the dialogue and complete the table with the correct forms of each verb.

Melanie: Hallo! Ich heiße Melanie. Wie heißt du?
Marco: Ich heiße Marco. Ich wohne in Straubing. Wo wohnst du?
Melanie: Ich wohne in Braunschweig. Wie alt bist du?
Marco: Ich bin zwölf Jahre alt. Wer ist das?
Melanie: Sie heißt Jessie. Sie wohnt in Leipzig und ist dreizehn Jahre alt.

wer = who

	heißen (to be called)	**wohnen** (to live)	**sein** (to be)
ich (I)		*wohne*	
du (you)			*bist*
er/sie/es (he/she/it)	*heißt*		

2 Write the missing word in each sentence and complete the crossword.

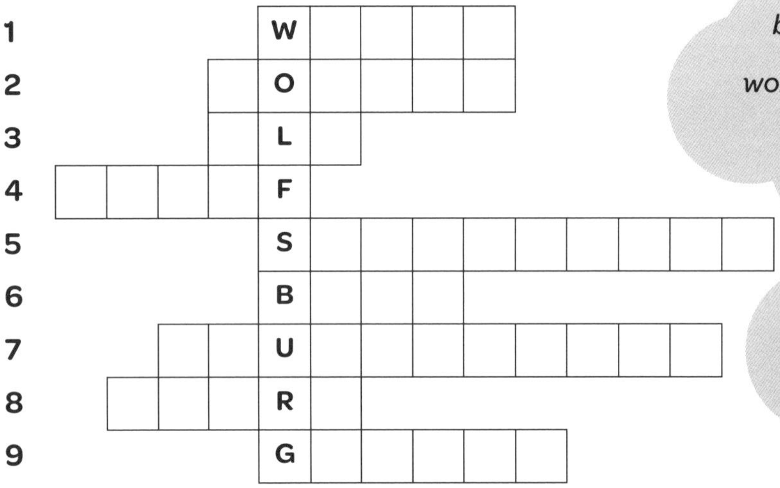

bist *zwölf* *wohne* *wohnst* *Jahre* *Schottland* *Deutschland* *geht's* *alt*

1 Ich ______________ in Manchester.
2 Wo ______________ du, Nick?
3 Wie ______________ ist er?
4 Er ist ______________ Jahre alt.
5 Glasgow ist in ______________ .
6 Wie alt ______________ du?
7 Ich wohne in Berlin. Das ist in ______________ .
8 Ich bin elf ______________ alt.
9 Wie ______________ ?

3 Research why the city of Wolfsburg is important to Germany.

1 **The printer has made four mistakes labelling the illustrations. Write *richtig* or *falsch* under each caption.**

1  Ich bin musikalisch.

____

2  Ich bin sehr launisch.

____

3  Ich bin ziemlich freundlich.

____

4  Ich bin kreativ.

____

5  Ich bin laut.

____

6  Ich bin lustig.

____

2 **Rewrite the false captions from exercise 1, correcting them so that they are true.**

____

____

____

____

faul
lustig
musikalisch
sportlich

3 **Separate out the words to form three sentences.**

meinelieblingsfußballmannschaftistbayernmünchen

meinlieblingssportisttennis

meinelieblingszahlistsieben

Remember that each sentence must start with a capital letter. Also, remember that nouns start with a capital letter.

1 ____

2 ____

3 ____

4 **Write a sentence about your favourite ...**

1 football team: __________________________________

2 sport: _______________________________________

3 number: _____________________________________

5 Meine Sachen (Seiten 16–17)

1 Write the German question word under its English translation.

Who?	What?	How?	Where?	Where from?

Wie? Was? Wo? Woher? Wer?

2 Write the correct question word in each question. You may use each word more than once.

1 ______________ bist du? Sportlich?

2 ______________ wohnt Shiva?

3 ______________ heißt du?

4 ______________ kommst du?

5 ______________ ist das? Ist das Max?

6 ______________ alt ist Michael?

7 ______________ ist Hannover? *Hannover ist in Deutschland!*

8 ______________ ist deine Lieblingsmusik?

3 Read the paragraph below. Pretend that you're Gabi, and answer each question in a complete German sentence.

Hallo! Ich heiße Gabi und ich bin vierzehn Jahre alt. Ich wohne in Kiel, in Deutschland, aber ich komme aus Swansea. Das ist in Wales. Wie bin ich? Ich bin sportlich, lustig und auch sehr laut! Mein Lieblingsmonat ist Dezember und meine Lieblingssendung ist ‚Die Simpsons'. Ich habe ein iPad und auch einen Computer. Tschüs!

1 Wie heißt du? ______________________________

2 Wo wohnst du? ______________________________

3 Woher kommst du? ______________________________

4 Wie bist du? ______________________________

5 Wie heißt deine Lieblingssendung? ______________________________

6 Was hast du? ______________________________

Ich über mich (Seiten 18–19)

1 Complete the table with the correct words.

	the	a	my	your
masculine: Sport				
feminine: Musik				
neuter: Auto				

2 Write each sentence or question in German. Tick the boxes when you've checked each part of your work.

Part of writing accurately in any language is going back over your work to check that there aren't any mistakes. Get into the habit now and watch both your English and German improve!

1 I'm called Osman.

____

2 I live in Germany.

____

3 I'm quite friendly and also creative.

____

____

4 I have a mobile phone.

____

5 Where do you live?

____

- ☐ Spelling of key phonics sound 'ei'
- ☐ Name has a capital
- ☐ Spelling of key phonics sound 'eu'
- ☐ Full stop at the end
- ☐ Check the qualifier
- ☐ Check the connective
- ☐ Capital on the noun
- ☐ Right word for 'a'
- ☐ Correct question word
- ☐ Verb in second position

3 Write a short paragraph about yourself. Use the sentences in exercise 2 as prompts. Check your work against the checklist below.

☐ genders ☐ qualifiers ☐ connectives ☐ verbs
☐ capital letters ☐ spelling ☐ question words

____

____

Wiederholung 1

1 Fill in the gaps by writing the German for the words in brackets.

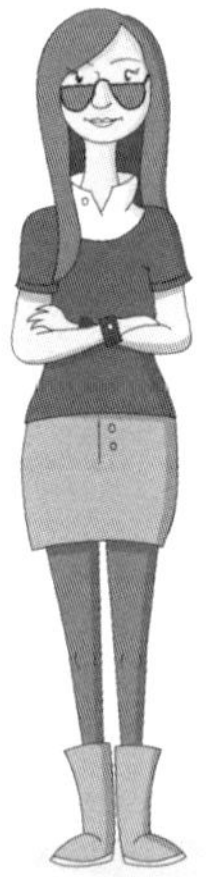

Hallo! Ich ______________ (am called) Marie und ich ______________ (live) in Walsrode. Das ist in ______________ (Germany). Ich bin fünfzehn ______________ (years) alt. Ich bin ______________ (very) sportlich und ______________ (quite) intelligent, ______________ (but) ich bin ______________ (also) faul. Mein ______________ (favourite sport) ist Hockey und ______________ (my) Lieblingsmusik ist Pop. Ich ______________ (have) einen Vogel aus Amerika. Er ist ______________ (very) freundlich, aber ______________ (not) laut!

2 Crack the code and write the sentences correctly.

a 18/24/19 4/12/19/13/22 18/13 20/28/7/7/18/13/20/22/13

Ich wohne in Göttingen.

b 22/9 18/8/7 20/26/13/1 21/9/22/6/13/23/15/18/24/19

____

c 14/22/18/13/22 15/18/22/25/15/18/13/20/8/14/6/8/18/16 18/8/7 14/12/1/26/9/7

____

____

ä = 27 ü = 29
ö = 28 ß = 30

3 Make up a coded sentence in German for a classmate to solve. Don't forget to provide a key.

4 Write the questions you would ask to get these answers.

1 *Wie heißt du?*

Ich heiße Elaine.

2 ______________________________

Mein Lieblingssport ist Tennis.

3 ______________________________

Sami ist musikalisch und intelligent, aber sehr launisch.

4 ______________________________

Alwin ist vierzehn Jahre alt.

Wiederholung 2

1 **Read the website entries.**

Ich heiße **Franzi** und suche Freunde aus England, Irland oder Nordirland. Ich habe eine Schlange zu Hause! Sie ist sechs Jahre alt. Ich wohne in Wien. Das ist in Österreich. Ich bin sehr kreativ und intelligent! Schreib mir bitte!

Hallo! Ich heiße **Hannah** und ich wohne in London, in England. Ich lerne Deutsch. Ich suche Freunde aus Deutschland, Österreich und auch aus der Schweiz. Ich bin sportlich und spiele Fußball und auch Tennis, aber ich bin sehr faul! Meine Lieblingsmusik ist Rock. Schreib mir!

Mein Name ist **Felix** und ich wohne in der Schweiz, aber ich komme aus Dortmund in Deutschland. Zu Hause habe ich eine Wii und mein Lieblingsspiel ist FIFA. Meine Lieblingsfußballmannschaft ist Bayern-München. Ich suche Freunde aus Schottland und Wales.

Hi! Ich bin **Muhammad** und ich wohne in Cardiff. Das ist in Wales. Ich bin sechzehn Jahre alt. Meine Lieblingssache ist Technologie. Ich habe zu Hause einen Computer, ein Handy und auch ein iPad. Ich bin nicht sehr sportlich, aber sehr freundlich. Mein Lieblingsland ist Deutschland und ich suche dort Freunde.

Write the name of the person who …

1 is looking for friends from Switzerland. Hannah

2 supports a football team. ________

3 has a pet. ________

4 is just looking for friends from Germany. ________

5 lives in a different place from where they were born. ________

6 does not particularly like sport. ________

7 lives in Switzerland. ________

suche = seek
Schreib mir (bitte)! = Write to me (please)!
dort = there

2 **Write your own profile for the website. Use as much German as you can from *Kapitel 1* to describe yourself.**

____

____

____

____

Grammatik (Seiten 22–23)

1 Write a sentence using the correct German word for 'a' for each item.

1  2  3  4  5 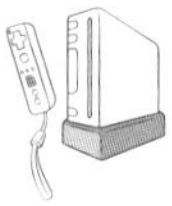 6  7  8 

1 Das ist ein Computer.
2 ______
3 ______
4 ______
5 ______
6 ______
7 ______
8 ______

die Gitarre · *das Handy* · *der iPod* · *der Computer* · *das Skateboard* · *das Keyboard* · *der Fußball* · *die Wii*

Grammatik
masculine – *ein*
feminine – *eine*
neuter – *ein*

2 Circle the correct verb form to complete each sentence.

1 Lukas **habe / hat / hast** einen Computer.
2 Ich **heiße / habe / hat** einen Vogel zu Hause.
3 Wo **bist / ist / wohnst** er?
4 Er **ist / komme / bin** musikalisch und sportlich.
5 Julia **bin / ist / wohnt** fünfzehn Jahre alt.
6 Wie alt **wohnst / bist / bin** du?
7 Wo **hast / bist / bin** ich?

Grammatik
You can use the pronouns *er* ('he') or *sie* ('she') instead of writing someone's name. Both need the *er*/*sie*/*es* form of the verb.

3 Complete the table with the correct forms of each regular verb.

wohnen (to live)	**kommen** (to come)	**heißen** (to be called)
ich wohne	ich	ich
du	du kommst	du
er/sie/es	er/sie/es	er/sie/es heißt

Now use the table to write the correct verb in each gap.

1 Mein Handy ______ aus China.
2 Meine Schlange ______ Sissel.
3 Du ______ Gabi.
4 ______ du aus Berlin?
5 ______ Monika in Hamburg?
6 Deine Lieblingssendung ______ ‚EastEnders'.
7 Ich ______ Wolfgang.
8 Wo ______ du?

Mein Fortschritt

1 **Record your levels for *Kapitel* 1.**

2 **Look at the level descriptors on pages 59–60 and set your targets for *Kapitel* 2.**

3 **Fill in what you need to do to achieve these targets.**

Listening 	I have reached Level ______ in **Listening**. In *Kapitel* 2, I want to reach Level ______ I need to ____ ____ ____ ____
Speaking 	I have reached Level ______ in **Speaking**. In *Kapitel* 2, I want to reach Level ______ I need to ____ ____ ____ ____
Reading 	I have reached Level ______ in **Reading**. In *Kapitel* 2, I want to reach Level ______ I need to ____ ____ ____ ____
Writing 	I have reached Level ______ in **Writing**. In *Kapitel* 2, I want to reach Level ______ I need to ____ ____ ____ ____

Wörter

Hallo! • Meeting and greeting

Wie heißt du?	*What's your name?*
Ich heiße ...	*My name is ...*
Hallo!	*Hello! / Hi!*
Guten Tag!	*Hello!*
Wie geht's?	*How are you?*
Gut, danke. Und dir?	*Fine, thanks. And you?*
Nicht schlecht.	*Not bad.*
Tschüs!	*Bye!*
Auf Wiedersehen!	*Goodbye!*

Die Zahlen 1–19 • Numbers 1–19

eins	*1*
zwei	*2*
drei	*3*
vier	*4*
fünf	*5*
sechs	*6*
sieben	*7*
acht	*8*
neun	*9*
zehn	*10*
elf	*11*
zwölf	*12*
dreizehn	*13*
vierzehn	*14*
fünfzehn	*15*
sechzehn	*16*
siebzehn	*17*
achtzehn	*18*
neunzehn	*19*
Wie alt bist du?	*How old are you?*
Ich bin ... Jahre alt.	*I am ... years old.*
Wie alt ist (Julia)?	*How old is (Julia)?*
(Julia) ist ... Jahre alt.	*(Julia) is ... years old.*

Wo wohnst du? • Where do you live?

Ich wohne in ...	*I live in ...*
Er/Sie/Es wohnt in ...	*He/She/It lives in ...*
... England	*England*
... Irland	*Ireland*
... Nordirland	*Northern Ireland*
... Schottland	*Scotland*
... Wales	*Wales*
... Deutschland	*Germany*
... Österreich	*Austria*
... der Schweiz	*Switzerland*

Wie bist du? • What are you like?

Ich bin ...	*I am ...*
Er/Sie ist ...	*He/She is ...*
faul	*lazy*
freundlich	*friendly*
intelligent	*intelligent*
kreativ	*creative*
launisch	*moody*
laut	*loud*
lustig	*funny*
musikalisch	*musical*
sportlich	*sporty*

Lieblingssachen • Favourite things

Mein Lieblingssport ist ...
My favourite sport is ...

Mein Lieblingsmonat ist ...
My favourite month is ...

Meine Lieblingsmusik ist ...
My favourite music is ...

Meine Lieblingszahl ist ...
My favourite number is ...

Meine Lieblingssendung ist ...
My favourite programme is ...

Meine Lieblingsfußballmannschaft ist ...
My favourite football team is ...

Mein Lieblingsspiel ist ...
My favourite game is ...

Mein Lieblingsland ist ...
My favourite country is ...

Mein Lieblingsauto ist ...
My favourite car is ...

Was ist dein Lieblingssport?
What's your favourite sport?

Was ist deine Lieblingszahl?
What's your favourite number?

Was ist dein Lieblingsland?
What's your favourite country?

Hast du einen Computer? • Have you got a computer?

Ich habe ...	*I have ...*
einen Computer	*a computer*
einen iPod	*an iPod*
einen Fußball	*a football*
eine Gitarre	*a guitar*
eine Wii	*a Wii*
eine Schlange	*a snake*
ein Handy	*a mobile phone*
ein Keyboard	*a keyboard*
ein Skateboard	*a skateboard*

Fragewörter • Question words

Wie?	*How?*
Was?	*What?*
Wo?	*Where?*
Woher?	*Where ... from?*
Wer?	*Who?*

Oft benutzte Wörter • High-frequency words

und	*and*
(und) auch	*(and) also*
aber	*but*
sehr	*very*
ziemlich	*quite*
nicht	*not*
Was denkst du?	*What do you think?*
Ich denke, ...	*I think ...*
Ich auch!	*Me too!*
Ich nicht!	*Not me!/That's not what I think!*
Was? Du spinnst!	*What? You're joking!*

1 Extreme Haustiere (Seiten 30–31)

1 Complete the sentences about the pets. Write the correct words in the gaps. Remember to think about the gender of each animal.

1 Ich habe *ein* ________ Pferd. *Es* ______ ist groß und heißt Romeo.
2 Ich habe ________ Kaninchen. ______ ist niedlich und heißt Timmo.
3 Ich habe ________ Katze. ______ ist intelligent und heißt Mieze.
4 Max hat ________ Schlange. ______ ist zwei Jahre alt.
5 Gabi hat ________ Pferd. ______ ist launish.
6 Ich habe ________ Hund. ______ ist freundlich und heißt Prinz.
7 Susi hat ________ Goldfisch. ______ heißt Nemo.

Grammatik
Remember: after *haben* the masculine word for 'a' changes from *ein* to *einen*.

Grammatik
m. der / ein → **er**
f. die / eine → **sie**
n. das / ein → **es**

2 Tina Tierfan has lots of pets! Write Tina's answers to the interviewer's questions about how many of each animal she has.

Grammatik

Hund (-e)	Pferd (-e)
Katze (-n)	Goldfisch (-e)
Schlange (-n)	Maus (Mäuse)

1 Hast du einen Hund? *Nein! Ich habe drei Hunde.*
2 Hast du ein Pferd? ________________________
3 Hast du eine Katze? ________________________
4 Hast du einen Goldfisch? ________________________
5 Hast du eine Schlange? ________________________
6 Hast du eine Maus? ________________________

2 Supertiere (Seiten 32–33)

1 **Complete the sentences about the animals. Write the correct name in each gap.**

Hermann

Minnie

Sisi

Kizzi

Moto

Millie

1 ____________ ist schnell.

2 ____________ ist süß.

3 ____________ ist gemein.

4 ____________ ist superintelligent.

5 ____________ ist cool.

6 ____________ ist kräftig.

2 **Write a sentence to say what each of the *Supertiere* can do.**

1

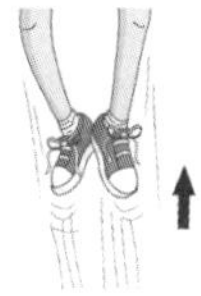

Hermann

2

Sisi

3

Minnie

4

Kizzi

5

Millie

6

Moto

1 Hermann kann springen.

2 ______________________________

3 ______________________________

4 ______________________________

5 ______________________________

6 ______________________________

Grammatik
The verb *kann* is always followed by an infinitive verb.

3 **Read the text below, then translate it into English.**

Günther Goldfisch ist mein Lieblingstier. Er ist ein Jahr alt. Er ist sehr lustig und kräftig, aber auch ziemlich süß. Er kann schwimmen, springen und auch im Aquarium tanzen! Günther hat einen Freund: er ist sehr cool und schlau.

3 Meine Familie (Seiten 34–35)

1 Find the numbers in the puzzle, and write them next to the correct numeral.

v	i	e	r	u	n	d	s	e	c	h	z	i	g	m	e
b	a	l	c	o	e	z	n	f	w	i	r	d	s	k	s
s	e	c	h	s	u	n	d	d	r	e	i	ß	i	g	a
q	g	n	a	j	n	x	i	n	d	m	h	t	g	ü	o
h	a	c	h	t	u	n	d	f	ü	n	f	z	i	g	i
u	e	i	n	u	n	d	a	c	h	t	z	i	g	p	b
n	t	e	r	i	d	f	b	n	ß	e	d	z	g	d	s
d	r	e	i	u	n	d	v	i	e	r	z	i	g	w	e
e	v	h	f	r	e	a	m	ß	p	l	s	j	a	q	c
r	d	r	e	i	u	n	d	z	w	a	n	z	i	g	h
t	z	a	n	j	n	x	o	u	e	y	g	r	e	v	z
k	c	p	f	s	z	d	l	b	n	l	a	i	h	m	i
i	b	z	w	e	i	u	n	d	s	i	e	b	z	i	g
a	g	b	n	ü	g	y	i	a	z	o	m	e	d	h	e

100 ______________________

64 ______________________

99 ______________________

43 ______________________

72 ______________________

36 ______________________

58 ______________________

81 ______________________

60 ______________________

23 ______________________

2 Describe each of the families. Fill in the gaps for the first family. Write the whole description for the second family.

Ich heiße Tom. Ich bin vierzehn Jahre alt. Es gibt vier Personen in meiner Familie. Meine Mutter ist ______________________ Jahre alt. Ich habe einen Bruder. ____ ist ________ Jahre alt. Ich habe eine Schwester. ______ ist ____________ Jahre alt. Wir wohnen in ________ .

____

____

____

____

____

____

3 Write about your family (real or imaginary). Use the descriptions in exercise 2 to help you.

der Stiefbruder = stepbrother
die Halbschwester = half-sister
Ich bin Einzelkind. = I am an only child.

1 Describe each person's hair and eyes.

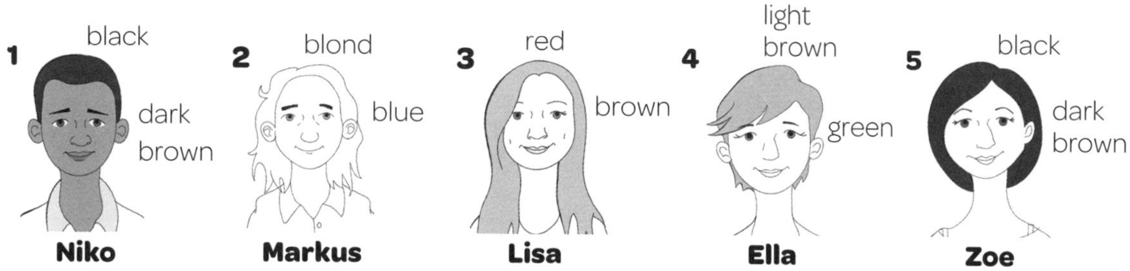

Grammatik
When you describe hair and eyes, the adjectives (colour, length) need an ***e*** on the end.

hell = light
dunkel = dark
hellbraun = light brown
dunkelblau = dark blue

1 Er heißt Niko. Er hat kurze, schwarze Haare und dunkelbraune Augen.

2 ____

3 ____

4 ____

5 ____

2 Complete the text by choosing the correct words from the cloud to fill the gaps. There are more words than you need.

Es gibt fünf __________ in meiner Familie. Wir __________ in Braunschweig. Das ist in __________________ . Meine __________ heißt Emma und sie ist neunundvierzig __________ alt. Sie ist sehr freundlich und hat __________ , schwarze Haare. Mein Vater __________ auch neunundvierzig und er hat kurze, dunkelbraune Haare und braune __________ .

Ich habe zwei __________ : einen Bruder und eine Schwester. __________ Bruder heißt Mehmet und er ist __________ Jahre alt. Er ist launisch aber __________ lustig. __________ Schwester, Isla, hat grüne Augen und __________ Haare. Sie ist sechzehn Jahre alt, sehr klein und __________________ .

Deutschland alt Augen Personen braune wohnen sportlich Meine Mutter Jahre lange Geschwister zwölf auch Mein blau ist

Read the text for gist first. For each sentence, think about whether you need a noun, a verb, a connective or an adjective.

5 Alles Gute! (Seiten 38–39)

1 Reorder the words to make correct sentences. Don't forget the full stop!

1 am | Mai | Ich | Geburtstag | habe | neunzehnten

____

2 hat | Oktober | am | Oma | Geburtstag | elften | Meine

____

3 Geburtstag | Stiefbruder | Dezember | am | Dein | dritten | hat

____

4 hast | Geburtstag | einunddreißigsten | Juli | Du | am

____

5 und | Geburtstag | haben | achten | am | Michael | Juni | Monika

____

2 Complete each sentence by writing the date. Write each holiday in English.

Neujahr ist am *ersten Januar*. *New Year*

Der Maifeiertag ist am ______________________. ____________

Der Tag der Deutschen Einheit ist am ______________________. *German Unity Day*

Weihnachten ist am ______________________. ____________

Silvester ist am ______________________. ____________

3 Read the short profile about Yannic and write a summary in the table.

Er heißt Yannic Spiller. Er ist dreizehn Jahre alt und kommt aus Trier. Trier ist in Deutschland. Yannic hat am siebten Januar Geburtstag. Er hat einen Bruder, Tim. Tim ist achtzehn Jahre alt. Yannic hat auch eine Schwester. Sie heißt Steffi und ist sechzehn Jahre alt. Die Familie Spiller hat zwei Haustiere: einen Hund und eine Katze.

Name:		Geschwister:	
Alter:			
Wohnt in:		Haustiere:	
Geburtstag:			

4 Now write a short profile about yourself.

6 Speaking Skills
Eine Superfamilie (Seiten 40–41)

1 Rescue the question words from the alphabet soup. Write each one on a line and use it to write a question.

Wie viele Brüder hast du?

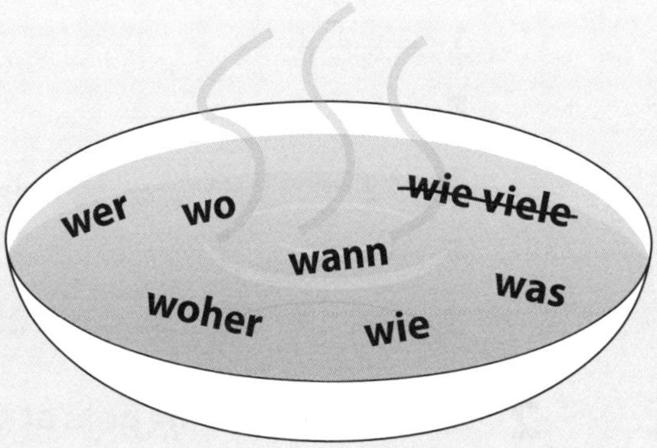

2 The police have written a summary about a crime suspect. Write six questions for a journalist to ask the suspect. The questions should cover all the information in the summary.

1 Wie heißt du?
2
3
4
5
6

Martin Kolwitz ist 24 Jahre alt. Er hat am achten November Geburtstag. Er wohnt in Hamburg, in Deutschland. Er hat einen Bruder. Er hat auch Haustiere: zwei Hunde.

Remember: the verb usually goes straight after the question word.

3 Use these notes to write questions to Martin about his accomplice, Sophie.

1 Wie heißt sie?
2
3
4
5

Sophie Meyer
19
Ebbingen, Deutschland
Haare – kurz, Augen – blau
Geb. 21.10.

Remember to use the correct part of the verb with the pronoun *sie*.

4 Write a summary about Sophie, like the one the police wrote about Martin in exercise 2.

Wiederholung 1

1 Complete the sentences. Choose the correct word from the cloud to fill in each gap.

1 ________________ Mutter ist sehr freundlich und intelligent.

2 Hast du ________________ Meerschweinchen?

3 Wir haben ________________ Haustier.

4 Wo ist ________________ Vogel?

5 Ich habe ________________ Bruder.

dein *kein*
ein *meine*
einen

2 You are describing pets at a pet show. Use the owners' notes to write what sort of pet they have, what the pet is like and what it can do.

Mareike

mouse
Pippa
cute, fast
fly, swim

Mareike hat ________________.

Sie heißt ________________.

Sie ist ________________.

Sie kann ________________.

Aaron

cat
Mieze
intelligent, cool, mean
jump, play football

________________.

________________.

________________.

________________.

________________.

3 Decscribe the animal you'll be entering in the pet show by writing a similar description.

Example: Ich habe …

Wiederholung 2

1 Read the texts below.

Hallo! Ich heiße **Anna** und ich bin fünfzehn Jahre alt. Ich habe am elften Februar Geburtstag. Ich wohne in Klagenfurt, in Österreich. Ich bin ziemlich groß und schlank und habe kurze, schwarze Haare und blaue Augen. Ich habe keine Geschwister – ich bin Einzelkind. Ich habe einen Goldfisch und einen Wellensittich. Ich kann Flöte spielen und Italienisch sprechen.

Hi! Ich bin **Noah** und ich komme aus Aachen. Das ist in Deutschland. Ich habe am zweiten November Geburtstag und bin vierzehn Jahre alt. Ich liebe Haustiere! Ich habe zwei Hunde, drei Katzen und eine Maus. Ich habe eine große Familie. Ich habe einen Halbbruder (er ist ein Baby) und zwei Schwestern. Mein Halbbruder ist sehr süß und klein. Er hat schwarze Haare und blaue Augen.

a Complete the sentences by writing *Anna* or *Noah*.

1 ________ lives in Austria.
2 ________ can play the flute.
3 ________'s birthday is on the 02.11.
4 ________ has a half-brother.
5 ________ is 15 years old.
6 ________ has cats.

b Write *richtig* or *falsch* next to each statement.

1 Anna hat einen Halbbruder. ________
2 Anna kann auch Englisch sprechen. ________
3 Noahs Halbbruder hat blaue Augen. ________
4 Klagenfurt ist nicht in Deutschland. ________
5 Anna hat am fünfzehnten Februar Geburtstag. ________
6 Anna hat keine Geschwister. ________

2 Translate these sentences into German.

1 My birthday is on the first of May. ________________
2 She can speak German. ________________
3 My guinea pig is very cute. ________________
4 Your sister has light blue eyes. ________________
5 My grandparents live in Southampton.
____
6 My brother can fly.
____

Grammatik (Seiten 44–45)

1 Complete the table by writing the correct form of *haben* for each pronoun.

haben *hast* *habt* *hat* *haben* *habe*

Words for 'you':
du (speaking to one family member or friend)
ihr (speaking to two or more family members or friends)
Sie (speaking to people you don't know or adults)

ich	du	er/sie/es	wir	ihr	Sie/sie

Now complete the sentences with the correct form of *haben*.

1 Katja, hast ____________ du eine Katze?
2 Tom und Niko, ____________ ihr einen Hund?
3 ____________ Sie eine Schlange, Herr Brand?
4 Ich ____________ ein Pferd.
5 Frau Gerber, ____________ Sie eine Maus?
6 Herr Alexander ____________ ein Pferd.

2 Join each pronoun to a verb. There is more than one possible verb for some of the pronouns. Then write a question or a sentence with each pair.

1 ich	a macht	1 ____________
2 du	b heißen	2 ____________
3 er	c wohnst	3 ____________
4 wir	d heiße	4 ____________
5 ihr	e spielt	5 ____________
6 Sie	f spielen	6 ____________

3 Rewrite the sentences so they include the verb *kann*.

1 Mein Bruder fliegt. Mein Bruder kann fliegen.
2 Ich spiele Flöte. ____________
3 Meine Mutter schwimmt. ____________
4 Mein Vater springt. ____________
5 Ich tanze. ____________
6 Er singt gut. ____________

Mein Fortschritt

1 Record your levels for *Kapitel* 2.

2 Look at the level descriptors on pages 59–60 and set your targets for *Kapitel* 3.

3 Fill in what you need to do to achieve these targets.

Listening 	I have reached Level ______ in **Listening**. In *Kapitel* 3, I want to reach Level ______ I need to ______________________________ ______________________________ ______________________________ ______________________________
Speaking 	I have reached Level ______ in **Speaking**. In *Kapitel* 3, I want to reach Level ______ I need to ______________________________ ______________________________ ______________________________ ______________________________
Reading 	I have reached Level ______ in **Reading**. In *Kapitel* 3, I want to reach Level ______ I need to ______________________________ ______________________________ ______________________________ ______________________________
Writing 	I have reached Level ______ in **Writing**. In *Kapitel* 3, I want to reach Level ______ I need to ______________________________ ______________________________ ______________________________ ______________________________

Haustiere • Pets

Hast du ein Haustier?	*Have you got a pet?*
Ich habe ...	*I have ...*
einen Goldfisch	*a goldfish*
einen Hamster	*a hamster*
einen Hund	*a dog*
ein Kaninchen	*a rabbit*
eine Katze	*a cat*
eine Maus	*a mouse*
ein Meerschweinchen	*a guinea pig*
ein Pferd	*a horse*
eine Schlange	*a snake*
einen Wellensittich	*a budgie*
kein Haustier	*no pet*

Eigenschaften • Qualities

Wie ist er/sie/es?	*What is he/she/ it like?*
Er/Sie/Es ist ...	*He/She/It is ...*
dick/schlank	*fat/thin*
frech/niedlich	*cheeky/cute*
gemein/süß	*mean/sweet*
groß/klein	*big/small*
kräftig	*strong*
schlau	*cunning*
(super)lustig	*(really) funny*
Er/Sie/Es kann ...	*He/She/It can ...*
Italienisch sprechen	*speak Italian*
fliegen	*fly*
Flöte/Fußball/Wii spielen	*play the flute/ football/on the Wii*
(schnell) laufen	*run (fast)*
lesen	*read*
Rad fahren	*ride a bike*
schwimmen	*swim*
singen	*sing*
springen	*jump*
tanzen	*dance*

Die Zahlen 20–100 • Numbers 20–100

zwanzig	*twenty*
dreißig	*thirty*
vierzig	*forty*
fünfzig	*fifty*
sechzig	*sixty*
siebzig	*seventy*
achtzig	*eighty*
neunzig	*ninety*
hundert	*hundred*
einundzwanzig	*twenty-one*
zweiundzwanzig	*twenty-two*

Meine Familie • My family

Es gibt ... Personen in meiner Familie.	*There are ... people in my family.*
meine Mutter	*my mother*
mein Vater	*my father*
mein Bruder	*my brother*
mein Stiefbruder/ Halbbruder	*my stepbrother/ half-brother*
meine Schwester	*my sister*
meine Stiefschwester/ Halbschwester	*my stepsister/ half-sister*
meine Eltern	*my parents*
meine Großeltern	*my grandparents*
Hast du Geschwister?	*Have you any brothers and sisters?*
Ich habe zwei Brüder.	*I have two brothers.*
Ich habe drei Schwestern.	*I have three sisters.*
Ich bin Einzelkind.	*I'm an only child.*
Ich habe keine Geschwister.	*I have no brothers and sisters.*

Die Farben • Colours

schwarz	*black*
weiß	*white*
grau	*grey*
braun	*brown*
rot	*red*
orange	*orange*
gelb	*yellow*
grün	*green*
blau	*blue*
indigoblau	*indigo*
violett	*violet*
lila	*purple*
rosa	*pink*
bunt	*brightly coloured*
hellblau/dunkelblau	*light blue/dark blue*

Haare und Augen • Hair and eyes

Er/Sie hat ...	*He/She has ...*
schwarze/braune/ blonde/rote Haare	*black/brown/ blond/red hair*
kurze/lange/ mittellange Haare	*short/long/ mid length hair*
blaue/braune/grüne/ graue Augen	*blue/brown/green/ grey eyes*

Die Monate • The months

Januar	*January*
Februar	*February*
März	*March*
April	*April*
Mai	*May*
Juni	*June*
Juli	*July*
August	*August*
September	*September*
Oktober	*October*
November	*November*
Dezember	*December*

Das Datum • The date

Wann hast du Geburtstag?	*When is your birthday?*
am 1. (ersten) Januar	*on 1 January*
am 3. (dritten) Februar	*on 3 February*
am 7. (siebten) März	*on 7 March*
am 8. (achten) April	*on 8 April*
am 15. (fünfzehnten) Mai	*on 15 May*
am 29. (neunund-zwanzigsten) Juni	*on 29 June*
Ich habe (heute) Geburtstag.	*It's my birthday (today).*

Oft benutzte Wörter • High-frequency words

und	*and*
aber	*but*
oder	*or*
ziemlich	*fairly, quite*
sehr	*very*

1 Bist du sportlich? (Seiten 54–55)

1 **Look at the survey results in the table. Then answer the questions using full German sentences.**

Ahmed	☺☺			☹			😐
Nicole		☺☺			☹		
Christa	☺		☺☺				😐
Torsten		☹		☺☺		☺	
Herr und Frau Meyer	☺☺			☺	☹	😐	

☺☺ = sehr gern ☺ = gern 😐 = ziemlich gern ☹ = nicht gern

1 Wer spielt sehr gern Fußball? *Nicole spielt sehr gern Fußball.*
2 Wer spielt gern Tischtennis? ______
3 Was spielt Christa sehr gern? ______
4 Was spielen Herr und Frau Meyer gern? ______
5 Wer spielt Basketball nicht gern? ______
6 Wer spielt ziemlich gern Handball? (2) ______
7 Und du? Was spielst du gern? ______

2 **Write three questions and three answers about the other people and sports in the table in exercise 1. Use the questions above as a model.**

______
______
______
______
______
______

2 Freizeit ist toll! (Seiten 56–57)

1 Write the words from the cloud in the grid. Translate the code word into English.

furchtbar
Eishockey
schlecht
spielst
irre
stinklangweilig
langweilig
Tischtennis
toll

2 Read about all the activities Hannes and Lola are involved in. Then write *richtig* or *falsch* next to each statement.

Hallo! Ich heiße **Hannes**. Ich finde Sport fantastisch. Ich spiele Tennis und schwimme. Schwimmen finde ich total super. Ich reite mit meiner Freundin, aber das finde ich langweilig. Fußball finde ich cool. Ich fahre auch gern Skateboard und lese sehr gern Sport- und Fitnessmagazine.

Meine Freundin heißt **Lola.** Sie findet Tischtennis toll. Lola fährt auch gern Rad – das ist sehr gesund! Sie findet schwimmen auch gut, aber Fußball findet sie nervig. Sie kann nicht Ski fahren. Im Winter spielt sie Eishockey und sie sieht sehr gern Eishockey im Fernsehen.

meine Freundin = my girlfriend
gesund = healthy
Fernsehen = television

1 Both Hannes and Lola participate in winter sports. ______________

2 Lola watches ice hockey on television. ______________

3 Hannes really likes swimming. ______________

4 Lola thinks skiing is fantastic. ______________

5 Lola plays ice hockey in winter. ______________

6 Hannes doesn't enjoying horse riding. ______________

7 Lola thinks football is exciting. ______________

8 Hannes watches sports programmes on television. ______________

3 In meiner Freizeit (Seiten 58–59)

1 Separate the words to form five time phrases and write them below. Number the phrases in order of frequency, starting with 1 for the most frequent. Translate the phrases into English.

jedenTagdreimalproWocheeinmalproMonatamWochenendesechsmalproMonat

☐ ______________________ ______________________

☐ ______________________ ______________________

☐ ______________________ ______________________

☐ ______________________ ______________________

☐ ______________________ ______________________

2 Use the time phrases from exercise 1 to answer the questions about yourself. Write your answers in full sentences.

1 Gehst du ins Kino? ______________________

2 Machst du Sport? ______________________

3 Gehst du einkaufen? ______________________

4 Hörst du Musik? ______________________

5 Spielst du Wii? ______________________

6 Chillst du mit deinen Freunden? ______________________

nie = never

3 Join up the sentence halves. Rewrite each sentence so that it starts with the time phrase.

1 Ich höre am — **a** Tag Sport.

2 Ich chille am — **b** Abend Musik.

3 Ich spiele sehr — **c** pro Woche Pizza.

4 Ich mache jeden — **d** Monat ins Kino.

5 Ich esse einmal — **e** oft Xbox.

6 Ich gehe einmal pro — **f** Wochenende.

Remember the 'verb in second place' rule.

4 Ich bin online (Seiten 60–61)

1 Unscramble and write down the time phrase in each sentence. Then translate the sentences into English.

Grammatik
You can use the present tense with a future time phrase to say what you are going to do – just as in English.

1 Wir machen ähncset eoWhc Filme. *nächste Woche*

We are going to make …

2 Ich suche ma Mtanog Infos im Internet. ______

______

3 Wir sehen ma eneneoWhcd Katzenvideos auf YouTube. ______

______

4 Ich chatte nejde denbA auf Facebook. ______

______

5 Stefan spielt ni iezw cnoWhe Wii Sport. ______

______

6 Ich lade gomrne Musik herunter. ______

______

2 Underline all the verbs in the text. Circle the words that are in first position in the sentences. Write a sentence about what you notice.

Hey du!

Franzi hier! Jetzt sind wir Freunde auf Facebook! Jeden Tag spiele ich Wii. Jede Woche schreibt mein Vater ein Blog, aber das finde ich langweilig. Am Abend lese ich gern E-Books. Morgen telefoniere ich mit Freunden in Kanada über Skype. Das finde ich cool! Im Sommer fahren wir nach Vancouver. Fantastisch! Was machst du am Computer und wie oft?

______

3 Reply to the question Franzi has asked you in his chat.

Use as many time phrases as you can in your reply.

1 What type of word is needed to fill the gap in each sentence? Complete each sentence by writing an appropriate German word or words in the gap.

verb *noun* *time/frequency phrase* *connective* *adjective*

	Type of word
1 Ich finde ______ Tennis toll.	verb
2 Meine Schwester findet Tischtennis ______ .	______
3 Wir sehen ______ fern.	______
4 Herr Peters spielt nächste Woche Tennis ______ Fußball.	______
5 Mein Bruder schreibt ein ______ .	______

2 Answer the questions about German grammar.

Use the sentences in exercise 1 to help you answer these questions.

1 Where in a sentence do verbs usually go?
______

2 What often goes after a verb? ______

3 What can you expect to go after *ein/eine*? ______

4 Which German verb suggests you're giving an opinion? ______

3 Replace the underlined word(s) with something else: a different noun, adjective or time phrase.

1 Ich finde Tischtennis <u>furchtbar</u>. Ich finde Tischtennis langweilig.

2 Ich spiele nicht gern <u>Fußball</u>. ______

3 Micha spielt gern <u>Wii</u>. ______

4 Er macht <u>einmal pro Monat</u> Judo. ______

5 Olli findet E-Books <u>fantastisch</u>. ______

6 Ich sehe <u>jede Woche</u> fern. Meine Schwester sieht <u>jeden Tag</u> Videos auf YouTube.

______

Remember that you'll keep the reader's interest if you use a variety of different words and phrases.

4 Write about your friends' hobbies.

Remember to include:
- opinions
- time/frequency phrases
- connectives
- 'verb in second place' rule

Wiederholung 1

1 Put the words in the correct order to make sentences or questions. Don't forget to insert a full stop or question mark.

1 fern gern sehr Ich sehe ____________________

2 einkaufen er Wochenende geht Am ____________________

3 Hausaufgaben Ich Infos lese die für ____________________

4 in Wie Stadt oft du fährst die ____________________

5 Woche Kai Wasserball Nächste spielt ____________________

6 herunter Videos Ich lade Musik und ____________________

2 Rewrite each sentence, beginning with a time phrase. Then translate the sentences into English.

1 Ich spiele Volleyball. (at the weekend) *Am Wochenende spiele ich Volleyball.*

At the weekend I am going to play volleyball.

2 Er spielt Basketball. (on Monday) ____________________

____

3 Du spielst Tischtennis. (every week) ____________________

____

4 Rosa spielt Fußball. (today) ____________________

____

5 Ich telefoniere mit Sam. (next week) ____________________

____

6 Sophie liest das Buch. (tomorrow) ____________________

____

3 Underline the regular verbs and circle the irregular verbs.

Ich spiele nicht gern Tennis. Ich finde Tennis langweilig. Fußball spiele ich dreimal pro Woche. Mein Bruder spielt sehr gern Tennis. Er fährt auch gern Rad. Radfahren findet er toll. Meine Schwester sieht ziemlich gern fern. Meine Mutter liest ziemlich gern. Oft liest sie Blogs im Internet. Ich lese auch oft. Mein Vater fährt gern Ski und spielt Gitarre.

Wiederholung 2

1 Read the email. Find the German for the following words and phrases in the text.

1 I think ______
2 about ______
3 but ______
4 New Zealand ______
5 comedies ______
6 Best wishes ______

Lieber Anish,

wie geht's? Danke für deine E-Mail.

Ich denke, Technologie ist toll. Ich bin sehr oft online. Ich chatte sehr gern mit Freunden auf Facebook. Facebook finde ich super und ich sehe oft Videos über Fußball auf YouTube.

Ich spiele Computerspiele nicht gern, aber ich suche ziemlich oft Infos für die Hausaufgaben. Meine Cousine, Connie, wohnt in Neuseeland und wir telefonieren ziemlich oft über Skype. Kannst du auch über Skype telefonieren?

Ich mache viel Sport mit meinen Freunden: Wir schwimmen zweimal pro Woche und wir spielen am Abend Basketball. Im Winter fahre ich auch Ski.

Ich esse manchmal am Wochenende mit meinen Freunden Pizza, und dann gehen wir ins Kino. Ich sehe gern Komödien. Nächste Woche sehen wir *Skyfall*.

Liebe Grüße,

Tibor

2 Answer the questions in complete German sentences.

1 Spielt Tibor gern Computerspiele? ______
2 Was macht Tibor auf Facebook? ______
3 Wer wohnt in Neuseeland? ______
4 Wie telefoniert Tibor mit seiner Cousine? ______
5 Wie oft schwimmt Tibor? ______
6 Was machen Tibor und seine Freunde am Wochenende?

______

3 Write a reply to Tibor's email about your hobbies and activities.

Grammatik (Seiten 68–69)

1 Complete the verb table.

	fahren (to go/travel)	**sehen** (to see)	**lesen** (to read)
ich			
du	fährst		liest
er/sie/es		sieht	
wir			
ihr			
Sie			
sie			

2 Complete the sentences by writing the correct form of the verb in brackets.

1 Ich ________________ das Auto. (waschen)
2 ________________ du gern Mangabücher? (lesen)
3 Er ________________ im Schlafzimmer. (schlafen)
4 Thomas ________________ nach Stockholm in Schweden. (fahren)
5 ________________ du morgen Torsten? (sehen)
6 ________________ du eine Schuluniform? (tragen)

Verbs like fahren:
tragen = to wear
schlafen = to sleep
waschen = to wash

die Schuluniform = school uniform

3 Write the question for each reply.

1 ________________ Ja, ich spiele Gitarre.
2 ________________ Nein, ich spiele nicht gern Wasserball.
3 ________________ Ja, Michael schläft im Bett.
4 ________________ Ja, ich fahre nach Bremen.
5 ________________ Ja, ich lese gern E-Books.
6 ________________ Nein, ich sehe nicht gern fern.
7 ________________ Ja, ich bin sportlich!
8 Was ________________ Ich trage morgen Jeans und ein T-Shirt.
9 ________________ Michael trägt eine Schuluniform.

Remember, to form a question you put the verb before the subject:
Du spielst gern Tennis. → Spielst du gern Tennis?

Mein Fortschritt

1 Record your levels for *Kapitel* 3.

2 Look at the level descriptors on pages 59–60 and set your targets for *Kapitel* 4.

3 Fill in what you need to do to achieve these targets.

Listening 	I have reached Level _____ in **Listening**. In *Kapitel* 4, I want to reach Level _____ I need to ______________________________ ______________________________ ______________________________ ______________________________
Speaking 	I have reached Level _____ in **Speaking**. In *Kapitel* 4, I want to reach Level _____ I need to ______________________________ ______________________________ ______________________________ ______________________________
Reading 	I have reached Level _____ in **Reading**. In *Kapitel* 4, I want to reach Level _____ I need to ______________________________ ______________________________ ______________________________ ______________________________
Writing 	I have reached Level _____ in **Writing**. In *Kapitel* 4, I want to reach Level _____ I need to ______________________________ ______________________________ ______________________________ ______________________________

Bist du sportlich? • Are you sporty?

Ich bin (sehr/ziemlich/ nicht sehr) sportlich.	*I am (very/quite/ not very) sporty.*
Was spielst du?	*What do you play?*
Ich spiele ...	*I play ...*
Ich spiele gern ...	*I like playing ...*
Ich spiele ziemlich gern ...	*I quite like playing ...*
Ich spiele nicht gern ...	*I don't like playing ... playing ...*
Badminton	*badminton*
Basketball	*basketball*
Eishockey	*ice hockey*
Fußball	*football*
Handball	*handball*
Tennis	*tennis*
Tischtennis	*table tennis*
Volleyball	*volleyball*
Wasserball	*water polo*

Was machst du gern? • What do you like doing?

Was machst du gern?	*What do you like doing?*
Ich fahre Rad.	*I ride my bike.*
Ich fahre Skateboard.	*I go skateboarding.*
Ich fahre Ski.	*I ski.*
Ich fahre Snowboard.	*I snowboard.*
Ich lese.	*I read.*
Ich mache Judo.	*I do judo.*
Ich mache Karate.	*I do karate.*
Ich reite.	*I go horse riding.*
Ich schwimme.	*I swim.*
Ich sehe fern.	*I watch TV.*
Ich spiele Gitarre.	*I play the guitar.*
Ich tanze.	*I dance.*

Wie findest du das? • What do you think of it?

Ich finde es ...	*I think it's ...*
Es ist ...	*It's ...*
irre	*amazing*
super	*super*
toll	*great*
cool	*cool*
gut	*good*
nicht schlecht	*not bad*
okay	*okay*
langweilig	*boring*
nervig	*annoying*
stinklangweilig	*deadly boring*
furchtbar	*awful*

Was machst du in deiner Freizeit? • What do you do in your free time?

Ich chille.	*I chill out.*
Ich esse Pizza oder Hamburger.	*I eat pizza or hamburgers.*
Ich gehe einkaufen.	*I go shopping.*
Ich gehe ins Kino.	*I go to the cinema.*
Ich gehe in den Park.	*I go to the park.*
Ich gehe in die Stadt.	*I go into town.*
Ich höre Musik.	*I listen to music.*
Ich mache Sport.	*I do sport.*
Ich spiele Xbox oder Wii.	*I play Xbox or on the Wii.*

Wörter

Ich bin online • I'm online

Was machst du am Computer?	*What do you do on the computer?*
Was machst du auf deinem Handy?	*What do you do on your mobile?*
Ich chatte mit Freunden auf Facebook.	*I chat with friends on Facebook.*
Ich lade Musik herunter.	*I download music.*
Ich mache Fotos oder Filme.	*I take photos or make films.*
Ich sehe Videos.	*I watch videos.*
Ich simse.	*I text.*
Ich spiele Computerspiele.	*I play computer games.*
Ich suche und lese Infos für die Hausaufgaben.	*I look for and read information for my homework.*
Ich surfe im Internet.	*I surf the internet.*
Ich telefoniere mit Freunden.	*I call my friends.*
Ich mache ziemlich viel auf meinem Handy.	*I do quite a lot of things on my mobile.*

Oft benutzte Wörter • High-frequency words

Wie oft?	*How often?*
(sehr/ziemlich/nicht so) oft	*(very/quite/not so) often*
einmal/zweimal/dreimal pro Woche/pro Monat	*once/twice/three times a week/a month*
jeden Tag	*every day*
jeden Morgen	*every morning*
manchmal	*sometimes*
immer	*always*
nie	*never*
Wann?	*When?*
am Wochenende	*at the weekend*
am Abend	*in the evening*
heute	*today*
morgen	*tomorrow*
am Montag	*on Monday*
nächste Woche	*next week*
in zwei Wochen	*in two weeks*

1 Ich mag Deutsch! (Seiten 76–77)

1 **Write a sentence for each illustration.**

1

2

3

4

5

6

1 Ich mag ______________________________

2 ______________________________

3 ______________________________

4 ______________________________

5 ______________________________

6 ______________________________

> **ich liebe** 🙂🙂
> **ich mag** 🙂
> **ich mag ... nicht** ☹
> **ich hasse** ☹☹

2 **Read the forum entries giving people's opinions about school subjects. Then answer the questions below.**

Hallo Leute! Mein Lieblingsfach ist Englisch! Ich liebe Englisch, weil es total interessant ist. Ich lese sehr gern Bücher auf Spanisch und auf Deutsch. Mathe finde ich langweilig. **Pedro**
Hi Pedro! Ich mag Englisch nicht. Es ist sehr schwierig, aber ich mag Mathe und Naturwissenschaften. Ich finde Mathe supercool. **Nadine**
Grüezi aus der Schweiz! Ich liebe Theater und Kunst. Ich mag Kunst sehr gern, weil ich total kreativ bin. Informatik finde ich sehr langweilig, und Geschichte und Erdkunde sind nutzlos. **Marta**

Who ...

1 is very creative? ______________

2 enjoys reading? ______________

3 doesn't like English? ______________

4 thinks ICT is boring? ______________

5 likes maths? ______________

6 can read Spanish? ______________

7 loves art? ______________

8 doesn't like geography? ______________

3 **Rewrite each sentence in exercise 1, adding *weil* and an opinion. Use the examples in exercise 2 to help you with word order.**

2 Was und wann? (Seiten 78–79)

1 Look at the timetable. Write *richtig* or *falsch* next to each statement.

	Montag	**Dienstag**	**Mittwoch**	**Donnerstag**	**Freitag**
8.15	Mathe	Erdkunde	Englisch	Deutsch	Technik
9.15	Englisch	Informatik	Theater	Mathe	Deutsch
10.45	Kunst	Mathe	Deutsch	Kunst	Naturwissenschaften
11.45	Naturwissenschaften	Mathe	Naturwissenschaften	Geschichte	Theater
13.30	Deutsch	Sport	Technik	Musik	Englisch

vor = before **nach** = after **die Doppelstunde** = double period

1 Am Mittwoch habe ich Deutsch. __________

2 Wir haben am Freitag nach der Pause Technik. __________

3 Am Montag vor der Pause haben wir Englisch. __________

4 Theater ist am Mittwoch und am Donnerstag. __________

5 Ich habe am Donnerstag nach der Mittagspause Musik. __________

6 Am Dienstag habe ich eine Doppelstunde Mathe. __________

2 At what time do you have the following subjects? Write a sentence for each.

1 *Ich habe Englisch um neun Uhr zehn.* — 09:10

2 __________ — 10:05

3 __________ — 11:15

4 __________ — 12:10

5 __________ — 13:20

6 __________ — 14:15

um acht Uhr = at 8 o'clock

3 Look at the timetable in exercise 1 and describe one school day. Try to add interest to your sentences by giving opinions about some subjects.

Example: Am Montag um acht Uhr fünfzehn habe ich Mathe. Ich mag Mathe, weil es interessant ist.

Ich finde Mathe ...
= I find maths ...

3 Lehrer und Lehrerinnen (Seiten 80–81)

1 Write a description for each of the teachers.

1 *Mein Sportlehrer heißt Herr Huber.*
Er ist cool, aber sehr unpünktlich.

2 ____________________
____

3 ____________________
____

4 ____________________
____

Use some qualifiers in your descriptions: *sehr, zu, ziemlich, ein bisschen, nicht*

2 Complete the text by writing the correct word from the cloud in each gap.

Mein ____________ an der Schule ist Geschichte, ____________ meine Geschichtelehrerin sehr lustig ist! Sie ____________ nur ein Haustier, aber ihr Haustier ist eine Schlange!

Am ____________ und am Freitag haben wir Kunst. Ich finde Kunst ziemlich langweilg, weil es schwierig ____________. Mein Kunstlehrer ____________ Herr Ackermann. ____________ Schwester ist auch Kunstlehrerin an meiner ____________! Sie heißt Frau Ackermann! Meine Sportlehrerin ist ____________ freundlich. Sie heißt Frau Krause und ____________ Lieblingssport ist Volleyball. Ich mag Sport, weil ich sehr ____________ bin.

heißt hat Mittwoch Lieblingsfach ist
sehr Schule Seine sportlich weil ihr

3 Write the correct word for 'his' or 'her' in each sentence.

1 ____________ Bruder lernt Hindi. (his)
2 ____________ Schwester ist Lehrerin. (her)
3 ____________ Hobby ist Gitarre spielen. (his)
4 ____________ Lieblingsfach ist Kunst. (her)
5 ____________ Schuluniform ist fantastisch. (his)
6 ____________ Bruder ist 19 Jahre alt. (her)

Grammatik
sein = his **ihr** = her (for masculine and neuter nouns)
seine = his **ihre** = her (for feminine nouns)
Check the gender of the noun if you are unsure.

4 Im Klassenzimmer (Seiten 82–83)

1 Draw a simple picture to show where each of these things is.

1 Der Musiklehrer ist im Klassenzimmer.
2 Das Buch ist neben dem Computer.
3 Das Poster ist an der Wand.
4 Der Stuhl ist auf dem Tisch und neben der Tür.

1	2	3	4

2 What is there in the classroom? Start each sentence with *Es gibt* (there is/there are). Write the numbers as words.

12  Es gibt zwölf Tische im Klassenzimmer.

6  ______________________

24  ______________________

2  ______________________

4 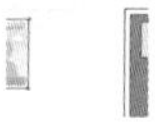 ______________________

5  ______________________

Look at the vocabulary on page 47 for the plurals of the nouns.

3 Answer the questions using the information in the pictures.

@peta_ush Darfst du dein Handy in der Schule benutzen?

____

@tara_winkel Darfst du im Klassenzimmer schnell laufen?

____

@e_atch Darfst du in der Pause Musik hören?

____

@janet_mc Darfst du dein Handy in der Mittagspause benutzen?

____

ich darf   du darfst   er/sie/es darf

Mein Lieblingstag (Seiten 84–85)

1 Most of the verbs you've seen end in –*en* in the infinitive. Write the infinitive form of each verb in the table. Then try to work out its meaning from the context.

If the context doesn't help you, use a German–English dictionary.

verb	**infinitive**	**meaning in English**
Er **geht** in die Schule.	*gehen*	*to go, to walk*
Er **kauft** ein Auto.		
Er **steht** auf dem Tisch.		
Warum **redest** du so schnell?		
Ich **wasche** meinen Hund.		
Ich **nehme** das Buch.		

2 Guess the meaning of these compound nouns by separating out the words. Look up the compound nouns in a dictionary to find their gender and meaning.

The second word in each compound noun gives the gender.

compound noun	**word 1**	**word 2**	**gender**	**meaning**
Fußballfeld	*Fußball*		*das*	
Arbeitstag				
Sporthalle				
Klassenarbeit				
Lehrerzimmer				

3 Now write a short German sentence using each compound noun from exercise 2.

1 *Das Fußballfeld ist sehr grün und …*

2 ______

3 ______

4 ______

5 ______

Wiederholung 1

1 Mimi's description of her school day is in the wrong time order! Number the sentences 1–6 in the correct order of time.

☐ Ich habe um dreizehn Uhr fünfundzwanzig Musik.

☐ Die Pause beginnt um elf Uhr zehn.

☐ Die erste Stunde beginnt um acht Uhr vierzig.

☐ Der Bus kommt um fünfzehn Uhr siebenundvierzig.

☐ Ich komme um sechzehn Uhr dreißig nach Hause.

☐ Wir haben Mathe um elf Uhr fünfundzwanzig.

2 The school is running 20 minutes late today. Rewrite each of the six sentences in exercise 1 with the time that each activity begins today.

3 Complete the sentences by writing the correct possessive pronoun in each gap.

! **sein** = his (for masculine and neuter nouns) **seine** = his (for feminine nouns)
ihr = her (for masculine and neuter nouns) **ihre** = her (for feminine nouns)

1 ________ Bruder heißt Pawel und ________ Schwester heißt Aga.

2 ________ Lieblingssport ist Eishockey.

3 ________ Katze ist braun, aber ________ Hund ist weiß.

4 ________ Schule ist in Hannover.

5 ________ Lieblingssport ist Reiten und ________ Lieblingsfach ist Mathe.

6 ________ Computer ist neu.

7 ________ Erdkundelehrerin ist sehr streng.

8 ________ Mutter wohnt in Salzburg, aber ________ Vater wohnt in Wien.

4 Describe where each of the items is located in the classroom.

1 Der Computer ist auf dem Tisch.

2 Das Poster ________________

3 Das Whiteboard ________________

4 Der Lehrer ________________

5 Der Stuhl ________________

6 Die Spinne ________________

Wiederholung 2

1 Read the texts. Use your knowledge of vocabulary to help you to find these new phrases. Write each German phrase next to the English.

1 My name is ______________________

2 her favourite artist ______________________

3 unfortunately ______________________

4 My brother also goes ______________________

5 an indoor pool ______________________

6 a pot plant ______________________

Hallo! Mein Name ist **Maik** und ich wohne in München, in Deutschland. Meine Schule heißt Mathias Brauer Gymnasium und ich finde sie toll. An meiner Schule lerne ich sehr gern Englisch und Geschichte, aber mein Lieblingsfach ist Kunst. Ich mag Kunst, weil ich total kreativ bin. Ich finde meine Kunstlehrerin auch sehr nett. Sie heißt Frau Weber und ihr Lieblingskünstler ist Dürer.

Ich mag nicht Sport, weil ich nicht sehr sportlich bin. Leider habe ich am Montag und auch am Mittwoch Sport. Morgen spielen wir Tennis. Das finde ich nicht so schlecht.

lernen = to learn

Hallo Leute! Ich heiße **Sabine** und ich wohne in Zürich, in der Schweiz. Meine Schule ist sehr groß. Mein Bruder geht auch auf meine Schule.

Mein Lieblingsfach ist Musik und dieses Fach haben wir am Dienstag in der zweiten Stunde und auch am Donnerstag in der vierten Stunde. Sport mag ich auch, weil der Sportlehrer total lustig ist. Sein Lieblingssport ist Schwimmen und wir haben ein Hallenbad in der Schule. Wir haben Sport am Mittwoch in der fünften Stunde und auch am Freitag in der zweiten Stunde.

Mein Klassenzimmer ist sehr schön. Wir haben zehn Computer, ein Whiteboard neben der Tür, viele Poster an der Wand und eine Topfpflanze am Fenster!

2 Answer the questions about the texts in exercise 1. Write complete sentences in German for your answers.

1 Wie heißt Maiks Schule? ______________________

2 Was mag Maik? ______________________

3 Was lernt Maik nicht gern? ______________________

4 Wann hat Maik Sport? ______________________

5 Wo ist Zürich? ______________________

6 Was hat Sabine am Donnerstag in der vierten Stunde?

____

7 Warum mag Sabine Sport? ______________________

8 Wo ist die Topfpflanze? ______________________

Grammatik (Seiten 90–91)

1 Answer the questions in full sentences, using *weil* and the reason given.

1 Warum magst du Kunst? (it's creative)

Ich mag Kunst, weil es kreativ ist.

2 Warum magst du Englisch? (it's interesting)

3 Warum spielst du Tennis? (I'm sporty)

4 Warum hasst du Sport? (it's difficult)

5 Warum findest du Erdkunde toll? (it's easy)

2 Put the words in the right order to make sentences.

Remember the 'verb in second place' rule.

1 der in Geschichte dritten wir Stunde haben

2 habe Pause ich nach der Kunst

3 Fußball spiele heute ich

4 gibt Klassenzimmer Computer und viele einen es im Poster

5 Montag ich vierten Stunde habe in am der Mathe

3 Write the following school rules in sentences in German.

Example: Man darf am Montag ...

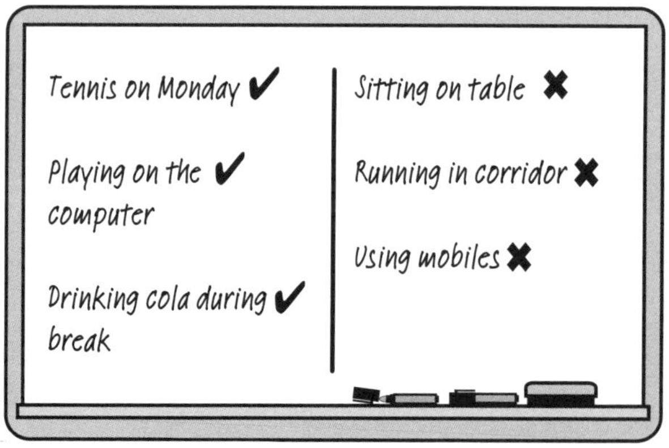

Man darf is often used to mean 'you/we are allowed to'.

Remember to use the correct preposition and the correct word for 'the' after it.

Mein Fortschritt

1 Record your levels for *Kapitel* 4.

2 Look at the level descriptors on pages 59–60 and set your targets for *Kapitel* 5.

3 Fill in what you need to do to achieve these targets.

Listening 	I have reached Level ______ in **Listening**. In *Kapitel* 5, I want to reach Level ______ I need to ______________________ ______________________ ______________________ ______________________
Speaking  	I have reached Level ______ in **Speaking**. In *Kapitel* 5, I want to reach Level ______ I need to ______________________ ______________________ ______________________ ______________________
Reading 	I have reached Level ______ in **Reading**. In *Kapitel* 5, I want to reach Level ______ I need to ______________________ ______________________ ______________________ ______________________
Writing 	I have reached Level ______ in **Writing**. In *Kapitel* 5, I want to reach Level ______ I need to ______________________ ______________________ ______________________ ______________________

Wörter

Schulfächer • School subjects

Deutsch	*German*
Englisch	*English*
Erdkunde	*geography*
Geschichte	*history*
Informatik	*ICT*
Kunst	*art*
Mathe	*maths*
Musik	*music*
Naturwissenschaften	*science*
Sport	*sport, PE*
Technik	*technology*
Theater	*drama*

Meinungen • Opinions

mein Lieblingsfach ist ...	*my favourite subject is ...*
ich mag ... (sehr)	*I like ... (a lot)*
ich liebe	*I love*
ich mag ... nicht	*I don't like ...*
ich hasse	*I hate*
gut	*good*
toll	*great*
furchtbar	*awful*
einfach	*easy*
schwierig	*difficult*
interessant	*interesting*
langweilig	*boring*
nützlich	*useful*
nutzlos	*useless*
faszinierend	*fascinating*
nervig	*irritating*
supercool	*really cool*
stinklangweilig	*dead boring*

Die Wochentage • The days of the week

Montag (Mo.)	*Monday*
Dienstag (Di.)	*Tuesday*
Mittwoch (Mi.)	*Wednesday*
Donnerstag (Do.)	*Thursday*
Freitag (Fr.)	*Friday*
Samstag (Sa.)	*Saturday*
Sonntag (So.)	*Sunday*
Was hast du am Montag?	*What do you have on Monday?*
Am Dienstag habe ich ...	*I have ... on Tuesday*
Am Sonntag haben wir keine Schule.	*We have no school on Sunday.*

Die Zeit • Time

Wann?	*When?*
Um wie viel Uhr?	*At what time?*
Um 8:30 Uhr (acht Uhr dreißig).	*At 8:30.*
Wie viel Uhr ist es?	*What time is it?*
Es ist 9:50 Uhr (neun Uhr fünfzig).	*It's 9:50.*
in der ersten Stunde	*in the first lesson*
vor der Pause	*before break*
nach der Mittagspause	*after the lunch break*

Eigenschaften • Characteristics

Er/Sie ist ...	*He/She is ...*
alt	*old*
fair	*fair*
freundlich	*friendly*
jung	*young*
launisch	*moody*
lustig	*funny*
nervig	*annoying*
streng	*strict*
unpünktlich	*unpunctual*

In der Schule • In school

die Lehrerin(-nen)	*teacher (female)*
die Deutsch-lehrerin(-nen)	*German teacher (female)*
der Lehrer(–)	*teacher (male)*
der Sportlehrer(–)	*sports teacher (male)*
Was gibt es?	*What is there?*
Es gibt einen/eine/ein ...	*There is a ...*
Es gibt viele ...	*There are lots of ...*
das Klassenzimmer(–)	*classroom*
der Tisch(-e)	*table*
der Stuhl(¨-e)	*chair*
der Computer(–)	*computer*
das Whiteboard(-s)	*whiteboard*
das Poster(–)	*poster*
das Fenster(–)	*window*
die Wand(¨-e)	*wall*
die Tür(-en)	*door*
der Korridor(-e)	*corridor*

Wo ist das? • Where is it?

in der Schule	*in the school*
im Klassenzimmer	*in the classroom*
im Korridor	*in the corridor*
an der Wand	*on the wall*
am Fenster	*by the window*
am Tisch	*at the table*
auf dem Tisch	*on the table*
neben der Tür	*near/next to the door*

Oft benutzte Wörter • High-frequency words

weil	*because*
sein/seine	*his*
ihr/ihre	*her*
zu	*too*
sehr	*very*
ziemlich	*quite, fairly*
ein bisschen	*a bit*
nicht	*not*
haben	*to have*
sein	*to be*
in	*in*
an	*at, by, on (wall)*
auf	*on (top of)*
neben	*near, next to*
heute	*today*
morgen	*tomorrow*
vor	*before*
nach	*after*

1 In der Stadt (Seiten 98–99)

1 Write sentences to say what there is and isn't in the town.

1 Es gibt hier ______________________________________.

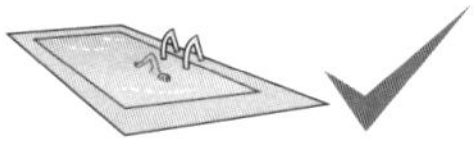

2 Hier gibt es ______________________________________.

3 In der Stadt gibt es ______________________________________.

4 Es gibt ______________________________________ hier.

Grammatik
der→einen/keinen **die**→eine/keine **das**→ein/kein

2 Read the texts. Tick the things there are in each person's town and cross the things there aren't.

Monika: *Ich wohne in Celle. Meine Stadt ist nicht sehr groß. Es gibt hier ein Schloss und auch einen Marktplatz. Leider gibt es kein Schwimmbad und auch keine Kegelbahn.*

leider = unfortunately

Erik: *Die Touristen kommen gern nach Verden, weil es eine Kirche und auch einen Marktplatz gibt. Ein Schloss gibt es auch, aber leider gibt es kein Schwimmbad und keine Imbissstube.*

Aisha: *Ich wohne in Neustadt, in der Nähe vom Titisee. Neustadt ist ganz klein, aber sehr schön. Es gibt hier kein Schloss, keine Kegelbahn und leider auch kein Kino. Wir haben aber einen Bahnhof, eine Kirche und auch einen alten Marktplatz. Wir haben kein Schwimmbad, aber man kann im Sommer im Titisee schwimmen!*

	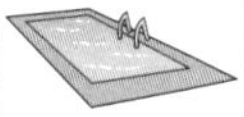			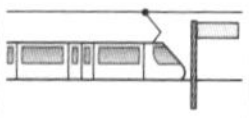				
Monika								
Erik								
Aisha								

3 Write two or three sentences about what there is to do where you live, as well as what there isn't. Use the texts in exercise 2 to help you.

2 Wir gehen einkaufen! (Seiten 100–101)

1 Write what the customers in the souvenir shop would like. Start your sentences with *Ich möchte*.

1 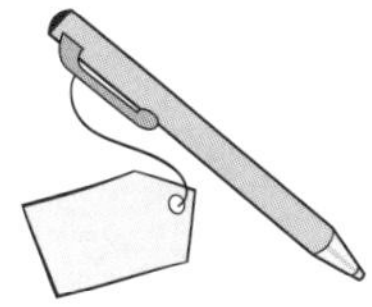
2 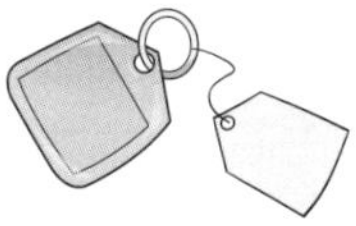
3 
4 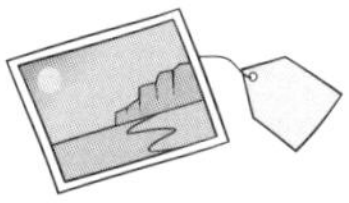
5 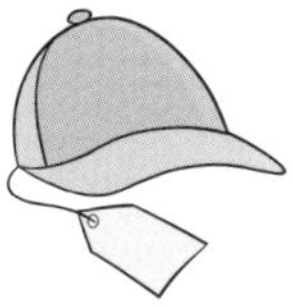
6 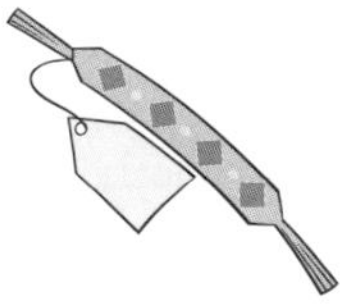
7 
8 

Look at the vocabulary on page 57 if you need to check which words to use.

1 Ich möchte einen Kuli.
2 ______________________
3 ______________________
4 ______________________
5 ______________________
6 ______________________
7 ______________________
8 ______________________

2 Complete the dialogue with words from the cloud below. Then number the lines of the conversation in the correct order 1–11.

☐ Guten Tag! ______________ ich dir helfen?
☐ Welche ______________? Wir haben blau, rot oder schwarz.
☐ Ja, klar! Dieser ______________, zum Beispiel, kostet nur €18,95.
☐ Super!
☐ Danke. Auf ______________.
☐ Sonst noch etwas?
☐ Alles ______________ kostet das €38,95.
☐ Guten Tag! Ich möchte ein Souvenir ______________, vielleicht ein Kuscheltier. Haben Sie ______________?
☐ Bitte sehr.
☐ Ja. Ich möchte ein ______________ für meine Schwester.
☐ Schwarz, bitte. Wie viel ______________ das?

*zusammen   Elefant   Kuscheltiere
Wiedersehen   Kann
kostet   Fußballtrikot   kaufen
Farbe*

3 Mmm, lecker! (Seiten 102–103)

1 Write four short conversations between hungry customers and the owner of the snack stand. The price of each individual item is shown: don't forget to add up the total price.

1

× 1
drei Euro zehn

× 1
zwei Euro fünfunddreißig

2

× 2
zwei Euro sechzig

× 2
zwei Euro fünfundzwanzig

3

× 3
drei Euro zwanzig

× 1
ein Euro neunzig

4

× 4
drei Euro fünfundneunzig

× 1
zwei Euro zehn

Ich möchte .../Ich hätte gern ...	I'd like ...
Das kostet alles zusammen ...	All together that costs ...

1 *Guten Tag! Ich möchte einmal Hamburger und einmal Bratwurst, bitte.*
Das kostet alles zusammen € ...

2 ______________________________
____

3 ______________________________
____

4 ______________________________
____

2 Write a short review of the menu, saying what there is to eat and drink and what you do and don't like.

Hamburger

Bratwurst

Pommes
Salat
Eis
Tee
Cola
Mineralwasser

Man kann ... trinken/essen.	You can eat/drink ...
Ich esse/trinke gern ...	I like eating/drinking ...
Ich esse/trinke nicht gern ...	I don't like eating/drinking ...
Ich mag ...	I like ....
Ich mag nicht ...	I don't like .....

____
____
____

4 In den Sommerferien (Seiten 104–105)

1 Circle the correct option to complete each sentence from the choices given. Then write the missing words in the gaps.

1 Ich __________ im See baden.

a wirst　　b werden　　c werde

2 Wir werden im __________ schwimmen.

a Meer　　b windsurfen　　c Bratwurst

3 __________ du nach Innsbruck fahren?

a Wird　　b Wirst　　c Bist

4 Er __________ nicht nach Hannover __________ .

a werden; fahre　　b kann; fährt　　c wird; fahren

5 Tobi __________ in den __________ nach Portugal fahren.

a werde; Park　　b wird; Bahnhof　　c wird; Sommerferien

6 Wohin __________ wir __________ ?

a werden; gehen　　b kann; gehen　　c darf; fahren

2 Read the sentences and write the correct words from the cloud in the gaps. There are more words than you need.

1 Ich werde eine Kappe __________ meinen Vater kaufen.

2 Ich __________ ein Trikot kaufen.

3 In den __________ fahren wir nach Rom.

4 Es __________ ein Schwimmbad und ein Kino in Walsrode.

5 Wir __________ nach Magdeburg fahren.

6 Ich möchte in den Bergen __________ gehen.

für
gibt
möchte
nächste Woche
Sommerferien
wandern
werde
werden

3 Write about your plans for the summer holidays. Use the questions and illustrations to help you.

- Wohin wirst du fahren?

- Wer kommt mit?

- Was wirst du dort machen?

- Was wird dein Bruder / deine Schwester machen

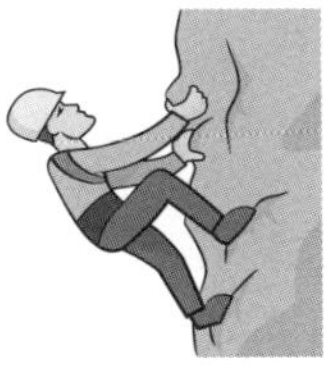

- Wirst du Souvenirs kaufen?

1 Rewrite each sentence. Swap the adjective in bold for an alternative adjective with a similar meaning.

1 Das Mozart Museum ist **faszinierend**. ______

2 Der Marktplatz ist **historisch**. ______

3 Das Schwimmbad ist **modern**.

______

4 Die Kegelbahn ist **toll**. ______

2 Join up the sentence halves to describe a trip to Vienna.

1 In den Sommerferien werde	a Tage in Wien bleiben.
2 Dort gibt es einen	b ich nach Wien fahren.
3 Am Montag kann	c Wien fantastisch.
4 Ich finde	d Marktplatz, aber keinen See.
5 Wir werden vier	e man das Mozart Museum besuchen.

Now rewrite the sentences, varying the sentence structure. Remember that in German you always need the verb as the second idea.

Example: **1** Ich werde in den Sommerferien ...

3 Read the text about Hahndorf. Try to work out what the words in bold mean from the context. If you can't work out the meanings, look them up in a dictionary.

Hahndorf ist eine kleine Stadt in Südaustralien, in der Nähe von Adelaide. Es gibt dort deutsche **Einwanderer**. Die Stadt ist klein, aber **fein**! Hahndorf ist toll für Kinder und auch für **Erwachsene**. Dort gibt es viele deutsche Restaurants und Cafés. Am Mittwoch und am Sonntag gibt es immer einen Markt auf dem Marktplatz. Man kann hier Schokolade, **Kuchen** und **Kleidung** kaufen. **Wein** aus der Region kann man auch dort trinken. Ich werde **nächstes Jahr** mit meiner Schule nach Hahndorf fahren.

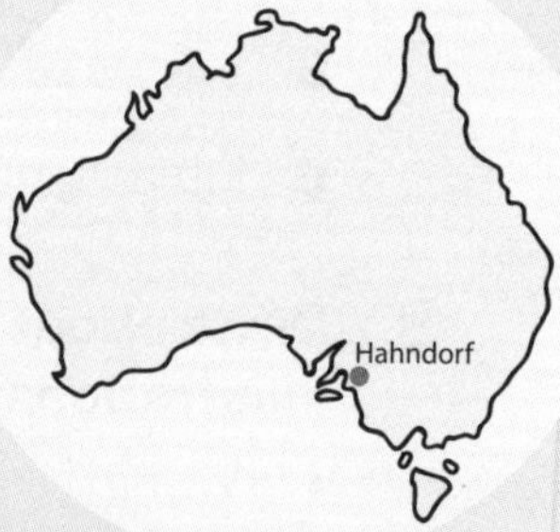

4 Write about a city or town of your choice. Adapt some of the words and phrases from the text in exercise 3.

Remember to include: the future tense, opinions, linking words, qualifiers, frequency expressions and inverted word order.

Wiederholung 1

1 Decide which souvenir you would buy for each person and write the price in words.

Grammatik

der → *er*   *die* → *sie*   *das* → *es*

Remember, *der* changes to *den* for masculine nouns.

1 Meine Mutter: Ich werde die Tasse für meine Mutter kaufen. Sie kostet sieben Euro fünfundfünfzig.

2 Onkel Karl: ______________________________

3 Meine Schwester: ______________________________

4 Meine Freundin: ______________________________

5 Frau Roberts: ______________________________

2 Peter is in the tourist office in Munich. Read the dialogue, then answer the questions in full German sentences.

Tourist guide: Guten Tag! Willkommen in München!

Peter: Guten Tag! Danke schön! Was gibt es hier in München?

Tourist guide: Hier gibt es viel zu tun! Man kann in München alles sehen!

Peter: Gibt es hier einen Marktplatz?

Tourist guide: Natürlich! Er heißt Marienplatz. Er ist sehr groß und total schön.

Peter: Wunderbar! Und kann man in München Ski fahren?

Tourist guide: Also ... nicht direkt in München, aber in der Nähe von hier kann man sehr gut Ski fahren.

Peter: Super. Und gibt es hier ein gutes Restaurant? Ich möchte gern Pizza essen.

Tourist guide: Ja, das gibt es! Es heißt *Robertos*. Dort kann man gut Pizza essen.

Peter: Vielen Dank. Ich werde im Restaurant *Robertos* essen. Auf Wiedersehen!

1 Was kann man in München machen?
2 Wie heißt der Marktplatz?
3 Wie ist er?
4 Wo kann man Ski fahren?
5 Was möchte Peter essen?
6 Was ist *Robertos*?

Wiederholung 2

1 Rewrite the sentences in the future tense. Identify the subject to help you change the form of *werden*.

1 Wir tauchen im Meer. Wir werden im Meer tauchen.

2 Wir baden im See. ____________________

3 Ich gehe an den Strand. ____________________

4 Lena und Michael klettern am Samstag in den Bergen.

____

5 Er kauft ein Kuscheltier für seine kleine Schwester.

____

6 Kaufst du eine Kappe als Souvenir? ____________________

7 Wir gehen am Wochenende mit meinen Freunden einkaufen.

____

2 Read the postcard and answer the questions in full German sentences.

Liebe Oma und Lieber Opa!

Hallo aus Mallorca in Spanien! Wir bleiben zwei Wochen hier, weil wir Sommerferien haben. Es gibt hier alles – einen Wasserpark, ein Schloss und auch einen Markt. Jeden Tag schwimmen wir im Meer. Im Hotel gibt es ein Schwimmbad und wir schwimmen auch hier. Man kann windsurfen und auch tauchen. Mallorca ist auch für das Essen sehr bekannt.

Nächste Woche werden wir in den Bergen klettern. Ich möchte auch segeln. Ich werde auch Souvenirs kaufen!

Alles Liebe,

Tamika

1 Warum ist Tamika in Spanien? ____________________

2 Was gibt es in Mallorca? ____________________

3 Was kann man machen? ____________________

4 Ist Mallorca bekannt für das Museum? ____________________

5 Was wird Tamika nächste Woche machen? ____________________

3 Write four true/false statements in English about the text in exercise 2. Then ask a friend to write 'True' or 'False' next to each statement.

Example: The postcard is to Tamika's parents. False

Grammatik (Seiten 112–113)

1 Rewrite the sentences to make them negative.

Use *keinen/keine/kein* to say what there is or isn't. Use *nicht* to say what you can't or don't like doing.

1 Es gibt in Düsseldorf einen Marktplatz.

____

2 Er mag Wasserball.

____

3 Beni kann Fußball spielen, weil er einen Ball hat.

____

4 In der Stadt gibt es ein Kino und auch eine Kirche.

____

5 Man darf hier schwimmen. ______________________________

2 Write the different forms of *möchten* in the table.

möchten
möchte
möchten
möchtest
möchte
möchtet
möchten

ich		wir	
du		ihr	
er/sie/es		Sie	
		sie	

Complete the sentences by writing the correct form of *möchten* in each gap. Then translate the sentences into English.

1 ____________ du ein Schokoladeneis?

2 Nein, aber ich ____________ gern ein Vanilleeis.

3 Anne ____________ nach Kapstadt in Südafrika fahren.

4 ____________ ihr auch nach Windhuk in Namibia fahren?

5 Wir ____________ zweimal Salat und zweimal Mineralwasser, bitte.

6 Frau Winkelmann, ____________ Sie eine Tasse Tee?

3 Fill in the gaps to complete the different forms of *werden*.

ich __e__de

du w__r__t

er/sie/es __ir__

wir we__ de__

ihr __er__e__

Sie/sie w__r__en

4 Write sentences about what you and your family/friends will do on your next holiday.

Example: Ich werde jeden Tag in Frankreich wandern. Mein Bruder ... /Steffi ...

Jahresbilanz

Record your levels for *Kapitel* 5.

Listening	I have reached Level ______ in **Listening**.
Speaking	I have reached Level ______ in **Speaking**.
Reading	I have reached Level ______ in **Reading**.
Writing	I have reached Level ______ in **Writing**.

Look back through your workbook and note down the level you achieved in each skill by the end of each *Kapitel*.

	Listening	**Speaking**	**Reading**	**Writing**
1 Meine Welt und ich				
2 Familie und Tiere				
3 Freizeit – juhu!				
4 Schule ist klasse!				
5 Gute Reise!				

You now have a record of your progress in German for the whole year.

In der Stadt • In town

Es gibt ...	*There is ... / There are ...*
Es gibt ein/eine/einen ...	*There is/are a ...*
Es gibt kein/keine/keinen ...	*There isn't/aren't ...*
in der Nähe von ...	*near to*
in der Nähe ...	*nearby*
der Bahnhof(¨-e)	*railway station(s)*
der Imbiss(-e)/die Imbissstube(-n)	*snack stand(s)*
die Kegelbahn(-en)	*bowling alley(s)*
das Kino(-s)	*cinema(s)*
die Kirche(-n)	*church(es)*
der Marktplatz(¨-e)	*market square(s)*
der Park(-s)	*park(s)*
das Schloss(¨-er)	*castle(s)*
das Schwimmbad(¨-er)	*swimming pool(s)*
die Eisbahn(-en)	*ice rink(s)*
der Fischmarkt(¨-e)	*fish market(s)*
das Kindertheater(-)	*children's theatre(s)*
der Radweg(-e)	*cycle path(s)*
das Sportzentrum (die Sportzentren)	*sports centre (sports centres)*
der Stadtpark(-s)	*city/town park(s)*
der Wasserpark(-s)	*water park(s)*

Verkaufsgespräch • Sales conversation

Ich gehe einkaufen.	*I am going shopping.*
Ich möchte ...	*I would like ...*
Ich möchte ... kaufen.	*I would like to buy ...*
Haben Sie ...?	*Do you have ...?*
Kann ich dir helfen?	*Can I help you?*
Sonst noch etwas?	*Anything else?*
alles zusammen	*all together*

Souvenirs • Souvenirs

der Aufkleber	*sticker*
das Freundschaftsband	*friendship bracelet*
die Kappe	*(baseball) cap*
der Kuli	*biro*
das Kuscheltier	*cuddly toy*
die Postkarte	*postcard*
der Schlüsselanhänger	*key ring*
die Tasse	*mug/cup*
das Trikot	*(football) shirt*
Wie viel kostet ...?	*How much does ... cost?*
Wie viel kostet das?	*How much does it cost?*
Es kostet €16.	*It costs 16 Euros.*

Snacks und Getränke kaufen • Buying snacks and drinks

die Bratwurst	*fried sausage*
der Hamburger	*hamburger*
die Pizza	*pizza*
die Pommes	*chips*
der Salat	*salad*
das Eis	*ice cream*
die Cola	*cola*
das Mineralwasser	*mineral water*
der Tee	*tea*
das Fleisch	*meat*
der Ketchup	*ketchup*
die Mayo(nnaise)/Majonäse	*mayo(nnaise)*
der Senf	*mustard*
Ich möchte einmal/zweimal/dreimal ...	*I would like one/two/three ...*
Ich hätte gern ...	*I would like ...*
Das macht €8.	*That's €8.*
Ich esse ... gern.	*I like eating ... .*
Ich trinke ... gern.	*I like drinking ... .*

Wörter

In den Sommerferien • During the summer holidays

Was wirst du machen?	*What will you do?*
Ich werde ...	*I will ...*
Wir werden ...	*We will ...*
klettern	*climb*
im Meer schwimmen	*swim in the sea*
rodeln	*toboggan*
im See baden	*bathe in the lake*
segeln	*sail*
an den Strand gehen	*go to the beach*
tauchen	*dive*
wandern	*hike*
windsurfen	*windsurf*
Was kann man dort machen?	*What can you do there?*
Man kann ... besuchen.	*'One'/People/ You can visit ...*
Die Stadt ist bekannt für ...	*The town is well known for ...*
Ich werde (eine Woche) bleiben.	*I will stay (for a week).*

Oft benutzte Wörter • High-frequency words

am Montag	*on Monday*
am Dienstag	*on Tuesday*
am Mittwoch	*on Wednesday*
am Donnerstag	*on Thursday*
am Freitag	*on Friday*
am Wochenende	*at the weekend*
sehr	*very*
nicht sehr	*not very*
ziemlich	*quite*
immer	*always*
nicht immer	*not always*
oft	*often*
nicht oft	*not often*
nie	*never*
alles	*everything*
dort	*there*
teuer	*expensive*

Level descriptors

Listening

Level 1	I can understand some familiar spoken words and phrases.
Level 2	I can understand a range of familiar spoken phrases.
Level 3	I can understand the main points of short spoken passages and note people's answers to questions.
Level 4	I can understand the main points of spoken passages and some of the detail.
Level 5	I can understand the main points and opinions in spoken passages about different topics. I can recognise if people are speaking about the future **OR** the past as well as the present.

Speaking

Level 1	I can say single words and short phrases.
Level 2	I can answer simple questions and use set phrases.
Level 3	I can ask questions and use short phrases to answer questions about myself.
Level 4	I can take part in conversations. I can express my opinions. I can use grammar to change phrases to say something new.
Level 5	I can give short talks, in which I express my opinions. I can take part in conversations giving information, opinions and reasons. I can speak about the future **OR** the past as well as the present.

Level descriptors

Reading

Level 1	I can understand familiar words and phrases.
Level 2	I can understand familiar phrases. I can read aloud familiar words and phrases. I can use a vocabulary list to check meanings.
Level 3	I can understand the main points and people's answers to questions in short written texts.
Level 4	I can understand the main points in short texts and some of the detail. Sometimes I can work out the meaning of new words.
Level 5	I can understand the main points and opinions in texts about different topics. I can recognise if the texts are about the future **OR** the past as well as the present.

Writing

Level 1	I can write or copy single words correctly.
Level 2	I can copy short sentences correctly and write some words from memory.
Level 3	I can answer questions about myself. I can write short phrases from memory. I can write short sentences with help.
Level 4	I can write short texts on familiar topics. I can use grammar to change phrases to write something new.
Level 5	I can write short texts on a range of familiar topics. I can write about the future **OR** the past as well as the present.

Notes

Notes

Published by Pearson Education Limited, Edinburgh Gate, Harlow, Essex, CM20 2JE.

www.pearsonschoolsandfecolleges.co.uk

Edited by Melanie Birdsall
Designed by Kamae Design

Illustrated by Caron at KJA Artists and Lisa Hunt

First published 2013

2022
17

British Library Cataloguing in Publication Data
A catalogue record for this book is available from the British Library

ISBN 978 1 447 94654 0

Printed in Great Britain by Bell and Bain Ltd, Glasgow

Acknowledgements

We would like to thank Melissa Weir, Angelika Libera, Janet Soame and Frances Reynolds for their invaluable help in the development of this course.

Every effort has been made to contact copyright holders of material reproduced in this book. Any omissions will be rectified in subsequent printings if notice is given to the publishers.

www.pearsonschools.co.uk
myorders@pearson.com
T 0845 630 33 33
F 0845 630 77 77

ISBN 978-1-4479-4654-0

Stimmt! 1

Übungsheft B

Malcolm Pacey

ALWAYS LEARNING

PEARSON

1 Hallo! (Seiten 8–9)

1 **Two of the words in each set have a sound that is the same. Circle the word with a different sound from the other two.**

1	*Schlange*	*Porsche*	*Buch*
2	*Bär*	*Löwe*	*Röntgenbild*
3	*Wildwassersport*	*Auf Wiedersehen*	*Tür*
4	*Biene*	*heiße*	*Eis*

2 **Join up the sentence halves.**

1	Gut, danke. Und	**a**	Wiedersehen.
2	Auf	**b**	Ben. Wie heißt du?
3	Ich heiße	**c**	geht's, Ben?
4	Hallo! Wie heißt	**d**	du?
5	Ich heiße Nadia. Wie	**e**	schlecht.
6	Nicht	**f**	dir?

3 **Write the sentences from exercise 2 in the correct order for the conversation. Then translate them into English.**

1 ______________________ ______________________

2 ______________________ ______________________

3 ______________________ ______________________

4 ______________________ ______________________

5 *Nicht schlecht.* *Not bad.*

6 ______________________ ______________________

4 **Unscramble the inventions. Look at the definite article (word for 'the') for each word. Then write each invention with the indefinite article (word for 'a').**

1 sad ngbönReltid *das ...* *ein ...*

2 erd reelmiDtoos ______________ ______________

3 sda toF3rMmPa- ______________ ______________

4 sad PeuAsotrcoh ______________ ______________

5 ied sAMrkdadiae ______________ ______________

2 Eins, zwei, drei … (Seiten 10–11)

1 The bank has sent texts to customers with their coded PIN numbers. Solve the maths problems in German to work out the PINs. Then write each customer's new PIN below the phone.

1

Meine Bank

zehn – acht = zwei

vier + drei = sieben

zwei + drei = ______

fünf + eins = ______

2 7 _ _

2

Meine Bank

sechs + zwei = ______

zehn – neun = ______

sieben – drei = ______

eins + vier = ______

_ _ _ _

3

Meine Bank

sieben – vier = ______

acht + eins = ______

drei + sechs = ______

fünf + zwei = ______

_ _ _ _

2 Write the winning lottery numbers in words.

1 13 ______

2 11 ______

3 16 ______

4 18 ______

5 12 ______

6 17 ______

3 Write two sentences for each speaker. Give the speaker's age and the age of his/her friend.

er ist = he is
sie ist = she is

1

Ich bin dreizehn Jahre alt.

Sie ist zwölf Jahre alt.

2

______

______

3

______

______

3 Ich wohne in Deutschland (Seiten 12–13)

1 Read the dialogue and complete the table with the correct forms of each verb.

Melanie: Hallo! Ich heiße Melanie. Wie heißt du?
Marco: Ich heiße Marco. Ich wohne in Straubing. Wo wohnst du?
Melanie: Ich wohne in Braunschweig. Wie alt bist du?
Marco: Ich bin zwölf Jahre alt. Wer ist das?
Melanie: Sie heißt Jessie. Sie wohnt in Leipzig und ist dreizehn Jahre alt.

wer = who

	heißen (to be called)	**wohnen** (to live)	**sein** (to be)
ich (I)		*wohne*	
du (you)			*bist*
er/sie/es (he/she/it)	*heißt*		

2 Write the missing word in each sentence and complete the crossword.

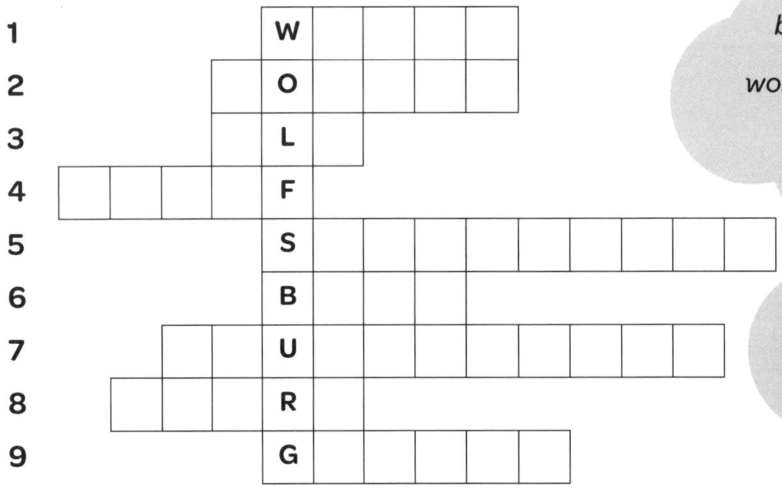

bist *zwölf* *wohne* *wohnst* *Jahre* *Schottland* *Deutschland* *geht's* *alt*

1 Ich ______________ in Manchester.
2 Wo ______________ du, Nick?
3 Wie ______________ ist er?
4 Er ist ______________ Jahre alt.
5 Glasgow ist in ______________ .
6 Wie alt ______________ du?
7 Ich wohne in Berlin. Das ist in ______________ .
8 Ich bin elf ______________ alt.
9 Wie ______________ ?

3 Research why the city of Wolfsburg is important to Germany.

4 Meine Welt ist wunderbar! (Seiten 14–15)

1 **The printer has made four mistakes labelling the illustrations. Write *richtig* or *falsch* under each caption.**

1 
Ich bin musikalisch.
____

2 
Ich bin sehr launisch.
____

3 
Ich bin ziemlich freundlich.
____

4 
Ich bin kreativ.
____

5 
Ich bin laut.
____

6 
Ich bin lustig.
____

2 **Rewrite the false captions from exercise 1, correcting them so that they are true.**

____

____

____

____

faul
lustig
musikalisch
sportlich

3 **Separate out the words to form three sentences.**

meinelieblingsfußballmannschaftistbayernmünchen

meinlieblingssportisttennis

meinelieblingszahlistsieben

Remember that each sentence must start with a capital letter. Also, remember that nouns start with a capital letter.

1 ____

2 ____

3 ____

4 **Write a sentence about your favourite ...**

1 football team: ________________________________

2 sport: ________________________________

3 number: ________________________________

5 Meine Sachen (Seiten 16–17)

1 Write the German question word under its English translation.

Who?	What?	How?	Where?	Where from?

Wie? Was? Wo? Woher? Wer?

2 Write the correct question word in each question. You may use each word more than once.

1 ________________ bist du? Sportlich?

2 ________________ wohnt Shiva?

3 ________________ heißt du?

4 ________________ kommst du?

5 ________________ ist das? Ist das Max?

6 ________________ alt ist Michael?

7 ________________ ist Hannover? *Hannover ist in Deutschland!*

8 ________________ ist deine Lieblingsmusik?

3 Read the paragraph below. Pretend that you're Gabi, and answer each question in a complete German sentence.

Hallo! Ich heiße Gabi und ich bin vierzehn Jahre alt. Ich wohne in Kiel, in Deutschland, aber ich komme aus Swansea. Das ist in Wales. Wie bin ich? Ich bin sportlich, lustig und auch sehr laut! Mein Lieblingsmonat ist Dezember und meine Lieblingssendung ist ‚Die Simpsons'. Ich habe ein iPad und auch einen Computer. Tschüs!

1 Wie heißt du? ________________________________

2 Wo wohnst du? ________________________________

3 Woher kommst du? ________________________________

4 Wie bist du? ________________________________

5 Wie heißt deine Lieblingssendung? ________________________________

6 Was hast du? ________________________________

6 Ich über mich (Seiten 18–19)

1 Complete the table with the correct words.

	the	a	my	your
masculine: Sport				
feminine: Musik				
neuter: Auto				

2 Write each sentence or question in German. Tick the boxes when you've checked each part of your work.

Part of writing accurately in any language is going back over your work to check that there aren't any mistakes. Get into the habit now and watch both your English and German improve!

1 I'm called Osman.

____

2 I live in Germany.

____

3 I'm quite friendly and also creative.

____

____

4 I have a mobile phone.

____

5 Where do you live?

____

- ☐ Spelling of key phonics sound 'ei'
- ☐ Name has a capital
- ☐ Spelling of key phonics sound 'eu'
- ☐ Full stop at the end
- ☐ Check the qualifier
- ☐ Check the connective
- ☐ Capital on the noun
- ☐ Right word for 'a'
- ☐ Correct question word
- ☐ Verb in second position

3 Write a short paragraph about yourself. Use the sentences in exercise 2 as prompts. Check your work against the checklist below.

☐ genders ☐ qualifiers ☐ connectives ☐ verbs
☐ capital letters ☐ spelling ☐ question words

____

____

Wiederholung 1

1 Fill in the gaps by writing the German for the words in brackets.

Hallo! Ich ____________ (am called) Marie und ich ____________ (live) in Walsrode. Das ist in ____________ (Germany). Ich bin fünfzehn ____________ (years) alt. Ich bin ____________ (very) sportlich und ____________ (quite) intelligent, ____________ (but) ich bin ____________ (also) faul. Mein ____________ (favourite sport) ist Hockey und ____________ (my) Lieblingsmusik ist Pop. Ich ____________ (have) einen Vogel aus Amerika. Er ist ____________ (very) freundlich, aber ____________ (not) laut!

2 Crack the code and write the sentences correctly.

a 18/24/19 4/12/19/13/22 18/13 20/28/7/7/18/13/20/22/13

Ich wohne in Göttingen.

ä = 27 ü = 29
ö = 28 ß = 30

b 22/9 18/8/7 20/26/13/1 21/9/22/6/13/23/15/18/24/19

____

c 14/22/18/13/22 15/18/22/25/15/18/13/20/8/14/6/8/18/16 18/8/7 14/12/1/26/9/7

____

____

3 Make up a coded sentence in German for a classmate to solve. Don't forget to provide a key.

4 Write the questions you would ask to get these answers.

1 *Wie heißt du?*

Ich heiße Elaine.

2 ____________________

Mein Lieblingssport ist Tennis.

3 ____________________

Sami ist musikalisch und intelligent, aber sehr launisch.

4 ____________________

Alwin ist vierzehn Jahre alt.

Wiederholung 2

1 **Read the website entries.**

Ich heiße **Franzi** und suche Freunde aus England, Irland oder Nordirland. Ich habe eine Schlange zu Hause! Sie ist sechs Jahre alt. Ich wohne in Wien. Das ist in Österreich. Ich bin sehr kreativ und intelligent! Schreib mir bitte!

Hallo! Ich heiße **Hannah** und ich wohne in London, in England. Ich lerne Deutsch. Ich suche Freunde aus Deutschland, Österreich und auch aus der Schweiz. Ich bin sportlich und spiele Fußball und auch Tennis, aber ich bin sehr faul! Meine Lieblingsmusik ist Rock. Schreib mir!

Mein Name ist **Felix** und ich wohne in der Schweiz, aber ich komme aus Dortmund in Deutschland. Zu Hause habe ich eine Wii und mein Lieblingsspiel ist FIFA. Meine Lieblingsfußballmannschaft ist Bayern-München. Ich suche Freunde aus Schottland und Wales.

Hi! Ich bin **Muhammad** und ich wohne in Cardiff. Das ist in Wales. Ich bin sechzehn Jahre alt. Meine Lieblingssache ist Technologie. Ich habe zu Hause einen Computer, ein Handy und auch ein iPad. Ich bin nicht sehr sportlich, aber sehr freundlich. Mein Lieblingsland ist Deutschland und ich suche dort Freunde.

Write the name of the person who ...

1 is looking for friends from Switzerland. Hannah

2 supports a football team. ____________

3 has a pet. ____________

4 is just looking for friends from Germany. ____________

5 lives in a different place from where they were born. ____________

6 does not particularly like sport. ____________

7 lives in Switzerland. ____________

suche = seek
Schreib mir (bitte)! = Write to me (please)!
dort = there

2 **Write your own profile for the website. Use as much German as you can from *Kapitel 1* to describe yourself.**

____

____

____

____

Grammatik (Seiten 22–23)

1 Write a sentence using the correct German word for 'a' for each item.

1  2  3  4  5 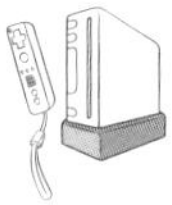 6  7  8 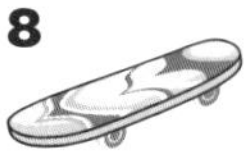

1 Das ist ein Computer. ______

2 ______

3 ______

4 ______

5 ______

6 ______

7 ______

8 ______

die Gitarre
der iPod
das Skateboard
der Fußball
das Handy
der Computer
das Keyboard
die Wii

Grammatik
masculine – *ein*
feminine – *eine*
neuter – *ein*

2 Circle the correct verb form to complete each sentence.

1 Lukas **habe / hat / hast** einen Computer.
2 Ich **heiße / habe / hat** einen Vogel zu Hause.
3 Wo **bist / ist / wohnst** er?
4 Er **ist / komme / bin** musikalisch und sportlich.
5 Julia **bin / ist / wohnt** fünfzehn Jahre alt.
6 Wie alt **wohnst / bist / bin** du?
7 Wo **hast / bist / bin** ich?

Grammatik
You can use the pronouns *er* ('he') or *sie* ('she') instead of writing someone's name. Both need the *er/sie/es* form of the verb.

3 Complete the table with the correct forms of each regular verb.

wohnen (to live)	**kommen** (to come)	**heißen** (to be called)
ich wohne	ich	ich
du	du kommst	du
er/sie/es	er/sie/es	er/sie/es heißt

Now use the table to write the correct verb in each gap.

1 Mein Handy ______ aus China.
2 Meine Schlange ______ Sissel.
3 Du ______ Gabi.
4 ______ du aus Berlin?
5 ______ Monika in Hamburg?
6 Deine Lieblingssendung ______ ‚EastEnders'.
7 Ich ______ Wolfgang.
8 Wo ______ du?

Mein Fortschritt

1 **Record your levels for *Kapitel* 1.**

2 **Look at the level descriptors on pages 59–60 and set your targets for *Kapitel* 2.**

3 **Fill in what you need to do to achieve these targets.**

Listening 	I have reached Level ______ in **Listening**. In *Kapitel* 2, I want to reach Level ______ I need to ______________________________ ______________________________ ______________________________ ______________________________
Speaking  	I have reached Level ______ in **Speaking**. In *Kapitel* 2, I want to reach Level ______ I need to ______________________________ ______________________________ ______________________________ ______________________________
Reading 	I have reached Level ______ in **Reading**. In *Kapitel* 2, I want to reach Level ______ I need to ______________________________ ______________________________ ______________________________ ______________________________
Writing 	I have reached Level ______ in **Writing**. In *Kapitel* 2, I want to reach Level ______ I need to ______________________________ ______________________________ ______________________________ ______________________________

wörter

Hallo! • Meeting and greeting

Wie heißt du?	*What's your name?*
Ich heiße ...	*My name is ...*
Hallo!	*Hello! / Hi!*
Guten Tag!	*Hello!*
Wie geht's?	*How are you?*
Gut, danke. Und dir?	*Fine, thanks. And you?*
Nicht schlecht.	*Not bad.*
Tschüs!	*Bye!*
Auf Wiedersehen!	*Goodbye!*

Die Zahlen 1–19 • Numbers 1–19

eins	*1*
zwei	*2*
drei	*3*
vier	*4*
fünf	*5*
sechs	*6*
sieben	*7*
acht	*8*
neun	*9*
zehn	*10*
elf	*11*
zwölf	*12*
dreizehn	*13*
vierzehn	*14*
fünfzehn	*15*
sechzehn	*16*
siebzehn	*17*
achtzehn	*18*
neunzehn	*19*
Wie alt bist du?	*How old are you?*
Ich bin ... Jahre alt.	*I am ... years old.*
Wie alt ist (Julia)?	*How old is (Julia)?*
(Julia) ist ... Jahre alt.	*(Julia) is ... years old.*

Wo wohnst du? • Where do you live?

Ich wohne in ...	*I live in ...*
Er/Sie/Es wohnt in ...	*He/She/It lives in ...*
... England	*England*
... Irland	*Ireland*
... Nordirland	*Northern Ireland*
... Schottland	*Scotland*
... Wales	*Wales*
... Deutschland	*Germany*
... Österreich	*Austria*
... der Schweiz	*Switzerland*

Wie bist du? • What are you like?

Ich bin ...	*I am ...*
Er/Sie ist ...	*He/She is ...*
faul	*lazy*
freundlich	*friendly*
intelligent	*intelligent*
kreativ	*creative*
launisch	*moody*
laut	*loud*
lustig	*funny*
musikalisch	*musical*
sportlich	*sporty*

Lieblingssachen • Favourite things

Mein Lieblingssport ist ...
My favourite sport is ...

Mein Lieblingsmonat ist ...
My favourite month is ...

Meine Lieblingsmusik ist ...
My favourite music is ...

Meine Lieblingszahl ist ...
My favourite number is ...

Meine Lieblingssendung ist ...
My favourite programme is ...

Meine Lieblingsfußballmannschaft ist ...
My favourite football team is ...

Mein Lieblingsspiel ist ...
My favourite game is ...

Mein Lieblingsland ist ...
My favourite country is ...

Mein Lieblingsauto ist ...
My favourite car is ...

Was ist dein Lieblingssport?
What's your favourite sport?

Was ist deine Lieblingszahl?
What's your favourite number?

Was ist dein Lieblingsland?
What's your favourite country?

Hast du einen Computer? • Have you got a computer?

Ich habe ...	*I have ...*
einen Computer	*a computer*
einen iPod	*an iPod*
einen Fußball	*a football*
eine Gitarre	*a guitar*
eine Wii	*a Wii*
eine Schlange	*a snake*
ein Handy	*a mobile phone*
ein Keyboard	*a keyboard*
ein Skateboard	*a skateboard*

Fragewörter • Question words

Wie?	*How?*
Was?	*What?*
Wo?	*Where?*
Woher?	*Where ... from?*
Wer?	*Who?*

Oft benutzte Wörter • High-frequency words

und	*and*
(und) auch	*(and) also*
aber	*but*
sehr	*very*
ziemlich	*quite*
nicht	*not*
Was denkst du?	*What do you think?*
Ich denke, ...	*I think ...*
Ich auch!	*Me too!*
Ich nicht!	*Not me!/That's not what I think!*
Was? Du spinnst!	*What? You're joking!*

1 **Complete the sentences about the pets. Write the correct words in the gaps. Remember to think about the gender of each animal.**

1 Ich habe *ein* ________ Pferd. *Es* ____ ist groß und heißt Romeo.

2 Ich habe ________ Kaninchen. ____ ist niedlich und heißt Timmo.

3 Ich habe ________ Katze. ____ ist intelligent und heißt Mieze.

4 Max hat ________ Schlange. ____ ist zwei Jahre alt.

5 Gabi hat ________ Pferd. ____ ist launish.

6 Ich habe ________ Hund. ____ ist freundlich und heißt Prinz.

7 Susi hat ________ Goldfisch. ____ heißt Nemo.

Grammatik

Remember: after *haben* the masculine word for 'a' changes from *ein* to *einen*.

Grammatik

m. der / ein → **er**

f. die / eine → **sie**

n. das / ein → **es**

2 **Tina Tierfan has lots of pets! Write Tina's answers to the interviewer's questions about how many of each animal she has.**

Grammatik

Hund (-e)	Pferd (-e)
Katze (-n)	Goldfisch (-e)
Schlange (-n)	Maus (Mäuse)

1 Hast du einen Hund? *Nein! Ich habe drei Hunde.*

2 Hast du ein Pferd? ________________________

3 Hast du eine Katze? ________________________

4 Hast du einen Goldfisch? ________________________

5 Hast du eine Schlange? ________________________

6 Hast du eine Maus? ________________________

2 Supertiere (Seiten 32–33)

1 Complete the sentences about the animals. Write the correct name in each gap.

Hermann 

Minnie 

Sisi 

Kizzi 

Moto 

Millie 

1 __________ ist schnell.

2 __________ ist süß.

3 __________ ist gemein.

4 __________ ist superintelligent.

5 __________ ist cool.

6 __________ ist kräftig.

2 Write a sentence to say what each of the *Supertiere* can do.

1 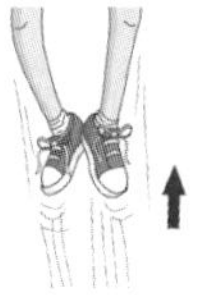
Hermann

2 
Sisi

3 
Minnie

4 

Kizzi

5 
Millie

6 
Moto

1 Hermann kann springen.

2 ______________________________

3 ______________________________

4 ______________________________

5 ______________________________

6 ______________________________

Grammatik
The verb *kann* is always followed by an infinitive verb.

3 Read the text below, then translate it into English.

Günther Goldfisch ist mein Lieblingstier. Er ist ein Jahr alt. Er ist sehr lustig und kräftig, aber auch ziemlich süß. Er kann schwimmen, springen und auch im Aquarium tanzen! Günther hat einen Freund: er ist sehr cool und schlau.

3 Meine Familie (Seiten 34–35)

1 **Find the numbers in the puzzle, and write them next to the correct numeral.**

v	i	e	r	u	n	d	s	e	c	h	z	i	g	m	e
b	a	l	c	o	e	z	n	f	w	i	r	d	s	k	s
s	e	c	h	s	u	n	d	d	r	e	i	ß	i	g	a
q	g	n	a	j	n	x	i	n	d	m	h	t	g	ü	o
h	a	c	h	t	u	n	d	f	ü	n	f	z	i	g	i
u	e	i	n	u	n	d	a	c	h	t	z	i	g	p	b
n	t	e	r	i	d	f	b	n	ß	e	d	z	g	d	s
d	r	e	i	u	n	d	v	i	e	r	z	i	g	w	e
e	v	h	f	r	e	a	m	ß	p	l	s	j	a	q	c
r	d	r	e	i	u	n	d	z	w	a	n	z	i	g	h
t	z	a	n	j	n	x	o	u	e	y	g	r	e	v	z
k	c	p	f	s	z	d	l	b	n	l	a	i	h	m	i
i	b	z	w	e	i	u	n	d	s	i	e	b	z	i	g
a	g	b	n	ü	g	y	i	a	z	o	m	e	d	h	e

100 ______________________

64 ______________________

99 ______________________

43 ______________________

72 ______________________

36 ______________________

58 ______________________

81 ______________________

60 ______________________

23 ______________________

2 **Describe each of the families. Fill in the gaps for the first family. Write the whole description for the second family.**

Oban

Ich heiße Tom. Ich bin vierzehn Jahre alt. Es gibt vier Personen in meiner Familie. Meine Mutter ist ______________________ Jahre alt. Ich habe einen Bruder. ____ ist ________ Jahre alt. Ich habe eine Schwester. ______ ist ____________ Jahre alt. Wir wohnen in ________ .

Köln

____

____

____

____

____

____

3 **Write about your family (real or imaginary). Use the descriptions in exercise 2 to help you.**

der Stiefbruder = stepbrother
die Halbschwester = half-sister
Ich bin Einzelkind. = I am an only child.

4 Die Farben der Welt (Seiten 36–37)

1 Describe each person's hair and eyes.

Grammatik
When you describe hair and eyes, the adjectives (colour, length) need an ***e*** on the end.

hell = light　　**hellbraun** = light brown
dunkel = dark　　**dunkelblau** = dark blue

1 Er heißt Niko. Er hat kurze, schwarze Haare und dunkelbraune Augen.

2 ______________________________

3 ______________________________

4 ______________________________

5 ______________________________

2 Complete the text by choosing the correct words from the cloud to fill the gaps. There are more words than you need.

Es gibt fünf __________ in meiner Familie. Wir __________ in Braunschweig. Das ist in __________________. Meine __________ heißt Emma und sie ist neunundvierzig __________ alt. Sie ist sehr freundlich und hat __________, schwarze Haare. Mein Vater __________ auch neunundvierzig und er hat kurze, dunkelbraune Haare und braune __________.

Ich habe zwei __________: einen Bruder und eine Schwester. __________ Bruder heißt Mehmet und er ist __________ Jahre alt. Er ist launisch aber __________ lustig. __________ Schwester, Isla, hat grüne Augen und __________ Haare. Sie ist sechzehn Jahre alt, sehr klein und __________________.

Deutschland alt Augen Personen braune wohnen sportlich Meine Mutter Jahre lange Geschwister zwölf auch Mein blau ist

Read the text for gist first. For each sentence, think about whether you need a noun, a verb, a connective or an adjective.

5 Alles Gute! (Seiten 38–39)

1 Reorder the words to make correct sentences. Don't forget the full stop!

1 am | Mai | Ich | Geburtstag | habe | neunzehnten

____

2 hat | Oktober | am | Oma | Geburtstag | elften | Meine

____

3 Geburtstag | Stiefbruder | Dezember | am | Dein | dritten | hat

____

4 hast | Geburtstag | einunddreißigsten | Juli | Du | am

____

5 und | Geburtstag | haben | achten | am | Michael | Juni | Monika

____

2 Complete each sentence by writing the date. Write each holiday in English.

Neujahr ist am *ersten Januar* ______________________. *New Year*

Der Maifeiertag ist am ______________________. ______________

Der Tag der Deutschen Einheit ist am *German Unity Day*

______________________.

Weihnachten ist am ______________________. ______________

Silvester ist am ______________________. ______________

3 Read the short profile about Yannic and write a summary in the table.

Er heißt Yannic Spiller. Er ist dreizehn Jahre alt und kommt aus Trier. Trier ist in Deutschland. Yannic hat am siebten Januar Geburtstag. Er hat einen Bruder, Tim. Tim ist achtzehn Jahre alt. Yannic hat auch eine Schwester. Sie heißt Steffi und ist sechzehn Jahre alt. Die Familie Spiller hat zwei Haustiere: einen Hund und eine Katze.

Name:		Geschwister:	
Alter:			
Wohnt in:		Haustiere:	
Geburtstag:			

4 Now write a short profile about yourself.

6 Speaking Skills Eine Superfamilie (Seiten 40–41)

1 **Rescue the question words from the alphabet soup. Write each one on a line and use it to write a question.**

Wie viele Brüder hast du?

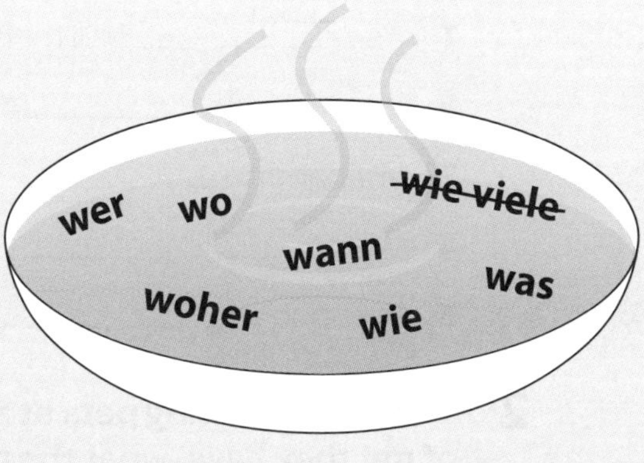

2 **The police have written a summary about a crime suspect. Write six questions for a journalist to ask the suspect. The questions should cover all the information in the summary.**

1 *Wie heißt du?*
2
3
4
5
6

Martin Kolwitz ist 24 Jahre alt. Er hat am achten November Geburtstag. Er wohnt in Hamburg, in Deutschland. Er hat einen Bruder. Er hat auch Haustiere: zwei Hunde.

Remember: the verb usually goes straight after the question word.

3 **Use these notes to write questions to Martin about his accomplice, Sophie.**

1 *Wie heißt sie?*
2
3
4
5

Sophie Meyer
19
Ebbingen, Deutschland
Haare – kurz, Augen – blau
Geb. 21.10.

Remember to use the correct part of the verb with the pronoun *sie*.

4 **Write a summary about Sophie, like the one the police wrote about Martin in exercise 2.**

Wiederholung 1

1 **Complete the sentences. Choose the correct word from the cloud to fill in each gap.**

1 ________________ Mutter ist sehr freundlich und intelligent.

2 Hast du ________________ Meerschweinchen?

3 Wir haben ________________ Haustier.

4 Wo ist ________________ Vogel?

5 Ich habe ________________ Bruder.

dein *kein*
ein *meine*
einen

2 **You are describing pets at a pet show. Use the owners' notes to write what sort of pet they have, what the pet is like and what it can do.**

Mareike

mouse
Pippa
cute, fast
fly, swim

Mareike hat ________________________________.

Sie heißt ________________________________.

Sie ist ________________________________.

Sie kann ________________________________.

Aaron

cat
Mieze
intelligent, cool, mean
jump, play football

________________________________.

________________________________.

________________________________.

________________________________.

________________________________.

3 **Decscribe the animal you'll be entering in the pet show by writing a similar description.**

Example: Ich habe ...

Wiederholung 2

1 Read the texts below.

Hallo! Ich heiße **Anna** und ich bin fünfzehn Jahre alt. Ich habe am elften Februar Geburtstag. Ich wohne in Klagenfurt, in Österreich. Ich bin ziemlich groß und schlank und habe kurze, schwarze Haare und blaue Augen. Ich habe keine Geschwister – ich bin Einzelkind. Ich habe einen Goldfisch und einen Wellensittich. Ich kann Flöte spielen und Italienisch sprechen.

Hi! Ich bin **Noah** und ich komme aus Aachen. Das ist in Deutschland. Ich habe am zweiten November Geburtstag und bin vierzehn Jahre alt. Ich liebe Haustiere! Ich habe zwei Hunde, drei Katzen und eine Maus. Ich habe eine große Familie. Ich habe einen Halbbruder (er ist ein Baby) und zwei Schwestern. Mein Halbbruder ist sehr süß und klein. Er hat schwarze Haare und blaue Augen.

a Complete the sentences by writing *Anna* or *Noah*.

1 __________ lives in Austria.

2 __________ can play the flute.

3 __________'s birthday is on the 02.11.

4 __________ has a half-brother.

5 __________ is 15 years old.

6 __________ has cats.

b Write *richtig* or *falsch* next to each statement.

1 Anna hat einen Halbbruder. __________

2 Anna kann auch Englisch sprechen. __________

3 Noahs Halbbruder hat blaue Augen. __________

4 Klagenfurt ist nicht in Deutschland. __________

5 Anna hat am fünfzehnten Februar Geburtstag. __________

6 Anna hat keine Geschwister. __________

2 Translate these sentences into German.

1 My birthday is on the first of May. __________

2 She can speak German. __________

3 My guinea pig is very cute. __________

4 Your sister has light blue eyes. __________

5 My grandparents live in Southampton.

____

6 My brother can fly.

____

Grammatik (Seiten 44–45)

1 Complete the table by writing the correct form of *haben* for each pronoun.

haben *hast* *habt* *hat* *haben* *habe*

Words for 'you':
du (speaking to one family member or friend)
ihr (speaking to two or more family members or friends)
Sie (speaking to people you don't know or adults)

ich	du	er/sie/es	wir	ihr	Sie/sie

Now complete the sentences with the correct form of *haben*.

1 Katja, hast ________ du eine Katze?

2 Tom und Niko, ________ ihr einen Hund?

3 ________ Sie eine Schlange, Herr Brand?

4 Ich ________ ein Pferd.

5 Frau Gerber, ________ Sie eine Maus?

6 Herr Alexander ________ ein Pferd.

2 Join each pronoun to a verb. There is more than one possible verb for some of the pronouns. Then write a question or a sentence with each pair.

1 ich — **a** macht — **1** ________

2 du — **b** heißen — **2** ________

3 er — **c** wohnst — **3** ________

4 wir — **d** heiße — **4** ________

5 ihr — **e** spielt — **5** ________

6 Sie — **f** spielen — **6** ________

3 Rewrite the sentences so they include the verb *kann*.

1 Mein Bruder fliegt. Mein Bruder kann fliegen.

2 Ich spiele Flöte. ________

3 Meine Mutter schwimmt. ________

4 Mein Vater springt. ________

5 Ich tanze. ________

6 Er singt gut. ________

Mein Fortschritt

1 **Record your levels for *Kapitel* 2.**

2 **Look at the level descriptors on pages 59–60 and set your targets for *Kapitel* 3.**

3 **Fill in what you need to do to achieve these targets.**

Listening 	I have reached Level ______ in **Listening**. In *Kapitel* 3, I want to reach Level ______ I need to ________________________________ ________________________________ ________________________________ ________________________________
Speaking 	I have reached Level ______ in **Speaking**. In *Kapitel* 3, I want to reach Level ______ I need to ________________________________ ________________________________ ________________________________ ________________________________
Reading 	I have reached Level ______ in **Reading**. In *Kapitel* 3, I want to reach Level ______ I need to ________________________________ ________________________________ ________________________________ ________________________________
Writing 	I have reached Level ______ in **Writing**. In *Kapitel* 3, I want to reach Level ______ I need to ________________________________ ________________________________ ________________________________ ________________________________

Haustiere • Pets

Hast du ein Haustier?	*Have you got a pet?*
Ich habe ...	*I have ...*
einen Goldfisch	*a goldfish*
einen Hamster	*a hamster*
einen Hund	*a dog*
ein Kaninchen	*a rabbit*
eine Katze	*a cat*
eine Maus	*a mouse*
ein Meerschweinchen	*a guinea pig*
ein Pferd	*a horse*
eine Schlange	*a snake*
einen Wellensittich	*a budgie*
kein Haustier	*no pet*

Eigenschaften • Qualities

Wie ist er/sie/es?	*What is he/she/ it like?*
Er/Sie/Es ist ...	*He/She/It is ...*
dick/schlank	*fat/thin*
frech/niedlich	*cheeky/cute*
gemein/süß	*mean/sweet*
groß/klein	*big/small*
kräftig	*strong*
schlau	*cunning*
(super)lustig	*(really) funny*
Er/Sie/Es kann ...	*He/She/It can ...*
Italienisch sprechen	*speak Italian*
fliegen	*fly*
Flöte/Fußball/Wii spielen	*play the flute/ football/on the Wii*
(schnell) laufen	*run (fast)*
lesen	*read*
Rad fahren	*ride a bike*
schwimmen	*swim*
singen	*sing*
springen	*jump*
tanzen	*dance*

Die Zahlen 20–100 • Numbers 20–100

zwanzig	*twenty*
dreißig	*thirty*
vierzig	*forty*
fünfzig	*fifty*
sechzig	*sixty*
siebzig	*seventy*
achtzig	*eighty*
neunzig	*ninety*
hundert	*hundred*
einundzwanzig	*twenty-one*
zweiundzwanzig	*twenty-two*

Meine Familie • My family

Es gibt ... Personen in meiner Familie.	*There are ... people in my family.*
meine Mutter	*my mother*
mein Vater	*my father*
mein Bruder	*my brother*
mein Stiefbruder/ Halbbruder	*my stepbrother/ half-brother*
meine Schwester	*my sister*
meine Stiefschwester/ Halbschwester	*my stepsister/ half-sister*
meine Eltern	*my parents*
meine Großeltern	*my grandparents*
Hast du Geschwister?	*Have you any brothers and sisters?*
Ich habe zwei Brüder.	*I have two brothers.*
Ich habe drei Schwestern.	*I have three sisters.*
Ich bin Einzelkind.	*I'm an only child.*
Ich habe keine Geschwister.	*I have no brothers and sisters.*

Die Farben • Colours

schwarz	*black*
weiß	*white*
grau	*grey*
braun	*brown*
rot	*red*
orange	*orange*
gelb	*yellow*
grün	*green*
blau	*blue*
indigoblau	*indigo*
violett	*violet*
lila	*purple*
rosa	*pink*
bunt	*brightly coloured*
hellblau/dunkelblau	*light blue/dark blue*

Haare und Augen • Hair and eyes

Er/Sie hat ...	*He/She has ...*
schwarze/braune/ blonde/rote Haare	*black/brown/ blond/red hair*
kurze/lange/ mittellange Haare	*short/long/ mid length hair*
blaue/braune/grüne/ graue Augen	*blue/brown/green/ grey eyes*

Die Monate • The months

Januar	*January*
Februar	*February*
März	*March*
April	*April*
Mai	*May*
Juni	*June*
Juli	*July*
August	*August*
September	*September*
Oktober	*October*
November	*November*
Dezember	*December*

Das Datum • The date

Wann hast du Geburtstag?	*When is your birthday?*
am 1. (ersten) Januar	*on 1 January*
am 3. (dritten) Februar	*on 3 February*
am 7. (siebten) März	*on 7 March*
am 8. (achten) April	*on 8 April*
am 15. (fünfzehnten) Mai	*on 15 May*
am 29. (neunund-zwanzigsten) Juni	*on 29 June*
Ich habe (heute) Geburtstag.	*It's my birthday (today).*

Oft benutzte Wörter • High-frequency words

und	*and*
aber	*but*
oder	*or*
ziemlich	*fairly, quite*
sehr	*very*

1 Bist du sportlich? (Seiten 54–55)

1 **Look at the survey results in the table. Then answer the questions using full German sentences.**

Ahmed	☺☺			☹			😐
Nicole		☺☺			☹		
Christa	☺		☺☺				😐
Torsten		☹		☺☺		☺	
Herr und Frau Meyer	☺☺			☺	☹	😐	

☺☺ = sehr gern ☺ = gern 😐 = ziemlich gern ☹ = nicht gern

1 Wer spielt sehr gern Fußball? *Nicole spielt sehr gern Fußball.*
2 Wer spielt gern Tischtennis? ____________
3 Was spielt Christa sehr gern? ____________
4 Was spielen Herr und Frau Meyer gern? ____________
5 Wer spielt Basketball nicht gern? ____________
6 Wer spielt ziemlich gern Handball? (2) ____________
7 Und du? Was spielst du gern? ____________

2 **Write three questions and three answers about the other people and sports in the table in exercise 1. Use the questions above as a model.**

____
____
____
____
____
____

2 Freizeit ist toll! (Seiten 56–57)

1 **Write the words from the cloud in the grid. Translate the code word into English.**

furchtbar
Eishockey
schlecht
spielst
irre
stinklangweilig
langweilig
Tischtennis
toll

2 **Read about all the activities Hannes and Lola are involved in. Then write *richtig* or *falsch* next to each statement.**

Hallo! Ich heiße **Hannes**. Ich finde Sport fantastisch. Ich spiele Tennis und schwimme. Schwimmen finde ich total super. Ich reite mit meiner Freundin, aber das finde ich langweilig. Fußball finde ich cool. Ich fahre auch gern Skateboard und lese sehr gern Sport- und Fitnessmagazine.

Meine Freundin heißt **Lola.** Sie findet Tischtennis toll. Lola fährt auch gern Rad – das ist sehr gesund! Sie findet schwimmen auch gut, aber Fußball findet sie nervig. Sie kann nicht Ski fahren. Im Winter spielt sie Eishockey und sie sieht sehr gern Eishockey im Fernsehen.

meine Freundin = my girlfriend
gesund = healthy
Fernsehen = television

1 Both Hannes and Lola participate in winter sports. ____________

2 Lola watches ice hockey on television. ____________

3 Hannes really likes swimming. ____________

4 Lola thinks skiing is fantastic. ____________

5 Lola plays ice hockey in winter. ____________

6 Hannes doesn't enjoying horse riding. ____________

7 Lola thinks football is exciting. ____________

8 Hannes watches sports programmes on television. ____________

1 Separate the words to form five time phrases and write them below. Number the phrases in order of frequency, starting with 1 for the most frequent. Translate the phrases into English.

JedenTagdreimalproWocheeinmalproMonatamWochenendesechsmalproMonat

☐ ______________________ ______________________

☐ ______________________ ______________________

☐ ______________________ ______________________

☐ ______________________ ______________________

☐ ______________________ ______________________

2 Use the time phrases from exercise 1 to answer the questions about yourself. Write your answers in full sentences.

1 Gehst du ins Kino? ______________________

2 Machst du Sport? ______________________

3 Gehst du einkaufen? ______________________

4 Hörst du Musik? ______________________

5 Spielst du Wii? ______________________

6 Chillst du mit deinen Freunden? ______________________

! **nie** = never

3 Join up the sentence halves. Rewrite each sentence so that it starts with the time phrase.

1	Ich höre am	**a**	Tag Sport.
2	Ich chille am	**b**	Abend Musik.
3	Ich spiele sehr	**c**	pro Woche Pizza.
4	Ich mache jeden	**d**	Monat ins Kino.
5	Ich esse einmal	**e**	oft Xbox.
6	Ich gehe einmal pro	**f**	Wochenende.

! Remember the 'verb in second place' rule.

4 Ich bin online (Seiten 60–61)

1 Unscramble and write down the time phrase in each sentence. Then translate the sentences into English.

Grammatik
You can use the present tense with a future time phrase to say what you are going to do – just as in English.

1 Wir machen änhcset eoWhc Filme. nächste Woche
We are going to make …

2 Ich suche ma Mtanog Infos im Internet. ____________

____

3 Wir sehen ma eneneoWhcd Katzenvideos auf YouTube. ____________

____

4 Ich chatte nejde denbA auf Facebook. ____________

____

5 Stefan spielt ni iezw cnoWhe Wii Sport. ____________

____

6 Ich lade gomrne Musik herunter. ____________

____

2 Underline all the verbs in the text. Circle the words that are in first position in the sentences. Write a sentence about what you notice.

Hey du!
Franzi hier! Jetzt sind wir Freunde auf Facebook! Jeden Tag spiele ich Wii. Jede Woche schreibt mein Vater ein Blog, aber das finde ich langweilig. Am Abend lese ich gern E-Books. Morgen telefoniere ich mit Freunden in Kanada über Skype. Das finde ich cool! Im Sommer fahren wir nach Vancouver. Fantastisch! Was machst du am Computer und wie oft?

____

3 Reply to the question Franzi has asked you in his chat.

Use as many time phrases as you can in your reply.

Brieffreunde (Seiten 64–65)

1 What type of word is needed to fill the gap in each sentence? Complete each sentence by writing an appropriate German word or words in the gap.

verb *noun* *time/frequency phrase* *connective* *adjective*

	Type of word
1 Ich finde ______ Tennis toll.	verb
2 Meine Schwester findet Tischtennis ______ .	______
3 Wir sehen ______ fern.	______
4 Herr Peters spielt nächste Woche Tennis ______ Fußball.	______
5 Mein Bruder schreibt ein ______ .	______

2 Answer the questions about German grammar.

Use the sentences in exercise 1 to help you answer these questions.

1 Where in a sentence do verbs usually go?
______

2 What often goes after a verb? ______

3 What can you expect to go after *ein/eine*? ______

4 Which German verb suggests you're giving an opinion? ______

3 Replace the underlined word(s) with something else: a different noun, adjective or time phrase.

1 Ich finde Tischtennis furchtbar. Ich finde Tischtennis langweilig.

2 Ich spiele nicht gern Fußball. ______

3 Micha spielt gern Wii. ______

4 Er macht einmal pro Monat Judo. ______

5 Olli findet E-Books fantastisch. ______

6 Ich sehe jede Woche fern. Meine Schwester sieht jeden Tag Videos auf YouTube.
______

Remember that you'll keep the reader's interest if you use a variety of different words and phrases.

4 Write about your friends' hobbies.

Remember to include:
- opinions
- time/frequency phrases
- connectives
- 'verb in second place' rule

Wiederholung 1

1 **Put the words in the correct order to make sentences or questions. Don't forget to insert a full stop or question mark.**

1. fern gern sehr Ich sehe ______
2. einkaufen er Wochenende geht Am ______
3. Hausaufgaben Ich Infos lese die für ______
4. in Wie Stadt oft du fährst die ______
5. Woche Kai Wasserball Nächste spielt ______
6. herunter Videos Ich lade Musik und ______

2 **Rewrite each sentence, beginning with a time phrase. Then translate the sentences into English.**

1. Ich spiele Volleyball. (at the weekend) *Am Wochenende spiele ich Volleyball.*
   At the weekend I am going to play volleyball.
2. Er spielt Basketball. (on Monday) ______
3. Du spielst Tischtennis. (every week) ______
4. Rosa spielt Fußball. (today) ______
5. Ich telefoniere mit Sam. (next week) ______
6. Sophie liest das Buch. (tomorrow) ______

3 **Underline the regular verbs and circle the irregular verbs.**

Ich spiele nicht gern Tennis. Ich finde Tennis langweilig. Fußball spiele ich dreimal pro Woche. Mein Bruder spielt sehr gern Tennis. Er fährt auch gern Rad. Radfahren findet er toll. Meine Schwester sieht ziemlich gern fern. Meine Mutter liest ziemlich gern. Oft liest sie Blogs im Internet. Ich lese auch oft. Mein Vater fährt gern Ski und spielt Gitarre.

Wiederholung 2

1 Read the email. Find the German for the following words and phrases in the text.

1 I think ____________
2 about ____________
3 but ____________
4 New Zealand ____________
5 comedies ____________
6 Best wishes ____________

Lieber Anish,

wie geht's? Danke für deine E-Mail.

Ich denke, Technologie ist toll. Ich bin sehr oft online. Ich chatte sehr gern mit Freunden auf Facebook. Facebook finde ich super und ich sehe oft Videos über Fußball auf YouTube.

Ich spiele Computerspiele nicht gern, aber ich suche ziemlich oft Infos für die Hausaufgaben. Meine Cousine, Connie, wohnt in Neuseeland und wir telefonieren ziemlich oft über Skype. Kannst du auch über Skype telefonieren?

Ich mache viel Sport mit meinen Freunden: Wir schwimmen zweimal pro Woche und wir spielen am Abend Basketball. Im Winter fahre ich auch Ski.

Ich esse manchmal am Wochenende mit meinen Freunden Pizza, und dann gehen wir ins Kino. Ich sehe gern Komödien. Nächste Woche sehen wir *Skyfall*.

Liebe Grüße,

Tibor

2 Answer the questions in complete German sentences.

1 Spielt Tibor gern Computerspiele? ____________
2 Was macht Tibor auf Facebook? ____________
3 Wer wohnt in Neuseeland? ____________
4 Wie telefoniert Tibor mit seiner Cousine? ____________
5 Wie oft schwimmt Tibor? ____________
6 Was machen Tibor und seine Freunde am Wochenende?

____

3 Write a reply to Tibor's email about your hobbies and activities.

Grammatik (Seiten 68–69)

1 **Complete the verb table.**

	fahren (to go/travel)	**sehen** (to see)	**lesen** (to read)
ich			
du	fährst		liest
er/sie/es		sieht	
wir			
ihr			
Sie			
sie			

2 **Complete the sentences by writing the correct form of the verb in brackets.**

1 Ich ________________ das Auto. (waschen)

2 ________________ du gern Mangabücher? (lesen)

3 Er ________________ im Schlafzimmer. (schlafen)

4 Thomas ________________ nach Stockholm in Schweden. (fahren)

5 ________________ du morgen Torsten? (sehen)

6 ________________ du eine Schuluniform? (tragen)

Verbs like fahren:
tragen = to wear
schlafen = to sleep
waschen = to wash

die Schuluniform = school uniform

3 **Write the question for each reply.**

1 ________________ Ja, ich spiele Gitarre.

2 ________________ Nein, ich spiele nicht gern Wasserball.

3 ________________ Ja, Michael schläft im Bett.

4 ________________ Ja, ich fahre nach Bremen.

5 ________________ Ja, ich lese gern E-Books.

6 ________________ Nein, ich sehe nicht gern fern.

7 ________________ Ja, ich bin sportlich!

8 Was ________________ Ich trage morgen Jeans und ein T-Shirt.

9 ________________ Michael trägt eine Schuluniform.

Remember, to form a question you put the verb before the subject:
Du spielst gern Tennis. → Spielst du gern Tennis?

Mein Fortschritt

1 Record your levels for *Kapitel* 3.

2 Look at the level descriptors on pages 59–60 and set your targets for *Kapitel* 4.

3 Fill in what you need to do to achieve these targets.

Listening

I have reached Level ______ in **Listening**.

In *Kapitel* 4, I want to reach Level ______

I need to ______________________________

____

____

____

Speaking

I have reached Level ______ in **Speaking**.

In *Kapitel* 4, I want to reach Level ______

I need to ______________________________

____

____

____

Reading

I have reached Level ______ in **Reading**.

In *Kapitel* 4, I want to reach Level ______

I need to ______________________________

____

____

____

Writing

I have reached Level ______ in **Writing**.

In *Kapitel* 4, I want to reach Level ______

I need to ______________________________

____

____

____

Bist du sportlich? • Are you sporty?

Ich bin (sehr/ziemlich/ nicht sehr) sportlich.	*I am (very/quite/ not very) sporty.*
Was spielst du?	*What do you play?*
Ich spiele ...	*I play ...*
Ich spiele gern ...	*I like playing ...*
Ich spiele ziemlich gern ...	*I quite like playing ...*
Ich spiele nicht gern ...	*I don't like playing ... playing ...*
Badminton	*badminton*
Basketball	*basketball*
Eishockey	*ice hockey*
Fußball	*football*
Handball	*handball*
Tennis	*tennis*
Tischtennis	*table tennis*
Volleyball	*volleyball*
Wasserball	*water polo*

Was machst du gern? • What do you like doing?

Was machst du gern?	*What do you like doing?*
Ich fahre Rad.	*I ride my bike.*
Ich fahre Skateboard.	*I go skateboarding.*
Ich fahre Ski.	*I ski.*
Ich fahre Snowboard.	*I snowboard.*
Ich lese.	*I read.*
Ich mache Judo.	*I do judo.*
Ich mache Karate.	*I do karate.*
Ich reite.	*I go horse riding.*
Ich schwimme.	*I swim.*
Ich sehe fern.	*I watch TV.*
Ich spiele Gitarre.	*I play the guitar.*
Ich tanze.	*I dance.*

Wie findest du das? • What do you think of it?

Ich finde es ...	*I think it's ...*
Es ist ...	*It's ...*
irre	*amazing*
super	*super*
toll	*great*
cool	*cool*
gut	*good*
nicht schlecht	*not bad*
okay	*okay*
langweilig	*boring*
nervig	*annoying*
stinklangweilig	*deadly boring*
furchtbar	*awful*

Was machst du in deiner Freizeit? • What do you do in your free time?

Ich chille.	*I chill out.*
Ich esse Pizza oder Hamburger.	*I eat pizza or hamburgers.*
Ich gehe einkaufen.	*I go shopping.*
Ich gehe ins Kino.	*I go to the cinema.*
Ich gehe in den Park.	*I go to the park.*
Ich gehe in die Stadt.	*I go into town.*
Ich höre Musik.	*I listen to music.*
Ich mache Sport.	*I do sport.*
Ich spiele Xbox oder Wii.	*I play Xbox or on the Wii.*

Wörter

Ich bin online • I'm online

Was machst du am Computer?	*What do you do on the computer?*
Was machst du auf deinem Handy?	*What do you do on your mobile?*
Ich chatte mit Freunden auf Facebook.	*I chat with friends on Facebook.*
Ich lade Musik herunter.	*I download music.*
Ich mache Fotos oder Filme.	*I take photos or make films.*
Ich sehe Videos.	*I watch videos.*
Ich simse.	*I text.*
Ich spiele Computerspiele.	*I play computer games.*
Ich suche und lese Infos für die Hausaufgaben.	*I look for and read information for my homework.*
Ich surfe im Internet.	*I surf the internet.*
Ich telefoniere mit Freunden.	*I call my friends.*
Ich mache ziemlich viel auf meinem Handy.	*I do quite a lot of things on my mobile.*

Oft benutzte Wörter • High-frequency words

Wie oft?	*How often?*
(sehr/ziemlich/nicht so) oft	*(very/quite/not so) often*
einmal/zweimal/dreimal pro Woche/pro Monat	*once/twice/three times a week/a month*
jeden Tag	*every day*
jeden Morgen	*every morning*
manchmal	*sometimes*
immer	*always*
nie	*never*
Wann?	*When?*
am Wochenende	*at the weekend*
am Abend	*in the evening*
heute	*today*
morgen	*tomorrow*
am Montag	*on Monday*
nächste Woche	*next week*
in zwei Wochen	*in two weeks*

1 Ich mag Deutsch! (Seiten 76–77)

1 Write a sentence for each illustration.

1 

2 

3 

4 

5 

6 

1 Ich mag ____________________
2 ____________________
3 ____________________
4 ____________________
5 ____________________
6 ____________________

!
ich liebe 🙂🙂
ich mag 🙂
ich mag ... nicht 🙁
ich hasse 🙁🙁

2 Read the forum entries giving people's opinions about school subjects. Then answer the questions below.

Hallo Leute! Mein Lieblingsfach ist Englisch! Ich liebe Englisch, weil es total interessant ist. Ich lese sehr gern Bücher auf Spanisch und auf Deutsch. Mathe finde ich langweilig. **Pedro**

Hi Pedro! Ich mag Englisch nicht. Es ist sehr schwierig, aber ich mag Mathe und Naturwissenschaften. Ich finde Mathe supercool. **Nadine**

Grüezi aus der Schweiz! Ich liebe Theater und Kunst. Ich mag Kunst sehr gern, weil ich total kreativ bin. Informatik finde ich sehr langweilig, und Geschichte und Erdkunde sind nutzlos. **Marta**

Who ...

1 is very creative? ____________
2 enjoys reading? ____________
3 doesn't like English? ____________
4 thinks ICT is boring? ____________
5 likes maths? ____________
6 can read Spanish? ____________
7 loves art? ____________
8 doesn't like geography? ____________

3 Rewrite each sentence in exercise 1, adding *weil* and an opinion. Use the examples in exercise 2 to help you with word order.

2 Was und wann? (Seiten 78–79)

1 Look at the timetable. Write *richtig* or *falsch* next to each statement.

	Montag	Dienstag	Mittwoch	Donnerstag	Freitag
8.15	Mathe	Erdkunde	Englisch	Deutsch	Technik
9.15	Englisch	Informatik	Theater	Mathe	Deutsch
10.45	Kunst	Mathe	Deutsch	Kunst	Naturwissenschaften
11.45	Naturwissenschaften	Mathe	Naturwissenschaften	Geschichte	Theater
13.30	Deutsch	Sport	Technik	Musik	Englisch

vor = before **nach** = after **die Doppelstunde** = double period

1 Am Mittwoch habe ich Deutsch. ______

2 Wir haben am Freitag nach der Pause Technik. ______

3 Am Montag vor der Pause haben wir Englisch. ______

4 Theater ist am Mittwoch und am Donnerstag. ______

5 Ich habe am Donnerstag nach der Mittagspause Musik. ______

6 Am Dienstag habe ich eine Doppelstunde Mathe. ______

2 At what time do you have the following subjects? Write a sentence for each.

1 *Ich habe Englisch um neun Uhr zehn.* — 09:10

2 ______ — 10:05

3 ______ — 11:15

4 ______ — 12:10

5 ______ — 13:20

6 ______ — 14:15

um acht Uhr = at 8 o'clock

3 Look at the timetable in exercise 1 and describe one school day. Try to add interest to your sentences by giving opinions about some subjects.

Example: Am Montag um acht Uhr fünfzehn habe ich Mathe. Ich mag Mathe, weil es interessant ist.

Ich finde Mathe ...
= I find maths ...

3 Lehrer und Lehrerinnen (Seiten 80–81)

1 Write a description for each of the teachers.

1 Mein Sportlehrer heißt Herr Huber.
Er ist cool, aber sehr unpünktlich.

2 ____________________
____

3 ____________________
____

4 ____________________
____

! Use some qualifiers in your descriptions: *sehr, zu, ziemlich, ein bisschen, nicht*

2 Complete the text by writing the correct word from the cloud in each gap.

Mein ____________________ an der Schule ist Geschichte, ____________________ meine Geschichtelehrerin sehr lustig ist! Sie ____________________ nur ein Haustier, aber ihr Haustier ist eine Schlange!

Am ____________________ und am Freitag haben wir Kunst. Ich finde Kunst ziemlich langweilg, weil es schwierig ____________________. Mein Kunstlehrer ____________________ Herr Ackermann. ____________________ Schwester ist auch Kunstlehrerin an meiner ____________________! Sie heißt Frau Ackermann! Meine Sportlehrerin ist ____________________ freundlich. Sie heißt Frau Krause und ____________________ Lieblingssport ist Volleyball. Ich mag Sport, weil ich sehr ____________________ bin.

heißt hat Mittwoch Lieblingsfach ist sehr Schule Seine sportlich weil ihr

3 Write the correct word for 'his' or 'her' in each sentence.

1 ____________ Bruder lernt Hindi. (his)
2 ____________ Schwester ist Lehrerin. (her)
3 ____________ Hobby ist Gitarre spielen. (his)
4 ____________ Lieblingsfach ist Kunst. (her)
5 ____________ Schuluniform ist fantastisch. (his)
6 ____________ Bruder ist 19 Jahre alt. (her)

Grammatik
sein = his **ihr** = her (for masculine and neuter nouns)
seine = his **ihre** = her (for feminine nouns)
Check the gender of the noun if you are unsure.

4 Im Klassenzimmer (Seiten 82–83)

1 Draw a simple picture to show where each of these things is.

1 Der Musiklehrer ist im Klassenzimmer.
2 Das Buch ist neben dem Computer.
3 Das Poster ist an der Wand.
4 Der Stuhl ist auf dem Tisch und neben der Tür.

1	2	3	4

2 What is there in the classroom? Start each sentence with *Es gibt* (there is/there are). Write the numbers as words.

12  Es gibt zwölf Tische im Klassenzimmer.

6  __________

24  __________

2  __________

4 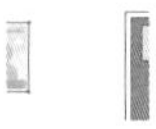 __________

5  __________

Look at the vocabulary on page 47 for the plurals of the nouns.

3 Answer the questions using the information in the pictures.

@peta_ush Darfst du dein Handy in der Schule benutzen?

____

@tara_winkel Darfst du im Klassenzimmer schnell laufen?

____

@e_atch Darfst du in der Pause Musik hören?

____

@janet_mc Darfst du dein Handy in der Mittagspause benutzen?

____

ich darf   du darfst   er/sie/es darf

Mein Lieblingstag (Seiten 84–85)

1 **Most of the verbs you've seen end in *–en* in the infinitive. Write the infinitive form of each verb in the table. Then try to work out its meaning from the context.**

If the context doesn't help you, use a German–English dictionary.

verb	**infinitive**	**meaning in English**
Er **geht** in die Schule.	*gehen*	*to go, to walk*
Er **kauft** ein Auto.		
Er **steht** auf dem Tisch.		
Warum **redest** du so schnell?		
Ich **wasche** meinen Hund.		
Ich **nehme** das Buch.		

2 **Guess the meaning of these compound nouns by separating out the words. Look up the compound nouns in a dictionary to find their gender and meaning.**

The second word in each compound noun gives the gender.

compound noun	**word 1**	**word 2**	**gender**	**meaning**
Fußballfeld	*Fußball*		*das*	
Arbeitstag				
Sporthalle				
Klassenarbeit				
Lehrerzimmer				

3 **Now write a short German sentence using each compound noun from exercise 2.**

1 *Das Fußballfeld ist sehr grün und …* ________

2 ________

3 ________

4 ________

5 ________

Wiederholung 1

1 **Mimi's description of her school day is in the wrong time order! Number the sentences 1–6 in the correct order of time.**

- [ ] Ich habe um dreizehn Uhr fünfundzwanzig Musik.
- [ ] Die Pause beginnt um elf Uhr zehn.
- [ ] Die erste Stunde beginnt um acht Uhr vierzig.
- [ ] Der Bus kommt um fünfzehn Uhr siebenundvierzig.
- [ ] Ich komme um sechzehn Uhr dreißig nach Hause.
- [ ] Wir haben Mathe um elf Uhr fünfundzwanzig.

2 **The school is running 20 minutes late today. Rewrite each of the six sentences in exercise 1 with the time that each activity begins today.**

3 **Complete the sentences by writing the correct possessive pronoun in each gap.**

!
sein = his (for masculine and neuter nouns) **seine** = his (for feminine nouns)
ihr = her (for masculine and neuter nouns) **ihre** = her (for feminine nouns)

1 ________ Bruder heißt Pawel und ________ Schwester heißt Aga.

2 ________ Lieblingssport ist Eishockey.

3 ________ Katze ist braun, aber ________ Hund ist weiß.

4 ________ Schule ist in Hannover.

5 ________ Lieblingssport ist Reiten und ________ Lieblingsfach ist Mathe.

6 ________ Computer ist neu.

7 ________ Erdkundelehrerin ist sehr streng.

8 ________ Mutter wohnt in Salzburg, aber ________ Vater wohnt in Wien.

4 **Describe where each of the items is located in the classroom.**

1 Der Computer *ist auf dem Tisch.*

2 Das Poster ________________

3 Das Whiteboard ________________

4 Der Lehrer ________________

5 Der Stuhl ________________

6 Die Spinne ________________

Wiederholung 2

1 Read the texts. Use your knowledge of vocabulary to help you to find these new phrases. Write each German phrase next to the English.

1 My name is ____________
2 her favourite artist ____________
3 unfortunately ____________
4 My brother also goes ____________
5 an indoor pool ____________
6 a pot plant ____________

Hallo! Mein Name ist **Maik** und ich wohne in München, in Deutschland. Meine Schule heißt Mathias Brauer Gymnasium und ich finde sie toll. An meiner Schule lerne ich sehr gern Englisch und Geschichte, aber mein Lieblingsfach ist Kunst. Ich mag Kunst, weil ich total kreativ bin. Ich finde meine Kunstlehrerin auch sehr nett. Sie heißt Frau Weber und ihr Lieblingskünstler ist Dürer.

Ich mag nicht Sport, weil ich nicht sehr sportlich bin. Leider habe ich am Montag und auch am Mittwoch Sport. Morgen spielen wir Tennis. Das finde ich nicht so schlecht.

lernen = to learn

Hallo Leute! Ich heiße **Sabine** und ich wohne in Zürich, in der Schweiz. Meine Schule ist sehr groß. Mein Bruder geht auch auf meine Schule.

Mein Lieblingsfach ist Musik und dieses Fach haben wir am Dienstag in der zweiten Stunde und auch am Donnerstag in der vierten Stunde. Sport mag ich auch, weil der Sportlehrer total lustig ist. Sein Lieblingssport ist Schwimmen und wir haben ein Hallenbad in der Schule. Wir haben Sport am Mittwoch in der fünften Stunde und auch am Freitag in der zweiten Stunde.

Mein Klassenzimmer ist sehr schön. Wir haben zehn Computer, ein Whiteboard neben der Tür, viele Poster an der Wand und eine Topfpflanze am Fenster!

2 Answer the questions about the texts in exercise 1. Write complete sentences in German for your answers.

1 Wie heißt Maiks Schule? ____________
2 Was mag Maik? ____________
3 Was lernt Maik nicht gern? ____________
4 Wann hat Maik Sport? ____________
5 Wo ist Zürich? ____________
6 Was hat Sabine am Donnerstag in der vierten Stunde? ____________
7 Warum mag Sabine Sport? ____________
8 Wo ist die Topfpflanze? ____________

Grammatik (Seiten 90–91)

1 Answer the questions in full sentences, using *weil* and the reason given.

1 Warum magst du Kunst? (it's creative)

Ich mag Kunst, weil es kreativ ist.

2 Warum magst du Englisch? (it's interesting)

____

3 Warum spielst du Tennis? (I'm sporty)

____

4 Warum hasst du Sport? (it's difficult)

____

5 Warum findest du Erdkunde toll? (it's easy)

____

2 Put the words in the right order to make sentences.

Remember the 'verb in second place' rule.

1 der in Geschichte dritten wir Stunde haben

____

2 habe Pause ich nach der Kunst ______________________

3 Fußball spiele heute ich ______________________

4 gibt Klassenzimmer Computer und viele einen es im Poster

____

5 Montag ich vierten Stunde habe in am der Mathe

____

3 Write the following school rules in sentences in German.

Example: Man darf am Montag …

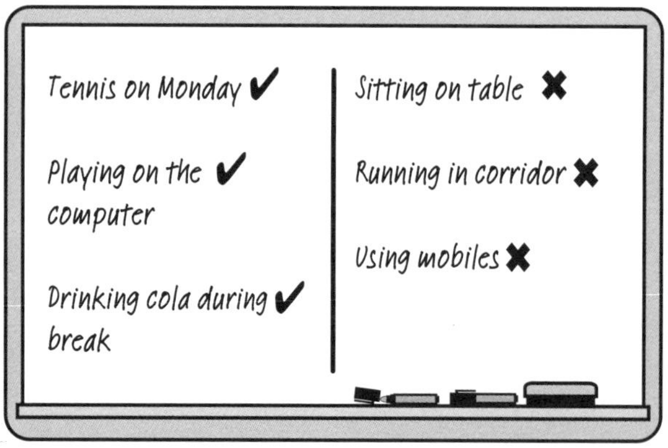

Man darf is often used to mean 'you/we are allowed to'.

Remember to use the correct preposition and the correct word for 'the' after it.

Mein Fortschritt

1 **Record your levels for *Kapitel* 4.**

2 **Look at the level descriptors on pages 59–60 and set your targets for *Kapitel* 5.**

3 **Fill in what you need to do to achieve these targets.**

Listening 	I have reached Level ______ in **Listening**. In *Kapitel* 5, I want to reach Level ______ I need to ____________________ ____________________ ____________________ ____________________
Speaking 	I have reached Level ______ in **Speaking**. In *Kapitel* 5, I want to reach Level ______ I need to ____________________ ____________________ ____________________ ____________________
Reading 	I have reached Level ______ in **Reading**. In *Kapitel* 5, I want to reach Level ______ I need to ____________________ ____________________ ____________________ ____________________
Writing 	I have reached Level ______ in **Writing**. In *Kapitel* 5, I want to reach Level ______ I need to ____________________ ____________________ ____________________ ____________________

Schulfächer • School subjects

Deutsch	*German*
Englisch	*English*
Erdkunde	*geography*
Geschichte	*history*
Informatik	*ICT*
Kunst	*art*
Mathe	*maths*
Musik	*music*
Naturwissenschaften	*science*
Sport	*sport, PE*
Technik	*technology*
Theater	*drama*

Meinungen • Opinions

mein Lieblingsfach ist ...	*my favourite subject is ...*
ich mag ... (sehr)	*I like ... (a lot)*
ich liebe	*I love*
ich mag ... nicht	*I don't like ...*
ich hasse	*I hate*
gut	*good*
toll	*great*
furchtbar	*awful*
einfach	*easy*
schwierig	*difficult*
interessant	*interesting*
langweilig	*boring*
nützlich	*useful*
nutzlos	*useless*
faszinierend	*fascinating*
nervig	*irritating*
supercool	*really cool*
stinklangweilig	*dead boring*

Die Wochentage • The days of the week

Montag (Mo.)	*Monday*
Dienstag (Di.)	*Tuesday*
Mittwoch (Mi.)	*Wednesday*
Donnerstag (Do.)	*Thursday*
Freitag (Fr.)	*Friday*
Samstag (Sa.)	*Saturday*
Sonntag (So.)	*Sunday*
Was hast du am Montag?	*What do you have on Monday?*
Am Dienstag habe ich ...	*I have ... on Tuesday*
Am Sonntag haben wir keine Schule.	*We have no school on Sunday.*

Die Zeit • Time

Wann?	*When?*
Um wie viel Uhr?	*At what time?*
Um 8:30 Uhr (acht Uhr dreißig).	*At 8:30.*
Wie viel Uhr ist es?	*What time is it?*
Es ist 9:50 Uhr (neun Uhr fünfzig).	*It's 9:50.*
in der ersten Stunde	*in the first lesson*
vor der Pause	*before break*
nach der Mittagspause	*after the lunch break*

Eigenschaften • Characteristics

Er/Sie ist ...	*He/She is ...*
alt	*old*
fair	*fair*
freundlich	*friendly*
jung	*young*
launisch	*moody*
lustig	*funny*
nervig	*annoying*
streng	*strict*
unpünktlich	*unpunctual*

In der Schule • In school

die Lehrerin(-nen)	*teacher (female)*
die Deutsch-lehrerin(-nen)	*German teacher (female)*
der Lehrer(–)	*teacher (male)*
der Sportlehrer(–)	*sports teacher (male)*
Was gibt es?	*What is there?*
Es gibt einen/eine/ein ...	*There is a ...*
Es gibt viele ...	*There are lots of ...*
das Klassenzimmer(–)	*classroom*
der Tisch(-e)	*table*
der Stuhl(¨-e)	*chair*
der Computer(–)	*computer*
das Whiteboard(-s)	*whiteboard*
das Poster(–)	*poster*
das Fenster(–)	*window*
die Wand(¨-e)	*wall*
die Tür(-en)	*door*
der Korridor(-e)	*corridor*

Wo ist das? • Where is it?

in der Schule	*in the school*
im Klassenzimmer	*in the classroom*
im Korridor	*in the corridor*
an der Wand	*on the wall*
am Fenster	*by the window*
am Tisch	*at the table*
auf dem Tisch	*on the table*
neben der Tür	*near/next to the door*

Oft benutzte Wörter • High-frequency words

weil	*because*
sein/seine	*his*
ihr/ihre	*her*
zu	*too*
sehr	*very*
ziemlich	*quite, fairly*
ein bisschen	*a bit*
nicht	*not*
haben	*to have*
sein	*to be*
in	*in*
an	*at, by, on (wall)*
auf	*on (top of)*
neben	*near, next to*
heute	*today*
morgen	*tomorrow*
vor	*before*
nach	*after*

1 In der Stadt (Seiten 98–99)

1 Write sentences to say what there is and isn't in the town.

1 Es gibt hier __________________________________.

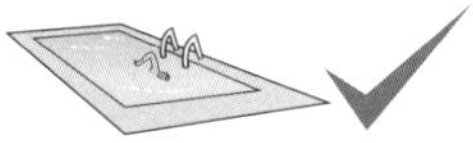

2 Hier gibt es __________________________________.

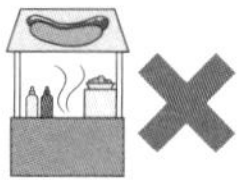

3 In der Stadt gibt es __________________________________.

4 Es gibt __________________________________ hier.

Grammatik

der→einen/keinen **die**→eine/keine **das**→ein/kein

2 Read the texts. Tick the things there are in each person's town and cross the things there aren't.

Monika: *Ich wohne in Celle. Meine Stadt ist nicht sehr groß. Es gibt hier ein Schloss und auch einen Marktplatz. Leider gibt es kein Schwimmbad und auch keine Kegelbahn.*

leider = unfortunately

Erik: *Die Touristen kommen gern nach Verden, weil es eine Kirche und auch einen Marktplatz gibt. Ein Schloss gibt es auch, aber leider gibt es kein Schwimmbad und keine Imbissstube.*

Aisha: *Ich wohne in Neustadt, in der Nähe vom Titisee. Neustadt ist ganz klein, aber sehr schön. Es gibt hier kein Schloss, keine Kegelbahn und leider auch kein Kino. Wir haben aber einen Bahnhof, eine Kirche und auch einen alten Marktplatz. Wir haben kein Schwimmbad, aber man kann im Sommer im Titisee schwimmen!*

	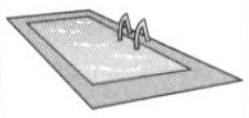			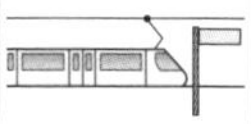				
Monika								
Erik								
Aisha								

3 Write two or three sentences about what there is to do where you live, as well as what there isn't. Use the texts in exercise 2 to help you.

2 Wir gehen einkaufen! (Seiten 100–101)

1 **Write what the customers in the souvenir shop would like. Start your sentences with *Ich möchte*.**

1 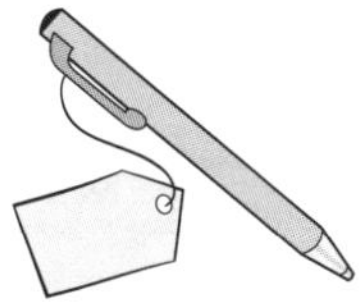
2 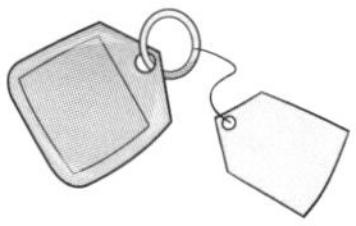
3 
4 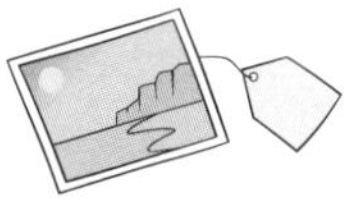
5 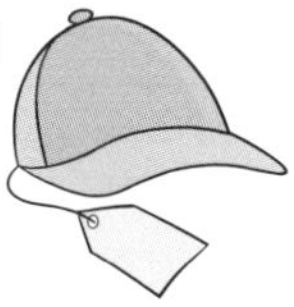
6 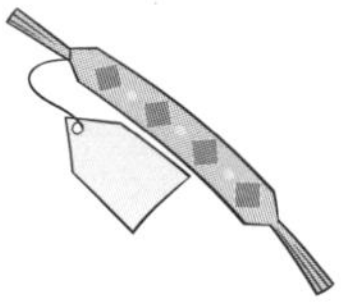
7 
8 

Look at the vocabulary on page 57 if you need to check which words to use.

1 Ich möchte einen Kuli.
5 ______________________
2 ______________________
6 ______________________
3 ______________________
7 ______________________
4 ______________________
8 ______________________

2 **Complete the dialogue with words from the cloud below. Then number the lines of the conversation in the correct order 1–11.**

☐ Guten Tag! ______________ ich dir helfen?
☐ Welche ______________? Wir haben blau, rot oder schwarz.
☐ Ja, klar! Dieser ______________, zum Beispiel, kostet nur €18,95.
☐ Super!
☐ Danke. Auf ______________.
☐ Sonst noch etwas?
☐ Alles ______________ kostet das €38,95.
☐ Guten Tag! Ich möchte ein Souvenir ______________, vielleicht ein Kuscheltier. Haben Sie ______________?
☐ Bitte sehr.
☐ Ja. Ich möchte ein ______________ für meine Schwester.
☐ Schwarz, bitte. Wie viel ______________ das?

zusammen *Elefant* *Kuscheltiere* *Wiedersehen* *Kann* *kostet* *Fußballtrikot* *kaufen* *Farbe*

3 Mmm, lecker! (Seiten 102–103)

1 Write four short conversations between hungry customers and the owner of the snack stand. The price of each individual item is shown: don't forget to add up the total price.

1

× 1
drei Euro zehn

× 1
zwei Euro fünfunddreißig

2

× 2
zwei Euro sechzig

× 2
zwei Euro fünfundzwanzig

3

× 3
drei Euro zwanzig

× 1
ein Euro neunzig

4

× 4
drei Euro fünfundneunzig

× 1
zwei Euro zehn

Ich möchte .../Ich hätte gern ...	I'd like ...
Das kostet alles zusammen ...	All together that costs ...

1 *Guten Tag! Ich möchte einmal Hamburger und einmal Bratwurst, bitte.*

Das kostet alles zusammen € ...

2 ______________________________

____

3 ______________________________

____

4 ______________________________

____

2 Write a short review of the menu, saying what there is to eat and drink and what you do and don't like.

- Hamburger 
- Bratwurst
- Pommes 
- Salat
- Eis
- Tee
- Cola
- Mineralwasser

Man kann ... trinken/essen.	You can eat/drink ...
Ich esse/trinke gern ...	I like eating/drinking ...
Ich esse/trinke nicht gern ...	I don't like eating/drinking ...
Ich mag ...	I like ....
Ich mag nicht ...	I don't like .....

____

____

____

4 In den Sommerferien (Seiten 104–105)

1 Circle the correct option to complete each sentence from the choices given. Then write the missing words in the gaps.

1 Ich ______________ im See baden.

a wirst b werden c werde

2 Wir werden im ______________ schwimmen.

a Meer b windsurfen c Bratwurst

3 ______________ du nach Innsbruck fahren?

a Wird b Wirst c Bist

4 Er ______________ nicht nach Hannover ______________ .

a werden; fahre b kann; fährt c wird; fahren

5 Tobi ______________ in den ______________ nach Portugal fahren.

a werde; Park b wird; Bahnhof c wird; Sommerferien

6 Wohin ______________ wir ______________ ?

a werden; gehen b kann; gehen c darf; fahren

2 Read the sentences and write the correct words from the cloud in the gaps. There are more words than you need.

1 Ich werde eine Kappe ______________ meinen Vater kaufen.
2 Ich ______________ ein Trikot kaufen.
3 In den ______________ fahren wir nach Rom.
4 Es ______________ ein Schwimmbad und ein Kino in Walsrode.
5 Wir ______________ nach Magdeburg fahren.
6 Ich möchte in den Bergen ______________ gehen.

für
gibt
möchte
nächste Woche
Sommerferien
wandern
werde
werden

3 Write about your plans for the summer holidays. Use the questions and illustrations to help you.

- Wohin wirst du fahren?

- Wer kommt mit?

- Was wirst du dort machen?

- Was wird dein Bruder / deine Schwester machen

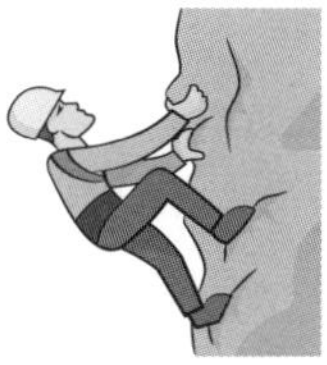

- Wirst du Souvenirs kaufen?

Willkommen! (Seiten 108–109)

1 Rewrite each sentence. Swap the adjective in bold for an alternative adjective with a similar meaning.

1 Das Mozart Museum ist **faszinierend**. ______________________

2 Der Marktplatz ist **historisch**. ______________________

3 Das Schwimmbad ist **modern**.

____

4 Die Kegelbahn ist **toll**. ______________________

2 Join up the sentence halves to describe a trip to Vienna.

1 In den Sommerferien werde	**a** Tage in Wien bleiben.
2 Dort gibt es einen	**b** ich nach Wien fahren.
3 Am Montag kann	**c** Wien fantastisch.
4 Ich finde	**d** Marktplatz, aber keinen See.
5 Wir werden vier	**e** man das Mozart Museum besuchen.

Now rewrite the sentences, varying the sentence structure. Remember that in German you always need the verb as the second idea.

Example: **1** Ich werde in den Sommerferien ...

3 Read the text about Hahndorf. Try to work out what the words in bold mean from the context. If you can't work out the meanings, look them up in a dictionary.

Hahndorf ist eine kleine Stadt in Südaustralien, in der Nähe von Adelaide. Es gibt dort deutsche **Einwanderer**. Die Stadt ist klein, aber **fein**! Hahndorf ist toll für Kinder und auch für **Erwachsene**. Dort gibt es viele deutsche Restaurants und Cafés. Am Mittwoch und am Sonntag gibt es immer einen Markt auf dem Marktplatz. Man kann hier Schokolade, **Kuchen** und **Kleidung** kaufen. **Wein** aus der Region kann man auch dort trinken. Ich werde **nächstes Jahr** mit meiner Schule nach Hahndorf fahren.

4 Write about a city or town of your choice. Adapt some of the words and phrases from the text in exercise 3.

Remember to include: the future tense, opinions, linking words, qualifiers, frequency expressions and inverted word order.

Wiederholung 1

1 **Decide which souvenir you would buy for each person and write the price in words.**

Grammatik

der → er *die → sie* *das → es*

Remember, *der* changes to *den* for masculine nouns.

1 Meine Mutter: Ich werde die Tasse für meine Mutter kaufen. Sie kostet sieben Euro fünfundfünfzig.

2 Onkel Karl: ______________________________

3 Meine Schwester: ______________________________

4 Meine Freundin: ______________________________

5 Frau Roberts: ______________________________

2 **Peter is in the tourist office in Munich. Read the dialogue, then answer the questions in full German sentences.**

Tourist guide: Guten Tag! Willkommen in München!

Peter: Guten Tag! Danke schön! Was gibt es hier in München?

Tourist guide: Hier gibt es viel zu tun! Man kann in München alles sehen!

Peter: Gibt es hier einen Marktplatz?

Tourist guide: Natürlich! Er heißt Marienplatz. Er ist sehr groß und total schön.

Peter: Wunderbar! Und kann man in München Ski fahren?

Tourist guide: Also ... nicht direkt in München, aber in der Nähe von hier kann man sehr gut Ski fahren.

Peter: Super. Und gibt es hier ein gutes Restaurant? Ich möchte gern Pizza essen.

Tourist guide: Ja, das gibt es! Es heißt *Robertos*. Dort kann man gut Pizza essen.

Peter: Vielen Dank. Ich werde im Restaurant *Robertos* essen. Auf Wiedersehen!

1 Was kann man in München machen?
2 Wie heißt der Marktplatz?
3 Wie ist er?
4 Wo kann man Ski fahren?
5 Was möchte Peter essen?
6 Was ist *Robertos*?

Wiederholung 2

1 Rewrite the sentences in the future tense. Identify the subject to help you change the form of *werden*.

1 Wir tauchen im Meer. *Wir werden im Meer tauchen.*

2 Wir baden im See. ______

3 Ich gehe an den Strand. ______

4 Lena und Michael klettern am Samstag in den Bergen.

______

5 Er kauft ein Kuscheltier für seine kleine Schwester.

______

6 Kaufst du eine Kappe als Souvenir? ______

7 Wir gehen am Wochenende mit meinen Freunden einkaufen.

______

2 Read the postcard and answer the questions in full German sentences.

Liebe Oma und Lieber Opa!

Hallo aus Mallorca in Spanien! Wir bleiben zwei Wochen hier, weil wir Sommerferien haben. Es gibt hier alles – einen Wasserpark, ein Schloss und auch einen Markt. Jeden Tag schwimmen wir im Meer. Im Hotel gibt es ein Schwimmbad und wir schwimmen auch hier. Man kann windsurfen und auch tauchen. Mallorca ist auch für das Essen sehr bekannt.

Nächste Woche werden wir in den Bergen klettern. Ich möchte auch segeln. Ich werde auch Souvenirs kaufen!

Alles Liebe,

Tamika

1 Warum ist Tamika in Spanien? ______

2 Was gibt es in Mallorca? ______

3 Was kann man machen? ______

4 Ist Mallorca bekannt für das Museum? ______

5 Was wird Tamika nächste Woche machen? ______

3 Write four true/false statements in English about the text in exercise 2. Then ask a friend to write 'True' or 'False' next to each statement.

Example: The postcard is to Tamika's parents. False

Grammatik (Seiten 112–113)

1 Rewrite the sentences to make them negative.

Use *keinen/keine/kein* to say what there is or isn't. Use *nicht* to say what you can't or don't like doing.

1 Es gibt in Düsseldorf einen Marktplatz.

____

2 Er mag Wasserball.

____

3 Beni kann Fußball spielen, weil er einen Ball hat.

____

4 In der Stadt gibt es ein Kino und auch eine Kirche.

____

5 Man darf hier schwimmen. ______________________________

2 Write the different forms of *möchten* in the table.

ich		wir	
du		ihr	
er/sie/es		Sie	
		sie	

möchten
möchte
möchten
möchtest
möchte
möchtet
möchten

Complete the sentences by writing the correct form of *möchten* in each gap. Then translate the sentences into English.

1 ____________ du ein Schokoladeneis?

2 Nein, aber ich ____________ gern ein Vanilleeis.

3 Anne ____________ nach Kapstadt in Südafrika fahren.

4 ____________ ihr auch nach Windhuk in Namibia fahren?

5 Wir ____________ zweimal Salat und zweimal Mineralwasser, bitte.

6 Frau Winkelmann, ____________ Sie eine Tasse Tee?

3 Fill in the gaps to complete the different forms of *werden*.

ich __e__de	wir we__de__
du w__r__t	ihr __er__e__
er/sie/es __ir__	Sie/sie w__r__en

4 Write sentences about what you and your family/friends will do on your next holiday.

Example: Ich werde jeden Tag in Frankreich wandern. Mein Bruder … /Steffi …

Jahresbilanz

Record your levels for *Kapitel* 5.

Listening	I have reached Level ______ in **Listening**.
Speaking	I have reached Level ______ in **Speaking**.
Reading	I have reached Level ______ in **Reading**.
Writing	I have reached Level ______ in **Writing**.

Look back through your workbook and note down the level you achieved in each skill by the end of each *Kapitel*.

	Listening	**Speaking**	**Reading**	**Writing**
1 Meine Welt und ich				
2 Familie und Tiere				
3 Freizeit – juhu!				
4 Schule ist klasse!				
5 Gute Reise!				

You now have a record of your progress in German for the whole year.

Wörter

In der Stadt • In town

Es gibt ...	*There is ... / There are ...*
Es gibt ein/eine/einen ...	*There is/are a ...*
Es gibt kein/keine/keinen ...	*There isn't/aren't ...*
in der Nähe von ...	*near to*
in der Nähe ...	*nearby*
der Bahnhof(¨e)	*railway station(s)*
der Imbiss(-e)/die Imbissstube(-n)	*snack stand(s)*
die Kegelbahn(-en)	*bowling alley(s)*
das Kino(-s)	*cinema(s)*
die Kirche(-n)	*church(es)*
der Marktplatz(¨e)	*market square(s)*
der Park(-s)	*park(s)*
das Schloss(¨er)	*castle(s)*
das Schwimmbad(¨er)	*swimming pool(s)*
die Eisbahn(-en)	*ice rink(s)*
der Fischmarkt(¨e)	*fish market(s)*
das Kindertheater(-)	*children's theatre(s)*
der Radweg(-e)	*cycle path(s)*
das Sportzentrum (die Sportzentren)	*sports centre (sports centres)*
der Stadtpark(-s)	*city/town park(s)*
der Wasserpark(-s)	*water park(s)*

Verkaufsgespräch • Sales conversation

Ich gehe einkaufen.	*I am going shopping.*
Ich möchte ...	*I would like ...*
Ich möchte ... kaufen.	*I would like to buy ...*
Haben Sie ...?	*Do you have ...?*
Kann ich dir helfen?	*Can I help you?*
Sonst noch etwas?	*Anything else?*
alles zusammen	*all together*

Souvenirs • Souvenirs

der Aufkleber	*sticker*
das Freundschaftsband	*friendship bracelet*
die Kappe	*(baseball) cap*
der Kuli	*biro*
das Kuscheltier	*cuddly toy*
die Postkarte	*postcard*
der Schlüsselanhänger	*key ring*
die Tasse	*mug/cup*
das Trikot	*(football) shirt*
Wie viel kostet ...?	*How much does ... cost?*
Wie viel kostet das?	*How much does it cost?*
Es kostet €16.	*It costs 16 Euros.*

Snacks und Getränke kaufen • Buying snacks and drinks

die Bratwurst	*fried sausage*
der Hamburger	*hamburger*
die Pizza	*pizza*
die Pommes	*chips*
der Salat	*salad*
das Eis	*ice cream*
die Cola	*cola*
das Mineralwasser	*mineral water*
der Tee	*tea*
das Fleisch	*meat*
der Ketchup	*ketchup*
die Mayo(nnaise)/Majonäse	*mayo(nnaise)*
der Senf	*mustard*
Ich möchte einmal/zweimal/dreimal ...	*I would like one/two/three ...*
Ich hätte gern ...	*I would like ...*
Das macht €8.	*That's €8.*
Ich esse ... gern.	*I like eating ... .*
Ich trinke ... gern.	*I like drinking ... .*

Wörter

In den Sommerferien • During the summer holidays

Was wirst du machen?	*What will you do?*
Ich werde ...	*I will ...*
Wir werden ...	*We will ...*
klettern	*climb*
im Meer schwimmen	*swim in the sea*
rodeln	*toboggan*
im See baden	*bathe in the lake*
segeln	*sail*
an den Strand gehen	*go to the beach*
tauchen	*dive*
wandern	*hike*
windsurfen	*windsurf*
Was kann man dort machen?	*What can you do there?*
Man kann ... besuchen.	*'One'/People/ You can visit ...*
Die Stadt ist bekannt für ...	*The town is well known for ...*
Ich werde (eine Woche) bleiben.	*I will stay (for a week).*

Oft benutzte Wörter • High-frequency words

am Montag	*on Monday*
am Dienstag	*on Tuesday*
am Mittwoch	*on Wednesday*
am Donnerstag	*on Thursday*
am Freitag	*on Friday*
am Wochenende	*at the weekend*
sehr	*very*
nicht sehr	*not very*
ziemlich	*quite*
immer	*always*
nicht immer	*not always*
oft	*often*
nicht oft	*not often*
nie	*never*
alles	*everything*
dort	*there*
teuer	*expensive*

Level descriptors

Listening

Level 1	I can understand some familiar spoken words and phrases.
Level 2	I can understand a range of familiar spoken phrases.
Level 3	I can understand the main points of short spoken passages and note people's answers to questions.
Level 4	I can understand the main points of spoken passages and some of the detail.
Level 5	I can understand the main points and opinions in spoken passages about different topics. I can recognise if people are speaking about the future **OR** the past as well as the present.

Speaking

Level 1	I can say single words and short phrases.
Level 2	I can answer simple questions and use set phrases.
Level 3	I can ask questions and use short phrases to answer questions about myself.
Level 4	I can take part in conversations. I can express my opinions. I can use grammar to change phrases to say something new.
Level 5	I can give short talks, in which I express my opinions. I can take part in conversations giving information, opinions and reasons. I can speak about the future **OR** the past as well as the present.

Level descriptors

Reading

Level 1	I can understand familiar words and phrases.
Level 2	I can understand familiar phrases. I can read aloud familiar words and phrases. I can use a vocabulary list to check meanings
Level 3	I can understand the main points and people's answers to questions in short written texts.
Level 4	I can understand the main points in short texts and some of the detail. Sometimes I can work out the meaning of new words.
Level 5	I can understand the main points and opinions in texts about different topics. I can recognise if the texts are about the future **OR** the past as well as the present.

Writing

Level 1	I can write or copy single words correctly.
Level 2	I can copy short sentences correctly and write some words from memory.
Level 3	I can answer questions about myself. I can write short phrases from memory. I can write short sentences with help.
Level 4	I can write short texts on familiar topics. I can use grammar to change phrases to write something new.
Level 5	I can write short texts on a range of familiar topics. I can write about the future **OR** the past as well as the present.

Notes

Notes

Published by Pearson Education Limited, Edinburgh Gate, Harlow, Essex, CM20 2JE.

www.pearsonschoolsandfecolleges.co.uk

Edited by Melanie Birdsall
Designed by Kamae Design

Illustrated by Caron at KJA Artists and Lisa Hunt

First published 2013

2022
17

British Library Cataloguing in Publication Data
A catalogue record for this book is available from the British Library

ISBN 978 1 447 94654 0

Printed in Great Britain by Bell and Bain Ltd, Glasgow

Acknowledgements

We would like to thank Melissa Weir, Angelika Libera, Janet Soame and Frances Reynolds for their invaluable help in the development of this course.

Every effort has been made to contact copyright holders of material reproduced in this book. Any omissions will be rectified in subsequent printings if notice is given to the publishers.

www.pearsonschools.co.uk
myorders@pearson.com

T 0845 630 33 33
F 0845 630 77 77

ISBN 978-1-4479-4654-0

Stimmt! 1

Übungsheft B

Malcolm Pacey

PEARSON

1 Hallo! (Seiten 8–9)

1 Two of the words in each set have a sound that is the same. Circle the word with a different sound from the other two.

1	*Schlange*	*Porsche*	*Buch*
2	*Bär*	*Löwe*	*Röntgenbild*
3	*Wildwassersport*	*Auf Wiedersehen*	*Tür*
4	*Biene*	*heiße*	*Eis*

2 Join up the sentence halves.

1	Gut, danke. Und	a	Wiedersehen.
2	Auf	b	Ben. Wie heißt du?
3	Ich heiße	c	geht's, Ben?
4	Hallo! Wie heißt	d	du?
5	Ich heiße Nadia. Wie	e	schlecht.
6	Nicht	f	dir?

3 Write the sentences from exercise 2 in the correct order for the conversation. Then translate them into English.

1 ______________________ ______________________

2 ______________________ ______________________

3 ______________________ ______________________

4 ______________________ ______________________

5 Nicht schlecht. Not bad.

6 ______________________ ______________________

4 Unscramble the inventions. Look at the definite article (word for 'the') for each word. Then write each invention with the indefinite article (word for 'a').

1	sad ngbönReltid	das …	ein …
2	erd reelmiDtoos		
3	sda toF3rMmPa-		
4	sad PeuAsotrcoh		
5	ied sAMrkdadiae		

2 Eins, zwei, drei … (Seiten 10–11)

1 The bank has sent texts to customers with their coded PIN numbers. Solve the maths problems in German to work out the PINs. Then write each customer's new PIN below the phone.

1

Meine Bank

zehn – acht = zwei

vier + drei = sieben

zwei + drei = ______

fünf + eins = ______

2 7 _ _

2

Meine Bank

sechs + zwei = ______

zehn – neun = ______

sieben – drei = ______

eins + vier = ______

_ _ _ _

3

Meine Bank

sieben – vier = ______

acht + eins = ______

drei + sechs = ______

fünf + zwei = ______

_ _ _ _

2 Write the winning lottery numbers in words.

1 

______

2 

______

3 

______

4 

______

5 

______

6 

______

3 Write two sentences for each speaker. Give the speaker's age and the age of his/her friend.

er ist = he is
sie ist = she is

1 

Ich bin dreizehn Jahre alt.
Sie ist zwölf Jahre alt.

2 ______
______

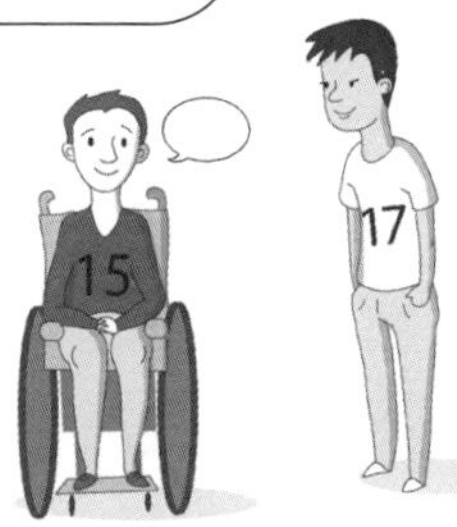

3 

______
______

3 Ich wohne in Deutschland (Seiten 12–13)

1 Read the dialogue and complete the table with the correct forms of each verb.

Melanie: Hallo! Ich heiße Melanie. Wie heißt du?
Marco: Ich heiße Marco. Ich wohne in Straubing. Wo wohnst du?
Melanie: Ich wohne in Braunschweig. Wie alt bist du?
Marco: Ich bin zwölf Jahre alt. Wer ist das?
Melanie: Sie heißt Jessie. Sie wohnt in Leipzig und ist dreizehn Jahre alt.

wer = who

	heißen (to be called)	**wohnen** (to live)	**sein** (to be)
ich (I)		*wohne*	
du (you)			*bist*
er/sie/es (he/she/it)	*heißt*		

2 Write the missing word in each sentence and complete the crossword.

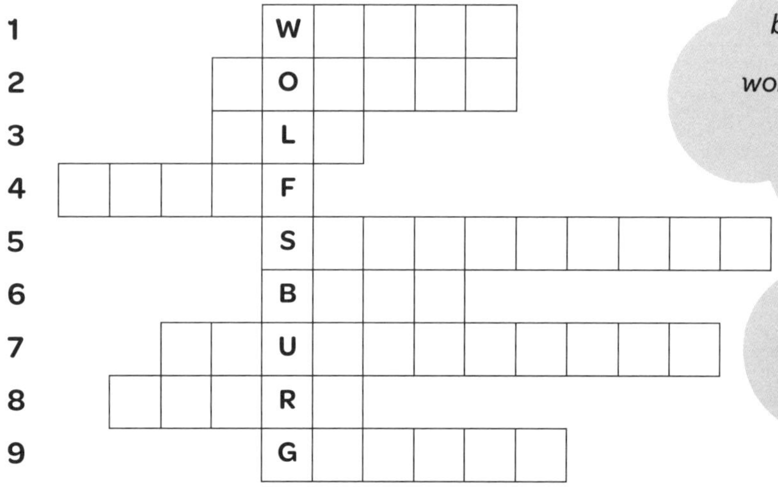

bist *zwölf* *wohne* *wohnst* *Jahre* *Schottland* *Deutschland* *geht's* *alt*

1 Ich ______________ in Manchester.
2 Wo ______________ du, Nick?
3 Wie ______________ ist er?
4 Er ist ______________ Jahre alt.
5 Glasgow ist in ______________ .
6 Wie alt ______________ du?
7 Ich wohne in Berlin. Das ist in ______________ .
8 Ich bin elf ______________ alt.
9 Wie ______________ ?

3 Research why the city of Wolfsburg is important to Germany.

4 Meine Welt ist wunderbar! (Seiten 14–15)

1 **The printer has made four mistakes labelling the illustrations. Write *richtig* or *falsch* under each caption.**

1 
Ich bin musikalisch.

____

2 
Ich bin sehr launisch.

____

3 
Ich bin ziemlich freundlich.

____

4 
Ich bin kreativ.

____

5 
Ich bin laut.

____

6 
Ich bin lustig.

____

2 **Rewrite the false captions from exercise 1, correcting them so that they are true.**

____

____

____

____

faul
lustig
musikalisch
sportlich

3 **Separate out the words to form three sentences.**

meinelieblingsfußballmannschaftistbayernmünchen

meinlieblingssportisttennis

meinelieblingszahlistsieben

Remember that each sentence must start with a capital letter. Also, remember that nouns start with a capital letter.

1 ______________________________________

2 ______________________________________

3 ______________________________________

4 **Write a sentence about your favourite …**

1 football team: ______________________________

2 sport: ______________________________

3 number: ______________________________

5 Meine Sachen (Seiten 16–17)

1 Write the German question word under its English translation.

Who?	What?	How?	Where?	Where from?

Wie? Was? Wo? Woher? Wer?

2 Write the correct question word in each question. You may use each word more than once.

1 ______________ bist du? Sportlich?

2 ______________ wohnt Shiva?

3 ______________ heißt du?

4 ______________ kommst du?

5 ______________ ist das? Ist das Max?

6 ______________ alt ist Michael?

7 ______________ ist Hannover? *Hannover ist in Deutschland!*

8 ______________ ist deine Lieblingsmusik?

3 Read the paragraph below. Pretend that you're Gabi, and answer each question in a complete German sentence.

Hallo! Ich heiße Gabi und ich bin vierzehn Jahre alt. Ich wohne in Kiel, in Deutschland, aber ich komme aus Swansea. Das ist in Wales. Wie bin ich? Ich bin sportlich, lustig und auch sehr laut! Mein Lieblingsmonat ist Dezember und meine Lieblingssendung ist ‚Die Simpsons'. Ich habe ein iPad und auch einen Computer. Tschüs!

1 Wie heißt du? ______________________________

2 Wo wohnst du? ______________________________

3 Woher kommst du? ______________________________

4 Wie bist du? ______________________________

5 Wie heißt deine Lieblingssendung? ______________________________

6 Was hast du? ______________________________

Ich über mich (Seiten 18–19)

1 **Complete the table with the correct words.**

	the	a	my	your
masculine: Sport				
feminine: Musik				
neuter: Auto				

2 **Write each sentence or question in German. Tick the boxes when you've checked each part of your work.**

Part of writing accurately in any language is going back over your work to check that there aren't any mistakes. Get into the habit now and watch both your English and German improve!

1 I'm called Osman.

____

2 I live in Germany.

____

3 I'm quite friendly and also creative.

____

____

4 I have a mobile phone.

____

5 Where do you live?

____

- ☐ Spelling of key phonics sound 'ei'
- ☐ Name has a capital
- ☐ Spelling of key phonics sound 'eu'
- ☐ Full stop at the end
- ☐ Check the qualifier
- ☐ Check the connective
- ☐ Capital on the noun
- ☐ Right word for 'a'
- ☐ Correct question word
- ☐ Verb in second position

3 **Write a short paragraph about yourself. Use the sentences in exercise 2 as prompts. Check your work against the checklist below.**

☐ genders ☐ qualifiers ☐ connectives ☐ verbs
☐ capital letters ☐ spelling ☐ question words

____

____

Wiederholung 1

1 Fill in the gaps by writing the German for the words in brackets.

Hallo! Ich __________ (am called) Marie und ich __________ (live) in Walsrode. Das ist in __________ (Germany). Ich bin fünfzehn __________ (years) alt. Ich bin __________ (very) sportlich und __________ (quite) intelligent, __________ (but) ich bin __________ (also) faul. Mein __________ (favourite sport) ist Hockey und __________ (my) Lieblingsmusik ist Pop. Ich __________ (have) einen Vogel aus Amerika. Er ist __________ (very) freundlich, aber __________ (not) laut!

2 Crack the code and write the sentences correctly.

a 18/24/19 4/12/19/13/22 18/13 20/28/7/7/18/13/20/22/13

Ich wohne in Göttingen.

b 22/9 18/8/7 20/26/13/1 21/9/22/6/13/23/15/18/24/19

____

ä = 27 ü = 29
ö = 28 ß = 30

c 14/22/18/13/22 15/18/22/25/15/18/13/20/8/14/6/8/18/16 18/8/7 14/12/1/26/9/7

____

____

3 Make up a coded sentence in German for a classmate to solve. Don't forget to provide a key.

4 Write the questions you would ask to get these answers.

1 *Wie heißt du?*

Ich heiße Elaine.

2 __________

Mein Lieblingssport ist Tennis.

3 __________

Sami ist musikalisch und intelligent, aber sehr launisch.

4 __________

Alwin ist vierzehn Jahre alt.

Wiederholung 2

1 **Read the website entries.**

Ich heiße **Franzi** und suche Freunde aus England, Irland oder Nordirland. Ich habe eine Schlange zu Hause! Sie ist sechs Jahre alt. Ich wohne in Wien. Das ist in Österreich. Ich bin sehr kreativ und intelligent! Schreib mir bitte!

Hallo! Ich heiße **Hannah** und ich wohne in London, in England. Ich lerne Deutsch. Ich suche Freunde aus Deutschland, Österreich und auch aus der Schweiz. Ich bin sportlich und spiele Fußball und auch Tennis, aber ich bin sehr faul! Meine Lieblingsmusik ist Rock. Schreib mir!

Mein Name ist **Felix** und ich wohne in der Schweiz, aber ich komme aus Dortmund in Deutschland. Zu Hause habe ich eine Wii und mein Lieblingsspiel ist FIFA. Meine Lieblingsfußballmannschaft ist Bayern-München. Ich suche Freunde aus Schottland und Wales.

Hi! Ich bin **Muhammad** und ich wohne in Cardiff. Das ist in Wales. Ich bin sechzehn Jahre alt. Meine Lieblingssache ist Technologie. Ich habe zu Hause einen Computer, ein Handy und auch ein iPad. Ich bin nicht sehr sportlich, aber sehr freundlich. Mein Lieblingsland ist Deutschland und ich suche dort Freunde.

Write the name of the person who …

1 is looking for friends from Switzerland. Hannah

2 supports a football team. ____________

3 has a pet. ____________

4 is just looking for friends from Germany. ____________

5 lives in a different place from where they were born. ____________

6 does not particularly like sport. ____________

7 lives in Switzerland. ____________

suche = seek
Schreib mir (bitte)! = Write to me (please)!
dort = there

2 **Write your own profile for the website. Use as much German as you can from *Kapitel 1* to describe yourself.**

____

____

____

____

Grammatik (Seiten 22–23)

1 **Write a sentence using the correct German word for 'a' for each item.**

1  2  3  4  5 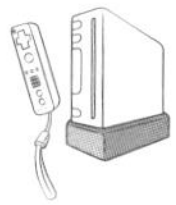 6  7  8 

1 Das ist ein Computer.
2 ______________________________
3 ______________________________
4 ______________________________
5 ______________________________
6 ______________________________
7 ______________________________
8 ______________________________

die Gitarre · *das Handy*
der iPod · *der Computer*
das Skateboard · *das Keyboard*
der Fußball · *die Wii*

Grammatik
masculine – *ein*
feminine – *eine*
neuter – *ein*

2 **Circle the correct verb form to complete each sentence.**

1 Lukas **habe / hat / hast** einen Computer.
2 Ich **heiße / habe / hat** einen Vogel zu Hause.
3 Wo **bist / ist / wohnst** er?
4 Er **ist / komme / bin** musikalisch und sportlich.
5 Julia **bin / ist / wohnt** fünfzehn Jahre alt.
6 Wie alt **wohnst / bist / bin** du?
7 Wo **hast / bist / bin** ich?

Grammatik
You can use the pronouns *er* ('he') or *sie* ('she') instead of writing someone's name. Both need the *er/sie/es* form of the verb.

3 **Complete the table with the correct forms of each regular verb.**

wohnen (to live)	**kommen** (to come)	**heißen** (to be called)
ich *wohne*	ich	ich
du	du *kommst*	du
er/sie/es	er/sie/es	er/sie/es *heißt*

Now use the table to write the correct verb in each gap.

1 Mein Handy ____________ aus China.
2 Meine Schlange ____________ Sissel.
3 Du ____________ Gabi.
4 ____________ du aus Berlin?
5 ____________ Monika in Hamburg?
6 Deine Lieblingssendung ____________ ‚EastEnders'.
7 Ich ____________ Wolfgang.
8 Wo ____________ du?

Mein Fortschritt

1 **Record your levels for *Kapitel* 1.**

2 **Look at the level descriptors on pages 59–60 and set your targets for *Kapitel* 2.**

3 **Fill in what you need to do to achieve these targets.**

Listening 	I have reached Level ______ in **Listening**. In *Kapitel* 2, I want to reach Level ______ I need to ______
Speaking 	I have reached Level ______ in **Speaking**. In *Kapitel* 2, I want to reach Level ______ I need to ______
Reading 	I have reached Level ______ in **Reading**. In *Kapitel* 2, I want to reach Level ______ I need to ______
Writing 	I have reached Level ______ in **Writing**. In *Kapitel* 2, I want to reach Level ______ I need to ______

Wörter

Hallo! • Meeting and greeting

Wie heißt du?	*What's your name?*
Ich heiße ...	*My name is ...*
Hallo!	*Hello! / Hi!*
Guten Tag!	*Hello!*
Wie geht's?	*How are you?*
Gut, danke. Und dir?	*Fine, thanks. And you?*
Nicht schlecht.	*Not bad.*
Tschüs!	*Bye!*
Auf Wiedersehen!	*Goodbye!*

Die Zahlen 1–19 • Numbers 1–19

eins	*1*
zwei	*2*
drei	*3*
vier	*4*
fünf	*5*
sechs	*6*
sieben	*7*
acht	*8*
neun	*9*
zehn	*10*
elf	*11*
zwölf	*12*
dreizehn	*13*
vierzehn	*14*
fünfzehn	*15*
sechzehn	*16*
siebzehn	*17*
achtzehn	*18*
neunzehn	*19*
Wie alt bist du?	*How old are you?*
Ich bin ... Jahre alt.	*I am ... years old.*
Wie alt ist (Julia)?	*How old is (Julia)?*
(Julia) ist ... Jahre alt.	*(Julia) is ... years old.*

Wo wohnst du? • Where do you live?

Ich wohne in ...	*I live in ...*
Er/Sie/Es wohnt in ...	*He/She/It lives in ...*
... England	*England*
... Irland	*Ireland*
... Nordirland	*Northern Ireland*
... Schottland	*Scotland*
... Wales	*Wales*
... Deutschland	*Germany*
... Österreich	*Austria*
... der Schweiz	*Switzerland*

Wie bist du? • What are you like?

Ich bin ...	*I am ...*
Er/Sie ist ...	*He/She is ...*
faul	*lazy*
freundlich	*friendly*
intelligent	*intelligent*
kreativ	*creative*
launisch	*moody*
laut	*loud*
lustig	*funny*
musikalisch	*musical*
sportlich	*sporty*

Lieblingssachen • Favourite things

Mein Lieblingssport ist ...
My favourite sport is ...

Mein Lieblingsmonat ist ...
My favourite month is ...

Meine Lieblingsmusik ist ...
My favourite music is ...

Meine Lieblingszahl ist ...
My favourite number is ...

Meine Lieblingssendung ist ...
My favourite programme is ...

Meine Lieblingsfußballmannschaft ist ...
My favourite football team is ...

Mein Lieblingsspiel ist ...
My favourite game is ...

Mein Lieblingsland ist ...
My favourite country is ...

Mein Lieblingsauto ist ...
My favourite car is ...

Was ist dein Lieblingssport?
What's your favourite sport?

Was ist deine Lieblingszahl?
What's your favourite number?

Was ist dein Lieblingsland?
What's your favourite country?

Hast du einen Computer? • Have you got a computer?

Ich habe ...	*I have ...*
einen Computer	*a computer*
einen iPod	*an iPod*
einen Fußball	*a football*
eine Gitarre	*a guitar*
eine Wii	*a Wii*
eine Schlange	*a snake*
ein Handy	*a mobile phone*
ein Keyboard	*a keyboard*
ein Skateboard	*a skateboard*

Fragewörter • Question words

Wie?	*How?*
Was?	*What?*
Wo?	*Where?*
Woher?	*Where ... from?*
Wer?	*Who?*

Oft benutzte Wörter • High-frequency words

und	*and*
(und) auch	*(and) also*
aber	*but*
sehr	*very*
ziemlich	*quite*
nicht	*not*
Was denkst du?	*What do you think?*
Ich denke, ...	*I think ...*
Ich auch!	*Me too!*
Ich nicht!	*Not me!/That's not what I think!*
Was? Du spinnst!	*What? You're joking!*

1 Extreme Haustiere (Seiten 30–31)

1 **Complete the sentences about the pets. Write the correct words in the gaps. Remember to think about the gender of each animal.**

1. Ich habe _ein_ Pferd. _Es_ ist groß und heißt Romeo.
2. Ich habe ______ Kaninchen. ______ ist niedlich und heißt Timmo.
3. Ich habe ______ Katze. ______ ist intelligent und heißt Mieze.
4. Max hat ______ Schlange. ______ ist zwei Jahre alt.
5. Gabi hat ______ Pferd. ______ ist launish.
6. Ich habe ______ Hund. ______ ist freundlich und heißt Prinz.
7. Susi hat ______ Goldfisch. ______ heißt Nemo.

Grammatik
Remember: after *haben* the masculine word for 'a' changes from *ein* to *einen*.

Grammatik
m. der / ein → **er**
f. die / eine → **sie**
n. das / ein → **es**

2 **Tina Tierfan has lots of pets! Write Tina's answers to the interviewer's questions about how many of each animal she has.**

Grammatik

Hund (-e)	Pferd (-e)
Katze (-n)	Goldfisch (-e)
Schlange (-n)	Maus (Mäuse)

1. Hast du einen Hund? _Nein! Ich habe drei Hunde._
2. Hast du ein Pferd? ______
3. Hast du eine Katze? ______
4. Hast du einen Goldfisch? ______
5. Hast du eine Schlange? ______
6. Hast du eine Maus? ______

2 Supertiere (Seiten 32–33)

1 Complete the sentences about the animals. Write the correct name in each gap.

Hermann 

Minnie 

Sisi 

Kizzi 

Moto 

Millie 

1 __________ ist schnell.

2 __________ ist süß.

3 __________ ist gemein.

4 __________ ist superintelligent.

5 __________ ist cool.

6 __________ ist kräftig.

2 Write a sentence to say what each of the *Supertiere* can do.

1 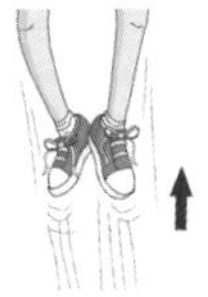

Hermann

2 

Sisi

3 

Minnie

4 

Kizzi

5 

Millie

6 

Moto

1 Hermann kann springen.

2 ______________________________

3 ______________________________

4 ______________________________

5 ______________________________

6 ______________________________

Grammatik
The verb *kann* is always followed by an infinitive verb.

3 Read the text below, then translate it into English.

Günther Goldfisch ist mein Lieblingstier. Er ist ein Jahr alt. Er ist sehr lustig und kräftig, aber auch ziemlich süß. Er kann schwimmen, springen und auch im Aquarium tanzen! Günther hat einen Freund: er ist sehr cool und schlau.

3 Meine Familie (Seiten 34–35)

1 **Find the numbers in the puzzle, and write them next to the correct numeral.**

v	i	e	r	u	n	d	s	e	c	h	z	i	g	m	e
b	a	l	c	o	e	z	n	f	w	i	r	d	s	k	s
s	e	c	h	s	u	n	d	d	r	e	i	ß	i	g	a
q	g	n	a	j	n	x	i	n	d	m	h	t	g	ü	o
h	a	c	h	t	u	n	d	f	ü	n	f	z	i	g	i
u	e	i	n	u	n	d	a	c	h	t	z	i	g	p	b
n	t	e	r	i	d	f	b	n	ß	e	d	z	g	d	s
d	r	e	i	u	n	d	v	i	e	r	z	i	g	w	e
e	v	h	f	r	e	a	m	ß	p	l	s	j	a	q	c
r	d	r	e	i	u	n	d	z	w	a	n	z	i	g	h
t	z	a	n	j	n	x	o	u	e	y	g	r	e	v	z
k	c	p	f	s	z	d	l	b	n	l	a	i	h	m	i
i	b	z	w	e	i	u	n	d	s	i	e	b	z	i	g
a	g	b	n	ü	g	y	i	a	z	o	m	e	d	h	e

100 ____________________

64 ____________________

99 ____________________

43 ____________________

72 ____________________

36 ____________________

58 ____________________

81 ____________________

60 ____________________

23 ____________________

2 **Describe each of the families. Fill in the gaps for the first family. Write the whole description for the second family.**

Oban

Ich heiße Tom. Ich bin vierzehn Jahre alt. Es gibt vier Personen in meiner Familie. Meine Mutter ist ____________________ Jahre alt. Ich habe einen Bruder. ____ ist ________ Jahre alt. Ich habe eine Schwester. ______ ist ____________ Jahre alt. Wir wohnen in ________ .

Köln

____

____

____

____

____

____

3 **Write about your family (real or imaginary). Use the descriptions in exercise 2 to help you.**

der Stiefbruder = stepbrother
die Halbschwester = half-sister
Ich bin Einzelkind. = I am an only child.

4 Die Farben der Welt (Seiten 36–37)

1 Describe each person's hair and eyes.

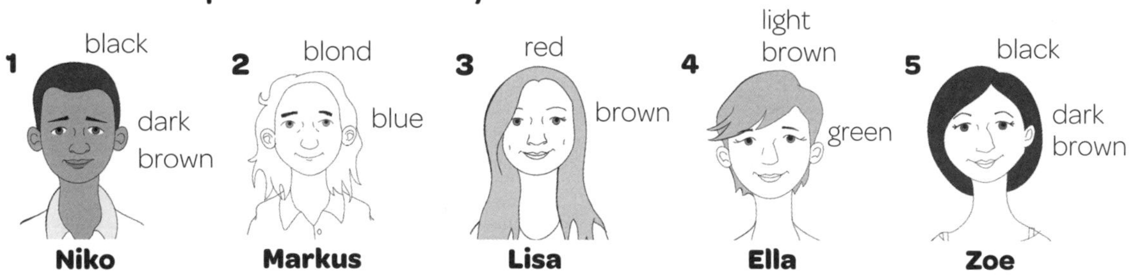

Grammatik
When you describe hair and eyes, the adjectives (colour, length) need an ***e*** on the end.

hell = light
dunkel = dark
hellbraun = light brown
dunkelblau = dark blue

1 Er heißt Niko. Er hat kurze, schwarze Haare und dunkelbraune Augen.

2 ______________________________

3 ______________________________

4 ______________________________

5 ______________________________

2 Complete the text by choosing the correct words from the cloud to fill the gaps. There are more words than you need.

Es gibt fünf __________ in meiner Familie. Wir __________ in Braunschweig. Das ist in __________________. Meine __________ heißt Emma und sie ist neunundvierzig __________ alt. Sie ist sehr freundlich und hat __________, schwarze Haare. Mein Vater __________ auch neunundvierzig und er hat kurze, dunkelbraune Haare und braune __________.

Ich habe zwei __________: einen Bruder und eine Schwester. __________ Bruder heißt Mehmet und er ist __________ Jahre alt. Er ist launisch aber __________ lustig. __________ Schwester, Isla, hat grüne Augen und __________ Haare. Sie ist sechzehn Jahre alt, sehr klein und __________________.

Deutschland alt Augen Personen
braune wohnen sportlich Meine
Mutter Jahre lange Geschwister
zwölf auch Mein blau ist

Read the text for gist first. For each sentence, think about whether you need a noun, a verb, a connective or an adjective.

5 Alles Gute! (Seiten 38–39)

1 Reorder the words to make correct sentences. Don't forget the full stop!

1 am | Mai | Ich | Geburtstag | habe | neunzehnten

____

2 hat | Oktober | am | Oma | Geburtstag | elften | Meine

____

3 Geburtstag | Stiefbruder | Dezember | am | Dein | dritten | hat

____

4 hast | Geburtstag | einunddreißigsten | Juli | Du | am

____

5 und | Geburtstag | haben | achten | am | Michael | Juni | Monika

____

2 Complete each sentence by writing the date. Write each holiday in English.

Neujahr ist am *ersten Januar*. *New Year*

Der Maifeiertag ist am ______________________________. ______________

Der Tag der Deutschen Einheit ist am ______________________________. *German Unity Day*

Weihnachten ist am ______________________________. ______________

Silvester ist am ______________________________. ______________

3 Read the short profile about Yannic and write a summary in the table.

Er heißt Yannic Spiller. Er ist dreizehn Jahre alt und kommt aus Trier. Trier ist in Deutschland. Yannic hat am siebten Januar Geburtstag. Er hat einen Bruder, Tim. Tim ist achtzehn Jahre alt. Yannic hat auch eine Schwester. Sie heißt Steffi und ist sechzehn Jahre alt. Die Familie Spiller hat zwei Haustiere: einen Hund und eine Katze.

Name:		Geschwister:	
Alter:			
Wohnt in:		Haustiere:	
Geburtstag:			

4 Now write a short profile about yourself.

1 **Rescue the question words from the alphabet soup. Write each one on a line and use it to write a question.**

Wie viele Brüder hast du?

____

____

____

____

____

____

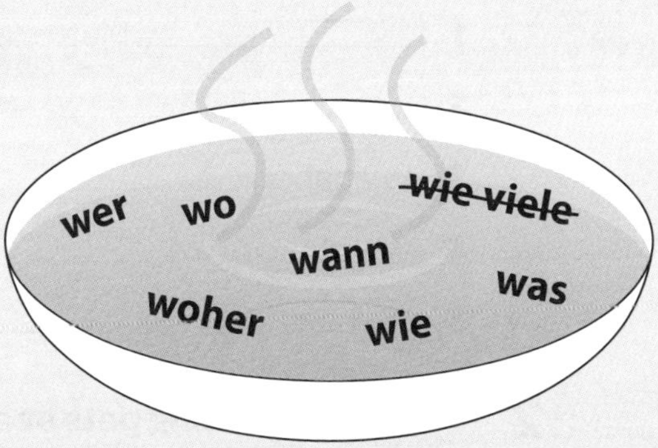

2 **The police have written a summary about a crime suspect. Write six questions for a journalist to ask the suspect. The questions should cover all the information in the summary.**

1 Wie heißt du?
2 ______________________
3 ______________________
4 ______________________
5 ______________________
6 ______________________

Martin Kolwitz ist 24 Jahre alt. Er hat am achten November Geburtstag. Er wohnt in Hamburg, in Deutschland. Er hat einen Bruder. Er hat auch Haustiere: zwei Hunde.

Remember: the verb usually goes straight after the question word.

3 **Use these notes to write questions to Martin about his accomplice, Sophie.**

1 Wie heißt sie?
2 ______________________
3 ______________________
4 ______________________
5 ______________________

Sophie Meyer
19
Ebbingen, Deutschland
Haare – kurz, Augen – blau
Geb. 21.10.

Remember to use the correct part of the verb with the pronoun *sie*.

4 **Write a summary about Sophie, like the one the police wrote about Martin in exercise 2.**

Wiederholung 1

1 **Complete the sentences. Choose the correct word from the cloud to fill in each gap.**

1 ________________ Mutter ist sehr freundlich und intelligent.

2 Hast du ________________ Meerschweinchen?

3 Wir haben ________________ Haustier.

4 Wo ist ________________ Vogel?

5 Ich habe ________________ Bruder.

dein *kein*
ein *meine*
einen

2 **You are describing pets at a pet show. Use the owners' notes to write what sort of pet they have, what the pet is like and what it can do.**

Mareike

mouse
Pippa
cute, fast
fly, swim

Mareike hat ________________________________.

Sie heißt ________________________________.

Sie ist ________________________________.

Sie kann ________________________________.

Aaron

cat
Mieze
intelligent, cool,
mean
jump, play football

________________________________.

________________________________.

________________________________.

________________________________.

________________________________.

3 **Decscribe the animal you'll be entering in the pet show by writing a similar description.**

Example: Ich habe ...

Wiederholung 2

1 Read the texts below.

Hallo! Ich heiße **Anna** und ich bin fünfzehn Jahre alt. Ich habe am elften Februar Geburtstag. Ich wohne in Klagenfurt, in Österreich. Ich bin ziemlich groß und schlank und habe kurze, schwarze Haare und blaue Augen. Ich habe keine Geschwister – ich bin Einzelkind. Ich habe einen Goldfisch und einen Wellensittich. Ich kann Flöte spielen und Italienisch sprechen.

Hi! Ich bin **Noah** und ich komme aus Aachen. Das ist in Deutschland. Ich habe am zweiten November Geburtstag und bin vierzehn Jahre alt. Ich liebe Haustiere! Ich habe zwei Hunde, drei Katzen und eine Maus. Ich habe eine große Familie. Ich habe einen Halbbruder (er ist ein Baby) und zwei Schwestern. Mein Halbbruder ist sehr süß und klein. Er hat schwarze Haare und blaue Augen.

a Complete the sentences by writing *Anna* or *Noah*.

1 ________ lives in Austria.
2 ________ can play the flute.
3 ________ 's birthday is on the 02.11.
4 ________ has a half-brother.
5 ________ is 15 years old.
6 ________ has cats.

b Write *richtig* or *falsch* next to each statement.

1 Anna hat einen Halbbruder. ________
2 Anna kann auch Englisch sprechen. ________
3 Noahs Halbbruder hat blaue Augen. ________
4 Klagenfurt ist nicht in Deutschland. ________
5 Anna hat am fünfzehnten Februar Geburtstag. ________
6 Anna hat keine Geschwister. ________

2 Translate these sentences into German.

1 My birthday is on the first of May. ________
2 She can speak German. ________
3 My guinea pig is very cute. ________
4 Your sister has light blue eyes. ________
5 My grandparents live in Southampton.
____
6 My brother can fly.
____

Grammatik (Seiten 44–45)

1 Complete the table by writing the correct form of *haben* for each pronoun.

haben *hast* *habt* *hat* *habe* *haben*

Words for 'you':
du (speaking to one family member or friend)
ihr (speaking to two or more family members or friends)
Sie (speaking to people you don't know or adults)

ich	du	er/sie/es	wir	ihr	Sie/sie

Now complete the sentences with the correct form of *haben*.

1 Katja, hast ______ du eine Katze?
2 Tom und Niko, ______ ihr einen Hund?
3 ______ Sie eine Schlange, Herr Brand?
4 Ich ______ ein Pferd.
5 Frau Gerber, ______ Sie eine Maus?
6 Herr Alexander ______ ein Pferd.

2 Join each pronoun to a verb. There is more than one possible verb for some of the pronouns. Then write a question or a sentence with each pair.

1 ich	a macht	1 ______
2 du	b heißen	2 ______
3 er	c wohnst	3 ______
4 wir	d heiße	4 ______
5 ihr	e spielt	5 ______
6 Sie	f spielen	6 ______

3 Rewrite the sentences so they include the verb *kann*.

1 Mein Bruder fliegt. Mein Bruder kann fliegen.
2 Ich spiele Flöte. ______
3 Meine Mutter schwimmt. ______
4 Mein Vater springt. ______
5 Ich tanze. ______
6 Er singt gut. ______

Mein Fortschritt

1 **Record your levels for *Kapitel* 2.**

2 **Look at the level descriptors on pages 59–60 and set your targets for *Kapitel* 3.**

3 **Fill in what you need to do to achieve these targets.**

Listening 	I have reached Level ______ in **Listening**. In *Kapitel* 3, I want to reach Level ______ I need to ______________________________ ______________________________ ______________________________ ______________________________
Speaking 	I have reached Level ______ in **Speaking**. In *Kapitel* 3, I want to reach Level ______ I need to ______________________________ ______________________________ ______________________________ ______________________________
Reading 	I have reached Level ______ in **Reading**. In *Kapitel* 3, I want to reach Level ______ I need to ______________________________ ______________________________ ______________________________ ______________________________
Writing 	I have reached Level ______ in **Writing**. In *Kapitel* 3, I want to reach Level ______ I need to ______________________________ ______________________________ ______________________________ ______________________________

Haustiere • Pets

Hast du ein Haustier?	*Have you got a pet?*
Ich habe ...	*I have ...*
einen Goldfisch	*a goldfish*
einen Hamster	*a hamster*
einen Hund	*a dog*
ein Kaninchen	*a rabbit*
eine Katze	*a cat*
eine Maus	*a mouse*
ein Meerschweinchen	*a guinea pig*
ein Pferd	*a horse*
eine Schlange	*a snake*
einen Wellensittich	*a budgie*
kein Haustier	*no pet*

Eigenschaften • Qualities

Wie ist er/sie/es?	*What is he/she/ it like?*
Er/Sie/Es ist ...	*He/She/It is ...*
dick/schlank	*fat/thin*
frech/niedlich	*cheeky/cute*
gemein/süß	*mean/sweet*
groß/klein	*big/small*
kräftig	*strong*
schlau	*cunning*
(super)lustig	*(really) funny*
Er/Sie/Es kann ...	*He/She/It can ...*
Italienisch sprechen	*speak Italian*
fliegen	*fly*
Flöte/Fußball/Wii spielen	*play the flute/ football/on the Wii*
(schnell) laufen	*run (fast)*
lesen	*read*
Rad fahren	*ride a bike*
schwimmen	*swim*
singen	*sing*
springen	*jump*
tanzen	*dance*

Die Zahlen 20–100 • Numbers 20–100

zwanzig	*twenty*
dreißig	*thirty*
vierzig	*forty*
fünfzig	*fifty*
sechzig	*sixty*
siebzig	*seventy*
achtzig	*eighty*
neunzig	*ninety*
hundert	*hundred*
einundzwanzig	*twenty-one*
zweiundzwanzig	*twenty-two*

Meine Familie • My family

Es gibt ... Personen in meiner Familie.	*There are ... people in my family.*
meine Mutter	*my mother*
mein Vater	*my father*
mein Bruder	*my brother*
mein Stiefbruder/ Halbbruder	*my stepbrother/ half-brother*
meine Schwester	*my sister*
meine Stiefschwester/ Halbschwester	*my stepsister/ half-sister*
meine Eltern	*my parents*
meine Großeltern	*my grandparents*
Hast du Geschwister?	*Have you any brothers and sisters?*
Ich habe zwei Brüder.	*I have two brothers.*
Ich habe drei Schwestern.	*I have three sisters.*
Ich bin Einzelkind.	*I'm an only child.*
Ich habe keine Geschwister.	*I have no brothers and sisters.*

Die Farben • Colours

schwarz	*black*
weiß	*white*
grau	*grey*
braun	*brown*
rot	*red*
orange	*orange*
gelb	*yellow*
grün	*green*
blau	*blue*
indigoblau	*indigo*
violett	*violet*
lila	*purple*
rosa	*pink*
bunt	*brightly coloured*
hellblau/dunkelblau	*light blue/dark blue*

Haare und Augen • Hair and eyes

Er/Sie hat ...	*He/She has ...*
schwarze/braune/ blonde/rote Haare	*black/brown/ blond/red hair*
kurze/lange/ mittellange Haare	*short/long/ mid length hair*
blaue/braune/grüne/ graue Augen	*blue/brown/green/ grey eyes*

Die Monate • The months

Januar	*January*
Februar	*February*
März	*March*
April	*April*
Mai	*May*
Juni	*June*
Juli	*July*
August	*August*
September	*September*
Oktober	*October*
November	*November*
Dezember	*December*

Das Datum • The date

Wann hast du Geburtstag?	*When is your birthday?*
am 1. (ersten) Januar	*on 1 January*
am 3. (dritten) Februar	*on 3 February*
am 7. (siebten) März	*on 7 March*
am 8. (achten) April	*on 8 April*
am 15. (fünfzehnten) Mai	*on 15 May*
am 29. (neunund-zwanzigsten) Juni	*on 29 June*
Ich habe (heute) Geburtstag.	*It's my birthday (today).*

Oft benutzte Wörter • High-frequency words

und	*and*
aber	*but*
oder	*or*
ziemlich	*fairly, quite*
sehr	*very*

1 Bist du sportlich? (Seiten 54–55)

1 **Look at the survey results in the table. Then answer the questions using full German sentences.**

Ahmed	🙂🙂			🙁			😐
Nicole		🙂🙂			🙁		
Christa	🙂		🙂🙂				😐
Torsten		🙁		🙂🙂		🙂	
Herr und Frau Meyer	🙂🙂			🙂	🙁	😐	

🙂🙂 = sehr gern 🙂 = gern 😐 = ziemlich gern 🙁 = nicht gern

1 Wer spielt sehr gern Fußball? *Nicole spielt sehr gern Fußball.*
2 Wer spielt gern Tischtennis? ______
3 Was spielt Christa sehr gern? ______
4 Was spielen Herr und Frau Meyer gern? ______
5 Wer spielt Basketball nicht gern? ______
6 Wer spielt ziemlich gern Handball? (2) ______
7 Und du? Was spielst du gern? ______

2 **Write three questions and three answers about the other people and sports in the table in exercise 1. Use the questions above as a model.**

______
______
______
______
______
______

2 Freizeit ist toll! (Seiten 56–57)

1 **Write the words from the cloud in the grid. Translate the code word into English.**

furchtbar
Eishockey
schlecht
spielst
irre
stinklangweilig
langweilig
Tischtennis
toll

2 **Read about all the activities Hannes and Lola are involved in. Then write *richtig* or *falsch* next to each statement.**

Hallo! Ich heiße **Hannes**. Ich finde Sport fantastisch. Ich spiele Tennis und schwimme. Schwimmen finde ich total super. Ich reite mit meiner Freundin, aber das finde ich langweilig. Fußball finde ich cool. Ich fahre auch gern Skateboard und lese sehr gern Sport- und Fitnessmagazine.

Meine Freundin heißt **Lola.** Sie findet Tischtennis toll. Lola fährt auch gern Rad – das ist sehr gesund! Sie findet schwimmen auch gut, aber Fußball findet sie nervig. Sie kann nicht Ski fahren. Im Winter spielt sie Eishockey und sie sieht sehr gern Eishockey im Fernsehen.

meine Freundin = my girlfriend
gesund = healthy
Fernsehen = television

1 Both Hannes and Lola participate in winter sports. ______________
2 Lola watches ice hockey on television. ______________
3 Hannes really likes swimming. ______________
4 Lola thinks skiing is fantastic. ______________
5 Lola plays ice hockey in winter. ______________
6 Hannes doesn't enjoying horse riding. ______________
7 Lola thinks football is exciting. ______________
8 Hannes watches sports programmes on television. ______________

3 In meiner Freizeit (Seiten 58–59)

1 **Separate the words to form five time phrases and write them below. Number the phrases in order of frequency, starting with 1 for the most frequent. Translate the phrases into English.**

jedenTagdreimalproWocheeinmalproMonatamWochenendesechsmalproMonat

☐ ______________________ ______________________

☐ ______________________ ______________________

☐ ______________________ ______________________

☐ ______________________ ______________________

☐ ______________________ ______________________

2 **Use the time phrases from exercise 1 to answer the questions about yourself. Write your answers in full sentences.**

1 Gehst du ins Kino? ______________________

2 Machst du Sport? ______________________

3 Gehst du einkaufen? ______________________

4 Hörst du Musik? ______________________

5 Spielst du Wii? ______________________

6 Chillst du mit deinen Freunden? ______________________

nie = never

3 **Join up the sentence halves. Rewrite each sentence so that it starts with the time phrase.**

1 Ich höre am	**a** Tag Sport.
2 Ich chille am	**b** Abend Musik.
3 Ich spiele sehr	**c** pro Woche Pizza.
4 Ich mache jeden	**d** Monat ins Kino.
5 Ich esse einmal	**e** oft Xbox.
6 Ich gehe einmal pro	**f** Wochenende.

Remember the 'verb in second place' rule.

4 Ich bin online (Seiten 60–61)

1 Unscramble and write down the time phrase in each sentence. Then translate the sentences into English.

Grammatik
You can use the present tense with a future time phrase to say what you are going to do – just as in English.

1 Wir machen ähncset eoWhc Filme. *nächste Woche*
We are going to make …

2 Ich suche ma Mtanog Infos im Internet. ______

3 Wir sehen ma eneneoWhcd Katzenvideos auf YouTube. ______

4 Ich chatte nejde denbA auf Facebook. ______

5 Stefan spielt ni iezw cnoWhe Wii Sport. ______

6 Ich lade gomrne Musik herunter. ______

2 Underline all the verbs in the text. Circle the words that are in first position in the sentences. Write a sentence about what you notice.

Hey du!

Franzi hier! Jetzt sind wir Freunde auf Facebook! Jeden Tag spiele ich Wii. Jede Woche schreibt mein Vater ein Blog, aber das finde ich langweilig. Am Abend lese ich gern E-Books. Morgen telefoniere ich mit Freunden in Kanada über Skype. Das finde ich cool! Im Sommer fahren wir nach Vancouver. Fantastisch! Was machst du am Computer und wie oft?

______

3 Reply to the question Franzi has asked you in his chat.

Use as many time phrases as you can in your reply.

1 What type of word is needed to fill the gap in each sentence? Complete each sentence by writing an appropriate German word or words in the gap.

verb *noun* *time/frequency phrase* *connective* *adjective*

	Type of word
1 Ich finde ______ Tennis toll.	verb
2 Meine Schwester findet Tischtennis ______.	
3 Wir sehen ______ fern.	
4 Herr Peters spielt nächste Woche Tennis ______ Fußball.	
5 Mein Bruder schreibt ein ______.	

2 Answer the questions about German grammar.

Use the sentences in exercise 1 to help you answer these questions.

1 Where in a sentence do verbs usually go? ______

2 What often goes after a verb? ______

3 What can you expect to go after *ein/eine*? ______

4 Which German verb suggests you're giving an opinion? ______

3 Replace the underlined word(s) with something else: a different noun, adjective or time phrase.

1 Ich finde Tischtennis furchtbar. Ich finde Tischtennis langweilig.

2 Ich spiele nicht gern Fußball. ______

3 Micha spielt gern Wii. ______

4 Er macht einmal pro Monat Judo. ______

5 Olli findet E-Books fantastisch. ______

6 Ich sehe jede Woche fern. Meine Schwester sieht jeden Tag Videos auf YouTube.

______

Remember that you'll keep the reader's interest if you use a variety of different words and phrases.

4 Write about your friends' hobbies.

Remember to include:
- opinions
- time/frequency phrases
- connectives
- 'verb in second place' rule

Wiederholung 1

1 **Put the words in the correct order to make sentences or questions. Don't forget to insert a full stop or question mark.**

1. fern gern sehr Ich sehe ______
2. einkaufen er Wochenende geht Am ______
3. Hausaufgaben Ich Infos lese die für ______
4. in Wie Stadt oft du fährst die ______
5. Woche Kai Wasserball Nächste spielt ______
6. herunter Videos Ich lade Musik und ______

2 **Rewrite each sentence, beginning with a time phrase. Then translate the sentences into English.**

1. Ich spiele Volleyball. (at the weekend) *Am Wochenende spiele ich Volleyball.*
   At the weekend I am going to play volleyball.
2. Er spielt Basketball. (on Monday) ______
   ______
3. Du spielst Tischtennis. (every week) ______
   ______
4. Rosa spielt Fußball. (today) ______
   ______
5. Ich telefoniere mit Sam. (next week) ______
   ______
6. Sophie liest das Buch. (tomorrow) ______
   ______

3 **Underline the regular verbs and circle the irregular verbs.**

Ich spiele nicht gern Tennis. Ich finde Tennis langweilig. Fußball spiele ich dreimal pro Woche. Mein Bruder spielt sehr gern Tennis. Er fährt auch gern Rad. Radfahren findet er toll. Meine Schwester sieht ziemlich gern fern. Meine Mutter liest ziemlich gern. Oft liest sie Blogs im Internet. Ich lese auch oft. Mein Vater fährt gern Ski und spielt Gitarre.

Wiederholung 2

1 Read the email. Find the German for the following words and phrases in the text.

1 I think ______________________
2 about ______________________
3 but ______________________
4 New Zealand ______________________
5 comedies ______________________
6 Best wishes ______________________

Lieber Anish,

wie geht's? Danke für deine E-Mail.

Ich denke, Technologie ist toll. Ich bin sehr oft online. Ich chatte sehr gern mit Freunden auf Facebook. Facebook finde ich super und ich sehe oft Videos über Fußball auf YouTube.

Ich spiele Computerspiele nicht gern, aber ich suche ziemlich oft Infos für die Hausaufgaben. Meine Cousine, Connie, wohnt in Neuseeland und wir telefonieren ziemlich oft über Skype. Kannst du auch über Skype telefonieren?

Ich mache viel Sport mit meinen Freunden: Wir schwimmen zweimal pro Woche und wir spielen am Abend Basketball. Im Winter fahre ich auch Ski.

Ich esse manchmal am Wochenende mit meinen Freunden Pizza, und dann gehen wir ins Kino. Ich sehe gern Komödien. Nächste Woche sehen wir *Skyfall*.

Liebe Grüße,

Tibor

2 Answer the questions in complete German sentences.

1 Spielt Tibor gern Computerspiele? ______________________
2 Was macht Tibor auf Facebook? ______________________
3 Wer wohnt in Neuseeland? ______________________
4 Wie telefoniert Tibor mit seiner Cousine? ______________________
5 Wie oft schwimmt Tibor? ______________________
6 Was machen Tibor und seine Freunde am Wochenende?

____

3 Write a reply to Tibor's email about your hobbies and activities.

Grammatik (Seiten 68–69)

1 Complete the verb table.

	fahren (to go/travel)	**sehen** (to see)	**lesen** (to read)
ich			
du	fährst		liest
er/sie/es		sieht	
wir			
ihr			
Sie			
sie			

2 Complete the sentences by writing the correct form of the verb in brackets.

1 Ich ________________ das Auto. (waschen)

2 ________________ du gern Mangabücher? (lesen)

3 Er ________________ im Schlafzimmer. (schlafen)

4 Thomas ________________ nach Stockholm in Schweden. (fahren)

5 ________________ du morgen Torsten? (sehen)

6 ________________ du eine Schuluniform? (tragen)

Verbs like fahren:
tragen = to wear
schlafen = to sleep
waschen = to wash

die Schuluniform = school uniform

3 Write the question for each reply.

1 ________________ Ja, ich spiele Gitarre.

2 ________________ Nein, ich spiele nicht gern Wasserball.

3 ________________ Ja, Michael schläft im Bett.

4 ________________ Ja, ich fahre nach Bremen.

5 ________________ Ja, ich lese gern E-Books.

6 ________________ Nein, ich sehe nicht gern fern.

7 ________________ Ja, ich bin sportlich!

8 Was ________________ Ich trage morgen Jeans und ein T-Shirt.

9 ________________ Michael trägt eine Schuluniform.

Remember, to form a question you put the verb before the subject:
Du spielst gern Tennis. → Spielst du gern Tennis?

Mein Fortschritt

1 Record your levels for *Kapitel* 3.

2 Look at the level descriptors on pages 59–60 and set your targets for *Kapitel* 4.

3 Fill in what you need to do to achieve these targets.

Listening 	I have reached Level ______ in **Listening**. In *Kapitel* 4, I want to reach Level ______ I need to ______________________________ ______________________________ ______________________________ ______________________________
Speaking 	I have reached Level ______ in **Speaking**. In *Kapitel* 4, I want to reach Level ______ I need to ______________________________ ______________________________ ______________________________ ______________________________
Reading 	I have reached Level ______ in **Reading**. In *Kapitel* 4, I want to reach Level ______ I need to ______________________________ ______________________________ ______________________________ ______________________________
Writing 	I have reached Level ______ in **Writing**. In *Kapitel* 4, I want to reach Level ______ I need to ______________________________ ______________________________ ______________________________ ______________________________

Bist du sportlich? • Are you sporty?

Ich bin (sehr/ziemlich/ nicht sehr) sportlich.	*I am (very/quite/ not very) sporty.*
Was spielst du?	*What do you play?*
Ich spiele ...	*I play ...*
Ich spiele gern ...	*I like playing ...*
Ich spiele ziemlich gern ...	*I quite like playing ...*
Ich spiele nicht gern ...	*I don't like playing ... playing ...*
Badminton	*badminton*
Basketball	*basketball*
Eishockey	*ice hockey*
Fußball	*football*
Handball	*handball*
Tennis	*tennis*
Tischtennis	*table tennis*
Volleyball	*volleyball*
Wasserball	*water polo*

Was machst du gern? • What do you like doing?

Was machst du gern?	*What do you like doing?*
Ich fahre Rad.	*I ride my bike.*
Ich fahre Skateboard.	*I go skateboarding.*
Ich fahre Ski.	*I ski.*
Ich fahre Snowboard.	*I snowboard.*
Ich lese.	*I read.*
Ich mache Judo.	*I do judo.*
Ich mache Karate.	*I do karate.*
Ich reite.	*I go horse riding.*
Ich schwimme.	*I swim.*
Ich sehe fern.	*I watch TV.*
Ich spiele Gitarre.	*I play the guitar.*
Ich tanze.	*I dance.*

Wie findest du das? • What do you think of it?

Ich finde es ...	*I think it's ...*
Es ist ...	*It's ...*
irre	*amazing*
super	*super*
toll	*great*
cool	*cool*
gut	*good*
nicht schlecht	*not bad*
okay	*okay*
langweilig	*boring*
nervig	*annoying*
stinklangweilig	*deadly boring*
furchtbar	*awful*

Was machst du in deiner Freizeit? • What do you do in your free time?

Ich chille.	*I chill out.*
Ich esse Pizza oder Hamburger.	*I eat pizza or hamburgers.*
Ich gehe einkaufen.	*I go shopping.*
Ich gehe ins Kino.	*I go to the cinema.*
Ich gehe in den Park.	*I go to the park.*
Ich gehe in die Stadt.	*I go into town.*
Ich höre Musik.	*I listen to music.*
Ich mache Sport.	*I do sport.*
Ich spiele Xbox oder Wii.	*I play Xbox or on the Wii.*

Wörter

Ich bin online • I'm online

Was machst du am Computer?	*What do you do on the computer?*
Was machst du auf deinem Handy?	*What do you do on your mobile?*
Ich chatte mit Freunden auf Facebook.	*I chat with friends on Facebook.*
Ich lade Musik herunter.	*I download music.*
Ich mache Fotos oder Filme.	*I take photos or make films.*
Ich sehe Videos.	*I watch videos.*
Ich simse.	*I text.*
Ich spiele Computerspiele.	*I play computer games.*
Ich suche und lese Infos für die Hausaufgaben.	*I look for and read information for my homework.*
Ich surfe im Internet.	*I surf the internet.*
Ich telefoniere mit Freunden.	*I call my friends.*
Ich mache ziemlich viel auf meinem Handy.	*I do quite a lot of things on my mobile.*

Oft benutzte Wörter • High-frequency words

Wie oft?	*How often?*
(sehr/ziemlich/nicht so) oft	*(very/quite/not so) often*
einmal/zweimal/dreimal pro Woche/pro Monat	*once/twice/three times a week/a month*
jeden Tag	*every day*
jeden Morgen	*every morning*
manchmal	*sometimes*
immer	*always*
nie	*never*
Wann?	*When?*
am Wochenende	*at the weekend*
am Abend	*in the evening*
heute	*today*
morgen	*tomorrow*
am Montag	*on Monday*
nächste Woche	*next week*
in zwei Wochen	*in two weeks*

1 Ich mag Deutsch! (Seiten 76–77)

1 **Write a sentence for each illustration.**

1

2

3

4

5

6

1 Ich mag ______________________

2 ______________________

3 ______________________

4 ______________________

5 ______________________

6 ______________________

> **!**
> ich liebe 🙂🙂
> ich mag 🙂
> ich mag … nicht ☹
> ich hasse ☹☹

2 **Read the forum entries giving people's opinions about school subjects. Then answer the questions below.**

Hallo Leute! Mein Lieblingsfach ist Englisch! Ich liebe Englisch, weil es total interessant ist. Ich lese sehr gern Bücher auf Spanisch und auf Deutsch. Mathe finde ich langweilig. **Pedro**

Hi Pedro! Ich mag Englisch nicht. Es ist sehr schwierig, aber ich mag Mathe und Naturwissenschaften. Ich finde Mathe supercool. **Nadine**

Grüezi aus der Schweiz! Ich liebe Theater und Kunst. Ich mag Kunst sehr gern, weil ich total kreativ bin. Informatik finde ich sehr langweilig, und Geschichte und Erdkunde sind nutzlos. **Marta**

Who …

1 is very creative? ____________

2 enjoys reading? ____________

3 doesn't like English? ____________

4 thinks ICT is boring? ____________

5 likes maths? ____________

6 can read Spanish? ____________

7 loves art? ____________

8 doesn't like geography? ____________

3 **Rewrite each sentence in exercise 1, adding *weil* and an opinion. Use the examples in exercise 2 to help you with word order.**

2 Was und wann? (Seiten 78–79)

1 **Look at the timetable. Write *richtig* or *falsch* next to each statement.**

	Montag	Dienstag	Mittwoch	Donnerstag	Freitag
8.15	Mathe	Erdkunde	Englisch	Deutsch	Technik
9.15	Englisch	Informatik	Theater	Mathe	Deutsch
10.45	Kunst	Mathe	Deutsch	Kunst	Naturwissenschaften
11.45	Naturwissenschaften	Mathe	Naturwissenschaften	Geschichte	Theater
13.30	Deutsch	Sport	Technik	Musik	Englisch

vor = before **nach** = after **die Doppelstunde** = double period

1 Am Mittwoch habe ich Deutsch. ________

2 Wir haben am Freitag nach der Pause Technik. ________

3 Am Montag vor der Pause haben wir Englisch. ________

4 Theater ist am Mittwoch und am Donnerstag. ________

5 Ich habe am Donnerstag nach der Mittagspause Musik. ________

6 Am Dienstag habe ich eine Doppelstunde Mathe. ________

2 **At what time do you have the following subjects? Write a sentence for each.**

1 *Ich habe Englisch um neun Uhr zehn.*

2 ________

3 ________

4 ________

5 ________

6 ________

um acht Uhr = at 8 o'clock

3 **Look at the timetable in exercise 1 and describe one school day. Try to add interest to your sentences by giving opinions about some subjects.**

Example: Am Montag um acht Uhr fünfzehn habe ich Mathe. Ich mag Mathe, weil es interessant ist.

Ich finde Mathe ... = I find maths ...

3 Lehrer und Lehrerinnen (Seiten 80–81)

1 Write a description for each of the teachers.

1 Mein Sportlehrer heißt Herr Huber.
Er ist cool, aber sehr unpünktlich.

2 ______________________________

____

3 ______________________________

____

4 ______________________________

____

Use some qualifiers in your descriptions: *sehr, zu, ziemlich, ein bisschen, nicht*

2 Complete the text by writing the correct word from the cloud in each gap.

Mein ______________ an der Schule ist Geschichte, ______________ meine Geschichtelehrerin sehr lustig ist! Sie ______________ nur ein Haustier, aber ihr Haustier ist eine Schlange!

Am ______________ und am Freitag haben wir Kunst. Ich finde Kunst ziemlich langweilg, weil es schwierig ______________. Mein Kunstlehrer ______________ Herr Ackermann. ______________ Schwester ist auch Kunstlehrerin an meiner ______________! Sie heißt Frau Ackermann! Meine Sportlehrerin ist ______________ freundlich. Sie heißt Frau Krause und ______________ Lieblingssport ist Volleyball. Ich mag Sport, weil ich sehr ______________ bin.

heißt hat Mittwoch Lieblingsfach ist
sehr Schule Seine sportlich weil ihr

3 Write the correct word for 'his' or 'her' in each sentence.

1 ______________ Bruder lernt Hindi. (his)
2 ______________ Schwester ist Lehrerin. (her)
3 ______________ Hobby ist Gitarre spielen. (his)
4 ______________ Lieblingsfach ist Kunst. (her)
5 ______________ Schuluniform ist fantastisch. (his)
6 ______________ Bruder ist 19 Jahre alt. (her)

Grammatik
sein = his **ihr** = her (for masculine and neuter nouns)
seine = his **ihre** = her (for feminine nouns)
Check the gender of the noun if you are unsure.

4 Im Klassenzimmer (Seiten 82–83)

1 Draw a simple picture to show where each of these things is.

1 Der Musiklehrer ist im Klassenzimmer.
2 Das Buch ist neben dem Computer.
3 Das Poster ist an der Wand.
4 Der Stuhl ist auf dem Tisch und neben der Tür.

1	2	3	4

2 What is there in the classroom? Start each sentence with *Es gibt* (there is/there are). Write the numbers as words.

12  *Es gibt zwölf Tische im Klassenzimmer.*

6  ______________________

24  ______________________

2  ______________________

4 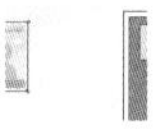 ______________________

5 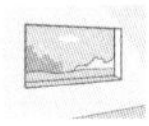 ______________________

! Look at the vocabulary on page 47 for the plurals of the nouns.

3 Answer the questions using the information in the pictures.

@peta_ush Darfst du dein Handy in der Schule benutzen?

____

@tara_winkel Darfst du im Klassenzimmer schnell laufen?

____

@e_atch Darfst du in der Pause Musik hören?

____

@janet_mc Darfst du dein Handy in der Mittagspause benutzen?

____

! ich darf du darfst er/sie/es darf

Mein Lieblingstag (Seiten 84–85)

1 Most of the verbs you've seen end in *–en* in the infinitive. Write the infinitive form of each verb in the table. Then try to work out its meaning from the context.

If the context doesn't help you, use a German–English dictionary.

verb	infinitive	meaning in English
Er **geht** in die Schule.	*gehen*	*to go, to walk*
Er **kauft** ein Auto.		
Er **steht** auf dem Tisch.		
Warum **redest** du so schnell?		
Ich **wasche** meinen Hund.		
Ich **nehme** das Buch.		

2 Guess the meaning of these compound nouns by separating out the words. Look up the compound nouns in a dictionary to find their gender and meaning.

The second word in each compound noun gives the gender.

compound noun	word 1	word 2	gender	meaning
Fußballfeld	*Fußball*		*das*	
Arbeitstag				
Sporthalle				
Klassenarbeit				
Lehrerzimmer				

3 Now write a short German sentence using each compound noun from exercise 2.

1 *Das Fußballfeld ist sehr grün und …*

2 ____________________

3 ____________________

4 ____________________

5 ____________________

Wiederholung 1

1 Mimi's description of her school day is in the wrong time order! Number the sentences 1–6 in the correct order of time.

- [ ] Ich habe um dreizehn Uhr fünfundzwanzig Musik.
- [ ] Die Pause beginnt um elf Uhr zehn.
- [ ] Die erste Stunde beginnt um acht Uhr vierzig.
- [ ] Der Bus kommt um fünfzehn Uhr siebenundvierzig.
- [ ] Ich komme um sechzehn Uhr dreißig nach Hause.
- [ ] Wir haben Mathe um elf Uhr fünfundzwanzig.

2 The school is running 20 minutes late today. Rewrite each of the six sentences in exercise 1 with the time that each activity begins today.

3 Complete the sentences by writing the correct possessive pronoun in each gap.

sein = his (for masculine and neuter nouns) **seine** = his (for feminine nouns)
ihr = her (for masculine and neuter nouns) **ihre** = her (for feminine nouns)

1 __________ Bruder heißt Pawel und __________ Schwester heißt Aga.
2 __________ Lieblingssport ist Eishockey.
3 __________ Katze ist braun, aber __________ Hund ist weiß.
4 __________ Schule ist in Hannover.

5 __________ Lieblingssport ist Reiten und __________ Lieblingsfach ist Mathe.
6 __________ Computer ist neu.
7 __________ Erdkundelehrerin ist sehr streng.
8 __________ Mutter wohnt in Salzburg, aber __________ Vater wohnt in Wien.

4 Describe where each of the items is located in the classroom.

1 Der Computer ist auf dem Tisch.
2 Das Poster __________
3 Das Whiteboard __________
4 Der Lehrer __________
5 Der Stuhl __________
6 Die Spinne __________

Wiederholung 2

1 Read the texts. Use your knowledge of vocabulary to help you to find these new phrases. Write each German phrase next to the English.

1 My name is ____________

2 her favourite artist ____________

3 unfortunately ____________

4 My brother also goes ____________

5 an indoor pool ____________

6 a pot plant ____________

Hallo! Mein Name ist **Maik** und ich wohne in München, in Deutschland. Meine Schule heißt Mathias Brauer Gymnasium und ich finde sie toll. An meiner Schule lerne ich sehr gern Englisch und Geschichte, aber mein Lieblingsfach ist Kunst. Ich mag Kunst, weil ich total kreativ bin. Ich finde meine Kunstlehrerin auch sehr nett. Sie heißt Frau Weber und ihr Lieblingskünstler ist Dürer.

Ich mag nicht Sport, weil ich nicht sehr sportlich bin. Leider habe ich am Montag und auch am Mittwoch Sport. Morgen spielen wir Tennis. Das finde ich nicht so schlecht.

lernen = to learn

Hallo Leute! Ich heiße **Sabine** und ich wohne in Zürich, in der Schweiz. Meine Schule ist sehr groß. Mein Bruder geht auch auf meine Schule.

Mein Lieblingsfach ist Musik und dieses Fach haben wir am Dienstag in der zweiten Stunde und auch am Donnerstag in der vierten Stunde. Sport mag ich auch, weil der Sportlehrer total lustig ist. Sein Lieblingssport ist Schwimmen und wir haben ein Hallenbad in der Schule. Wir haben Sport am Mittwoch in der fünften Stunde und auch am Freitag in der zweiten Stunde.

Mein Klassenzimmer ist sehr schön. Wir haben zehn Computer, ein Whiteboard neben der Tür, viele Poster an der Wand und eine Topfpflanze am Fenster!

2 Answer the questions about the texts in exercise 1. Write complete sentences in German for your answers.

1 Wie heißt Maiks Schule? ____________

2 Was mag Maik? ____________

3 Was lernt Maik nicht gern? ____________

4 Wann hat Maik Sport? ____________

5 Wo ist Zürich? ____________

6 Was hat Sabine am Donnerstag in der vierten Stunde?

____

7 Warum mag Sabine Sport? ____________

8 Wo ist die Topfpflanze? ____________

Grammatik (Seiten 90–91)

1 Answer the questions in full sentences, using *weil* and the reason given.

1 Warum magst du Kunst? (it's creative)

Ich mag Kunst, weil es kreativ ist.

2 Warum magst du Englisch? (it's interesting)

____

3 Warum spielst du Tennis? (I'm sporty)

____

4 Warum hasst du Sport? (it's difficult)

____

5 Warum findest du Erdkunde toll? (it's easy)

____

2 Put the words in the right order to make sentences.

Remember the 'verb in second place' rule.

1 der in Geschichte dritten wir Stunde haben

____

2 habe Pause ich nach der Kunst _______________

3 Fußball spiele heute ich _______________

4 gibt Klassenzimmer Computer und viele einen es im Poster

____

5 Montag ich vierten Stunde habe in am der Mathe

____

3 Write the following school rules in sentences in German.

Example: Man darf am Montag …

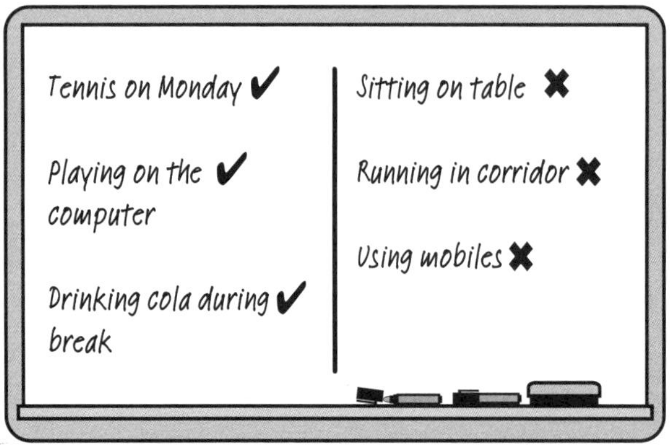

Man darf is often used to mean 'you/we are allowed to'.

Remember to use the correct preposition and the correct word for 'the' after it.

Mein Fortschritt

1 **Record your levels for *Kapitel* 4.**

2 **Look at the level descriptors on pages 59–60 and set your targets for *Kapitel* 5.**

3 **Fill in what you need to do to achieve these targets.**

Listening 	I have reached Level _____ in **Listening**. In *Kapitel* 5, I want to reach Level _____ I need to ______________________________ ______________________________ ______________________________ ______________________________
Speaking  	I have reached Level _____ in **Speaking**. In *Kapitel* 5, I want to reach Level _____ I need to ______________________________ ______________________________ ______________________________ ______________________________
Reading 	I have reached Level _____ in **Reading**. In *Kapitel* 5, I want to reach Level _____ I need to ______________________________ ______________________________ ______________________________ ______________________________
Writing 	I have reached Level _____ in **Writing**. In *Kapitel* 5, I want to reach Level _____ I need to ______________________________ ______________________________ ______________________________ ______________________________

Wörter

Schulfächer • School subjects

Deutsch	*German*
Englisch	*English*
Erdkunde	*geography*
Geschichte	*history*
Informatik	*ICT*
Kunst	*art*
Mathe	*maths*
Musik	*music*
Naturwissenschaften	*science*
Sport	*sport, PE*
Technik	*technology*
Theater	*drama*

Meinungen • Opinions

mein Lieblingsfach ist ...	*my favourite subject is ...*
ich mag ... (sehr)	*I like ... (a lot)*
ich liebe	*I love*
ich mag ... nicht	*I don't like ...*
ich hasse	*I hate*
gut	*good*
toll	*great*
furchtbar	*awful*
einfach	*easy*
schwierig	*difficult*
interessant	*interesting*
langweilig	*boring*
nützlich	*useful*
nutzlos	*useless*
faszinierend	*fascinating*
nervig	*irritating*
supercool	*really cool*
stinklangweilig	*dead boring*

Die Wochentage • The days of the week

Montag (Mo.)	*Monday*
Dienstag (Di.)	*Tuesday*
Mittwoch (Mi.)	*Wednesday*
Donnerstag (Do.)	*Thursday*
Freitag (Fr.)	*Friday*
Samstag (Sa.)	*Saturday*
Sonntag (So.)	*Sunday*
Was hast du am Montag?	*What do you have on Monday?*
Am Dienstag habe ich ...	*I have ... on Tuesday*
Am Sonntag haben wir keine Schule.	*We have no school on Sunday.*

Die Zeit • Time

Wann?	*When?*
Um wie viel Uhr?	*At what time?*
Um 8:30 Uhr (acht Uhr dreißig).	*At 8:30.*
Wie viel Uhr ist es?	*What time is it?*
Es ist 9:50 Uhr (neun Uhr fünfzig).	*It's 9:50.*
in der ersten Stunde	*in the first lesson*
vor der Pause	*before break*
nach der Mittagspause	*after the lunch break*

Wörter

Eigenschaften • Characteristics

Er/Sie ist ...	*He/She is ...*
alt	*old*
fair	*fair*
freundlich	*friendly*
jung	*young*
launisch	*moody*
lustig	*funny*
nervig	*annoying*
streng	*strict*
unpünktlich	*unpunctual*

In der Schule • In school

die Lehrerin(-nen)	*teacher (female)*
die Deutsch-lehrerin(-nen)	*German teacher (female)*
der Lehrer(–)	*teacher (male)*
der Sportlehrer(–)	*sports teacher (male)*
Was gibt es?	*What is there?*
Es gibt einen/eine/ein ...	*There is a ...*
Es gibt viele ...	*There are lots of ...*
das Klassenzimmer(–)	*classroom*
der Tisch(-e)	*table*
der Stuhl(¨-e)	*chair*
der Computer(–)	*computer*
das Whiteboard(-s)	*whiteboard*
das Poster(–)	*poster*
das Fenster(–)	*window*
die Wand(¨-e)	*wall*
die Tür(-en)	*door*
der Korridor(-e)	*corridor*

Wo ist das? • Where is it?

in der Schule	*in the school*
im Klassenzimmer	*in the classroom*
im Korridor	*in the corridor*
an der Wand	*on the wall*
am Fenster	*by the window*
am Tisch	*at the table*
auf dem Tisch	*on the table*
neben der Tür	*near/next to the door*

Oft benutzte Wörter • High-frequency words

weil	*because*
sein/seine	*his*
ihr/ihre	*her*
zu	*too*
sehr	*very*
ziemlich	*quite, fairly*
ein bisschen	*a bit*
nicht	*not*
haben	*to have*
sein	*to be*
in	*in*
an	*at, by, on (wall)*
auf	*on (top of)*
neben	*near, next to*
heute	*today*
morgen	*tomorrow*
vor	*before*
nach	*after*

1 In der Stadt (Seiten 98–99)

1 **Write sentences to say what there is and isn't in the town.**

1 Es gibt hier ______________________________________. 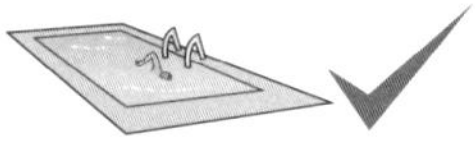

2 Hier gibt es ______________________________________. 

3 In der Stadt gibt es ______________________________________. 

4 Es gibt ______________________________________ hier. 

Grammatik
der→einen/keinen **die**→eine/keine **das**→ein/kein

2 **Read the texts. Tick the things there are in each person's town and cross the things there aren't.**

Monika: *Ich wohne in Celle. Meine Stadt ist nicht sehr groß. Es gibt hier ein Schloss und auch einen Marktplatz. Leider gibt es kein Schwimmbad und auch keine Kegelbahn.*

leider = unfortunately

Erik: *Die Touristen kommen gern nach Verden, weil es eine Kirche und auch einen Marktplatz gibt. Ein Schloss gibt es auch, aber leider gibt es kein Schwimmbad und keine Imbissstube.*

Aisha: *Ich wohne in Neustadt, in der Nähe vom Titisee. Neustadt ist ganz klein, aber sehr schön. Es gibt hier kein Schloss, keine Kegelbahn und leider auch kein Kino. Wir haben aber einen Bahnhof, eine Kirche und auch einen alten Marktplatz. Wir haben kein Schwimmbad, aber man kann im Sommer im Titisee schwimmen!*

	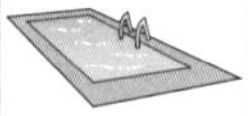			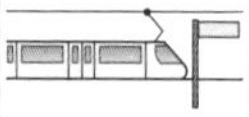				
Monika								
Erik								
Aisha								

3 **Write two or three sentences about what there is to do where you live, as well as what there isn't. Use the texts in exercise 2 to help you.**

2 Wir gehen einkaufen! (Seiten 100–101)

1 **Write what the customers in the souvenir shop would like. Start your sentences with *Ich möchte*.**

Look at the vocabulary on page 57 if you need to check which words to use.

1 Ich möchte einen Kuli. 5 ____________________

2 ____________________ 6 ____________________

3 ____________________ 7 ____________________

4 ____________________ 8 ____________________

2 **Complete the dialogue with words from the cloud below. Then number the lines of the conversation in the correct order 1–11.**

☐ Guten Tag! ____________ ich dir helfen?

☐ Welche ____________ ? Wir haben blau, rot oder schwarz.

☐ Ja, klar! Dieser ____________ , zum Beispiel, kostet nur €18,95.

☐ Super!

☐ Danke. Auf ____________ .

☐ Sonst noch etwas?

☐ Alles ____________ kostet das €38,95.

☐ Guten Tag! Ich möchte ein Souvenir ____________ , vielleicht ein Kuscheltier. Haben Sie ____________ ?

☐ Bitte sehr.

☐ Ja. Ich möchte ein ____________ für meine Schwester.

☐ Schwarz, bitte. Wie viel ____________ das?

zusammen *Elefant* *Kuscheltiere* *Wiedersehen* *Kann* *kostet* *Fußballtrikot* *kaufen* *Farbe*

3 Mmm, lecker! (Seiten 102–103)

1 **Write four short conversations between hungry customers and the owner of the snack stand. The price of each individual item is shown: don't forget to add up the total price.**

1

 × 1
drei Euro zehn

 × 1
zwei Euro fünfunddreißig

2

 × 2
zwei Euro sechzig

 × 2
zwei Euro fünfundzwanzig

3

 × 3
drei Euro zwanzig

 × 1
ein Euro neunzig

4

 × 4
drei Euro fünfundneunzig

× 1
zwei Euro zehn

Ich möchte .../Ich hätte gern ...	I'd like ...
Das kostet alles zusammen ...	All together that costs ...

1 *Guten Tag! Ich möchte einmal Hamburger und einmal Bratwurst, bitte.*

Das kostet alles zusammen € ...

2 ______________________________

____

3 ______________________________

____

4 ______________________________

____

2 **Write a short review of the menu, saying what there is to eat and drink and what you do and don't like.**

Hamburger 
Bratwurst
Pommes 
Salat
Eis
Tee
Cola
Mineralwasser

Man kann ... trinken/essen.	You can eat/drink ...
Ich esse/trinke gern ...	I like eating/drinking ...
Ich esse/trinke nicht gern ...	I don't like eating/drinking ...
Ich mag ...	I like ....
Ich mag nicht ...	I don't like .....

____

____

____

4 In den Sommerferien (Seiten 104–105)

1 Circle the correct option to complete each sentence from the choices given. Then write the missing words in the gaps.

1 Ich ______________ im See baden.

a wirst b werden c werde

2 Wir werden im ______________ schwimmen.

a Meer b windsurfen c Bratwurst

3 ______________ du nach Innsbruck fahren?

a Wird b Wirst c Bist

4 Er ______________ nicht nach Hannover ______________ .

a werden; fahre b kann; fährt c wird; fahren

5 Tobi ______________ in den ______________ nach Portugal fahren.

a werde; Park b wird; Bahnhof c wird; Sommerferien

6 Wohin ______________ wir ______________ ?

a werden; gehen b kann; gehen c darf; fahren

2 Read the sentences and write the correct words from the cloud in the gaps. There are more words than you need.

1 Ich werde eine Kappe ______________ meinen Vater kaufen.
2 Ich ______________ ein Trikot kaufen.
3 In den ______________ fahren wir nach Rom.
4 Es ______________ ein Schwimmbad und ein Kino in Walsrode.
5 Wir ______________ nach Magdeburg fahren.
6 Ich möchte in den Bergen ______________ gehen.

für
gibt
möchte
nächste Woche
Sommerferien
wandern
werde
werden

3 Write about your plans for the summer holidays. Use the questions and illustrations to help you.

- Wohin wirst du fahren?

- Wer kommt mit?

- Was wirst du dort machen?

- Was wird dein Bruder / deine Schwester machen

- Wirst du Souvenirs kaufen?

1 **Rewrite each sentence. Swap the adjective in bold for an alternative adjective with a similar meaning.**

1 Das Mozart Museum ist **faszinierend**. ________________

2 Der Marktplatz ist **historisch**. ________________

3 Das Schwimmbad ist **modern**.

____

4 Die Kegelbahn ist **toll**. ________________

2 **Join up the sentence halves to describe a trip to Vienna.**

1	In den Sommerferien werde	a	Tage in Wien bleiben.
2	Dort gibt es einen	b	ich nach Wien fahren.
3	Am Montag kann	c	Wien fantastisch.
4	Ich finde	d	Marktplatz, aber keinen See.
5	Wir werden vier	e	man das Mozart Museum besuchen.

Now rewrite the sentences, varying the sentence structure. Remember that in German you always need the verb as the second idea.

Example: **1** Ich werde in den Sommerferien ...

3 **Read the text about Hahndorf. Try to work out what the words in bold mean from the context. If you can't work out the meanings, look them up in a dictionary.**

Hahndorf ist eine kleine Stadt in Südaustralien, in der Nähe von Adelaide. Es gibt dort deutsche **Einwanderer**. Die Stadt ist klein, aber **fein**! Hahndorf ist toll für Kinder und auch für **Erwachsene**. Dort gibt es viele deutsche Restaurants und Cafés. Am Mittwoch und am Sonntag gibt es immer einen Markt auf dem Marktplatz. Man kann hier Schokolade, **Kuchen** und **Kleidung** kaufen. **Wein** aus der Region kann man auch dort trinken. Ich werde **nächstes Jahr** mit meiner Schule nach Hahndorf fahren.

4 **Write about a city or town of your choice. Adapt some of the words and phrases from the text in exercise 3.**

Remember to include: the future tense, opinions, linking words, qualifiers, frequency expressions and inverted word order.

Wiederholung 1

1 **Decide which souvenir you would buy for each person and write the price in words.**

Grammatik

der → *er* *die* → *sie* *das* → *es*

Remember, *der* changes to *den* for masculine nouns.

1 Meine Mutter: Ich werde die Tasse für meine Mutter kaufen. Sie kostet sieben Euro fünfundfünfzig.

2 Onkel Karl: __________

3 Meine Schwester: __________

4 Meine Freundin: __________

5 Frau Roberts: __________

2 **Peter is in the tourist office in Munich. Read the dialogue, then answer the questions in full German sentences.**

Tourist guide: Guten Tag! Willkommen in München!

Peter: Guten Tag! Danke schön! Was gibt es hier in München?

Tourist guide: Hier gibt es viel zu tun! Man kann in München alles sehen!

Peter: Gibt es hier einen Marktplatz?

Tourist guide: Natürlich! Er heißt Marienplatz. Er ist sehr groß und total schön.

Peter: Wunderbar! Und kann man in München Ski fahren?

Tourist guide: Also ... nicht direkt in München, aber in der Nähe von hier kann man sehr gut Ski fahren.

Peter: Super. Und gibt es hier ein gutes Restaurant? Ich möchte gern Pizza essen.

Tourist guide: Ja, das gibt es! Es heißt *Robertos*. Dort kann man gut Pizza essen.

Peter: Vielen Dank. Ich werde im Restaurant *Robertos* essen. Auf Wiedersehen!

1 Was kann man in München machen?
2 Wie heißt der Marktplatz?
3 Wie ist er?
4 Wo kann man Ski fahren?
5 Was möchte Peter essen?
6 Was ist *Robertos*?

Wiederholung 2

1 Rewrite the sentences in the future tense. Identify the subject to help you change the form of *werden*.

1 Wir tauchen im Meer. *Wir werden im Meer tauchen.*

2 Wir baden im See. ____________________

3 Ich gehe an den Strand. ____________________

4 Lena und Michael klettern am Samstag in den Bergen.

____

5 Er kauft ein Kuscheltier für seine kleine Schwester.

____

6 Kaufst du eine Kappe als Souvenir? ____________________

7 Wir gehen am Wochenende mit meinen Freunden einkaufen.

____

2 Read the postcard and answer the questions in full German sentences.

Liebe Oma und Lieber Opa!

Hallo aus Mallorca in Spanien! Wir bleiben zwei Wochen hier, weil wir Sommerferien haben. Es gibt hier alles – einen Wasserpark, ein Schloss und auch einen Markt. Jeden Tag schwimmen wir im Meer. Im Hotel gibt es ein Schwimmbad und wir schwimmen auch hier. Man kann windsurfen und auch tauchen. Mallorca ist auch für das Essen sehr bekannt.

Nächste Woche werden wir in den Bergen klettern. Ich möchte auch segeln. Ich werde auch Souvenirs kaufen!

Alles Liebe,

Tamika

1 Warum ist Tamika in Spanien? ____________________

2 Was gibt es in Mallorca? ____________________

3 Was kann man machen? ____________________

4 Ist Mallorca bekannt für das Museum? ____________________

5 Was wird Tamika nächste Woche machen? ____________________

3 Write four true/false statements in English about the text in exercise 2. Then ask a friend to write 'True' or 'False' next to each statement.

Example: The postcard is to Tamika's parents. False

Grammatik (Seiten 112–113)

1 Rewrite the sentences to make them negative.

Use *keinen/keine/kein* to say what there is or isn't. Use *nicht* to say what you can't or don't like doing.

1 Es gibt in Düsseldorf einen Marktplatz.

____

2 Er mag Wasserball.

____

3 Beni kann Fußball spielen, weil er einen Ball hat.

____

4 In der Stadt gibt es ein Kino und auch eine Kirche.

____

5 Man darf hier schwimmen. ______________________________

2 Write the different forms of *möchten* in the table.

ich		wir	
du		ihr	
er/sie/es		Sie	
		sie	

möchten
möchte
möchten
möchtest
möchte
möchtet
möchten

Complete the sentences by writing the correct form of *möchten* in each gap. Then translate the sentences into English.

1 ______________ du ein Schokoladeneis?

2 Nein, aber ich ______________ gern ein Vanilleeis.

3 Anne ______________ nach Kapstadt in Südafrika fahren.

4 ______________ ihr auch nach Windhuk in Namibia fahren?

5 Wir ______________ zweimal Salat und zweimal Mineralwasser, bitte.

6 Frau Winkelmann, ______________ Sie eine Tasse Tee?

3 Fill in the gaps to complete the different forms of *werden*.

ich _e_de	wir we_de_
du w_r_t	ihr _er_e_
er/sie/es _ir_	Sie/sie w_r_en

4 Write sentences about what you and your family/friends will do on your next holiday.

Example: Ich werde jeden Tag in Frankreich wandern. Mein Bruder ... /Steffi ...

Jahresbilanz

Record your levels for *Kapitel* 5.

Listening	I have reached Level ______ in **Listening**.
Speaking	I have reached Level ______ in **Speaking**.
Reading	I have reached Level ______ in **Reading**.
Writing	I have reached Level ______ in **Writing**.

Look back through your workbook and note down the level you achieved in each skill by the end of each *Kapitel*.

	Listening	**Speaking**	**Reading**	**Writing**
1 Meine Welt und ich				
2 Familie und Tiere				
3 Freizeit – juhu!				
4 Schule ist klasse!				
5 Gute Reise!				

You now have a record of your progress in German for the whole year.

In der Stadt • In town

Es gibt ...	*There is ... / There are ...*
Es gibt ein/eine/einen ...	*There is/are a ...*
Es gibt kein/keine/keinen ...	*There isn't/aren't ...*
in der Nähe von ...	*near to*
in der Nähe ...	*nearby*
der Bahnhof(¨-e)	*railway station(s)*
der Imbiss(-e)/die Imbissstube(-n)	*snack stand(s)*
die Kegelbahn(-en)	*bowling alley(s)*
das Kino(-s)	*cinema(s)*
die Kirche(-n)	*church(es)*
der Marktplatz(¨-e)	*market square(s)*
der Park(-s)	*park(s)*
das Schloss(¨-er)	*castle(s)*
das Schwimmbad(¨-er)	*swimming pool(s)*
die Eisbahn(-en)	*ice rink(s)*
der Fischmarkt(¨-e)	*fish market(s)*
das Kindertheater(-)	*children's theatre(s)*
der Radweg(-e)	*cycle path(s)*
das Sportzentrum (die Sportzentren)	*sports centre (sports centres)*
der Stadtpark(-s)	*city/town park(s)*
der Wasserpark(-s)	*water park(s)*

Verkaufsgespräch • Sales conversation

Ich gehe einkaufen.	*I am going shopping.*
Ich möchte ...	*I would like ...*
Ich möchte ... kaufen.	*I would like to buy ...*
Haben Sie ...?	*Do you have ...?*
Kann ich dir helfen?	*Can I help you?*
Sonst noch etwas?	*Anything else?*
alles zusammen	*all together*

Souvenirs • Souvenirs

der Aufkleber	*sticker*
das Freundschaftsband	*friendship bracelet*
die Kappe	*(baseball) cap*
der Kuli	*biro*
das Kuscheltier	*cuddly toy*
die Postkarte	*postcard*
der Schlüsselanhänger	*key ring*
die Tasse	*mug/cup*
das Trikot	*(football) shirt*
Wie viel kostet ...?	*How much does ... cost?*
Wie viel kostet das?	*How much does it cost?*
Es kostet €16.	*It costs 16 Euros.*

Snacks und Getränke kaufen • Buying snacks and drinks

die Bratwurst	*fried sausage*
der Hamburger	*hamburger*
die Pizza	*pizza*
die Pommes	*chips*
der Salat	*salad*
das Eis	*ice cream*
die Cola	*cola*
das Mineralwasser	*mineral water*
der Tee	*tea*
das Fleisch	*meat*
der Ketchup	*ketchup*
die Mayo(nnaise)/Majonäse	*mayo(nnaise)*
der Senf	*mustard*
Ich möchte einmal/zweimal/dreimal ...	*I would like one/two/three ...*
Ich hätte gern ...	*I would like ...*
Das macht €8.	*That's €8.*
Ich esse ... gern.	*I like eating ... .*
Ich trinke ... gern.	*I like drinking ... .*

In den Sommerferien • During the summer holidays

Was wirst du machen?	*What will you do?*
Ich werde ...	*I will ...*
Wir werden ...	*We will ...*
klettern	*climb*
im Meer schwimmen	*swim in the sea*
rodeln	*toboggan*
im See baden	*bathe in the lake*
segeln	*sail*
an den Strand gehen	*go to the beach*
tauchen	*dive*
wandern	*hike*
windsurfen	*windsurf*
Was kann man dort machen?	*What can you do there?*
Man kann ... besuchen.	*'One'/People/ You can visit ...*
Die Stadt ist bekannt für ...	*The town is well known for ...*
Ich werde (eine Woche) bleiben.	*I will stay (for a week).*

Oft benutzte Wörter • High-frequency words

am Montag	*on Monday*
am Dienstag	*on Tuesday*
am Mittwoch	*on Wednesday*
am Donnerstag	*on Thursday*
am Freitag	*on Friday*
am Wochenende	*at the weekend*
sehr	*very*
nicht sehr	*not very*
ziemlich	*quite*
immer	*always*
nicht immer	*not always*
oft	*often*
nicht oft	*not often*
nie	*never*
alles	*everything*
dort	*there*
teuer	*expensive*

Level descriptors

Listening

Level 1	I can understand some familiar spoken words and phrases.
Level 2	I can understand a range of familiar spoken phrases.
Level 3	I can understand the main points of short spoken passages and note people's answers to questions.
Level 4	I can understand the main points of spoken passages and some of the detail.
Level 5	I can understand the main points and opinions in spoken passages about different topics. I can recognise if people are speaking about the future **OR** the past as well as the present.

Speaking

Level 1	I can say single words and short phrases.
Level 2	I can answer simple questions and use set phrases.
Level 3	I can ask questions and use short phrases to answer questions about myself.
Level 4	I can take part in conversations. I can express my opinions. I can use grammar to change phrases to say something new.
Level 5	I can give short talks, in which I express my opinions. I can take part in conversations giving information, opinions and reasons. I can speak about the future **OR** the past as well as the present.

Level descriptors

Reading

Level 1	I can understand familiar words and phrases.
Level 2	I can understand familiar phrases. I can read aloud familiar words and phrases. I can use a vocabulary list to check meanings.
Level 3	I can understand the main points and people's answers to questions in short written texts.
Level 4	I can understand the main points in short texts and some of the detail. Sometimes I can work out the meaning of new words.
Level 5	I can understand the main points and opinions in texts about different topics. I can recognise if the texts are about the future **OR** the past as well as the present.

Writing

Level 1	I can write or copy single words correctly.
Level 2	I can copy short sentences correctly and write some words from memory.
Level 3	I can answer questions about myself. I can write short phrases from memory. I can write short sentences with help.
Level 4	I can write short texts on familiar topics. I can use grammar to change phrases to write something new.
Level 5	I can write short texts on a range of familiar topics. I can write about the future **OR** the past as well as the present.

Notes

Notes

Published by Pearson Education Limited, Edinburgh Gate, Harlow, Essex, CM20 2JE.

www.pearsonschoolsandfecolleges.co.uk

Edited by Melanie Birdsall
Designed by Kamae Design

Illustrated by Caron at KJA Artists and Lisa Hunt

First published 2013

2022
17

British Library Cataloguing in Publication Data
A catalogue record for this book is available from the British Library

ISBN 978 1 447 94654 0

Printed in Great Britain by Bell and Bain Ltd, Glasgow

Acknowledgements

We would like to thank Melissa Weir, Angelika Libera, Janet Soame and Frances Reynolds for their invaluable help in the development of this course.

Every effort has been made to contact copyright holders of material reproduced in this book. Any omissions will be rectified in subsequent printings if notice is given to the publishers.

www.pearsonschools.co.uk
myorders@pearson.com

T 0845 630 33 33
F 0845 630 77 77

ISBN 978-1-4479-4654-0